----- Contents -----

Photos © S. Cyd Read, Robert Keller; see "Acknowledgments" for details; also for Scripture quotations permissions, abbreviations, and our gratitude to the publishers.

Comments may be directed to the **author, Bob Keller,** at PO Box 5104, Hemet CA 92544 U.S.A. [This is Edition 1 version B]

Invitation: *Come with us to the place of peace, rest and renewal — of energy and wisdom.*

We were made to think, we were made for love, we were made for life.

What is *humanity's greatest discovery*? It is not the New World, not the human genome – it is not agriculture, fire, nor language. Humanity's greatest discovery is that there is a love at the heart of the universe which answers the question, "If someone dies, can that person live again?" The discovery flows from one true holy God Who is love. This discovery has a Trinitarian aspect to it — it has three parts, all of which are one, but all are different: first, that God is one (rather than many "gods"); second, that God is almighty; third, that God is love.

Perhaps we should say that we did not discover this; it was revealed to us. Compare the discovery of penicillin — Sir Alexander Fleming did not search it out, but when he saw the disease bacteria being killed in the culture dishes in his lab, he recognized what was happening, and penicillin became a powerful blessing to humanity. The key was his ability to genuinely *see* what came before his eyes...

We combine insights into the intellectual problems from a variety of material, with a story format to make it easy to move through and keep the mind traveling with it. (Our story is cast as a dialogue among hitchhikers on a cross-country trip to different destinations — with the faithful dog to pace the moods.)

Science is vital today and the right grasp on it, hand in hand with "religion," *rightly understood*, helps deeply. But science will not *show* us the depth of life and God's offer of love; when the searching mind is ready to proceed, the method must fit the realm of inquiry.

Indeed, any domain of knowledge needs to be approached with the right methodology — a microscope does not suffice to explore the heavens, nor a telescope to probe the cell. Prayer is a path of knowledge that the informed seeker will need to walk when the intellectual understanding is on correctly, and we have provided what helps and tips we can offer.

In whatever degree it succeeds, this book is a love song, translated into a hand running over the intellectual structure of our times with a gentle but healing touch. Lest we seem pompous, let us acknowledge explicitly that many others have done far better at greater length in various intellectual areas; but, we keep this book from going much over 300 pages, and we hope that our special mix serves you well.

A caution: Ours is a story without a plot. The characters are thrown together seemingly by chance. (Is it?) What transpires with them, is of concern only per the question on the front cover — and its implications for how we live now.

The **front cover photo** re-evokes the magic of a special moment, "*Purple mountain spirit*:" I was hiking, watching the sunset over a lake, with the beauty of the gold and purple light on the water - and I turned, and the snow-capped mountain was radiant in purple from the sunset's special light. It was indeed "breathtakingly" beautiful - and I realized, these are the awesome things that God does - God alone - and for others to share God's wonderfulness, *that* is the point of our communications. (see "Contents" for photo credit). Sunset reminds the sensitive of death, and the question comes, "Must all this beauty end?" — Bob Keller

> "*God is there to give you something, but you're not there to receive it.*" Athabascan Indian Chief Peter John (Interior of Alaska), p. 47 of his *The Gospel According to...*

Chapter One: "If someone dies, can that person live again?"

R_ was on an RV trip, not a philosophical journey. But the hitchhiker's question was riveting. "If people die, can they live again?" The hitchhiker was reading from a battered Bible – from the book of Job, thought by scholars to be the oldest book in the Bible.[1] Was this not humanity's oldest question?

R_ was a "legal Elder," well past the magic age of fifty-five. Should he have the wisdom to answer this? He had in fact seen a basic fact that was foundational to any answer. He turned momentarily from driving to advance the conversation: "A famous neurosurgeon said, 'It is clear that, in order to survive after death, the mind must establish a connection with a source of energy other than that of the brain.'[2]"

The second hitchhiker looked up as the RV swayed slightly. Was R_'s driving at fault, or did the magnitude of the ideas affect even a vehicle? The other hitchhiker interjected, "Hey, friend, any energy source like that would have to be a supernatural one. There's lots of energy in the cosmos, stars and supernova and all kinds of stuff — but they're all organized in their own trips, and they won't do it for us." She paused and looked at the first hitchhiker's battered Bible, and the equally-worn New Testament that R_ had on the dashboard, jammed against the windshield. "You guys with your Bibles have probably been thinking 'supernatural' already, right?"

The first hitchhiker was getting excited. It was an exciting prospect, undeniably so. "Yes," he spoke, seeming to try to slow himself down to maintain clarity. "That 'new source of energy for the mind' is what the Bible calls the 'new birth,'[3] and the One who created us in the first place has to be the best source of any unending energy for us to live on."

The second hitchhiker was unmoved. "What if I pull out a Qur'an? Maybe you guys call that 'Koran,' the old way. Can't I pull a 'higher power' from the life of trees? What if I have a Baha'i worship book? You Bible-folks have to admit your 'Trinity' is pretty spooky."

R_ took his eyes off the road long enough to give a glance that he hoped didn't seem like a dirty look. "Well, thousands and thousands of years of experience have brought humanity to being a majority 'monotheistic,' 'one God' believers.[4] They didn't start out that way — they started with 'gods' everywhere and of every type.[5] It's been the endless interaction with reality that has brought them to this new focus, to being more monotheist than anything else, 'one-God' believers."

R_ continued, trying not to be strident in tone: "And *you* have to admit that the 'Trinity' proves that Christianity is not a human invention — no one would come up with a concept like that if they wanted to make it easy to persuade people. Come on, now — you have to concede that we would certainly *expect* that there would be things about God that are beyond our conception, and Jesus in beginning the revelation of the Trinity gave us exactly that." (Note to reader: we deal with understanding the Trinity as reasonable — *one* God in "three persons" as the Father, Son and Spirit — in Part Four.)

The second hitchhiker was prepared to respond. "Jesus never said he was the 'Son of God,' so back off." R_ waited to see if the first hitchhiker would nail that one, then spoke softly, "Mark 14:61-62 and John 10:36." The second hitchhiker was in fact interested in the question of what was really so, and she waited while the first hitchhiker thumbed in his Bible to these Scriptures and read them. "OK, then Jesus did say that. I was told otherwise." Neither R_ nor the first hitchhiker was expecting an apology. We were all told a lot of stuff, and if "forgive them, for they know not what they do"[6] didn't apply today, what hope was there for anyone?

The second hitchhiker was evidently up for serious consideration of serious matters. "You guys talk about Jesus — what about people who never heard of him?" R_ had studied: "The

Bible tells us, 'God has compassion on all He* has made,' Psalm 145:9." The second hitchhiker had evidently been listening carefully to America's conversations about God. "So you think 'many paths' lead to God?" R_ pushed his shoulders against the seat. "No, I think God reaches to those on many paths and lifts them to Himself*."[7] (See endnote for Jesus, John 5:24). He knew that "sincerity" was worshipped in many quarters — but also that sincerity had to be correctly focused to do the job. "The New Testament tells us, 'everyone who loves has been born of God.' "[8]

The second hitchhiker looked conflicted — as if she wanted to be friends, but she had to bring something up if she were to be honest. "If all that is so, then think about your 'Trinity' – shouldn't some awareness of that deep matter have emerged somewhere among all these peoples that you say God loves and works with?" The first hitchhiker looked startled, and clutched his battered Bible a little closer. R_ dubbed the second hitchhiker "Thoughtful-Woman" in his mind for that probing question, and he straightened up a bit before he supplied some facts. "It's a deep and difficult matter. Coming to believe in One God has taken humanity a long time, a hard journey. But the Trinity *has* become known elsewhere. Among the ancient Cherokees, even before the Europeans arrived, there was among some a religious understanding which said that 'there existed above three beings who were always together and of the same mind... always one in sentiment and action... [who] created all things, were acquainted with all, were present everywhere, and governed all things... all prayers were directed to them.'[9] That's interesting, eh?"

---

* Throughout this book, we capitalize "He/Him/His" when referring to God. It is true, as so many Bible translators earnestly argue, that no special pronouns were used for the Deity in the original Hebrew and Greek Bible manuscripts. BUT the "pronoun wars" in our culture have fixated so much thought on "he" and "she" being distinctly and dividedly "masculine" and "feminine," that it seems necessary somehow to make the distinction that God is above this. The early Christian writer Aristides is cited on this at the beginning of the endnotes.

R_ kept his eyes on the road, trying to drive responsibly and think deeply at the same time. Death, the unbidden accompaniment to every human journey — would our understandings knit together for the good answer?

Chapter Two: The Convergence of Science and Religion

R_ was touched by the setting. A small campfire on a starry night... The hitchhikers had taken him up on his offer to expound a convergence of science and religion, and this setting – reminiscent of people since time immemorial, including the famous ancients Abraham and Sarah, and so many others – what a background!

R_ indulged himself in a throat-clearing to focus attention, and his beloved dog sat up attentively. "Generally unremarked on, there has been a remarkable convergence of the teachings of science and those of the received Bible. The Bible opens with, 'In the beginning, God created the heavens and the earth,' but for centuries, human thinking did not support this. It was easy to perceive the universe as 'just being there,' 'always has been.' St. Thomas Aquinas, one of the most learned people of his time, said about A.D. 1200 that we 'will never to be able to prove that the universe had a beginning, we must take it on faith.' Now, some 800 years later, science has come around to teaching that the universe we see, did in fact have a beginning, although you seldom hear anyone say that the Bible's "Genesis" was there first, three thousand years earlier." (We don't say that to criticize the science-expositors, but just to say, let's give credit where credit is due).

R_ was never sure what he had on his hands when he picked up hitchhikers, and these two people opened up a new scope. One leaned forward excitedly and said, "I was reading the newspaper one day, about science news. You know that the sun gets its energy by nuclear fusion, fusing hydrogen atoms into helium. Well, they said that when *that* fusion is completed and the sun burns through its hydrogen, then the reactions in the sun will proceed to fuse the helium into heavier elements, ultimately up to iron. They said that when that happens, the sun will expand and sear the earth into a lifeless ball."

R_ didn't share that excitement yet. *We might beat them to it with global warming*, he thought, but he wasn't about to say that.

The hitchhiker saw that it would be necessary to explain it all the way through. "St. Peter wrote 2,000 years ago that 'the heavens and earth that exist are stored up for fire."[10]

The mortality of the earth, the planet we inhabit and love, didn't strike R_ as a positive topic, and he moved on: "There's another convergence: Evolutionary biologists say that they have discovered that human societies became more 'fit' in evolutionary survival terms, when they began to respect their old people as sources of wisdom — 'Elders,' not just 'old folks.' The Bible's Moses was there first, writing, 'Stand up in the presence of the aged'[11] long before Christ."

The fire was dying down, and R_ was afraid his audience's interest might be doing the same. He wanted to go on — the testimony of scientists on religious matters can be of great interest. Some of the disdainers accuse believers of "taking up a crutch," of immersing themselves in a fantasy because the hope is so glorious. But the great British scientist Michael Faraday had said, "Nothing is too good to be true." [12]

Didn't that cover it? "Convergence" of science and religion about the earth and the universe having a beginning, about the earth's "end," and about human beings in between, the virtue of wisdom... R_ paused before he turned towards bed. Shouldn't he say something about the "amazing coincidences," the fundamental scientific constants that physicists had found in the construction of the universe, so perfectly tuned — in so many ways, as to defy imagination? (Note to the reader: we discuss this in Part Four, Chapter 15.) What if the skeptical hitchhiker took interest -- should he offer possible tips on prayer, pointers on difficult issues?

Chapter Three: The Gathering Storm
(issues and threads for further discussion)

Did grace smile upon them because of their concern for ultimate matters? They came upon a lovely place for breakfast. Fringes of snow around a sheltered lake caught the special riches of the colors of sunrise radiantly... Small patches of ice revolved in the breeze here and there out in the lake, accenting the colors on the water. As the sun rose, patches of snow began to catch the white light and glisten with little dots of red and blue and green, as water drops in the snow's crust gave diamond-like refraction.[13] The hitchhikers absorbed the loveliness of the lake as R_ cooked a simple breakfast for them. R_ was delighted with the scene — the cooking was basic enough not to tax his simple brain; being "host" gave him a generous feel, and it didn't cut deeply into his time or energy — what a perfect combination, in such a perfect place! Perhaps he should write an essay on how "perfection" was not purely hypothetical...

The dog stirred as a middle-aged man approached. "Say, you wouldn't be able to give a poor man a ride, would you?" he asked with a smile. R_'s sense of hospitality was enhanced rather than overtaxed, and he was glad to incorporate the man into their modest meal. "I would have waited till after you ate, but I was afraid you'd get away and I'd be stuck here — you're the first person here since yesterday morning," the man said. R_ offered him more coffee to affirm that he was indeed glad to have him as breakfast guest. "Remember to show hospitality, for some have entertained angels without being aware of it," an old Bible verse spoke to R_'s mind.[14] *Coffee is the major source of antioxidants in the American diet,* R_ thought to himself, *so this is a bit deeper favor than it appears!* The man had a backpack with a high-tech pack frame — *"engineering science meets the great outdoors,"* R_ thought. The man became "Sci-guy" in R_'s thoughts, due to this aspect of his appearance. Any fancy of his being an "angel" took an unexpected twist as he later became R_'s interrogator about science versus religion — but clarity and discussion were important, perhaps even "angelic"? The dog had found a friend, as the man petted him gently and steadily, and fed him a continuing stream of scraps.

R_ was glad to see the man had a good sleeping bag. "B-t" (as R_ mentally labeled his Bible-toting hitchhiker) voiced the obvious thought: "You must have been cold here last night." The new hitchhiker laughed. "It was cold, but the Indians saved me. They had a trick I had heard about. I scooped out the ground where I would sleep, built a fire, let it burn down to coals, spread them out and put the dirt over them, and I had heat enough for the night." B-t smiled in delight and said, "You were blessed by God," and R_ thought of the earlier discussion about God having compassion on all people and creatures. R_ thought of a Scripture, a Bible verse where God said, "My people are destroyed for lack of knowledge"[15] — that problem had been avoided *here*.

R_ took time to walk along the lake, accompanied only by the dog — honoring spiritual truth required sound management of the body, and "they" say to walk 45 minutes a day. As R_ pulled the RV back onto the highway, "Sci-guy" took the front passenger's seat, expressed his appreciation for both the meal and the ride, and told R_ that the other hitchhikers had briefed him on R_'s exposition on death, the core solution to it, and the "convergence" of science and religion. "Do you mind if I get obnoxious about that?" the new hitchhiker asked R_. His smile didn't match the wording of the question. "Tell me what you think," R_ replied, with a prayer in his spirit for grace on this discussion and all the reach of its impacts. "Well," Sci-guy began, "I agree with you that the possibility of a transformation after death, would be most important for us to consider. But how do you get into fixating on the Bible, then? And when I think about your Bible, the 'Adam and Eve' thing comes up first in my mind, and that stops me cold."

The dog came up and put his head on R_'s knee to be petted, which was a most welcome comfort for R_. "Adam and Eve are understood in many ways by Christians," R_ began. "Your question of 'fixating on the Bible' may be even more important. Let me hold forth for a moment on all this…" Sci-guy shrugged his shoulders cheerfully, and R_ began. "Adam and Eve got put into a special perspective for me when I read what the Luiseño Indians told the Spanish about their ancient understandings. The Bible's Genesis creation account has come in for a lot of heat, with many people saying you have to just read it as a parable — but one commentator said that if you read Genesis carefully to understand its creation account for what it is really *saying*, it matches what science is saying." Sci-guy's eyebrows arched and he looked to see if R_ could be serious.

R_ hastened on: "Let me just start with one of his key points. Genesis chapter one, verse two says that, 'The Spirit of God was moving over the face of the waters' of the early earth. This commentator says that with that statement, the perspective has shifted — from the cosmos as a whole, to the surface of the earth — and *that's* why the sun appears on the fourth 'day' in the creation account in the Bible's first chapter, Genesis 1, because science tells us that as a planet forms, the early atmosphere is opaque, keeping the sun from being seen until it clears."[16]

Sci-guy confined himself to a single word: "Interesting." B-t was more interested when R_ added, "People argue about the 'days' of creation in the Bible, but this person says that 'yom,' 'day,' is the only word that the ancient Hebrew language of the Old Testament, the first part of the Bible, had in its vocabulary for an era or an extended period of time."[17]

"Before I say any more about that," R_ continued, "remember that Einstein transformed science with his 'relativity.' And the transformations of relativity theory transformed at least one scientist's analysis of the 'six day' creation in Genesis chapter one (our chapter 16). Let me chart his analysis for you, and tell you how Einstein's insights can transform not only the beginning but the end of the Bible account. I need to draw a diagram for that, next time we stop." R_ was getting pumped up, and the dog had to nudge his hand to get him to resume petting. "Yes," R_ resumed, "do let me comment on those issues! But, what you called 'fixating on the Bible,' out of all the theories of afterlife, comes from a basic fact that reshapes our approach."

Sci-guy laughed — a friendly laugh, but with an incisive edge, a wariness: "If you can unstick my thoughts on all this, you should write a book!" The other hitchhikers had been listening, and they laughed too. "A book, a book!" one said, as if there were a shortage of books.[18]

The dog put his paw on R_'s leg, hoping this would be a friendly time among them all, and R_ patted the dog's chest. "Yes, a book," Thoughtful-Woman said. "You can tell everyone how the Luiseño Indians' ancient information illuminated Adam and Eve for you." There was a twinkle in her eye, and R_ interrupted, "And I would assess what Adam and Eve *did*, which the Sunday-school version doesn't do very well sometimes." "You promised us Einstein on the beginning and end of the Bible's discussions," Sci-guy smiled, and everyone laughed. Thoughtful-Woman asked, "How *would* you handle all this, if you wrote a book?" The dog had an anxious look, as if he feared that his beloved master would falter now.

"I would set out some of the basic understandings," R_ began, "with just enough discussion to chart the course, and I would make a section of some of the prayers that I have been blessed with. Then I would go in the other direction; I would expound more fully the analytic discussions, for those who relate to that sort of thing — the exposition of science and philosophy, the special information that has been blessed to me. I would try to make a short book of it all, and I would capsulate the books that have positively informed my thinking, so people could go to the ones that would do *them* good, for their particular outlooks."

Thoughtful-Woman felt R_ was wandering. "You would put in prayers?" she asked. "Yes," R_ responded, "talking information about God and making things make sense, removing intellectual obstacles[19] — that's fine, it's essential for some people, and there's a vast desert of barren cultural understandings that people have to get through somehow. But to grasp 'Humanity's Greatest Opportunity' is to go beyond intellectualizing about God. It's like seeing footprints and measuring them, but you don't meet the person until you follow the trail to real encounter." R_ looked around to see if anyone was with him on that concept.

"You haven't answered my issue about 'fixating on the Bible' — do I have to wait for your *book*?" Sci-guy laughed. "Well," R_ said, "you all got me going about the book idea." "You're putting in a variety of things," interjected Thoughtful-Woman. R_ pulled in even more variety: "I would have a chapter on poverty," he said firmly. Thoughtful-Woman was startled. "Why?" she asked. "Poverty is one of God's great concerns," R_ answered, "and you can't get close to the heart of God without caring about the poor. Yes," he said, "I guess I *am* roving over a variety of things.

"But to talk about the great discovery that comes out of the grinding and the agonies of humanity's millennia, the discovery that puts death back in its place, that *is* worth a book! To do it justice would take combining the intellectual matters, the practical steps of prayer, and referring people to further depths," R_ said. The dog looked like he was thinking, *What a mouthful*, but being a dog, he couldn't interject anything into the conversation.

Sci-guy's smile had grown weary and faded. "I wouldn't even look at your *book* unless you can answer my question about 'fixating on the Bible,' and you have to make me think you can deliver on some of your other promises," he said in a friendly but skeptical tone. "Like you said that there's a 'basic fact that reshapes our understanding' about religious things."

"Many religions talk about God or gods," R_ replied. "But Jesus showed us something unique. God came down to the human level, incarnate as a human in Jesus, to make the more definitive revelation — one beyond words, principles, precepts — a life lived among us, and with us in Spirit forevermore. *That* is what justifies 'fixating on the Bible,' out of all the books held to be sacred." Sci-guy gave R_ a wary look. The Bible-toting hitchhiker, whom R_ had begun to call "B-t" in his own thoughts, was also wary, undoubtedly for different reasons. Thoughtful-Woman was all ears. Only the faithful dog was unconcerned. "Jesus proved that almost-unbelievable special status by the miracles He did, claimed it in the words He spoke, and sealed it with the miracle He predicted — 'destroy this temple' — He spoke of His body, which was killed by crucifixion — 'and I will raise it again in three days.'[20] That's a life we need to listen to — and share in."

Sci-guy pushed himself back against the seat, hard. "Extraordinary claims require extraordinary proof," he quoted some philosopher from centuries past. "Jesus gave that," R_ affirmed. "That's why in the earliest days of the Church, they were able to preach Him to the local community as 'a man accredited by God to you by miracles, wonders and signs, which God did among you through him, as you yourselves know.'[21] Well, to give you the 'extraordinary proof' that you deserve, the best way might be to take you through the intensive analysis of the data that Lee Strobel did in *The Case for Easter* — Jesus' ultimate miracle — rising from the dead."

Sci-guy stared at R_ as if he had seen a space alien, and B-t tried to take the edge off the situation. "I read that book," he began cheerfully. "Strobel was a professional journalist, award-winning at a major paper, and with a legal degree from Yale — and as a hard-core atheist, he felt an evidence-based approach would be fruitful to counteract the betrayal he felt when his wife became a Christian. He wanted to be able to pry her out of what he considered a 'cult'! Strobel broke the issue down into three questions: Did Jesus really die on the cross? Was Jesus buried? (Some people claim otherwise!) Was Jesus seen by credible witnesses after such burial, or do hypotheses such as hallucinations make sense concerning the reported Resurrection?"

Sci-guy was morose in aspect, and Thoughtful-Woman took the next opportunity to move the conversation. "If you *do* write a book," she told R_, "put that in an appendix. Most people's eyes would cross and their minds go blank, long before they finished wading through whatever you might offer in such a regard." R_ looked like he was making a mental note...

Thoughtful-Woman smiled and reached for a more positive note. "Well, you've been reading, anyway!" R_ nodded, pleased. "The problem you have with your idea," she said, "is that you can't reproduce a hundred-page book in a couple paragraphs, and someone may hear your little 'guide-to-the-book' summary and dismiss it as not enough to be persuasive, and you will become a stumbling-block to them yourself." Now R_ was troubled — he felt even an appendix of several pages might have the same problem.[22] He turned to B-t, the only hope he had in this company. "Friend, will you join with me in the 'prayer of agreement'[23] for that not to happen?" B-t nodded, with an anxious mien, and they prayed.

Sci-guy suggested more: "That's right, you'll never do a hundred-page analysis of evidence any justice in a few paragraphs of your narratives, if you ever do write this 'book.' Put in an appendix, maybe five pages recapping the info, to let people see if they're interested in the in-depth exploration. If they *are*, they can use your Bibliography to get the book for themselves." Sci-guy believed in original research... [*the reader will note that it took us 7 pages to do the appendix. Oh well!*]

Sci-guy had been meditating on the scenery while all this conversation passed, and now he put his concerns front and center. "Remember that old conundrum about 'if a tree falls in the forest, and there is no one to hear it, does it make a sound?' Well, if someone 'falls' — dies — 'in the forest,' far from your Christian preaching, what hope is there for them, in what you are saying? If Jesus is 'the only way,' what of billions of people geographically and chronologically outside the reach of the ministry of His Name?" B-t frowned and R_ gripped the wheel. "His Name is a divine Name," R_ replied. "It undergirds all reality. 'All things were made through Him,* and without Him, was nothing made, of all the things that were made.'[24] People come into contact with His divine life when they read 'the book of nature' accurately to see the love, the power, the order given by wisdom — Romans 1:19-20, compare Psalms 19:1-4. That's how the 'unique Jesus' can be the 'one way to God' without being exclusionary to anyone." *But the more explicit knowledge of Him, the closer tracking of His word, the better,* R_ thought, and kicked himself later for not having said it.

B-t added that "In Biblical usage, 'name' is the character, the nature, of someone, not just a label. The essence, the reality..." R_ nodded, and resumed, "The Bible says that 'all who live in love are born of God.'[25] The heavens and the earth have been preaching God's love and making the knowledge of God available, but Jesus has clarified it and made a statement of it that all philosophy since has had to deal with."[26]

"A statement that no one really can get a grip on, if you're talking Trinity," Sci-guy replied. B-t thought that was evading the issue, when the saving Love offered through Jesus was the topic — a divine all-undergirding love offered in the fullest broadness.[27] However, R_ followed the thread: "When we stop and I can draw some diagrams to undergird a little presentation, let me discuss how the nature of being changes in higher dimensions, and let's see if we can make three-who-are-one make sense to you — not to define it, but at least to make it seem intelligible." Thoughtful-Woman looked interested; "God as three persons, all making one only," the "Trinity" of Father*, Son* and Spirit — that always perplexed her when she heard it.[28]

"I'll wait," said Sci-guy. A pleasant silence ensued, till Thoughtful-Woman said to B-t, "Weren't you going to ask him about that remark that 'Adam and Eve aren't presented well in Sunday School'?" R_ wished he could hide under a flat rock — far be it from him to knock Sunday School, and his grandmother had been a Sunday School teacher![29] "Well," he addressed B-t, "tell me, my friend, what did Adam and Eve do?" "The short version," B-t rejoined, "is that they ate the apple that had been forbidden to them, and were expelled from paradise, bringing death to the human race by their disobedience to God."

R_ braced himself between the wheel and the seat. "There's no apple tree in Genesis, the first book of the Bible," he said firmly. "That came from John Milton, the epic literary work *Paradise Lost*, interpreting the Bible's Genesis account for an audience of centuries past, for them to hear in their own cultural framework. Genesis says they 'ate the fruit of the tree of the knowledge of good and evil.' I've heard someone say, 'Well, Genesis doesn't tell us what kind of tree it was, whether it was an apple or a pomegranate or exactly what.' Nonsense! Genesis tells you *exactly* what kind of tree it was. It was the *tree of the knowledge of good and evil.* The Bible isn't shy about details — it tells you who King David committed adultery with, who her husband was, and how he was gotten out of the way — and it touches on that affair again, unnecessarily from a literary viewpoint, in the first page of the New Testament.[30] If it had been an apple tree or a pomegranate tree, the Bible would have said so. If your interpretative framework isn't up to handling 'the tree of the knowledge of good and evil,' you need to change your interpretative framework, not change what the Bible says."

The dog had a look on his face like "that's my beloved master," and B-t had a look like "you're trying to take us places nobody needs to go." B-t asked, "So you are saying we need to read Genesis as a parable, not a reality?"

R_ picked up on his earlier promise. "The Luiseño Indian data put it in a new perspective for me. In the Spanish Mission period in California, the Spanish authorities sent orders to document the old culture of the Native peoples. The priest who did the most thorough job of this was a Father Boscana. He had old Indian Elders as his sources, who had grown up before the Spanish missions arrived in their territory. They told Boscana that *at the time of creation, everything existed in a different level of reality.* Boscana, by the way, said that since they couldn't describe that 'reality,' it had to be considered imaginary. But of course they couldn't describe it, in terms of our language which is based on our reality! And the change in the nature of reality, which they are indicating, matches exactly what Genesis says about the condition of human life being transformed, by what Christian theology calls 'the Fall'."

Thoughtful-Woman wrinkled her face. "I never could get behind that 'eating the apple' — one act of disobedience and *pow,* 'you must die,' mortality reigns for all future generations. It sounds like if God had said, 'Don't spit on the sidewalk,' and they had spit on the sidewalk, they would have been condemned to be mortal and die, and all the later human beings also... It just never computed for me." R_ moved in while B-t frowned: "That doesn't portray it," R_ said. "The Bible says that they 'ate the fruit of the tree of the knowledge of good and evil' — that is, they set their own understanding up as the judge and guide of their conduct, they put their own egos and minds at the center of their understanding.

"This is the failure to recognize God as Lord, this is the fatal human-centeredness. It puts God in the place where He* can't reasonably sustain this off-the-best-place way of being for indefinite continuation, hence the imposition of mortality."

R_ paused, looking as if he wanted to say more but the problems didn't lend themselves to simple exposition. Sci-guy said, "You're not really giving me something I can take a firm grip on, but you do put it into a different place."

R_ had a perplexed look himself. "Here's another piece that moves it but doesn't give you an ending-up viewpoint:

an atheistic evolutionist, Carl Sagan... points out in _Dragons of Eden_ *that there is a remarkable correlation between the evolutionary development of man and the Genesis account of the Fall. A key observation in the fossil record is that there occurred a rapid [in evolutionary time ...] increase in the cranial capacity of hominids [per the scientific timeline, this increase occurs in mere hundreds of thousands of years among BILLIONS of years]. This increase represents the development of that portion of the brain used for abstract and analytical thought. For the first time, hominids could grasp the concept of a God and of right and wrong. A simple clear way of describing it is that man ate the fruit of the knowledge of good and evil. The consequences are direct: the increased cranial capacity led to a skull too large for the female pelvic structure and, therefore, inevitable pain at childbirth. No other mammal experiences such a pain. With the analytical mind, the struggle for survival meant a switch from brute-force food gathering to cunning and skill in cultivating food — the sweat of the brow. Above all, abstract thought led to the awareness of death and its inevitability and finality. Here, too, came the recognition of God and the beginning notions of what it meant to communicate with him. Some of the earliest signs of civilization are burial grounds with crude items of worship...*[31]

Thoughtful-Woman was living up to the name R_ had given her in the quiet of his own mind. "It does make you think," she said, "and I'm willing to meditate about these things and accept that they're not handed to me in a simplistic, neatly-wrapped package. So, tell me about these prayers that you would include if you do a book on these things we're discussing."

But unity of mind was not to be so easy. (Is it ever?) Sci-guy said, "Listening to you talk about the Bible reminds me of my first night on this trip. I was fed up with hitchhiking, which I hadn't done since I was a teenager. People are so uncaring and disdainful! I got myself a hotel room, I restored my mood in the bar — the next morning I was nursing a hangover, and I picked up the Gideon's Bible there in my hotel room and browsed in it — I hadn't ever read word one in the Bible. I came on something that was patently absurd — it would make "π" "pi" exactly 3 instead of 3.14159, and anybody who knows anything about science knows that's ridiculous and also that it's a key fact in the whole mathematical structure of the universe."

R_ could see that either he or Sci-guy would have to explain to Thoughtful-Woman and B-t what "π" was ("pi", pronounced "pie"). "OK," Thoughtful-Woman interrupted R_'s thoughts, "if this challenge is so sharp, go ahead on that, and *then* tell me about your prayers."

"I'm going to do the thing on 'poverty' first," R_ replied firmly. "Martin Luther King Jr. said, 'Life's most persistent and urgent question is, What are you doing for others?'"[32]

Chapter Four: Poverty: "Love your neighbor as yourself" incl. the BTD's (Better-To-Do)

"So you think God has a special concern for the poor," said Sci-guy. "The poor remind me of Abraham Lincoln's comment that God must love plain-looking people, 'because He made so many of them.' "

"The Bible speaks much of God's concern for the poor," R_ replied. "It says, 'Whoever oppresses the poor shows contempt for their Maker' (Prov. 14:31 NIV). And James, who chaired the Jerusalem Council — the first council of the Church (Bible, Acts 15), reproached in his epistle: 'You have dishonored the poor' (Bible, James 2:6 ESV). Rick Warren, who has become somewhat famous as a megachurch pastor now, said that upon his wife's getting breast cancer: 'It was like the blinders came off... I've got three advanced degrees. I went to two different seminaries and a Bible school. How did I miss the 2,000 verses in the Bible where it talks about the poor?'[33] The old hymn 'Good King Wenceslas' promised Christians 'rank or wealth possessing,' that 'You who will now bless the poor, shall yourselves find blessing.' " Sitting quietly after this exposition, then, R_ was thinking of his friend in Africa who wrote, "We are eating only every two or three days, and the children do not want to study because they are hungry." (Personal communication from Congo/D.R.C., 2009.)

"Wow," said Thoughtful-Woman. "Are there really 2,000 verses in the Bible on poverty?" R_ replied, "The Christian service organization Love INC (Love In the Name of Christ) had a PDF download on their website that listed Bible verses — and it had 13 pages of quotations."[34] B-t was glad to be able to contribute from core doctrine, being an earnest Bible-student himself: "Concern for the poor is a basic consequence of the commandment that Jesus taught: 'Do unto others as you would have them do unto you' (Matthew 7:12). Jesus put that into a deep-cutting form, action-oriented!"

Sci-guy was glum. "Some people would tell you that it will never work," he said. "One of Darwin's undeniable insights is that all forms of life tend to over-reproduce themselves, above the carrying-capacity of their environment, which is what creates the pressure for natural selection of the 'fittest.' Your dog, for example — no personal disrespect intended — can produce a litter of four to six puppies every year, making *dozens* of dogs for the next generation, and progressively escalating from there, generation by generation — and all living things tend to over-reproduce. Some people would say you're fighting the basic dynamics of nature."

R_ was convinced God has a better idea. "An African said that the best contraception is the knowledge that your children will live to be adults," he said. "People have lots of children so that enough will survive to take care of them in their old age. It isn't a mindless dynamic."[35]

Thoughtful-Woman wanted to go somewhere else with the conversation. "How would you help the poor?" she asked. R_ went back almost 1,000 years for his first answer: " 'Anticipate charity by preventing poverty; assist the reduced fellowman... so that he may earn an honest living... This is the highest step and summit of charity's golden ladder.' That's from Maimonides, about A.D. 1200."[36] Sci-guy appreciated the new direction of the analysis, adding, "Micro-credit is helping people in poorer countries to start small family businesses and get out of poverty. A few hundred dollars, in some cases, or a few thousand dollars for others, can often put a third-world family in a good income-earning situation for life, with a little equipment and technical help." "Some organizations are supplying livestock to people who couldn't buy their own, and achieving the same result," B-t added.

"So if we talk you into doing a book, you'll talk about the Bible's command to care, and organizations that people could support for real impact?" Thoughtful-Woman asked R_, almost playfully. The dog was brooding, stretched out flat on the floor — perhaps still contemplating the canine species as over-reproducers? R_ needed to answer her question, more than to reach to break the dog's mood. "I would set out *stewardship*, because the better-to-do people — 'BTD's,' I call them — will have to account for their stewardship of what was given to them. And I would pray for right respect and appreciation to be shown to them, when they *are* generous, and when they *do* productive development, so that they can be in a positive environment, not one of resentment or envy. Then, I would pray for them not to sink into worldly values, wrongly absorbed in the pleasures of this life, which tempts them to consume their resources instead of giving them the proper use."[37]

"You and the Pope," Sci-guy said. "He puts out a lot about economic justice and concern for the poor." B-t chimed in again, quoting " 'Happy are those who consider the poor; the LORD[38] delivers them in the day of trouble.' That's Psalm 41:1 NRSV." R_ remembered a grimmer Scripture about the poor, and quoted it for them: " 'For the LORD is their defender. He will ruin anyone who ruins them.'[39] That's Proverbs 22:23 in the Bible." Thoughtful-Woman was moved: "That sounds like what happened to the mortgage companies that lured poor people into buying houses they couldn't afford, with come-on low interest rates for the initial years..." They pondered in silence, till she added, "Well, until they got bailed out by the Government..."

Everyone laughed, and that brought the dog out of his funk. They stopped where the wind was whispering in the pine trees, and had a pleasant lunch — how sweet it is to be able to eat when you are hungry!

The dog lay stretched out nearby. As he watched the "two-leggeds," he wanted so badly to be able to say to R_, "If you ever do write this in a book, remind your readers to be always conscious of that 'sweetness' of provision!"

Chapter Five: Is It Absurd? Some aspects of the Bible — reported miracle of sun standing still, math error of π "pi" in Bible

The lunch and chat had been fun, with the wind whispering in the pine trees. But now, with the hitchhikers back in the RV and "the show on the road," R_ wondered: *would they take up the question(s) of life again?* How nice to be just a man and his dog on the road, soaking up the beauty of the glorious created world — the splendor made by a wise and loving Creator — even just the light itself, shining off the mountains and trees and flowers, shining on the waters — such a miracle, the "simple" light which contains all the colors... but the "Fallen-ness" of creation lurked throughout "Nature," and the perplexities of the human mind went with us in whatever splendors we might journey among...

The next day answered his question. Dawn broke over a desert landscape, painting it lavishly with reds and purples. The desert was in bloom, with the special intensity that cactus flowers manage to stage. It was a scene worthy of a Creator.

R_'s reverie was not long-lived. Perhaps Thoughtful-Woman had not slept well; she was sharper-edged this morning. "So you think the answer to death is the God who gave life to the world, and you think the Trinity in the Bible should draw us nearer to see, like the 'burning bush' drew Moses," she started up. "How can you take that seriously? After all you had to say, I started browsing in your friend's Bible" — she waved a hand toward B-t — "and I came on a story of how God helped his beleaguered people fight their enemies by making the sun stand still. How can you take an account like that seriously?"

Sci-guy also was more negative: "Remember that I told you, the first night I was travelling, I had a few beers. The next morning, I was fighting a mild headache, and I picked up the Gideon's Bible in the hotel room, and browsed a bit — *that* gave me a *terrible* headache. I was reading about a washing bowl used in their religious activities that was 'ten cubits measure across' and 'thirty cubits measure around' — that makes a ratio of *exactly* three-to-one for the diameter and circumference of a circle, and anybody who survived high school math knows that there is a ratio concerning the circle's measurements that is called "π" "pi," [pronounced "pie"] and it is 3.14159... — NOT three — and if this is real history, they must have measured over 31 cubits *around* the washing bowl! Careless or stupid or something, but not the text to guide my life, eh?"

Sci-guy closed with, "Every time I hear 'Bible,' it brings back that headache. Maybe you can cure it for me!" R_ reflected — the discussion had mentioned "Bible" quite often, and this was the first the man had complained. Sci-guy *was* a tolerant individual, actually!

The dog was watching R_ intently. R_ sighed. The desert was in bloom, but his day was not. "Yes," he said, "I have heard of these things. Jefferson wrote his nephew and said, 'Read the Bible like any other book. For the sun to stand still in the sky — now that we know the earth turns under the sun's rays — the rotation of the earth would have to stop, momentum would cause trees to tear out of the ground as the earth stopped beneath their continuing movement, buildings would fly apart for the same reason...' [40] The hitchhiker who had brought this issue up, smiled broadly. A nice scientific expansion of the dubious view she had stated... and with that added depth, surely irrefutable. Not that she wanted R_ to be wrong — but truth was truth, friend... R_ continued without taking his eyes off the road, "And the 'washing bowl' issue also... let me show you an analysis a scholar did of *that* text.

"I heard a preaching by Dr. James Sanders," R_ continued, "and Sanders said, 'Read the Bible critically *and* faithfully.' Yes, we grasp what Jefferson said, but instead of just tossing it out over a surface objection, we read 'faithfully' also and we ask, 'How could this be?' And if you do *that*, you get answers — sometimes simple ones, like the puzzle of *one* angel at Christ's empty tomb versus *two* angels [41] — sometimes ones of deep mystery, as we are, for all our science, still limited in our grasp.

"Jefferson has a point. So how could 'the sun stand still' for such a length of time as to help deliver God's struggling people? The answer would seem to be a 'lensing effect' in the upper atmosphere — a special touch of God's power bending the rays, more and more over time for a period of hours, so the light the people needed would be prolonged." Sci-guy brought a wiser perspective to *that*: "It would have to be in space, not the upper atmosphere," he said, "to get *hours* of added light. Do you think your God can reach into space and do changes?" R_ clearly thought so, even if he wasn't smart enough to think in terms of the thinness of the atmosphere in relation to the size of the earth, and B-t nodded enthusiastically, but neither voiced the obvious.

The hitchhikers were interested — R_ didn't really make explanations simple and clear, but it came through enough to do. The other question they had posed — "π" "pi," the ratio of a circle's two measurements — across and around — that was such a simple thing, once you thought about it, and so basic and far-reaching: R_ would have to climb more than the highest mountain to turn that universal ratio from 3.14159. [42]

The RV passed a small river — a stream, really, gurgling over rocks and splashing up around them — and R_ went back at his guests' request, so they could all play in the water for a while. The dog waded joyfully, but he wouldn't swim. When they resumed travel, R_ screwed up his determination and took on the topic of whether the Bible — a text whose millennium-plus of composition R_ believed had been watched over by the God it was intended to make known — whether *that* Bible could screw up so basic and reliable a thing as "π," the ratio of the measurements of a circle.

"Harold Lindsell looked at the Bible text about that 'washing bowl,' or 'bronze laver,' " R_ said, as he plunged into the issue. A glance in the rear-view mirror at a couple of blank faces told him he would have to recapitulate the opening question. "When you have a circle," R_ said, "it has two basic measurements.

The distance across is the diameter, and the distance around is the circumference." R_ was pleased to see Thoughtful-Woman make a quick sketch on a piece of paper, which the Bible-toting hitchhiker "B-t" eyeballed intently.

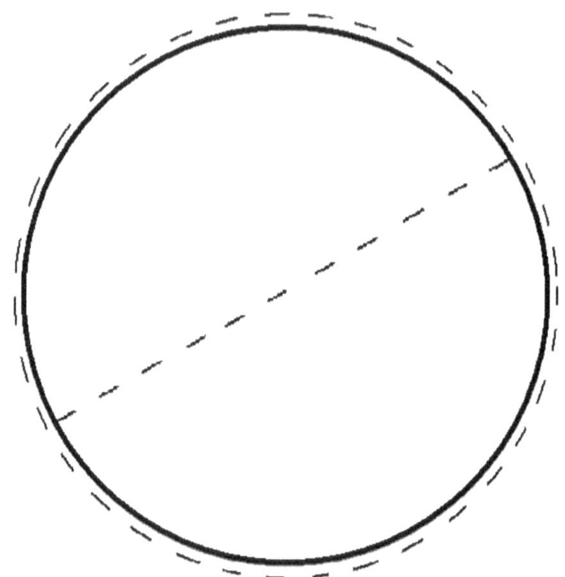

R_ didn't have an enthusiastic audience for this exposition. The Bible-toter's eyes were glazed over. Sci-guy didn't think R_ could pull this one "out of the fire," and it didn't really bother him. "π" was pretty basic, even if most of the citizenry were ignorant of it, and if the Bible couldn't handle "π" it was obviously the product of reality-illiterate human minds — and that was how he had thought about the Bible for a long time.

The RV swept past a lovely lake, and R_ reflected on days gone by. One May, in the far north, he had driven by such a lake — still capped with ice, a thin cap as Spring worked on it, but melted through only around the very edge of the lake. As the wind ruffled the water, the little waves moved the ice up and down and it tinkled beautifully like very fine wind chimes. The world, so awesome in all its beauty and wonder — yet marred, stained by blood and tears.

But how people viewed the larger issues of the world sometimes turned on some of the smaller issues, and while none of the hitchhikers were enthusiastic about the question of the "bronze laver" religious washing bowl and "π," it was time for R_ to lay that objection to rest — "to put that puppy to bed," to borrow a friend's phrase.

R_ parked the RV so everyone could stretch their legs, then gathered the discussion. A diagram was what he needed:

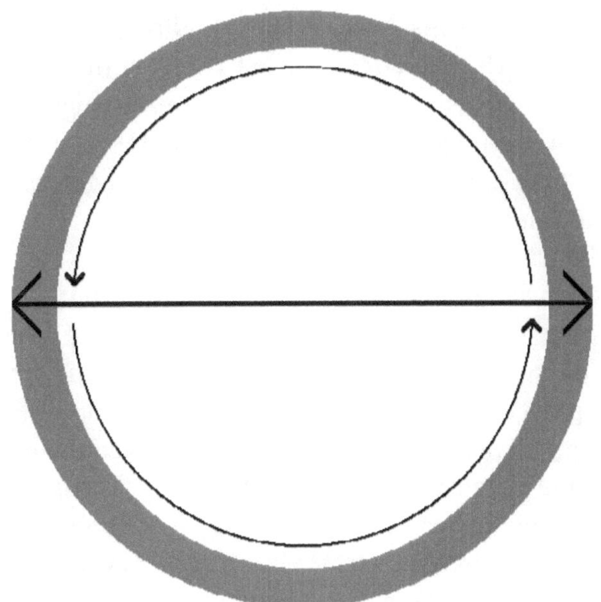

"The 10-cubit 'diameter' and 30-cubit 'circumference' come together because of the thickness of the 'bronze laver,' the washing bowl for the religious ceremonies," he began. "A commentator suggests that they measured the outer diameter by having guys stand on both sides and stretch the rope over the laver —thus including the thickness of the bronze walls on both sides. This would be the logical way to do it, if you're using ropes to measure, with guys on both sides holding the rope taut. And to measure the circumference, 'around,' well, the sides had decorative bronze figures all around the outside, so with that unevenness and the basic geometry to contend with, the easiest way to measure 'around' it would be to climb inside and push the measuring rope around the smooth inside. Well then, the Bible says what the thickness of the walls was, and when you deduct that from the 10-cubit 'diameter,' and *then* multiply by π = 3.14159, it matches the measured 'circumference' within eight hundredths of an inch, or an accuracy of one part in 1,000." [43]

Sci-guy took this in readily. It wasn't something that would sway much of his thinking, but it did show that what R_ had to say might be worth considering, to cut through some of the superficialities. The Bible-toter hadn't cared in the first place — "π" was never going to go deep with him. Thoughtful-Woman considered it carefully — once she understood the question, it was like a small rock that kept the train of her thought from rolling forward, to consider the Bible seriously.

The "π" "pi" question was like a small leak in the bottom of a ship — unglamorous work, but essential — but it must not distract from the larger issues of the voyage, the glory of the ocean, to pursue the metaphor. "*Take all my need and opportunity, Lord,*" R_ prayed quietly in the depth of his mind. "*Hold them in Your hands, and fulfill the good.*" People neglected the question of death, people became entangled in thickets of thought that held them from the light.[44] Hopefully this exposition cleared one bramble bush and gave interest to see that others could be cleared also. "*You have made these people so that they might find light, and live,*" R_ prayed.

The "obstacle" problem is more like a flat tire on your vehicle, R_ thought. *Can't go on till it's taken care of...* A sudden bang punctuated his thoughts, and the RV leaned to the right as the failing tire gave its last. The dog let out a short howl, which scrambled R_'s thoughts — he had never heard that from the creature, and it jolted R_'s attempt to concentrate as he pulled the stricken vehicle onto the shoulder. The shoulder was more steeply sloped than most, and Thoughtful-Woman's face showed alarm as the RV leaned sharply. Sci-guy's face reflected a mind processing slopes, angles, center-of-gravity, forces and balance. "If this thing rolls over, we're in trouble" — the thought could have been anyone's, and at least the dog had stopped howling. *Damn, damn, damn,* R_ thought; then *that* troubled his mind, for he was trying to be God's person in this situation, and what kind of impression would swearing make? B-t saved the day with a loud "Crap!"[45]

Sci-guy's whirling mind of forces, torques, and balancing led him to point to a more level spot twenty feet ahead, and there the jack held nicely as B-t helped R_ change the failed tire. Thoughtful-Woman's mind of concern led her to pet the dog reassuringly, and things were soon restored. *For once a positive and effective unity among us all,* R_ thought. Does it take trouble to bring that about? *Let us be formed by Your Spirit so we may be blessed without needing trouble,* R_ prayed in the depth of his mind.

As travel resumed, R_ was able to meditate on the beauty of the desert flowers for a while, then the discussion swept in again. "These kinds of issues are interesting, in a way," Thoughtful-Woman said, "but one of my philosophy professors delivered an angry lecture one day, about how the terrible sufferings and devastations in the world proved that there was no loving, all-powerful God like you describe." R_ understood, but replied, "When we get a perspective on the reality underlying 'Adam and Eve' that enables you to take up the meaning of that matter, I'll ask our Bible-studying friend for an exposition of the 'fallen-ness' of this present world. For now, let me just tell you what *God's statement* is about this world — it comes when He* talks about His followers, and He* says that because 'they desire a better country, that is, a heavenly one. Therefore God is not ashamed to be called their God' (Bible, Hebrews 11:16 ESV, NRSV). That shows the precise point: God agrees with you exactly that this world, as it is *now*, is not what it's supposed to be, not 'the best of all possible worlds,' and NOT how we are to remain. 'Reality should, could have been, otherwise,' said George Steiner.[46] A man named William Paul Young wrote a novel called *The Shack*, and in it he has the Trinitarian God saying, 'We're not justifying it, we're redeeming it.'[47] It isn't the way He* made it, it isn't the way He* wanted it to be, nor is it the way He* will let it remain."

Chapter Six: The rest of this book and you

When next they stopped to stretch, R_ let the hitchhikers go off into a flower-laden meadow, and he talked to the dog, in that strangely productive way that dog owners have with their cherished companions. "That idea of writing a book... What I would do: cover the basics, then give people who want to study the intellectual information places for more in-depth treatment — because these things, done thoroughly, take books of 150 to 600 pages on *each* area of concern, and what I would do, would be to capsulate the matters and give references for books I've found helpful. But *before* the in-depth discussions, I would put in the prayers, because people who *want* the intellectual considerations, are certainly smart enough to follow the multi-part layout — and people who read about the basic considerations and 'see the light,' would want the prayers — some of them would *not* want the extended 'intellectual' stuff, and it would only throw them off."

The dog was pleased, as dogs always are at being included in the conversation — their end of the matter is to care if their owners are "o.k.," and here it seemed that his owner, R_, was actually not only "o.k." but enjoying a broad new idea.

"Yes," R_ said enthusiastically, "that would be the layout, the table of contents would guide them to any specific interests once they saw my general structure for the book, and I would put an annotated bibliography that could help them focus if there was a particular area where they might be helped by what I have been reading." If the dog had had human intellect, he might have said, "Beloved master, the 80^{+} books you've worked through on these matters, are just a drop in the bucket in the world of books — but, hey, they might indeed be just the ticket for someone." Constrained by Nature to be silent, however, the dog smiled and nudged R_'s hand, and they went hiking after the others.

[Marijuana more prevalent, sometimes as "sacred freedom" in America now, → the caution in endnote 211; my 18 years' experience, page 126.]

Chapter Seven: Prayers Accordingly: We begin…

Thoughtful-Woman said, "Now it's time for the 'prayers' you said you would discuss. What would they be? I mean, if you *did* try to write a book." R_ shifted uncomfortably in the driver's seat of the RV, and B-t stepped into the pause: "My own favorite prayer is, 'Thank You Lord, that my troubles are so small and my blessings are so great.' As long as you're able to breathe a prayer — or even think one — there's truth in both clauses, when we look at eternal life with God by comparison with this mortal passage!"

R_ made a mental note, *write something about the importance of gratitude, how it's like plugging in to the power source…* R_ followed swiftly as B-t paused: "My own might be, 'Grant me to take the way of escape that You provide' — that's one I need to remember whenever there are problems and griefs, because God promised to always provide the way through them.[48] It's easy to forget and focus not-on-Him*."

Thoughtful-Woman smiled, but these obviously weren't going very deep with her. "If you went to seminary," she addressed R_, "you must have picked up some special prayers." R_ looked like he had been struck by a thought, as the dog swiveled to gaze in hope that his master had more to offer. "One is a single word from Biblical Hebrew that has stuck with me," he said. "It's ע מ ש א ESHma, it's in the Qal imperfect tense and it can be translated 'let me hear.' I use it in a special meaning, 'Let me hear You, receive Your voice and be what You desire.' B-t was on the case: "The verb 'to hear' in Hebrew also means 'to obey'," he said.[49] "Yes," replied R_ as the dog grinned and licked his hand, "I ask to do that. Some people's attitude to God is like a two-year old — the first word out of their mouth is 'No.' I think that my Creator has the best ideas about what I can be."[50]

Thoughtful-Woman petted the dog, which made him very happy. R_ took another cut: "I pray, 'To fulfill for You' — as His* child, there's something for me to be/do that is my part *for* His precious heart." B-t frowned slightly, and R_ went on, "It may sound pompous or presumptuous, but I think it has to be true, and so I want to be that, fully. It includes my joys — when they're right joys, He* shares them." "Your phrase 'right joys' means excluding exulting over a theft or getting jacked up on drugs, eh?" said Thoughtful-Woman. "Quite so," answered R_.[51]

"If you guys con me into writing a book," said R_ , "there would be two groups of prayers — prayers from the great tradition, and ones that have been given to me." *Where to go from there,* he thought. R_ was looking very serious, and Thoughtful-Woman was, too. "There are a lot of times when I just wouldn't have any idea how to pray," she said. "You might attend to the Lord's Prayer," R_ replied, "as Jesus Himself* taught us — He said, 'In this way, then, you are to pray:

Our Father in heaven,
Hallowed be Your Name (may Your holy name be honored).
Your kingdom come, Your will be done, on earth as it is in heaven.
Give us this day our daily bread, and forgive our sins, as we forgive those who wrong us.' "

R_ paused and looked to see if the hitchhikers were listening. "Here," he said, "I personally like to add, *Grant us to be so perfectly forgiving indeed, and put Your grace to absolve anywhere that we have not been!"* Then he returned to the main prayer:

"Do not lead us into hard testing, but deliver us from evil, for Yours is the kingdom and the power and the glory. Amen."

The Bible-toting hitchhiker that R_ thought of as "B-t" was upset. "That's not what it says! It starts off 'Our Father, who art in heaven...' " Sci-guy looked puzzled. "Who is 'Art,' and why would Jesus emphasize 'Art' being in heaven?" R_ said, "Let me just say that the New Testament was written in Greek, and my friend is quoting the old King James Bible, translated from the Greek in 1611, and I'm using my own modernized wording after studying enough Greek, and reading enough modern translations, to think it out a bit. 'Do not lead us into hard testing' is from one of the modern versions,[52] and there is an argument about whether 'deliver us from evil' should be 'deliver us from the Evil One'[53] — the Greek supports both versions there."

R_ tried to keep the conversation from lurching into a bottomless pit of argument by reaching for momentum. "Our Lord gave us two Great Commandments,[54] and 'one great opportunity' — so those turn into a good basic prayer:

"Grant me, Father, Lord, to love You with all my heart and mind and soul and strength, and to love my neighbor as myself, according to Your holy word. Grant me to worship You in SPIRIT *and in truth, perfectly so — grant US to do these things, in grace abounding!"*

B-t was aggravated. "If you're going to teach prayers, you *need* to teach first the prayer of acceptance, to receive Jesus as Savior and Lord, so that people can *have* the divine gift of spiritual life that you've been talking about." As he lapsed into aggrieved silence, Thoughtful-Woman took up a different aspect: "I like that 'in grace abounding' — I think we should ask for what we want, and that's good!"

R_ let the silence hang for a moment. *There are a lot of versions of the "sinner's prayer," for accepting Jesus as Savior,* he thought, *and do people recognize the problem of sin when the only time they see the word is on a restaurant menu offering "SINfully delicious desserts"? If they just come humbly to God, won't they be accepted, even if they haven't got their heads around some concepts? The Bible tells us that Hezekiah prayed, asking the Lord God to accept those who came "even if not in accordance with the Law"[55] — B-t's got a good point at some level,* R_ thought, *but are we at that level now?*

R_ took up where he had left off. "The 'great opportunity' to worship is stated in the Bible in John chapter 4, when Jesus talked with a Samaritan woman at a well — the first person He told that He was the promised Messiah, John 4:25-26 — He made that astounding revelation first to a woman, in an age when women's status was not so elevated, and to a Samaritan, an 'out-group' to the Jews of His day — ! He said that such worshipers are what 'the Father seeks' — we have the opportunity to be what the

Creator of the universe is looking for! John 4:23." B-t finally smiled, and R_ was glad. "If I came up with that idea, that we can be what God is looking for, I would be the most arrogant person in the history of the human race — but He* revealed it to us, and it's not for us to set aside! The NIV Bible[56], a top-selling modern translation, states that Scripture as 'worship the Father in the Spirit and in truth,' but if I ever do that book, I will write it as 'in SPIRIT and in truth.' The original Greek was written all in capital letters, before 'majuscule' writing segued to 'minuscule.' If you write it as 'in Spirit and in truth,' you see that it refers to the Holy Spirit, Whom we need to worship properly — our own spirits need to be involved also, and the small-capitals form leaves 'SPIRIT' as reading both ways — the human being's spirit and God's Holy Spirit." B-t smiled again — he had finally found something he could approve, but he was too busy praying in his head about unsolved problems to say so. He paused his praying and confirmed R_'s point by quoting the rest of the Bible verse that R_ had been discussing: "worship the Father* in spirit and truth, for the Father seeks such as these — John 4:23, NRSV Bible translation." It was R_'s turn to smile. Thoughtful-Woman looked like she was already trying out some prayers, and they rode in silence for miles.

"Done?" Thoughtful-Woman asked R_. "Next," R_ said, "*Grant me Lord, to abide in You*. That's a privilege Jesus held out to us in John, in the 'Upper Room discourse,' chapters 13 - 17 (especially 15:4), and it reflects His* coming to be our source of life and wisdom."

B-t was still wary about R_, but he was moved to favor by this exposition, so he chimed in: "My favorite — one which has served me in many, many situations — is 'Take words with you.' " Thoughtful-Woman was puzzled, so B-t said, "That's Bible, Hosea 14:2," and R_ recited it from memory: "Take words with you, and return to the LORD God; say to God, 'Forgive all our sins and receive us graciously, and we will praise You.' "[57] R_ liked "having the floor," so to speak, and so he held forth further: "Rev. James White in Alaska told me, 'You'll get a lot more from God by praising Him* than by endless asking.'[58]" Thoughtful-Woman wrinkled her nose.

"Your God sounds a little vain, I'm afraid," she said. B-t was pained. "No, it's more like turning your face towards the direction you want to see in — you receive the light when you face into it." *If I write a book, I must remember to expand on that remark so people can understand it clearly,*[59] R_ thought to himself.

"Do you have a favorite prayer?" Thoughtful-Woman asked R_. "Yes, *Hold me to Yourself,*" R_ answered, "*and guide and provide.* When it's just all too much," he continued, "I sometimes pray, 'See! Save!' — because Jesus said that He* does know our needs before we ask. But it's often important to 'pray through' — to wring our hearts out thoroughly — and honestly — before Him* (Psalm 62:8). It helps in 'casting all our care on Him*,' which the Bible tells us to do, and there's a promise He* gave us: *Do not be anxious about anything, but in every situation, by prayer and petition, with thanksgiving, present your requests to God. And the peace of God, which transcends all understanding, will guard your hearts and your minds in Christ Jesus (Philippians 4:6-7 NIV).*"

"I like that, I want that!" said Thoughtful-Woman. She looked like the idea made her happy enough to clap her hands, but she didn't.

========================

We mentioned in Chapter Six that the rest of this book involves a combination of intellectual material of relevance, with spiritual comments. If you find some of the following chapters becoming dense reading that you choose to skip in favor of material that more suits your personal interests, we acknowledge that we have tried to design this book to be like a website in that you can "jump" to portions that interest you... (Discussions of the intellectual controversies may be helpful to you in later periods, ?) We might urge you to take up the "prayer and petition with thanksgiving" as above, before your eyes leave this chapter, !

Chapter Eight: Destinations, Temporary; Apocalyptic Matters

"So where are you heading?" R_ asked Sci-guy. How had he managed not to ask one of his hitchhikers that already? "D.C., eventually," was the reply. R_ asked further: "Why?"

"I have a 300-page report in the bottom section of my backpack," Sci-guy answered. "Protected in cardboard and waterproofed with heavy plastic, of course, and two copies on DVDs. It's the final report of my last several years work — I got a National Science Foundation grant for the capstone of my career."

"Good for you!" R_ exclaimed. "And now you're hitchhiking?" Sci-guy smiled, a thin smile: "When the state budget cutbacks started to be so severe, the university made a policy decision to protect people's jobs — those of us that were able to get grants, would be switched to grant funding, and that way the layoffs wouldn't be as severe among the other people. Like a lot of the things they do now — like Arizona's idea of selling the State Capitol Building and leasing it back for use by the State Government[60] — these things help for the moment but make the long-term worse. At least for me — my grant ran out, the final report is due 90 days after the end of the funding, my wife won't let me use my unemployment check to pay for the trip to D.C. And I have to deliver the report in person; there is a panel that will meet with me for their initial review of it. So, from eminent professor to hitchhiker, and I had to borrow my teenager's backpack." He smiled, a little deeper smile now. The dog came up to nuzzle his hand and be petted, and Sci-guy seemed to find that mood-lifting.

"I'll take you to D.C.," R_ said. B-t's destination would be along the way. Thoughtful-Woman was going farther south — what of *that*? "If you get me to D.C., I can take the Amtrak," she said. Washington D.C., then — burned once by a foreign army, never entered by the Confederate armies[61] — was now the *goal* for all of them. *See the Smithsonian's wonderful gem and minerals collection*, R_ reminded himself. Now he, too, had his short-term *goal*. But, the trip would also make both R_ and the dog *tourists* at the White House — and participants!

The "*goal*" of life according to some evolutionary philosophers is to disseminate your genes. The *goal* of human life, per the Westminster Shorter Catechism, is "to glorify God and to enjoy Him* forever." The dog's *goal* [62] was to live the day in positive harmony with his "master" (his "human," other people would phrase it) — and, if possible, with the other folks around him... An <u>inexorable journey to a more distant destination</u>, *that* he left to the "two-leggeds" to process.

Apocalyptic Matters: Reflections from within a temporary destination

Thoughtful-Woman browsed more in B-t's Bible as the RV meandered along a river. When they all piled out to stretch, the dog led Sci-guy on a jaunt up a hillside, and Thoughtful-Woman asked about the Bible's "signs of the end." "War, earthquakes, rumors of wars — those have been going on for a long time," she said. "But what about 'the sign of the Son of Man will appear in the sky' — as Jesus said in Matthew 24:30 — ?" R_'s smile seemed out of touch with the seriousness of the subject. "I saw something in Alaska that I could call that," he said, and B-t started violently. "I was gazing at a low line of clouds that hung just above the setting sun, and the sun turned the bottom of the clouds into a glowing golden line above a stretch of the horizon — then, for just a few moments after the sun went behind the hills, a vertical ray of golden light went straight up from it, and the golden lines made a very clear and radiant cross."

Silence prevailed for several minutes, and then B-t chimed in regarding a different sign, "the moon turned blood red:"[63] "I read an account by a Native American Indian named Black Buffalo, who is also a Christian preacher. He said that in 1980, after he left a church where he preached, he was praying and rejoicing, praising God, when the sky started to turn red. At this point he was driving across open country in Texas. And in just a few minutes it was a brilliant, fluorescent red. He said, 'The sky, stars, and moon — all were red.' His wife asked if it was a forest fire and he 'explained we were between Pecos and nowhere. There was just sagebrush out there and they were three feet apart. It could not be a fire.' Black Buffalo said that a *front page newspaper article, the next morning, asked the question in its last paragraph*, 'Could this be what the Bible was talking about when it said the moon shall turn to blood?' "[64]

Thoughtful-Woman asked, "Shouldn't the 'sign' be seen all over the earth, not just by a few people or in one place?" R_ wasn't sure what to say to that. Jesus' "Incarnation"[65] came in one place and was then publicized all over...

Sci-guy was staring out the side window. This was not his sort of thing. But R_ had him in mind more than the others, with an interpretation that *could* be seen everywhere on earth if people took it to heart: "The full prophecy includes 'the sun will be turned to darkness... the stars will fall from the sky ... before the day of the LORD' (Mark 13:24-25). The day of His* return, the day of judgment. Look, now," R_ continued, "see if you can agree with me on this: For thousands of years, the sun and moon and stars served as 'signs,' just as Genesis 1:14 said — and beyond 'marking seasons, days and years' as Genesis said, they were seen by thoughtful people as signs of the great providing power of God, of God's love for beauty, God's wisdom and creativity, God's care for us — but now they are explained as naturalistic events — atoms and molecules in motion, fields of forces at work, 'that's what they do, that's just the way these things work' — seen that way, the sun and stars point to no greater realities beyond themselves. With that kind of 'scientific' consciousness, as 'signs' the sun *has* been 'turned to darkness,' the stars *have* 'fallen.' What do you think?"

Chapter Nine: Prayers, Further Considerations ("Still Trying")

Thoughtful-Woman went up to B-t when they stopped for gas. "What was that about a 'sinner's prayer' — a prayer to accept God into your life?" B-t felt it was the key thing for beginning life with God: "God gave us all free will, the freedom to choose Him* or to live without Him* and go our own way, which ends in death, because God is the only source of life," he told her. "So we have to make a decision to give God His* rightful — and fruitful — place in our lives. Here, listen, this is how the Gideon's New Testament phrases it:

'My Decision to Receive Christ As My Savior:

Confessing to God that I am a sinner, and believing that the Lord Jesus Christ died for my sins on the cross and was raised for my justification, I do now receive and confess Him as my personal Savior.' "

(Endnote 55 has another version)

Thoughtful-Woman felt it made sense, yet implications from it went out to great distances. "Jesus died for our sins, that's what you call 'atonement,' isn't it?" she asked B-t. "Yes," B-t replied, "it would take, at the very least, a chapter of a book to do it justice." "What do they say after that?" she asked B-t. "Well, they go on with the obvious fact that a new life demands nourishment," B-t replied. "Their next paragraph says:

'Seeking a Church:[66]

'After making your decision to receive Christ, we encourage you to prayerfully seek a local church, congregation or assembly that will assist you in growing as a new Christian by the clear teaching of the Bible. (Bible, 2 Pet. 3:18 : But grow in the grace and knowledge of our Lord and Savior Jesus Christ.)'

"They also give some Bible verses that document your 'Assurance As a Believer:' Romans 10:9, John 5:24, John 20:31.

These are things you can turn to when your new life gets stressful and you wonder if it's really at work in *you* (per Philippians 1:6)."

They walked silently back to join the RV as R_ prepared to hit the road again. R_ was waiting to tell them another favorite prayer that he felt almost everyone could use: "Do you feel that when you try to relate to God, an endless array of pressures and distractions come against you? An Alaskan gave me this prayer: 'Bring in our wandering minds, Lord.'[67]"

B-t said, "I usually read the King James Bible translation, but there's one verse where I really like the NIV wording: 'Bring to an end the violence of the wicked and make the righteous secure' — Psalm 7:9."

Then, B-t laughed as a thought struck him. The dog was startled. "Here's a 'general' one for you: I heard a preacher say, 'We serve time, but time serves God.'[68] That brings up the promise of the Bible: 'He* (the Lord God Almighty) will be the sure foundation of your times.' That's a promise to claim in your prayers!" Thoughtful-Woman looked very, very interested, so R_ opened his NIV Bible to Isa. 33:6 and she read out loud, "He (God) will be the sure foundation for your times, a rich store of salvation and wisdom and knowledge; the fear of the LORD is the key to this treasure." She frowned. "I don't like the idea of 'fearing' God," she said. R_ quoted Psalm 130:4 to her: "But with you [God] there is forgiveness; therefore you are feared." He went on, "There you see the difference between 'servile fear,' and the old meaning of the word. 'Servile fear' is fear as in 'fear and loathing,' the way we tend to use the word today — it's a bad thing, so we avoid it if we can. The old 'fear of God' is a different matter, holding great power in awe, giving awesome reverence."[69]

R_ addressed Thoughtful-Woman further with a "general prayer" that he took much to heart: "Send Your angels in full abundance, Lord, grant the whole armor of God to the whole people of God." B-t recognized the Scriptural (Bible) reference about the "armor of God"[70] but he wanted to talk about something else: "That kind of praying requires that a person has accepted God, taken Jesus as savior, committed to God." Thoughtful-Woman was somewhere else: "It feels incomplete. Is that all of it?" R_ nodded and said, "Actually, when I'm using that, I usually start with, 'Send the fullness of Your truth and Your light.' And often, 'Touch hearts and minds.' By the way, do you ever think about the way we close prayers with 'Amen'? It goes back to the early Hebrew of the Bible; it stayed the same in the Greek of the New Testament (αμην in Greek letters, 'amen') — the Hebrew root appears first in the Bible when it says that, 'Abraham *believed* God and it was credited to him as righteousness,' right standing with God, or as some modern versions translate it, 'God was pleased with him because of it' (Genesis 15:6, cf. CEV, GNT). That word 'believed' is from the Hebrew root אמן *aman*, which gives us 'amen.' "

Thoughtful-Woman asked R_, "So, are you going to pray about that idea of writing a book about all this?" R_ chuckled. "You've already got me composing prayers to go with a book endeavor," he said. "If it works out, remind me to pray: '*Gracious Lord, grant me to remember that it is Your glory that this has been done. Let my heart know that by myself I can do nothing*' — here I'm taking the thought from the Bible, John 15:4-5," R_ interrupted himself; then he continued the prayer "*For it is You who give strength and wisdom.*" (B-t was mentally adding footnotes, more Bible verses — Deu 8:16-18, 1 Sam. 2:7-9, Ps. 89:15-17, Isa 26:12 — but he kept quiet.) Thoughtful-Woman said, "That would be a good prayer after *any* attainment," and B-t grinned in agreement.

"So," B-t asked, "if you get psyched up enough to do a book, are you going to include the 'Jesus Prayer'?" Thoughtful-Woman's puzzled look led R_ to address her with an explanatory remark, "The simplest version is repeating the name of Jesus as you inhale and as you exhale, calling on Him* because He* knows your needs and has the power and wisdom and love. The extreme simplicity makes it very helpful in times of severe stress. No, my friend," R_ turned to B-t, "there are cautions about using that prayer extensively, discussed in *Christ the Eternal Tao*, where they discuss advanced forms of the Jesus Prayer, and I'm reluctant to go into it without the fuller exposition. Although I must say, it's done me a world of good."[71]

After they all passed a moment of meditative silence, R_ said, "As long as we're talking generalities, here are some broad-brush prayers: 'To make the most of every opportunity' — I'm keying off of Colossians 4:5 (NIV) — and Oswald Chambers gave me one: 'Lord, garrison the reaches of my being' — that is, for His* protecting, cleansing, perfecting even the depths of me where my own conscious mind cannot reach." B-t and Thoughtful-Woman looked at each other, and neither smiled at a moment like this. R_ added, "*Guide me and touch my heart, to be where You can bless me.*"[72]

===================

B-t saw R_ making notes for this chapter, and he again was not at peace with R_'s view. "If you're talking about teaching to pray, teach them to read the Bible for a foundation: tell them to read the 23rd Psalm; Matthew chapters 5 through 7, the "Sermon on the Mount;" 1 Corinthians 13 on "love;" chapter four of Philippians on joy and peace; Luke chapter two, the birth of Jesus; Matthew 27 & 28, the crucifixion and resurrection of Jesus; 1 Thessalonians four, the return of Christ; and Revelation 21 & 22 on heaven." R_ replied, "That's a nice 'short list,' but if anyone wants my recommendations, I'm going to recommend serious reading, all of Luke - John - Acts."

The dog watched intently. He seemed to sense the surface layer of disunity, *and* he seemed to sense a deeper, resolving unity between the two.

[An editorial note to our long-suffering reader: R_ penned a third chapter, Chapter 18, on prayer tips & considerations; in a burst of enthusiasm, some of the best information got cranked into endnote #277.]

Chapter 10: Notes on Watching Human Beings Think

"I enjoy hearing your prayers," Sci-guy said, "are you going to do a book full of them?" B-t answered before R_ could: "There are already books of prayers, the Book of Common Prayer, Martin Luther's prayers, devotional guides, etc. etc." R_, as usual, was elsewhere: "An American writer summarized the intellectual outlook — she said, 'Ignorant people believed, uncouth people believed, and we were heavily couth.'[73] If I get pumped up enough to do a book, the prayers I am moved to put in will co-exist with a modest intellectual defense." Thoughtful-Woman arched a quizzical eyebrow, and R_ elaborated, "Modest in the sense of stating basic things and referring people to books where they are elaborated in more detail. When one follows one's betters on an expedition, quotation with credit is the honest thing to do, and probably the most productive!"

Thoughtful-Woman laughed. "What can you 'footnote,' my friend," she asked, "to take the sting out of *uncouth*?" R_ sighed — it *was* asking a lot — and as B-t grimaced, he said, "Os Guinness followed that quotation of the American writer, by listing a couple lines of names of great authors, scientists, and writers who *were* people of faith."[74]

Sci-guy was an active listener, and he chimed in, "Many scientists, indeed — the majority of the great founders, some say! The founder of physics, Isaac Newton, being one of them. [75] He was a Bible student and wrote more on theology than on scientific matters." R_ nodded and added, "Guinness kept the list as short as possible while making the point, and he goes to hit some other key notes — that 'almost all great reforms in Western history — including the banning of infanticide, the abolition of slavery,[76] the rise of the women's movement, and progress in civil rights — have been inspired by faith and led by people of faith. Yet faith itself is commonly dismissed as reactionary. Still another fact is that secular ideologies, not religion, proved responsible in the last century for the Holocaust, the Gulag, and the killing fields.'[77] Interesting, eh? Rodney Stark goes deeper into the statistics on some of these things, but Guinness' survey is an antidote for the person who has had 'his brains go to his head.' The things I quoted of Guinness, he does all in one page."

Thoughtful-Woman was jolted. "How far does he go with a pace like that?" R_ answered, "He assesses the basic philosophical spectrum of humanity — Western 'monotheistic' religions, secular humanism, and Eastern religions. He quotes Alfred Nobel's writing, read at his funeral: 'Silent you stand before the altar of death! ... Eternity has the floor.'[78] Guinness talks about famous insights into human nature, how some celebrated thinkers were forced to confront the fact that we are not 'naturally good,' and he analyzes all the religious alternatives to undergird his conclusion that Jesus the Christ is the best answer in all the spectrum of the world's many and various religious alternatives and claims."

"You said he covered secular humanism as one available philosophy, right?" said Sci-guy. "Yes," R_ responded, "he says that 'there's no doubt that a secular form of humanism is one of the most powerful faiths in the modern world... dominant in educated circles.'[79] He quotes Sir Julian Huxley, 'Human knowledge worked over by human imagination is seen as the basis to human understanding and belief, and the ultimate guide to human progress.' " Thoughtful-Woman clapped her hands, "Hurray, doesn't that sound great?"

B-t was grimacing again, so R_ took up articulating what the poor man must be thinking: "We believers value human knowledge as much as anyone, but we feel divine wisdom is its underlying basis. The order of the universe stands out so clearly when you study it, that some moderns postulate an 'ordering principle' to dodge crediting God. And the unfolding of progress hasn't cheered: Guinness says the humanist's vision becomes darker with elaboration. He quotes the classic secular humanist author Bertrand Russell: 'I wrote with passion & force, because I really thought I had a gospel [your author's note: "gospel" means "good news"] ... Now I am cynical about the gospel [of his atheistic humanism] because it won't stand the test of life... the man who would face a hostile universe rather than lose his vision has become a man who will creep into the first hovel to escape the terror & splendour of the night.'[80] Russell's friend H. J. Blackham said, 'The most drastic objection to humanism is that it is too bad to be true. The world is one vast tomb if human lives are ephemeral and human life itself is doomed to ultimate extinction.' Well, *that* segues into what I call 'nice-dinner religion' — nothing better than a passing enjoyment, get well-fed and relax in being well-off, even if it can't last. Or lose yourself in 'causes,' to forget the ephemerality of your own passing existence..." "Eat, drink and be merry," B-t quoted his treasured Bible (Luke 12:19, the rich fool — later reading brought him to Isaiah 22:13: "Let us eat and drink ... for tomorrow we die"). B-t's "translation" of R_'s comment moved R_ to recall another phrase from Guinness: "the restlessness of perpetual craving."[81]

Sci-guy was staring out the window, and turned briefly to interject: "The issue is whether it's true, not whether it's bleak." He turned back to the landscape, as R_ replied, "I don't believe in God because I want to hope, I hope because I believe — because decades of life have brought me to see the love, to experience it in depths that were deeper than I knew they could be." Thoughtful-Woman took that as a cue to put the discussion back in motion: "So Guinness is one of the authors you are recommending for people to read, that you think can meet their seeking? He must have some interesting things to say when he gets to Christianity!"

R_ quoted Guinness for a while: "In contrast to those who think religious belief is a mere human projection,[82] the God of the Biblical story is not simply personal for us but a person in himself. He's personal because of his own nature, not because we need him to be personal. He isn't made in our image; we're made in his. And there's no other ground for justifying the preciousness and inalienable dignity of each human being... Because of its view of creation, the Christian faith — like humanism today and Confucianism in the past — openly affirms the world. It therefore builds hospitals, encourages the arts, pursues science, and is the most powerful animating force in history's most world-affirming civilization." But, he added, "Guinness also lays out the other side: '...there has consistently been one unanswerable objection to the Christian faith — Christians ... With a history that includes Richard Coeur de Lion's massacres in the Crusades, Torquemada's burning of Jews and heretics in the Spanish Inquisition, and the malignant pornocracy of the Borgia pope, Alexander VI, the case for the Christian faith must always be made with confession and humility.' The slaughter has been larger by others, in the number of victims, but Christians have always reflected the down-side of God's determination to work with human beings."[83]

B-t looked like he had sucked on a lemon. "Fairness, driver?" he began. "Remember the many others, less ballyhooed, far more numerous? The quiet toilers in countless charities, the mild parents who received home their prodigal offspring... When Roman soldiers came to arrest Polycarp and take him to martyrdom for his faith, his response was to ask if he might have an hour to pray — they said yes — can you imagine that in an arrest today? — and he spread his arms and prayed for two hours for everyone he had ever known. People who were there said, 'Why are they arresting such a sweet old man?' These people don't get the portrayal in the movies, but the true followers of Christ are known to those who trouble themselves to truly know the Christian community, who aren't too busy to seek out the mild-mannered, who don't deal in stereotypes and hostile put-downs. The question is whether people join them in following the One who said, 'Do unto others as you would have them do unto you' (Mat 7:12, Luke 6:31), or whether they join the hostile-niks in finding a rock to throw." A brief pause covered the group, during which the dog continued to stare at B-t.

Sci-guy's memory of a hangover triggered the next move in the conversation. "Guinness? Any connection to Guinness stout, the famous beer?" "Yes," R_ replied, "the family fortune enabled him to take up studying these matters. The biographer says that Os Guinness' ancestor 'brewed a healthy alternative to the dirty water and hard liquors plaguing seventeenth-century Ireland, invested his profits into workers and the needy, and along the way founded his country's first Sunday schools.' He calls them 'Ireland's first family of stout'[84] (beer)."

Sci-guy enjoyed the history. But R_ was asserting a relation to reality, so *that* called for comment. "You were going to talk about the intellectual side, so you think Guinness has done a good job of surveying the landscape? What about other people's thinking, huh?" "Well," R_ replied, "human beings have been thinking for a long time. More than five hundred years before Christ, the great Chinese sage Lao Zi (old spelling Lao Tzu) wrote:

> '*There exists a Being undifferentiated and complete,*
> *Born before heaven and earth.*
> *... Fathomless, it seems to be the source of all things.*
> *I do not know its name,*
> *But characterize it as the Tao.*'[85]

"Here, indeed, Lao Zi (Lao Tzu) seems to perceive what the New Testament revealed as *Christ the Logos of God*."[86] R_ had indeed been reading, and now was his moment. He continued without a pause: "The scholar who brought us this, in his book *Christ the Eternal Tao*, also notes what he calls 'the startling phrase' in chapter 42 of the Tao Teh Ching, in which Lao Zi writes, 'The Three produced all things.' Say," R_ went on, "While I am mentioning this awesome book, written by a Christian (Eastern Orthodox) monk, let's note for the seeker the monk's statement that, 'one can — upon becoming aware of the light of one's spirit — begin to worship it as God. This is the ultimate delusion... [This light] is the natural light peculiar to the mind of man created in God's image.' " [*for more on this, see endnote 196*]

R_ had been challenged to go beyond Guinness as a source, and he went where the people are: "China is busy thinking today, and doing an amazing job of it. Those thoughts have included some reassessment of Christianity, a religion that started in Western Asia, not Europe, and which arrived in China in A.D. 635 (C.E., for those who prefer that way of denominating years).[87] There was a fascinating statement of one conclusion of that thinking, related to visitors to China in 2002. One of mainland

China's top scholars told a visiting group of Western tourists (on a tour of ancient Chinese Christian sites):

'One of the things we were asked to look into was what accounted for the success, in fact, the pre-eminence of the West all over the world,' he said. 'We studied everything we could from the historical, political, economic, and cultural perspective. At first, we thought it was because you had more powerful guns than we had. Then we thought it was because you had the best political system. Next we focused on your economic system. But in the past twenty years, we have realized that the heart of your culture is your religion: Christianity. That is why the West has been so powerful. The Christian moral foundation of social and cultural life was what made possible the emergence of capitalism and then the successful transition to democratic politics. We don't have any doubt about this.' This was not coming from some ultra-conservative at a think-tank in Orange County, California ... This was a scholar from [one of] *China's premier academic research institutes..."* [88] [The report noted that the scholar asked not to be identified by name. N.B. also endnote 90.]

R_ made the mistake of pausing for breath, and B-t took the floor away from him. "Barry Lopez wrote a book called *Arctic Dreams: Imagination and Desire in a Northern Landscape*. If you lived in Alaska, did you read that? It was famous. One thing he said was that one of the oldest dreams of humanity is 'to find a dignity that might include all living things... The dignity we seek is one beyond that articulated by Enlightenment philosophers.'[89] When you get to understand the God of the New Testament properly, that's what you find, because His* care is for all the creation — 'that the creation itself will be liberated from its bondage to decay and brought into the freedom and glory of the children of God' (Romans 8:21 NIV). That's why Jesus told His disciples to 'preach the gospel [good news] to all creation' (Mark 16:15 NIV)." ["Good news" is what the word "gospel" means, in the Greek.]

"While we're talking about how people think about these things," R_ resumed, "let me mention another point from that Chinese vantage-point. One of the Chinese commentators says in

Christ the Eternal Tao that Westerners now have turned away from an 'attenuated' form of Christianity and are finding in ancient Chinese religion the echoes of Christ.[90] Let's take some time to focus in on the 'Atonement' performed by Jesus the Christ, and maybe you'll see some merit to his comment. Or maybe not!" R_ smiled at them all, and the look on their faces showed a clear consensus: *another day*. R_ was reminded of the cartoon where a student puts up his hand and says, "Professor, may I be excused? My brain is full."[91]

Thoughtful-Woman was the only one not mentally numbed by the flow of all this exposition, and now she weighed in: "When you talk about people doing the careful analysis, what you called 'watching human beings think' when you started this discussion, it makes *me* think — and I go back to what you said about that 'catechism,' that the purpose of human life was to 'glorify God and *enjoy Him* forever*.' My, oh, my!" R_ took his eyes off the road long enough to give her an appreciative smile, and said, "Timothy Keller says the Bible's Genesis creation account makes him feel it's like God is saying, 'Have a ball! Keep it going!' "[92]

Sci-guy was staring out the window again. *If I didn't need this ride so badly,* he thought to himself, *I'd like to do some conversation-dominating myself... I'd like to go over my findings and presentation. It would help me get in shape for what's waiting for me in D.C. That's what's important to ME in life.* After an appraising glance at R_, Sci-guy proceeded to do exactly that, spending five hours on rafts of information that none of them had ever heard a bit of before — and Thoughtful-Woman listened with rapt attention to it all, asked enough questions to begin to get some real insight, and enjoyed it as much as she enjoyed anything. It put B-t right to sleep; all he learned was the value of a nice nap — he knew that already, but a refresher course was always good...

Chapter 11: Notes on Watching Human Beings Argue

One of the small towns they went through had a solitary Chinese-food restaurant, and the hitchhikers urged R_ to stop. The look on the dog's face seemed to say, "What, they don't like his cooking?" Inside the restaurant, a pleasant meal lubricated conversation, and Thoughtful-Woman turned to the flow of recent history. "There was an old song," she said, "that said, 'I'm sorry for the things I didn't do… I'm sorry for the starving kids in China…' — *now*, after Mao's 'iron rice bowl' policy, it's 'the starving kids in Africa.' You guys [she looked at R_ and B-t] may think your God is the key thing, but it wasn't the missionaries that ended the hunger of Chinese peasants." *Nor was it they that blanketed China in coal smoke*, thought B-t, but he kept his peace.

"The missionaries fed so many people that the stereotype became 'rice Christians,' people coming to their places just so they could eat," R_ said. *Suddenly I'm glad I kept quiet*, B-t thought to himself. *After all, it was the capitalists that blanketed <u>London</u> in coal smoke*. "China brought to me a different aspect," R_ continued. "A Chinese person was preaching to fellow believers in that nation, who were complaining about how soft Westerners have it, compared to the persecution of believers in China. He told them, 'In China we have persecution, but in the West they have delusion.'[93] His point was that it's equally destructive, spiritually, to the individual."

Sci-guy laughed heartily but warily. "We have every spectrum of opinion in our 'free' countries — thousands of beliefs — so, simple logical analysis would tell you 'they can't all be right.' Concern for 'delusion' is going to cut a wide swath, if that concern ever gets loose in the 'West'!"[94] The dog sighed and put his jaw flat on the floor and went to sleep, and the restaurant owner looked over in alarm. She had felt very kind in letting the group bring in their beloved dog, but the sighing sound triggered a mental alarm. Some cultures eat dogs, and she was uneasy with the welter of varied opinions that sometimes swirl through a precariously-perched culture...

But laughter was the next input, as Thoughtful-Woman chimed in, "The word 'delusion' got a lot of play when Dawkins published *The God Delusion*." Sci-guy had seen people take that in eagerly: "Dawkins said that if God controls the universe, God must be more complex than the universe, so it's logically no explanation at all." B-t spoke: "It's a question of reality, not logical simplicity. God has revealed Himself* to those who care to receive it..."

B-t's voice trailed off as R_ made a different point: "Dawkins seems to be thinking in the old machine analogies, levers and so on for causing movement. Greg Koukl took the argument apart, noting the divine mind as being of a different nature and 'simple' per theology; Polkinghorne looked at the issue from the depths of physics, showing Einstein's equation of General Relativity — a compact equation from which flows all the complexity of the universe we see."[95]

"Put your response to Dawkins in a footnote," Sci-guy grumped, "or else write 300 pages about it. People get their heads so locked into these things that it takes quite a bit to move the mountain." *Move the mountain*, B-t thought — *can our friend be using a Biblical phrase*?

R_ was glad to see them all come to a pause, which he read as serious reflection on these difficult matters. The human mind struggles to grasp the universe, but it never seems to fit into our heads... Onward, then... "The issue of 'delusion' hinges, more than anything else, on the uniqueness of Jesus," said R_.

When they stopped for the night, R_ sat up after the others went to bed, writing furiously on how the key points of this might be pursued further. The dog sat unmoving, watching with curiosity and apprehension. *The uniqueness of Jesus is the key to so much of this*, R_ thought, and noted with his pen: *Jesus: Son of God, but also as the Gospels say in the Bible, the "Son of Man" ("the Human One"[96] in an "inclusive" translation of the New Testament by Oxford University Press, 1995). Jesus was fully God, eternal but now incarnate into human form; He was also, incarnate as the "God-*

man," fully human. The uniting of these two natures creates the new possibility for human beings. That should segue into summarizing Strobel's refutation of recent "new perspectives" and challenges on Jesus and Christian teaching. (R_ may be wrong again, just like he was when he thought his tires were all in fine shape; Lee Strobel's book *The Case for the Real Jesus* is probably better left to be read in the original; we summarize on p. 179 what it covers.)

People argue so much, one way and the other, R_ thought. *So much is a matter of perspective: So what if 90% of species are extinct? Compare the case of the buggy-whip, now long gone — but it was an intelligent design for its time. The human eye is slammed as suboptimal engineering but they use it perfectly well to read the attacks on God's handiwork — ! People say, "If God was doing this, it should have been this way..." but they don't have God's viewpoint.*

If I take their suggestion and try to write a book, R_ pondered, *I should write about the present day's privileging of skepticism: Skepticism has become an article of faith in some quarters;*[97] *belief is considered naïve — but the things that "must be believed to be seen" are a profound blessing that some of us have experienced with joyful wonder, and people should be free to "taste and see" as it says in Psalm 34:8 in the Bible. Coming out of the pre-scientific period, skepticism was indeed needed — as shown by the legend that the "Star of Bethlehem" shone brighter than the sun, which Scripture itself contradicts*[98] *— somebody went too far with misplaced enthusiasm. Note similarly the credulous presence in a European reliquary of the pre-Reformation period of the "skulls of the Three Wise Men" — complete with gold crowns to prove that these were kings from the East who came to worship the baby Jesus! Somebody made some money putting that one together, eh?* The dog suddenly let out a bark, although not a loud one, and R_ looked at him, startled.

R_ took up some of this when he and B-t had breakfast, as the others took their food with them on a short hike. B-t had been picking at his food — something was bothering him. "Delusion is a big word," he said, finally. "Mentioning it puts you in the realm of two Scriptures — a Bible verse that says, 'Rescue those who are perishing, staggering towards slaughter,' Prov. 24:11 — and another that says that when they refuse to love the truth and be saved, 'God sends them a powerful delusion' because they have deliberately rejected God, 2 Thess 2:11." (Compare Isaiah 47:10 in the Bible: "Your 'wisdom' and 'knowledge' mislead you.")

R_ took a break after breakfast to add to his notes about what could be, should be, might be written about "watching human beings argue." *Lee Strobel has written a series of books documenting the evidence for faith in Jesus; they are more accessible than some such books — and they have the human element of his own life-changing experience. The Case for Christ, The Case for Faith, The Case for the Real Jesus — each dealing with different problems. Luke Timothy Johnson wrote The Real Jesus, which is a different sort of work, valuable to people who have been exposed to too much "Bible criticism" and feel that the Gospels are not a reliable source concerning Jesus. "An Annotated Bibliography, that's what any book I might do would need."* R_ wrote a note, reminding himself to give the interested reader — if he could find such! — some specifics about the contents of these books, to guide the interested in further search.

R_ began to write almost frantically. *Brian Moynahan's The Faith: A History of Christianity offers much valuable information and perspective, especially on the fact that God's willingness to work with human beings has been the source of much suboptimal "Christian" activity. (History is important; do modern Americans know that 100 years after Muhammad's death, in A.D. 732, an Islamic army took the Islamic conquest drive into what is now France, where they were repulsed by an army under Charles Martel — thus allowing Europeans and Americans to have the Bible and Christianity — this all preceding the "Crusades" by centuries.*[99] *Violence has been a human characteristic, not a monotheistic one, as proven by Alexander the Great...)*

R_'s pen flew as his hand threatened to cramp in protest: *key points from The Faith history, from Rodney Stark's books — issues like Christian leadership in ending slavery, the real extent/death toll of the Inquisition versus the popular portrayal of it* [that became endnote 83], *and "witch hunts" — the Salem "witch hunts" were stopped by clergy!)*

Put all these arguments in context: yes, Christians often "established the first hospitals and clinics and schools" in many areas, as a crisp summary said in the *Encyclopedia of Catholicism,*[100] *but the key issue is Jesus: His* claims; His word "do unto others as you would have them do unto you" (Bible, Matthew 7:12, Luke 6:31); His offer of salvation and always-with-you Mt. 28:20 ("Mt." = Matthew; Appendix Six shows abbreviations that may not be obvious).*

Chapter 12: Atone/Shalom

Dawn often moves the birds to sing in chorus (Gordon Hempton went around the world recording the "Dawn Chorus" on all the continents, the chorus of the birds that moves around the world steadily every 24 hours as dawn sweeps the globe[101]). Our travelers were blessed with this as they breakfasted beside a tree-clad lake. But the driving afterwards brought them through a series of small towns, miles of nondescript buildings ungraced by architectural flair. The mind disengages from the scenery, and R_'s brain cycled to a previous conversation. "You asked about 'Atonement,' the central work of Jesus Christ," he said to Thoughtful-Woman. B-t looked up apprehensively — this was a hard area. The dog growled softly and went to sleep.

"I think we need to start with the word 'shalom,' to open that subject," R_ said. B-t was startled — "vicarious" or "substitutionary" he would have expected, as a long-time Western Protestant believer, but "shalom" — ? Thoughtful-Woman was a "citizen of the world," and her experience had gone there: "That's 'peace' in Hebrew," she said readily. She pronounced it correctly, "shal OHM." "Arabic 'salaam,' " she said to Sci-guy with a proud smile, and he made a mental note to find out what university she attended.

"Yes, but more," R_ replied. "Peace, harmony, well-being, wholeness — the good quality of life that God desired for all His* creatures when He first made the creation." R_ sent B-t to the back of the RV to get a book, *Not the Way It's Supposed to Be*, by Cornelius Plantinga. "Shalom, here's what it means in the Bible: 'the webbing together of God, humans, and all creation in justice, fulfillment and delight... *universal flourishing, wholeness and delight* ... a rich state of affairs in which natural needs are satisfied and natural gifts fruitfully employed, a state of affairs that inspires joyful wonder... the way things ought to be" (page 10, emphasis Plantinga's).

"That's *not* the way things are now, all right," Thoughtful-Woman assessed. Sci-guy looked over dourly, as if such a simple-minded beginning could not bode well for results. "No, it's not," R_ agreed with her, "and Augustine described it in a way that has stuck in my mind. Augustine was one of the most famous early bishops of the Western church, about A.D. 400," he added as Thoughtful-Woman looked at him quizzically.

"Augustine wrote about his own youth, before God got hold of him — he would steal from someone's fruit orchard and eat with great delight, feeling augmented by the action, but if someone stole from *him*, he felt violated and felt it wasn't right. That's a portrait in miniature of what the Bible calls 'the sinful nature.'[102] It's the 'self' locked in itself, serving itself, not 'doing unto others' [as you would have them do unto you, Jesus, Mat 7:12, Luke 6:31]. It's a transformation from what God intended creation to be, hence the term 'the Fall' for the transformation from the intended and initial reality into what we see now."

Sci-guy was staring out the side window again. "The reality we see now" was his world, the object of his and his colleagues' study, often wrapped in a dogmatic assertion that there *could be* nothing else. But he was listening — these ideas were data in their own right, and a scientist waits for data to take its rightful place; one does not trash it.

B-t had been browsing on R_'s two little bookshelves in the back of the RV. "That 'shalom' sounds like what one of the Sioux Indian students wrote in that pamphlet of poetry you have," he said. "*Where people live in perfect harmony ... walk and sing without laughter of putdowns; where someone greets you with words of joy, where loneliness and inequality become a speck of dirt...*"[103]

"No, that's not the reality we inhabit now," R_ responded. "Those are the ideals, God's plan;[104] Plantinga says sin is 'blamable human vandalism of these great realities.' He notes that, 'the veins of sin interlace through most of the rest of what is wrong with our lives... Third World children die daily from largely preventable diseases... Thousands of First World children are born drug addicts...' Many accidents are preventable, but 'somebody who needed to concentrate on his job in order to protect others... got drunk instead, or careless, or wholly preoccupied.' Granting that 'tornadoes, earthquakes, floods, forest fires, shark attacks' come from natural causes, the suffering often has much to do with human fault — 'People might have prepared... Shoddy bridge and building construction, bribery of inspectors... ignorant disdain' for known natural potentials 'sometimes cause or at least exacerbate the sufferings produced in a natural disaster. Sin usually plays at least some role in the kind and amount of evil we absorb from what we are used to thinking of as nonmoral events.'[105] So human sin is involved in evil beyond violence, oppression, exploitation and abuse." R_ paused, then added, "Remember, Plantinga said 'blamable,' not 'deliberate.' Our actions have consequences far beyond what we intend or see — but we are still the root cause of those."

The dog woke up and began to paw restlessly. Thoughtful-Woman picked up the thread: "OK, so humans do a lot of bad stuff, and all of us prove to be flawed, and human 'sin' is broader in its impact than we often concede when we talk about what's wrong with the world. But what's this, that God laid on Christ Jesus the iniquity [sin, wrong-doing] of us all?" B-t cringed — he had read her Isaiah 53:6 in the Bible in an earlier conversation, and he was hurt by the tone in her voice when she brought up the beginning step in the greatest kindness, the most encompassing benefit ever worked for human beings.

B-t was steeped in the Western view, and it made him swift to answer: "Every sin, every wrong, bears its penalty," he said. "It has to be paid for, counterbalanced with the love of God, so people can be forgiven and can live in unity with God." The dog was still now, staring alertly for some reason. *Can dogs read human emotions and feel the depth of our concern about these matters,* R_ asked himself in quiet inner thought. B-t continued: "Because Jesus was not just a human being, but He was God incarnate, both God and human fully, He alone could pay the penalty — for everyone, for all time and all the human race. That's why He could say, 'It is finished,' as death came to Him on the cross."

Thoughtful-Woman replied, "My friend's understanding of Christianity is that God was angry about sin and God needed somebody to beat on, so God beat on Jesus." B-t was pained. "It's the pain that God felt, watching people stubbornly do what was below what was possible and good — that's the pain that came to expression when Jesus agonized on the cross."

R_ understood a layer that lay within what B-t had just said: "Karl Rahner said that there is a 'cross of creation.' He said the cross where Jesus died, 'the Cross of 'Golgotha [is] only the visible form... [of the cross which] towers throughout the spaces of eternity.'[106] Golgotha was the hill in Jerusalem on which Jesus and two thieves were crucified, dying in the ancient Romans' most excruciatingly painful and degrading form of execution," R- added as Thoughtful-Woman continued to frown.

Sci-guy had heard about Jesus in a non-Church sort of way, and he had been doing his own thinking: "I think there's a simple, obvious answer to the question, 'Why did Jesus die?' He went around doing amazing things, and got on the wrong side of the establishment. He flouted the rules they considered most sacred and pulled down the public's opinion of these leaders.[107] There was a deep undercurrent fermenting for rebellion, and those people began to hope that Jesus would be the over-thrower of the Roman overlords. He began to be seen as a substantial threat to the powers-that-be, and they charted the road to Jesus' crucifixion."

"That makes all the sense in the world, at a secular level of human historical causation," R_ replied. "But Jesus said that He came to die, 'to give his life as a ransom for many' — that's Matthew 20:28 in the Bible.[108] Your analysis of 'paying the penalty' fits in with that, and it's one way of understanding it" — here R_ nodded to B-t — "but it's a way of understanding Jesus' vital work that evolved in the Western church as they spent centuries answering the demands of people for explanations that made human-level sense, in a feudal world where 'offended honor demanding payment' fit the spirit of the times. Where I have a problem with your 'satisfaction theory' view, Anselm of Canterbury's great formulation, is when I read my Bible carefully and I come to 1 Corinthians 15:17." B-t was thumbing his well-worn Bible as R_ continued: "If it was just a matter of paying the aggregate penalty, whether you view that as the infinite offendedness of an infinite Holy God or whether you think of it as the accumulated counterbalancing of each of ever-so-many wrong acts, the penalty of each wrong — thinking that way, Christ's death alone was the answer, and salvation would be achieved by His death alone. But 1 Cor 15:17 in the Bible says that if He did not rise from the dead, we would still be in our sins!" B-t grimaced, and the dog looked desperately sad.

"The early Church's understanding of the Incarnation,[109] Crucifixion and Resurrection was that the full flow of Jesus' life, death and rising again represented victory over sin and death. Because all people had proven to be sinners, with a warped nature that could not be part of God's plan of *shalom*, there had to be a fully righteous life — one we could share in, by His Spirit — and given the depth of humanity's waywardness, that had to be lived to the very depth, even to staying true to God's way in the face of an agonized and despised death.[110] Let me quote this: 'By taking up our broken humanity into himself [Incarnation], Christ restores it and, in the words of another Christmas hymn, *lifts up the fallen image* [the "image of God" in which humans were created, Gen 1:26]... But in a fallen and sinful world his love had to reach out yet further... The Cross signifies, in the most stark and uncompromising manner, that this act of sharing is carried to the utmost limits. God incarnate enters into all our experience. Jesus Christ our companion shares not only in the fullness of human life but also in the fullness of human death... *all* our griefs, *all* our sorrows (Isa 53:4)... by this act of voluntary self-offering he turns what would have been a piece of arbitrary violence, a judicial murder, into a redemptive sacrifice... [also] identifying himself with all the despair and mental pain of humanity... The Cross, understood as victory, sets before us the paradox of love's omnipotence... he has done for us something we should be altogether incapable of doing without him. At the same time, we should not say that Christ has suffered "instead of us," but rather that he has suffered *on our behalf*... love is openly shown to be stronger than hatred, and life to be stronger than death. God himself has died and risen from the dead, and so there is no more death: even death is filled with God.'[111] That's from an Eastern Orthodox Christian writer," R_ concluded. He was reading from some notes he had written after he heard B-t quoting Isaiah 53:4 from the Bible to Thoughtful-Woman. Did the pause of silence signify a positive touch of these words on his audience? Even the dog seemed cheered.

"You guys should look at that book *Christus Victor*," R_ resumed, gesturing at the bookshelf. "Christ's vital work as victory over sin and death: His Incarnation, Crucifixion, Resurrection and Ascension all working as part of an essential progressive work of overcoming the situation of humanity in its vast and terrible need.[112] His life, death and resurrection created a new life which is available to us through His spirit."

Sci-guy turned to dialogue with the little group. "You're giving me a picture of cosmic forces," he said. "It reminds me of the principles of conservation in science — conservation of energy, conservation of momentum, etc. Things go on until a transforming force is applied."

==

Now we turn once again to R_'s further notes, as he scribbled again to himself before bed, regarding how further to treat of these vast matters — what a poor author he would make, with all this endless desire to go on in many directions! R_ wrote by the small light: <u>*Christus Victor*</u> *opens a possible need to go into further references about "sacrifice" per citation there of Bishop F. C. N. Hicks' perspective-altering book* <u>*The Fullness of Sacrifice*</u> *(Macmillan and Co., 1930). People today see the agony and death as the sacrifice; Hicks' view takes them into the deeper layers of action that make a sacrifice the real thing. (It is the devotion and transformation of the life to the higher purpose that makes the sacrifice, that is the essence of the sacrifice.) Christianity also transformed the practice of "religion:" Guillebaud notes that, "Hostility towards the early Christians was often related to their [the early Christians] rejection of sacrifice" (p. 225 of Re-Founding...) [since Christ had made the ultimate and complete sacrifice, further sacrifices were unnecessary, and therefore cruel].*

*The much-processed Western understanding (Latin theology, Anselm et al, the "substitutionary" theory that an Eastern Orthodox priest said was "a purely Protestant invention" — Western, not Protestant, I think — that understanding of Christ's work, when carried to its extreme expressions, may be found to be "distilled like brandy, no longer the wine:" it travels well, and works fine among those who can receive the taste, but those who reject the taste might be receptive to the original "wine" instead — hence the importance of the Eastern Orthodox understanding of "**original sin**" — not standing on the aspect of "guilt" but seeing one of sickness, a condition needing positive transformation. (In that regard note the comment on page 23 of Christ the Eternal Tao: "[in the West] we were exposed to an attenuated form of Christianity.") The "what Adam and Eve did" item probably needs to be recapitulated here.* [See Index.] But another prior conversation came to mind:

B-t had glared at R_, "Jesus said on the cross, 'My God, my God, why have You forsaken me?' That shows that what you call the 'Western' view is right, doesn't it?" R_ sighed. He wasn't much for disputation, *but...* "The Psalms weren't numbered in Jesus' day," he said, "and you referred to a Psalm by citing the first line. The Eastern theology says that Jesus cited Psalm 22 by quoting that, which is its first line, and He was saying, this is the situation prophesied centuries earlier – look at verses 16, & 14, also 24."

B-t had seen that it made sense, but he had a deeper response. "The 'Western' view has brought countless millions of people to Christ, and people who came to see their own foul deeds saw, in its liberation from guilt, the transformation that they needed," he stated. R_ had felt that was right; he agreed: "Yes, it's a question of making both views available for people, because the background culture is shifting, and some people need different understandings, perhaps going back to the early Church, which worked in a strongly multi-cultural environment like ours..."

Then Thoughtful-Woman had asked, "Doesn't the whole thing turn on a deeper matter, that idea you were expounding that Jesus described Himself as 'a missionary from heaven'?" B-t had a Scripture list in his Bible and read it: "Here are 40 times Jesus said that: John 3:13, 3:34, 4:34, 5:23, 5:24, 5:30, 5:36, 5:37, 5:38, 6:29, 6:38, 6:39, 6:44, 6:57, 7:16, 7:28, 7:29, 7:33, 8:16, 8:18, 8:26, 8:29, 8:42, 9:4, 10:36, 11:42, 12:44, 12:45, 12:49, 13:20, 14:24, 15:21, 16:5, 17:3, 17:8, 17:18, 17:21, 17:23, 17:25, 20:21."

"Am I supposed to jot down all those numbers and look them up? Tell me what two or three of those verses say!" Thoughtful-Woman had snapped. R_ was hoping she smiled as she said it – things could be so tense... He couldn't look in the rear-view mirror and see, because a squirrel ran across the road in front of the RV at that moment. A little braking, a little steering, and the squirrel was neatly avoided... *Don't presume on the kindness of human beings, little squirrel,* R_ thought, *human beings can be cruel, and they often just don't pay attention.* Thinking about "the kindness of human beings" and the crucifixion sacrifice of Jesus Christ at the same time – that combination had driven R_ to prayer so intense he couldn't help mumbling under his breath as he drove.

B-t had answered Thoughtful-Woman's reasonable request: "Jesus told a crowd of people, 'I have come down from heaven not to do my will but to do the will of him who sent me,' John 6:38. He told the religious leader Nicodemus, 'No one has ever gone into heaven except the one who came from heaven – the Son of Man,' John 3:13. At the 'Last Supper,' the night before He gave His life that we might truly live, He told His disciples, 'I came from the Father and entered the world; now I am leaving the world and going back to the Father,' John 16:28. If you *do* take the time to look up all the other verses, you'll see that many of them show His 'missionary from Heaven' status by His declaration that

God the Father sent Him – as when He said, 'My teaching is not my own. It comes from the one who sent me,' John 7:16." Thoughtful-Woman had seemed a bit overwhelmed – it *was* a difficult thought, a status that put Jesus in a different place from every other religion founder, teacher, leader.

R_ pulled his mind back from the memory of that episode. A key point indeed, he thought, *who Jesus is*, in the full reality of it.

Then some remembered-reading overtook R_'s mind: *There was a minor media flap when genetic research showed that all humans did indeed share one common female ancestor (dubbed "mitochondrial Eve") and one common male ancestor (dubbed "Y-chromosome Adam"). The "standard model" of evolution has been expounded to include this smoothly, but it should cue people that there is going to be a resolution that includes the Bible...*[113]

British author G. K. Chesterton observed that "the doctrine of original sin — that something is radically awry at the heart of human nature — has been verified by thousands of years of human history." (Pearcey, p. 220 of Saving Leonardo).

Christus Victor may want more discussion than we gave it, and there are of course more recent books. The "conservation" point that 'Sci-guy' mentioned could be the key for expansion... [Endnote 112 as a brief exposition of *Christus Victor*; its last paragraph, book references and web articles that show "Western" understanding broadening toward grasping the Eastern Church's viewpoint]

Also, the "medical model," lifting the issue above the traditional Western "legal metaphor" to see it as a basic element of reality, including the idea that perhaps the divine pain from sin has to come to expression — ?? R_ paused. *I mentioned that to the people, didn't I? How much does it take to make something clear, and when the point is to receive the cure, not to understand the cure? Especially when there are different ways to understand it.* (He didn't bother to say the obvious, "and I am so limited in my own understanding"!) The dog was asleep, and R_ joined him.

Chapter 13: Trinity: interfacing the human mind with it

A long stretch of road, void of vehicles and scenery, left Sci-guy to muse. "I don't see how Jesus can be God and yet there is only One God — and you say the Holy Spirit is a separate person, so how can three Gods be *one* God?" "That's why some Muslims say Christians are 'innumerate,' unable to handle numbers, just as a person who can't handle letters is 'illiterate'," B-t responded. R_ grimaced at that and said, "The best I've seen on that, is the reflection on how the nature of being changes at higher dimensions of being — and the 'nature' of God's being is higher than ours by far."

Thoughtful-Woman put in a comment about the traditional philosopher's triad — "the good, the true, the beautiful" — "Isn't that a 'trinity' of sorts..." Her voice trailed off. This wasn't going any farther than the analogy of the human mind being one in three: intellect, will, memory. B-t was ready to jump in and say that the analogy of a clover-leaf with three lobes, or the analogy of water having three states — steam, water, ice — these analogies were "Modalism," a theological error that made God one Person in three manifestations instead of three Persons who were one Being. But, the situation didn't seem to call for it.

Instead, B-t threw in John Eddison's analogy of a book: "A book exists in three different and distinct ways at once — in the mind of the author, on the shelf in a library, and in the imagination of the reader."[114] He smiled, but R_ moved forward with the implacability of a bulldozer: "What I was saying about 'the nature of being' as becoming different in higher dimensions, can be illustrated in a rough form with some multi-dimensional mathematical discussion." B-t's eyes were glazed over, Thoughtful-Woman's brow was wrinkled, and Sci-guy looked skeptically amused. Even the dog sighed. *Oh, well,* R_ thought, *we can't always run on the enthusiasm of our environment.*

R_ pondered his words for a moment, and realized it would be better to yield to a master. He asked Thoughtful-Woman if she would bring the ALPHA course book, *Searching Issues,* from the bookshelf. He began to read from it C. S. Lewis's words on the Trinity, grateful that the absence of cars on this stretch of road gave him liberty to drive safely and do this.

[quoting Lewis:] "You know that in space you can move in three ways — to left or right, backwards or forwards, up or down. Every direction is either one of these three or a compromise between them. They are called the three Dimensions." Sci-guy rolled his eyes at such elementary material, but the other two seemed comfortable with it. R_ continued quoting Lewis: "Now notice this. If you are using only one dimension, you could draw only a straight line. If you are using two, you could draw a figure: say, a square. Now a step further. If you have three dimensions, you can then build what we call a solid body: say, a cube — a thing like a dice or a lump of sugar. And a cube is made up of six squares.

"Do you see the point? A world of one dimension would be a straight line. In a two-dimensional world, you still get straight lines, but many lines make one figure. In a three-dimensional world, you still get figures but many figures make one solid body. In other words, as you advance to more real and more complicated levels, you do not leave behind you the things you found on the simpler levels: you still have them, but combined in new ways — in ways you could not imagine if you knew only the simpler levels.

"Now the Christian account of God [as Trinity, three-who-are-one] involves just the same principle. The human level is a simple and rather empty level." Thoughtful-Woman frowned at that, and R_ paused to say that he didn't agree with Lewis about the "rather empty" characterization. But he plowed on with Lewis: "On the human level one person is one being, and any two persons are two separate beings — just as, in two dimensions (say on a flat sheet of paper) one square is one figure, and any two squares are two separate figures. On the Divine level you still find personalities; but up there you find them combined in new ways which we, who do not live on that level, cannot imagine. In God's dimension, so to speak, you find a being who is three Persons while remaining one Being, just as a cube is six squares while remaining one cube. Of course we cannot fully conceive a Being like that: just as, if we were so made that we perceived only two dimensions in space we could never properly imagine a cube. But we can get a sort of faint notion of it. And when we do, we are then, for the first time in our lives, getting some positive idea, however faint, of something super-personal — something more than a person. It is something we could never have guessed, and yet, once we have been told, one almost feels one ought to have been able to guess it because it fits in so well with all the things we know already." (R_ was very glad no one asked him what "things we know already" in this regard.)

[Lewis again:] "You may ask, 'If we cannot imagine a three-personal Being, what is the good of talking about Him?' Well, there isn't any good talking about Him. The thing that matters is being actually drawn into that three-personal life, and that may begin any time — tonight, if you like." R_ paused, then added that he found the ALPHA material some of the most helpful on a number of issues.

Silence followed, and B-t looked genuinely relieved that the exposition was over. Thoughtful-Woman proved herself an apt student: "When we started discussing, you talked about the 'minority religious opinion' among the ancient Cherokees that the three Divine Beings 'were always together and of the same mind ... always one in sentiment and action' — that's a unity that we can't conceive of among separate human 'persons' ..." Her voice trailed off, and Sci-guy looked like he felt he was doing the group a favor by not interjecting that modern theories of physics call for the existence of eleven dimensions in our universe. But he did make a more directly relevant contribution: "About 'natures of being' beyond our intuition, Alistair McGrath once commented on 'the nature of light... sometimes it seemed to behave as if it was a wave, and sometimes as if it was a particle... How could it be two totally different things? But eventually, through the development of the Quantum Theory, it was found that this contradiction expressed a fundamental difficulty in grasping what the nature of light really was… on account of our difficulties in conceiving it.'[115]"

B-t was also an apt student, although he read different books from those Thoughtful-Woman and Sci-guy read. "The greatest thinkers about the Trinity left us some wisdom early in Christian thought," he interjected. "Gregory of Nyssa said that the nature of God 'is beyond names or human speech.' Basil the Great similarly said that the Trinity is 'beyond either analysis or conceptualization.'[116] These people were in the 300's A.D., and we have to admit that they were right, for all the books written since."

Sci-guy's gaze swiveled past B-t. He grinned at R_. "I see you have Nabeel Qureshi's new book. You should tell people how he came to peace with 'Trinity' before he converted from Islam to Jesus as Christ!" He turned to Thoughtful-Woman and added, "I've always loved chemistry!"[117] The others were too tired to interrogate him, and the dog pawed the bookshelf as if he wished *he* could dig out the treasures hidden there.

Thoughtful-Woman stepped over the dog, now asleep, and picked up one of the books from R_'s shelf at the back of the RV. Was hers a magic touch? She opened it to read to them all: "Trinity … the basic truth… people are saved by God through Jesus Christ by the power of the Holy Spirit." Closing the volume and reshelving it with a thump, she reminded R_, "Well, you said that we would expect to find something about God beyond our comprehension. I think that you're right that the 'mind-warp' of the Trinity proves it's not a human invention!" She exercised the same magic touch and pulled another book, reading to the group, "The highest point of revelation is thus … a paradox that cannot be resolved through human powers."[118] The dog woke up and licked her hand as she reshelved that book.

Chapter 14: Evolution: An evolving non-consensus

> *A Note to the Reader*: We enter here into one of the major minefields of our time. Ours is in some ways a shallow foray — I have one book that takes one view, in 1200 pages, and another that takes a different view in 600 pages; but *Humanity's Greatest Discovery* will spend far less talk. Our narrative ending (p. 87-88) may reconfigure, or redeem, the matter for some readers.
>
> *For a more "conclusive" science view, and less dense reading, skip to Chapter 15.*

Only the dog was capable of traveling hundreds of miles in silence, and conversation broke out again. "You must have thought about the 'evolution' controversies a lot," Thoughtful-Woman said to Sci-guy. He smiled and replied, "A lot of people are surprised to find out that the religious establishment was generally fine with Darwin's thoughts, when he first came out with them, before more radical ram-rodding of extrapolations of the idea was done to them."[119] Thoughtful-Woman arched her eyebrows and Sci-guy expanded, "Oh, the main *early* opposition to Darwin came from paleontologists, who knew that the fossil record did not match what seemed to be the logical conclusion of his ideas, in their first-draft form — endless slow changes, accumulating very gradually into new species."

Thoughtful-Woman's arched eyebrows were matched by her mouth now falling open in unbelief, and Sci-guy expounded: "Darwin had only one graphic in *The Origin of Species.* It showed a branching tree — symbolizing forms of life continuously branching over time — but the fossil record shows long periods of stasis, a species continuing almost unchanged over enormous periods of time. Species appear suddenly, persist with little change for long periods of time, and then disappear suddenly. The fossils do *not*, in general, show the gradual, step-by-step changes that classical Darwinism led people to expect."[120]

Thoughtful-Woman had been paying attention to the world around her: "A friend told me that this is why the theory of 'punctuated equilibrium' was developed. Species are in equilibrium with their surroundings and stay as they are, but in some small area, some conditions will develop that are different and require change — and that's where the transition occurs, in a small sub-population. This accounts for the relatively small number of 'transitional' fossils."[121]

B-t was interested enough, although this whole field of analysis didn't intrigue him. "So where are we at now?" he asked. Sci-guy turned in the passenger seat of the RV as he answered: "Genetic work has shown where mutations in DNA sequences have been passed on along in species progressions. Possible step-by-step processes have been laid out that can account for complex organs previously thought impossible to derive by evolution — and a lot of analysis has gone on. Stephen Jay Gould, the late great paleontologist (died 2002), argued that the extinction of most departing species seems to be from catastrophic natural events — which have nothing to do with the 'fitness' of the various subspecies before the environmental change.[122] Sub-cellular microbiology has shown incredible complexity *within* the individual cell, structures of enormous complexity,[123] so whether that could 'evolve' without a guiding power/principle, is a major focus now. But everybody who's anybody, agrees that the 'creationists' have to be kept out of the science classroom."

R_ smiled at the last point. "Some disputed areas of purely scientific analysis underlie that last matter, don't they?" It was Sci-guy's turn to smile. "There has been a lot of argument about whether even talking about a possible active-intelligence, in shaping the forms of living things, is suitable in 'science.' I watched these arguments come onto the field, and I used to urge my friends to consider the scientific data if scientific aspects were being argued, instead of using shallow dismissals like 'intelligent design is just creationism in a cheap tuxedo.' I would see serious questions being raised - often leading to counter-analyses that were at least possible - but they did involve serious thought about scientific aspects." He turned to look at B-t. "After all," he continued, "if there *were* an intelligent agent causing 'creation,' you would think some aspects of the natural world might give a clue." B-t wanted to smile at this but he didn't dare; he knew that the "anti-" expositions were too heavy and the controversies were heated, intricate and difficult.

"Micro-analysis, macro-analysis, mathematical analysis, that's how I list them for my friends, when I was arguing for open-minded scientific consideration of the issues people were raising," Sci-guy said. "Micro-analysis: the overwhelming complexity of structures *within* the cell, which caused some competent professionals to feel that the evolutionary paradigm, in the absence of any guiding, cannot account for what we observe. Furthermore, the issue of creating the carefully-specified *information* that's in the genetic code, the amount of time compared to the rates of mutation... Darwin took the cell for granted — but we can't any more. You have to be very careful how you talk about these things, though, or you get lumped in with the 'crackpots.' Dr. Dean Kenyon was a world-renowned scientist when he wrote *Chemical Evolution*, analyzing how he thought the chemical structure needed for simple cells might 'evolve.' Then, he pursued the data further, realized it didn't work at all, and said so openly. Now he's labeled a sixth-rate scientist and was forbidden for a while to teach introductory biology at his university."

"By the way, the controversies over structures within the cell involves not only complexity, but issues of interlocking complexity among parts — where 'natural selection' can only favor the structure when enough of the various parts have evolved to make it functional, just like your car engine can't go anywhere with just pistons but no intake manifold. But every argument like that invokes intense counter-argument — supported by thick books of facts organized and viewed in such a way as to lock in with the argument. Since there are billions of facts out there, susceptible to varieties of viewpoints, it's quite a process. AND," he said with a strong voice as he looked at B-t, "those cell-structure arguments have 'evolved' into a whole system-wide counter-view, 'co-option' arguing that modifications, from earlier structures that served different purposes, can be adduced to explain the items that have been put forward in these discussions." Sci-guy swiveled his glance to R_, and continued, "None of that takes away from the 'information' argument, which rests on a different foundation, so you'll have to let me get into that more later." (Some readers may want to use the Index to jump to those expositions; this chapter gets intense in a lot of things that many people may want to avoid "bogging down" in, for those less concerned with this particular controversy, so we try to provide "jump points" for escape where those varying personal interests and concerns may warrant. Those less concerned with the "scientific" issue may want to "jump" to Chapter 17, "Hell and the Antidote," or Chapter 18's "more on prayer." [After all, dense reading and intellectual jungles are not everybody's thing!])

"Micro, macro, math – now I've begun, but just in case you think I'm making it easy for you, I'll take an aside" – Sci-Guy glanced at Thoughtful-Woman – "there's an issue that has emerged later, 'bio-inspiration.' Some profound engineering / product design problems have been solved by imitating structures in living creatures – if those structures were cobbled together by progressive chance mutations / co-option of prior structures, how do such elegant solutions come to be, things that our highly-developed intellects had not been able to devise... I'll go into some examples and let you chew on the issue, but I'm going to finish the analytic array I started!" Sci-guy obviously liked "having the floor," and the fact that the dog had not only gone to sleep, but was beginning to snore, didn't dampen the mood.

Thoughtful-Woman looked at B-t to see how he was weathering this, then returned a fascinated gaze to Sci-guy, who continued: "Macro-analysis, I call it, is the overall flow of species, the appearance and spread of new life forms. Darwin anticipated a continuous flow of variations building to new species. But as I mentioned, the fossil record has shown that wasn't the way things worked. One feature in particular has led to a lot of controversy as to whether it has demolished Darwin's projection of how the whole system of nature works — that's the discovery of the 'Cambrian explosion.' The full array of basic body plans for the advanced species appeared rather suddenly and without adequate precedent of variations, at the Cambrian period. For a while, it was argued that previous life forms were without adequate hard structure to make fossils, accounting for the absence of the 'lead-in,' but fossil beds were found that disproved *that* idea. So the unlikely pattern of the overall flow of species development, in my 'macro-analysis,' puts a crimp in the 'purely naturalistic' outlook."

Sci-guy eyed his audience appraisingly. *I should clarify, "rather suddenly" in terms of geologic time and the usual flow of such things,* he thought... *And "without adequate precedent" meaning, without the type of branching as expected by processes of chance variations and selection... But for this audience? No need to spout forth with all that,* he told himself.

He stuck his head out the window to spit, and added, "These are the things I tease my ideologically-severe colleagues with when they are telling me that the whole thing – *no room for any 'directing intelligence' in the development of forms of life* – is proven beyond any doubt. There's no consensus, other than keeping out 'creationism' and insisting on 'naturalistic' analyses. And the consensus that gaps in our understanding call for more funding." The wry character of his grin undoubtedly came from the pain of being personally part of the "cut-backs."

B-t wasn't grinning at all. "Don't slide over the major issue of 'information' — whether naturalistic means can create information, which is displayed immensely in the genetic code." His jaw was set, he wasn't going to let Sci-guy evade that. He had another wrinkle he wanted to throw in, that some scientists say the data shows not only that planet earth is designed for life, but also that the placement of the planet in the universe is made to sustain scientific observation – a touch from a God Who wants to be known, sought out, valued, in B-t's view. *Later,* he thought, *my turn will come...*

Thoughtful-Woman was more interested in Sci-guy's thoughts than B-t was. "By 'purely naturalistic,' you mean only natural forces and processes, no guiding intelligence involved, no higher principle that leads the course, above the physics and chemistry and biology, yes?" she asked Sci-guy. "That's a reasonable translation," he said with a warm smile, although he was tempted to object that "higher principles" were welcome as long as they didn't admit any "guiding intelligence." He moved on: "The other thing I listed, the 'mathematical analysis' is the issue of how rapidly mutations occur in nature, how often they are favorable versus how often they are destructive to the organism's functioning, and how long it then can be calculated to take for these higher organs to be developed by chance variation and natural selection of the 'fittest' forms."

Sci-guy's warm smile had faded, as his discourse demanded one detail amidst the forest of knowledge that his studies had given him. "It was an atheist, Fred Hoyle, if I remember right, who came up with the famous analogy that the mathematics show that the purely naturalistic origin of life as we know it, is about as likely as a tornado going over a junkyard and producing a 747 aircraft.[124] That's one of the reasons for the popularity in some circles of the 'multiverse' concept: If there are trillions of trillions of universes, it's easy — mathematically — for *one* of them to come through the statistical odds and produce life as we know it. With 'multiverse' theory, of course, you're back to having an explanation based on invisible and unobservable matters, beyond the reach of your experimentation."

B-t knew that his ideas weren't allowed in this universe of discourse, and he glowered while Thoughtful-Woman moved the conversation forward: "So don't those levels of analysis cover it pretty well — micro, macro, math? Is there an emerging consensus among people who are willing to face the facts?" she asked Sci-guy.

"Not so fast, my friend," he replied. "A lot of people feel that so much has been explained,[125] that we can count on making the basic ideas work through all the problems we haven't yet thrashed out. And whether sub-cellular complexity is inexplicable or not, depends on who you're listening to, and how much scope you give to their imaginative constructs about what is, after all, not available to us as data (the actual historical flow in full detail, that is). Further, a lot of people feel that science *has* to deal only in naturalistic causes, and so whatever explanation we have at that level, whether it satisfies fully or not, that explanation *is* the 'scientific' one. And you mentioned 'higher principle' — if you can't account for the marvelous order of things, you can say there's an 'ordering principle' and that settles it, without creating any underpinning for looking for a *personal* God."

B-t wasn't going to be an outsider any longer. "Two concepts of science lurk there, my friend," he interjected. "One says 'have the courage to follow the data wherever they lead' — like Copernicus and Galileo did. The other concept says 'naturalistic only,' inadequate or not. One is empiricism, the other is naturalism."[126] Sci-guy looked like he was mentally filing away this terminology for future discussion — after all, scientists are by definition always open to new ideas when they prove meritorious.

Thoughtful-Woman was again justifying her name: "By 'empiricism' you mean basing matters on the empirical data, the experimental and observed data, and by 'naturalism' you mean philosophically restricting your consideration to only naturalistic causations, right?" B-t nodded and drew the obvious consequences: "When you restrict your consideration to 'naturalistic' domains, you cannot guarantee that you do not omit something important. But it may take a thousand years for such matters to break through your filters." *Look at how many centuries it took science to break through presumptions and line up with the Bible's opening words, "It the beginning..."* he thought, but he didn't say it.

Neither Sci-guy nor Thoughtful-Woman wanted to join B-t in going there, but he added a juicy tidbit after a brief silence made everyone uneasy: "By the way, the 'multiverse' concept was written up about 1955 by C. S. Lewis, the great Christian lecturer of the mid-1900's. Also, a recent Christian commentator said he felt that an infinite Creator God might well be expected to have created such a vast number of universes."[127]

Rampant speculation was outside Sci-guy's domain, and he turned to peruse the passing landscape. But it brought to mind the stimulating insight he had promised earlier; he relieved his mental stress by petting the dog, and said to the group, "OK, time for 'bio-inspiration.' Philosophy has a tendency to interlock with matters of perceived reality, and Sci-guy had observations from the world of work.

"There's a new line of analysis, arising out of 'bio-inspiration,' also known as 'bio-mimetics.' That's from the word 'mimicry,' because human innovations have been very successfully and ingeniously based on 'mimicking' designs from nature. An unexpected result, if these 'natural systems' are the result of chance cobbling together pieces of prior systems that 'just happen' to succeed at new levels...

"When the super-high-speed 'bullet train' emerges from a tunnel, the shock wave is a major issue, a sonic boom," Sci-guy continued. "The design solution was found by studying a bird that dives into water for fish, the kingfisher's beak. Painless syringe needles for medical use were developed in Japan by studying the structure of mosquito mouthparts that are able to extract blood from the host animal with the least amount of nerve irritation. A 1997 book emphasized 'that biomimicry is leading the path to a new age of technological development by taking lessons from nature as the groundwork for products' (*Biomimicry*, Janine M Benyus).[128]

Sci-guy swiveled his gaze around the group before he finished this arena of exposition. "The basic question that arises here — how do roughly-cobbled-together systems, under no guiding intelligence, co-opting parts from earlier chance-mutated but workable structures, achieve such high levels of form that they move above what our own minds have developed? It brings me face-to-face with a Ph.D. biochemist's reaction to the intricate subcellular 'machines' — 'an elegance and ingenuity of an absolutely transcending quality,' which another scholar called 'transcendent brilliance of design' in molecular machines." He paused to look at the dog, who was grinning up at him, and he went on to recount: "Fazale Rana tells how, as a graduate student, he was 'agnostic,' not even pondering the question of 'God.' But, he says, "When I was confronted with the elegance and the sophistication, the beauty, the ingenuity, the cleverness of biochemical systems [within the cell] in terms of the way they're structured and the way they function, it convinced me that a Creator must exist."[129] [see endnote for his list of "decisive items"]

Sci-guy seemed energized by the faint smile on B-t's face. "Dr. Rana cites something else that's penetrating: advanced research found that 'the genetic code in nature resides near the global optimum for all possible genetic codes with respect to its error-minimization capacity… [Scientists who found this] have concluded that the rules of the genetic code cannot be accidental.'

"These things are very thought-provoking," Sci-guy continued, "but they don't *prove* what you guys want to establish." (He gestured at R_ and B-t.) "Give an example of amazing biology, and someone will finger something they think shows poor work by any 'Creator.' The human eye, for one: the way the optic nerve is structured, makes a 'blind spot,' so 'it should have been done differently.' " Sci-guy grinned as he added the obvious next point: "But the skeptics use their eyes perfectly well to read their scathing remarks against any 'Creator.' … I'll give you a stunning example to put in an endnote if you write this up, driver."[130]

B-t's eyes looked glazed — "too much information" is part of our vocabulary — but he had a clear thought: "If our minds 'evolved' according to survival and reproduction, 'natural selection,' how is it that we are able to comprehend math like infinite set theory, intricacies of biochemistry, transcendental beauty in symphonies and art, even abstractions like 'theory of evolution'?" Sci-guy glowered at him and silence covered the scene.

B-t took a deep breath and moved the conversation to a new peak: "Someone said, 'The universe is full of clues that point to a hidden God.' Maybe what He* is doing with nature, is just giving the opportunity to see the possibility, to seed the search, so people can come to a personal relationship — maybe the *personal* *relationship* is more important to Him* than mere intellectual perception of 'a Being without Whom no existence is possible.' That would make the science of nature the beginning, not the conclusion."

It was troubling to most of them that science seemed to fall short of a definitive answer, although establishing that science had *not* proven "no room for God" was an important point in the current intellectual climate. (Later, when Sci-guy went for a moonlight walk, Thoughtful-Woman hastened after him and went over this dialogue with him. "These often-loud scientific atheists... If they don't know what the 'hand of God' looks like, how can they 'know' that there's 'no room in the flow of nature' for the hand of God?" Her question made sense to him, but it put matters in terms outside his "concept-space," and Thoughtful-Woman was accompanied by the dog back to the RV, as the dog watched her struggle against going into a deep preoccupation with the question.) (But that evening's question was a later matter, and we return to the conversation that followed "bio-inspiration.")

Thoughtful-Woman was contemplative, and R_ broke his own unaccustomed silence: "A popular story tells us Mark Twain said that when he was sixteen, he was profoundly embarrassed at how ignorant his Dad was. When he became twenty-one, he was astonished at how much the old man had learned in just five short years." Thoughtful-Woman was puzzled, and R_ expounded: "The change, of course, was not in the old man, but in the arrogance of youth [would "headiness" be a better word, reader?] and its attitude toward what the old man knew, of domains outside the purview of adolescence. I bring it up, because I wonder if some present-day 'scientific' philosophy isn't taken with itself in the way that Twain was taken with his own wisdom when he was sixteen, and similarly to Twain's change of view, the vast domains now excluded a priori may come to receive a respect similar to the regard that a maturing Twain developed for his father's grasp."[131]

Thoughtful-Woman laughed. "You have the strangest RV I've ever seen," she said. "The two shelves of books you have in the back are nothing like what other people take 'on the road.' I was browsing in the book you have by Mary Midgley" — she noted B-t's disapproving glance and said to R_, "You told us we could look in any of them except the notebooks, which are personal. Midgley assessed Hume on skepticism in his day versus skepticism now, and Midgley said that 'once disbelief becomes fashionable' you reach the point we're at, where 'narrow-minded, conformist skeptics' are commonplace."[132]

Sci-guy was a "student of life," as a very special Native American Indian friend of your author had once labeled herself, and he had read some exposition at the philosophical level about how people are thinking now - the general posture and its implications - he brought that pondering to R_ privately, later when R_ was working over his notes (our "Postscript" to this chapter, p. 89).

The Next Day

Evolution never rests, and this discussion was not over. The question "where does that leave us" came to life and danced across the dashboard, as R_ asked Sci-guy for his own personal outlook. "There are three metaphysical positions among intellectual circles now," Sci-guy said. B-t didn't do "metaphysics" and Sci-guy explained the term: "Ideas about what are the deeper meanings of the scientific ideas, the greater and underlying realities that the ideas illuminate." Sci-guy listed the three positions: "Some people say evolution has explained things so successfully that there's no room for a Creator. Some say evolution explains much about the flow of life forms through time but doesn't debar the work of an intelligent and concerned Creator. Others say that the purely naturalistic explanation of life forms has collapsed, and thus a purely scientific analysis of the data shows that a guiding intelligence — 'Creator' or otherwise — is established scientifically."

Thoughtful-Woman was sharp and remembered the previous day's analysis: "When some people say 'naturalistic explanations have collapsed,' that's your 'micro/macro/math' triad of places where the naturalism assertedly doesn't work, right?" "Generally, yes," Sci-guy replied, "with all kinds of variations depending on who you are listening to."

"It sounded pretty conclusive to me," B-t said. "But what the analysis shows, has a lot to do with who is doing the analysis," Sci-guy replied. "Is the 'Cambrian explosion' inexplicable and intelligence-proving, or is it overblown, overstated, and just waiting for some more 'naturalistic' clarification? By the way, be prepared to talk about 'God-of-the-gaps'[133] if you take that material to heart." He paused with a twinkle in his eye as he took a glance at B-t and added, "Also, a new problem in the Cambrian explosion has emerged. Not only did the higher levels of life emerge in dramatic suddenness, not only have more fossil researches shown that the lack of the expected predecessors, and of long gradual changing, was *not* due to fossilization gaps — but also, the pattern of the emergence of the new forms was 'top-down' instead of Darwin's slow, gradual branching out."[134]

Sci-guy gave the others a searching gaze. "Now, remember: some people say Darwinian explanations don't work here, some people say they do, and if you study deeply and get the expertise to have an opinion on that issue, you won't settle it, you'll just add one person to the count in one of the camps."

Sci-guy brooded over the landscape for a while, then turned back to the silent little group. "One of my colleagues believes that the Cambrian 'explosion' shows just enough transitional forms [Reader: see endnotes 120, 121, 250], and so swiftly in emergence patterns, to make it look like an intelligence was working over the process — far swifter and in far different patterns than the groping gradualism of chance & necessity per Darwin. It seemed spooky to me that way, long before I met you guys." He sighed. "I'll guess we'll just have to wait for further..." His voice trailed off and he looked moodily away.

B-t was impatient with all the various "evolving" controversies. But he knew it was inescapable, so he had done his own browsing. "Your 'analytic overview' has not done justice to the question of information in the cell," he said, with a strong undertone in his voice. The dog sat up and his ears went straight up, as if he knew that undertone would translate into something powerful.

"Information? What are you talking about?" asked Thoughtful-Woman. Sci-guy did the exposition: "The hereditary material of genetics in the cell was once thought to be different, as a matter of course, for different life-forms. But the exploration of DNA in genes has shown that it's a code that can be represented by four letters A, T, C, G, with the precise sequencing of those in the genetic code being both crucial and *not determined* by the physics or chemistry of the molecules. The letters, by the way, stand for four 'bases:' adenine, thymine, guanine, and cytosine. The sequence of coded 'letters' has the character of information, just like letters in the alphabet arranging into words. Bill Gates himself said that 'DNA is like a computer program.' Francis Collins, the eminent scientist who oversaw the 'reading' of the human genome, said that the information in the human genome, printed 'in regular font size on normal bond paper and binding them all together would result in a tower the height of the Washington Monument.'[135] But that information exists within each human cell.

"That raises the question," Sci-guy continued, "of tracing the source of the information, given science's long-standing commitment to explaining observed effects in terms of causes known to produce such effects ('uniformitarianism' or 'principle of uniformity'). The argument is that we have a vast amount of experience with 'information,' from ancient writings to computer programs, and it's always from an active intelligence. (And, by the way," his voice softened like a parenthetical insertion, "Meyer explains that by definition, chemical affinities of molecules cannot create the ordering in the DNA that codes the information.)" [136]

The silence couldn't last. Thoughtful-Woman was looking at R_ questioningly. After being silent yesterday, would he emerge as a speaker again? "One thing people miss, is the issue of how God is involved with the world," R_ began. "They often think that if a 'naturalistic' cause can be shown, God is at best standing by watching, or perhaps set it up in the first place. But the God of the Bible is very much involved in 'natural' events: He* tells His people to ask Him 'for rain in the springtime,' per the Bible, Zechariah 10:1. The 'naturalist' would say, 'Raining is what it does naturally in the springtime! Why should we ask You?' And God says, 'Do the clouds rain by themselves?' Jeremiah 14:22.[137] People leave God out of the analysis, but the New Testament says that all things hold together by His* word of power (Heb 1:3). The Bible sees God as deeply involved in 'natural' processes, for example Psalm 147:8."

Thoughtful-Woman's face bore the obvious question, so R_ took it up: "People think, 'If He*'s involved in everything, why doesn't He stop the tsunami?' They want to rule Him* out because they think in terms of their interests[138] and their purposes, *their* analysis of what a God of love should be doing for them. But remember novelist William Paul Young's attribution of a quote to the Trinitarian God, Who says about the condition of the world, 'We're not justifying it, we're redeeming it.'[139] The important point about it, is that people who take the time to attune themselves to God, report that it results — overall — in a better well-being than results from 'living in the darkness.'[140] Let me give you an analysis that might help you keep an open mind.

"If fish had the collective intelligence to assess what causes the movements of a sailing ship, they would interpret it in terms of water currents, waves, the position of the rudder, and the rocking of the hull — the things they can see from underwater. The position of the sails would be outside of their underwater realm, outside the scope of their perceptions, so that would go untheorized. As the changes in the sails generally result in a listing of the hull down on one side, *that listing* would be the causative factor that would dominate their analysis of how the ship's course is affected." *Can I hope that these people can personify fish so heavily as to comprehend my comparison*, R_ thought in profound concern.

Thoughtful-Woman was patient, but not inexhaustibly so. "And your point would be?" she asked. R_ replied, "A woman said that 'the spiritual realm is causative,'[141] and when it's outside of your perception, you will explain everything without it. That's fine, as long as what you want is covered — if the fish want to stay out of the way of the ship, they know that when the hull leans ("lists" may be better nautical parlance) or the rudder turns, get out of the way of the new direction the ship will take. But if your analysis shows that your theories can explain everything, *precisely because you've been asking only a limited range of questions and satisfying yourself*, the true comprehensiveness of your explanation is at risk."

Sci-guy laughed. "True comprehensiveness at risk," he said. "That I have to remember. Say, remember the question, 'Where does all this leave us?' I'm ready to answer that, if anyone wants to hear me out!" Thoughtful-Woman was all ears; B-t was wary but wanted to hear it; R_ was interested. The dog sat up in response to the uplift in the humans' mood. "Three metaphysical positions about what the science implies," Sci-guy said: " 'A,' that 'we can explain everything by (naturalistic) evolution' and God has been ruled out by the data. 'B,' that evolution does or is likely to explain everything, at least to satisfy *our* analysis, but how God relates to the matters is another issue. 'C,' that scientific analysis shows that there is shepherding intelligence of some form."

A neat "A-B-C" goes over well after long discussions, and everyone was attentive as Sci-guy continued: "The state of science today — according to *me* — is that 'A' definitely does not follow. If you ever want a pointed discussion on *that*, read Berlinski's book on the 'scientific pretensions' of atheism."

"BY THE WAY," Sci-guy said, with a definitive tone in his voice, "remember when you assess this stuff, to think about what the terms mean and how the various levels of 'evolution' relate to the data that you're hearing about." He began to pet the dog vigorously. "Here's something from a widely-read critic: 'Evolution' can mean anything from the uncontroversial statement that bacteria "evolve" resistance to antibiotics to the grand metaphysical claim that the universe and mankind "evolved" entirely by purposeless mechanical forces. A word that elastic is likely to mislead, by implying that we know as much about the grand claim as we do about the small one.'[142] Be careful when clear proofs of some evolutionary facts become pillars for metaphysics debarring your God – not that I support your God, but I believe in clarity and truth."

B-t liked that caution, but he saw the state of science differently: "I've read some on the micro/macro/math breakdowns that you described yesterday as areas of contention, and it seems clear that strictly scientific analysis has shown that strictly 'naturalistic' evolution doesn't hold up." Sci-guy turned to glance at him, and replied, "If the science is so clear, why can't scientists see it?" B-t replied hesitantly: "An absorption in their own levels of analysis, which definitely do have their own merits, but are limited in scope; cultural conditioning; peer pressure; a reluctance to open the window to a vast unknown."

"Well," Sci-guy responded, "you have to admit, much as your own scientific studies prove intelligence at work to *you*, there are credible scientists who study the matter deeply and believe in God and give 'evolution' a good report."[143] Sci-guy looked away, out over the landscape, as he thought, *When I get good and ready, I'm going to give you a bombshell you won't forget.* He had found that R_ had a book with exactly the write-up that he wanted to show Thoughtful-Woman...

B-t had gotten stimulated, and he took another tack: "If it's possible to explain imaginatively all the emergence of life-forms by natural selection etc., even if you have to squint after reading Stephen Meyer on *information* in DNA – and *if, on the other hand,* it's possible to see all the scientific data with God still in view, you have a choice to make, not an intellectual forced-conclusion..." B-t's voice trailed off, and Sci-guy did, in fact, squint. "*Imaginatively*?" he asked. "Well," B-t said softly, "the purely-naturalistic 'explanation' involves a lot of extrapolation, some outright conjecture, and in addition, it comes down to mentally charting how one thinks it *could* have happened, which doesn't mean that that's how it actually *did* happen, historically."

As for the conversation's flow, it had stalled, and Thoughtful-Woman was ready to move on. She told Sci-guy with a definitive tone, "You're our resident scientist for this trip, so you're going to have to comment on Dawkins for me." She could see Sci-guy's mental wheels turning to prepare a later exposition,[144] and she turned the "evolution" of their discourse to "what are we going to do about dinner," which worked "naturally" for everyone.

Thoughtful-Woman was absorbed in silence for a while. She was contemplating a remark R_ had made, that the *progression of forms* would seem a reasonable way for a spiritual Creator to work with a material creation. She also remembered Sci-guy's comment that Darwin had put forward a *hypothesis* and, as a scientist, Darwin would have been glad to see the data-driven discussion evaluating it — the wide-ranging debate with facts from many areas of biology, with a *scientific* focus on the adequacy of the "purely naturalistic" hypothesis (the hypothesis that chance mutation plus natural selection could account for all life's forms).

Thoughtful-Woman pondered also R_'s larger caution — "methodological naturalism" as meaning that science will continue to work on no-intelligence-cited explanations. That's what they're expected to do, and it's fine as long as it doesn't slop over into "ontological naturalism," the presumption that this level of thinking means that there *is* no other realm or power (called "metaphysical naturalism" by some). It will mean that however convincing the analysis may seem to some people that "purely naturalistic" explanations have collapsed, many scientists will defer judgment to see what may be thought up in the future. (It is a different issue that some thinkers will take any "natural" explanation, whatever its shortcomings, in preference to considering that realities beyond naturalism may be in effect).

She pondered until Sci-guy fell asleep and began to snore, then she took out her smart-phone and began texting relatives. During the next travel break, as R_ walked the dog and B-t tried to see if he was still limber enough to climb a tree, Sci-guy showed Thoughtful-Woman the passage he had marked with a post-it in one of R_'s own books. She read it, her eyes widened, and she began to meditate again, preparing to "lay it on" B-t, R_, and the world in general...

Thoughtful-Woman waited till B-t had brewed himself a fresh cup of tea. She had watched him web-surfing a site that expounded at length, "Frequently raised but weak arguments against Intelligent Design" (uncommondescent.com/faq/). Sci-guy had primed her, out of R_'s books, with dramatically different material. After the cup of tea, she felt B-t would be awake for her "bombshell," and she addressed the group at somewhat elevated volume. "I can see why you guys like your I.D.iots," she said (as Sci-guy winced), "but that's not the only claim to a thoughtful scientific perspective." Sci-guy blushed as he realized that this harsh introduction was how she was going into the material *he* had pointed out, but there was no fine-tuning the situation. He watched B-t's expression to try to assess if B-t even knew what an "IDiot" was — the put-down shorthand for I.D. "Intelligent Design" thinkers.

"Open your minds, gentlemen," Thoughtful-Woman continued, "listen to a different scientist and grow in your perception. Here's Dr. Denis Alexander's framing of the situation: He asks, 'Does the evolutionary account display properties that are more consistent with a theistic or with an atheistic account of the world?' "[145] She waived R_'s copy of Dr. Alexander's book as she spoke.

"His answer is that 'recent biological discoveries clearly point to the theistic account as providing a more reasonable explanation for the existence of the overall story of evolution on planet earth...' Note that he is not 'I.D.' — he refutes 'intelligent design' in very strong language, stating that it takes usually about ten years to get a good evolutionary explanation of any of the 'inexplicable' conundrums that I.D. people assert, etc."[146]

Thoughtful-Woman was on a role, and B-t was wondering if she would have made a good schoolmarm. *Sexist term, got to rethink that,* he told himself. *Perhaps an excellent guest lecturer circulating at a group of colleges...* Thoughtful-Woman was focused on her text now, and had no time for reading anyone's expression. She brought out the point of interest to B-t and R_: "But while he [Dr. Alexander] believes fully that evolution explains the flow of the forms of life, he believes very assertively that God is sovereign and present over all of it; and he assesses the characteristics of the evolutionary account to show the 'theistic consistency.' This is some of what he says: 'Look at evolutionary history as a whole... the idea of progress is inescapable.' Also, 'the mechanisms of life look highly constrained... all living things are united... by possessing an elegant and highly restricted set of protein structures.' Elegant! I like that," she said. Sci-Guy interjected, "That 'highly constrained, highly restricted set' is empirical data, and it tends to show that what we see does not result from chemical possibilities simply wandering around randomly wherever." The dog looked anxiously at R_, then at B-t. He pawed R_'s leg gently, hoping to be petted, as the atmosphere seemed inexplicably tense.

Thoughtful-Woman cleared her throat to refocus attention, and continued her exposition: "Adding in a discussion of convergence, he concludes that, 'atheists seek to support their disbelief in God based on interpretations of scientific data which appear initially plausible due to lack of knowledge about the data... [but] less believable as our understanding... becomes more complete.'[147] That's not what you like to think about 'inability of naturalistic explanations' but it's a whole higher order of thought than what you've been reading."

B-t wanted to glare at her, but he wasn't willing to let himself go to do that, until he had taken time to try to think through what she was reading to them. He decided she would indeed make a good guest lecturer when she concluded, "The person interested in the controversy will appreciate that Dr. Alexander concludes his chapter refuting I.D. with the observation that, 'The more we look at Darwinian evolution taken as a whole, the more it seems to display precisely the signs of intelligence that I.D. proponents believe are located in those hidden non-Darwinian gaps.'"[148] *R_ made a mental note that if he ever wrote a book, that comment should be elaborated with Plantinga on science as a whole bespeaking theism... (see endnote).*

==================

Postscript to Chapter 14: This was another topic area that moved R_ to sitting alone in the back of the RV while the others slept, jotting furiously about what he might compile into narratives. *Age of the earth material shows the need for* *<u>thinking</u>* *in interpreting Bible ("love God with all ... your* *<u>mind</u>*" *— Jesus' command in Matthew 22:37, Mark 12:30, Luke 10:27). Copernicus opposed by mis-interpretation of the Bible, "Earth cannot be moved" (1 Chron 16:30; Psa 93:1, 96:10, 104:5) — an example of Augustine's insight that Christians ignorant of the science, thinking they see from Scripture, make Scripture look bad.*

Recounting the key insights of Hugh Ross helps put Genesis on the throne with science in harmony [e.g. our p. 13 earlier; also chapter 16 on the "six days" matter]. *Websites dedicated to these issues include a science association of scientists who are Christians, website asa3.org (see the last five paragraphs of note 113 for a caution re this). Note D. Falk, F. Collins books. Collins on projections from evolutionary theory bearing fruit, shows that there are areas of proven validity to evolutionary thinking.* R_ paused and refocused his tired eyes by gazing at some distant trees. He remembered Sci-guy's remark to B-t that "the reason you need a new flu shot every fall is that the germs are constantly evolving — so evolution is a proven fact." *At certain levels, indubitably,* he thought, and *onward...*[149]

"Up, eyes, and back to work" R_ muttered, and wrote: *Bishop Ussher's 4004 B.C. stands as a famous miscalculation of the date of Creation per Genesis — compare the great Christian theologian Augustine's caution (about A.D. 400!) not to make Scripture into scientific data when things are open to varying interpretations. Falk's book shows solid science (tree rings, sediment layers in lakes, etc.) taking indisputable dating back far beyond 4004 B.C.* (On misinterpreting Genesis for the age of the human race, some Bible facts in endnote 262).

"Creation," the "how" of the universe's history, unsettles people, perhaps because we are in too much of a hurry to feel that we have complete understanding? This is how I would put it, R_ thought: *"Look, think about the creation of a car. There are two*

stories you can tell about that: one involves enormous power-shovels bringing tons of iron ore out of the earth, huge steel furnaces making usable metal, great presses forming the metal under enormous pressure. The second version, by contrast, is extremely quiet, with only the muted, disciplined energy of people bending over desks and sketching designs, sketching curves of car body shapes and other matters... These two stories would seem totally different and irreconcilable, if you didn't know how they come together.

The two are one, and we know how — but that is because we are in the realm above-these-processes, where it all comes together. The spiritual story told in Genesis 1-3 and the scientific story of the Big Bang and the fast-moving atoms, may have a similar situation of incongruity that escapes our understanding — until the clarification. And that may not come until we are moved ourselves into higher levels of being! The dog came back from a jaunt and paused to be petted and gaze lovingly at his "master," and R_ was startled to realize he had run that last "insight" repeatedly through his mind, at least three times in a row, without its getting any more profound. Oh well!

Shouldn't people be equipped with Meyer's counter-argument to the "God of the gaps" issue, R_ thought, but he wrote nothing. If people say that when "unexplainable" structures are found in living things, that proves "God made it," they are told that their God is just a "gap" waiting for the explanation to be found, and such a "God" will disappear at that point. Meyers says the issue isn't "gaps," it's a wide pattern of "inference to the best explanation." *Let them read Meyer*, R_ thought, as he massaged his aching writing-hand.[150]

R_ paused, and the dog put his paw on R_'s knee as if he were expecting something. *Sci-guy mentioned the issue of the "information" in the genetic code (DNA), and then he just left it hanging*, R_ thought. *It may be the most profound manifestation that creation has of the deep intelligence that formed it. Like anything else that's claimed to point to God, some people immediately run in every other direction — they claim "information" is just a metaphor re the genetic code, but Meyer shows that it matches exactly his dictionary's definition of information* (p. 86 of Meyer, *Signature...*; his dictionary is Webster's). "Oh well," R_ muttered, and the dog's eyes saddened.

More writing, though, as the dog stretched out: *Polkinghorne (John Polkinghorne spent 30 years as a high-energy-particle physicist, then became an Anglican priest; he is one of the "big names" in the field of "science and religion") says that the fundamental equations/structure of quantum mechanics have been shown to have an alternate solution, alternate to the standard model that* <u>*is*</u> *physics today. Are there any implications of that in the philosophical things we hear about regarding physics and the nature of the universe?*

The principle of uniformity or "uniformitarianism"[151] *is an assumption, not a proven fact or a theoretical necessity. And when people accumulate thousands of observations compatible with that assumption, it doesn't prove that the assumption really delimits the nature of the universe — it just proves that this is what people have busied themselves observing.* R_ stopped writing to remark to himself, "I must get the PBS DVD on the 'Scablands' counter-example to uniformitarianism. A scientist who interpreted evidence in eastern Washington State as showing a swift, incredibly large flood, was treated as totally out-of-bounds by the scientific establishment of his day, due to the commitment to "uniformitarian" thinking. Postulated catastrophes like the Bible's 'Flood' are not the way Nature is to be explained! But the evidence eventually proved him correct; now it's accepted and part of the scientific view, and there's more room for such massive events in the thinking." (R_ told B-t later about this issue, "It's an example of getting one's head stuck in a scientific paradigm, and over-extending it." *That* reminded R_ of Midgley's comment about "bad science vs. bad religion" but he couldn't find it then to share it (endnote 132 here).

R_ made another note, which he circled and put asterisks beside: *The idea that forms of life become progressively better adapted to their environment, would appear most definitely NOT to conflict with the idea that a benevolent Creator is presiding over their progress!*

R_'s lonely authoring was interrupted by a whisper: "Can I disturb you and tell you some of my own reading?" Sci-guy spoke softly to let the others go on sleeping; only the dog woke up to watch this conversation.

"A Canadian academic, Charles Taylor, wrote an intense magnum opus *A Secular Age,* almost 900 pages, which James Smith made accessible in *How (Not) to Be Secular: Reading Charles Taylor,* bringing it down to 160 pages. One thing I found most thought-provoking: the discussion of how we think, what I might call our 'concept-space,' our basic viewpoint underlying our thinking about these issues." He pulled out a well-worn note and read from Smith/Taylor: "...rather than seeing ourselves positioned within a hierarchy of forms (in which case we wouldn't be surprised if 'higher levels' are mysterious and inscrutable), we now adopt a God-like, dispassionate 'gaze' that deigns to survey the whole. ...it is in this context that the project of *theodicy* ramps up: we now expect an answer to whatever puzzles us, including the problem of evil. Nothing should be inscrutable... while earlier the terrors and burdens of evil and disaster would have cast us on the help of a Savior, now that we think we see how it all works, the argument gets displaced. People in coffee-houses and salons [and philosophy classes?] begin to express their disaffection in reflections on divine justice, and the theologians begin to feel this is the challenge they must meet to fight back the coming wave of unbelief."[152]

R_ made a few quick notes, holding his hand so that Sci-guy could not see him write "read Smith's 'condensed' book, not the huge original"... Sci-guy was a person who tried to hear all the sectors, and he had heard B-t expound on how "pride" could be an evil thing in Bible terms (although the Bible also has Godly pride, see "Pride" references in Appendix One.) "This more-demanding, ourselves-at-the-top viewpoint that Taylor & Smith describe, makes me uneasy about 'pride' as a conceptual blinder. Also, they discuss how the concept-space of our society, the way we conceptualize the scope of reality, makes it easy to omit consideration of the 'supernatural.' Those levels of reality, the 'hierarchy of forms'... They discuss how people take up 'unbelief' not from proof but from the 'form of the *story* that science tells and the self-image that comes with it... the stance of maturity, of courage..." Sci-guy paused, then gave a repressed twitch as he saw that R_'s little bookshelf had a book he himself had pondered. "That analysis reminds me of what your friend Guillebaud said," and he gestured toward the book. "Guillebaud talked against '...the closed universe of scientism [where] scientific rationality, as a mode of knowledge, is endowed with an authority that discredits all others ... "totalitarian" in the sense that it refuses any legitimacy to other ways of apprehending reality — intuitive, poetic, metaphysical, mystical, and so on. It literally closes off the horizon of knowledge.' That made me think, but you can't prove anything with that."[153] Sci-guy paused, seemed rigid, and the dog stared intently at him, as if the next gesture would define something important. "Well, it makes me cautious, but you can't push back the science-ideologues with those kinds of philosophical ruminations."

After Sci-guy went out to star-gaze, R_ made some notes about a conversation the whole group had had earlier in the day. (He thought about running after Sci-guy to ask him if he had read D. B. Hart's *The Experience of God*, another "magnum opus" which many might find "inaccessible," but a thought-provoking analysis of how "being" itself, consciousness, and more, point toward God [see Annotated Bibliography, Deeper Philosophy]. R_ decided he had too much to meditate about from the earlier group conversation, and he stayed focused on that: Thoughtful-Woman was a person who followed the flow of ideas over the mind of the people, and she had brought up **Stephen Hawking's** much-ballyhooed conclusion that the laws of physics are adequate to create the universe and God is unnecessary. "Hawking is doing what people have been doing at least since the time of Aristotle, over 2,000 years ago," R_ had said softly, sadly. "They take the universe as something that 'just is,' it's 'one of those things...'

Hawking has taken the top layer off: he applies this outlook to the deeper layers only — he doesn't take the universe itself for granted, but he takes the laws of physics for granted. The laws of physics are said to account for everything, to create the universe and order it, and those laws need no law-giver, no law maker, they just are."[154]

All the expositions had produced a period of silent absorption, and then Sci-guy had asked B-t, "What do you think of all this?" B-t had put down his fork, swallowed hard and said, "We Bible-believers are often accused of being 'ignorant.' Someone will 'prove' it to us by citing some recent study they think proves something of deep importance, some study which we of course have never heard of, and that does indeed show that — relative to the issue of that study — we *are* 'ignorant.' But that's a relative ignorance, and the God-deniers are ignorant at an absolute level — ignorant of the one absolute fact of all reality, ignorant of the most important matter, the love and power of God. I prefer to be relatively ignorant rather than to be absolutely ignorant."

"That makes sense," Sci-guy had grunted. But Thoughtful-Woman had seen in his eyes that he was more taken with what he knew, than with what might remain to be discovered in the spiritual and ultimate realm. "They close their eyes and they shut their ears,"[155] the New Testament says, but she was "relatively ignorant" of that Scripture, so she could not ponder its applicability.

Yes, that earlier conversation touched on a lot, R_ thought. R_ paused, and the dog suddenly sat up as he felt a new tension in his beloved "master." R_ took down James Gleick's massive 2011 tome, *The Information: A History, A Theory, A Flood*. A different conversation came back for meditation. "Sci-guy mentioned the question of DNA being clearly *coded information*, not set in place by physics or chemistry," he told the alert dog, in a solemn tone. "But we left the implications hanging." He found the validation of his concern: [By the 1990s] "the technical jargon of biologists included the words *alphabet, library, editing, proofreading, transcription, translation, nonsense, synonym* and *redundancy*" (his

p. 299).** And Gleick sharpened the issue on p. 241, citing that "materialism" has to admit that information is "not matter or energy." He looked at the dog, who was still sharply alert. "There it is, then — the fact of 'information' in the cell, in the genetic code, throughout the system, has been established, has become *a commonplace*." The dog put a sympathetic paw on R_'s thigh as R_ leaned back slightly in his chair. "So Meyer's comment becomes inescapable: 'Today we buy information, we sell it... we send it down wires and bounce it off satellites -- and we know that it invariably comes from intelligent agents. So what do we make of the fact that there's information in life?' " R_ took the dog for a moon-lit walk, on which he told the dog, "P. Fong said in 1973 that, 'The question of the ultimate source of **information** is not trivial. In fact it is the basic and central philosophical and theoretical problem.'[156]" (Woodward's comments on pp. 174-175 here will interest the reader concerned for the "information" issue.) The dog was busy gathering information about the trace of a squirrel's scent.

Pondering as they walked, R_ thoughts went to method: *Any domain of knowledge needs to be approached with the right methodology — a microscope does not suffice to explore the heavens, nor a telescope to probe the cell. The analytic method is not the way to "get to know" a person; this issue of methodology applies to getting to know God. Praying is a method that is needed here, aside from all the intellectual considerations that so many authors have been incisively bringing up recently — and room for consideration of revelation. "Seek Him*," the Bible says! Prayer, Word of God, right Christian community...* "You're back to the uniqueness of Jesus," B-t told him when he brought this up later.

** Excerpts from THE INFORMATION: A HISTORY, A THEORY, A FLOOD by James Gleick, copyright © 2011 by James Gleick. Used by permission of Pantheon Books, an imprint of the Knopf Doubleday Publishing Group, a division of Random House LLC. All rights reserved. Any third party use of this material, outside of this publication, is prohibited. Interested parties must apply directly to Random House LLC for permission. [*That's required language, obviously; your author adds, they're friendly and good to work with. In case that helps you.* Re **Gleick & the nature of reality**, see endnote 226.]

Chapter 15: The Universe and You: notes on studying it

A rainy, gloomy day — no lightning to add interest and variety... Thoughtful-Woman looked out on the darkness for hours, pondering: *That day when the snow caught the sunrise colors and the ice chunks in the lake glinted in the sun's rays as they rotated in the wind and currents — what was it our driver quoted Barry Lopez as saying? "So beautiful it made you afraid"*[157] *— about some Arctic landscape scene Lopez had seen. Lopez saw such beauty that it made him feel, sense, perceive the presence of a different, deeper, very powerful reality — that's what "afraid" must mean there,* she thought. *Some people sense transcendence in the order of nature, some feel it in the beauty — that's where the eminent scientist Dr. Francis Collins found it.*[158] Her ponderings trailed off inconclusively and she started to turn to mental planning for her meeting with her relatives.

Sci-guy had seen her brooding, and he asked cheerfully, "Studying the landscape?" Thoughtful-Woman replied, "Studying the world around us is what science is all about, isn't it?" Her smile rewarded his attempt to cheer her. The warming mood let her mind return to an earlier conversation, and she asked Sci-guy, "What was that our Bible-toting friend was saying about 'fine-tuning' in the universe?"

Sci-guy was glad to be on solid ground, above the sway of contention.[159] "There are a dozen or so fundamental 'constants' in the physics of the universe, fundamental numbers that define how things are set up, which have to be almost exactly where they actually are, for life to be possible," he expounded. "Things like the numerical value of the gravitational constant — a shade larger, and no living things of any size could exist; but if it were slightly smaller, the galaxies, stars and planets wouldn't have formed. The ratio of the size of fundamental particles — protons and neutrons, is another critical number — it 'just happens' to be just right for a universe that life as we know it can inhabit. But these numbers are experimental results, not values set by basic laws of nature. They could be other values; no theory constrains them to be what they are! However, they 'happen' to be just right for life to be possible. Given how small the range of 'workable' values is for these fundamentals,[160] given how many of them there are, given that they 'just happen' to be 'just so,' the whole thing becomes most amazing, if you think that chance ruled the set-up of the universe."

Sci-guy was glad to see the smile still lingering on Thoughtful-Woman's face, deeper in some ways but also quizzical now. "What do you see in the night sky?" he asked her, to thread the next twist of the conversation. "Stars, moon, flashing lights of planes..." she answered.

"The moon! That's another 'just so' item," Sci-guy exclaimed. "It 'just happens' to move in the plane where it can eclipse the sun — and it 'just happens' to be exactly the right size, for its distance from the sun, to fit the sun perfectly for the eclipse. Not just that the light of the sun is blocked — the fit is so amazingly right that *the very fringe of the sun* remains visible, a very thin ring of light that enables us to study the sun's upper 'atmosphere.' An eclipse in the late 1800s led to the discovery of helium on the sun, part of how we discovered how the sun 'works' — all thanks to this amazing 'coincidence' of the moon's orbit and size being so incredibly 'perfect' for the eclipse phenomenon. Another eclipse, early 1900s, enabled us to verify Einstein's prediction that the gravity of the sun bends the light from distant stars. That showed a deep interconnection in the workings of the universe, and again the 'miracle' of how the moon fits against the sun in the sky is what made the discovery possible. That bending of light by gravity was a key element in proving Einstein's theory of General Relativity."

B-t had awakened, and he came from the back of the RV to join them — accompanied by the faithful dog, whose smile was as pleasant as Thoughtful-Woman's but without the quizzical undertone. "Cosmology, eh?" B-t chimed in. "Some people argue that there's an uncanny overlap between the special factors that make earth habitable, and those that make it an optimal platform for scientific discovery. Like the location — not near the center of the galaxy, where too much radiation, supernovas, and so on make a planet uninhabitable; not too far out, where there are not the heavier elements needed for living beings. But, the Earth's actual location not only serves habitability, it makes the proper platform for observing the universe, because nearer the center, it would be hard to differentiate between what's in our galaxy and what's outside, while if the planet were farther out in the spiral arms of the galaxy, observation would be obscured by stardust, and so on."

Sci-guy laughed. "You've been reading Gonzalez & Richards," he said. "Yes," B-t responded, "and they say that there are more than a dozen such 'overlaps' between the special factors that make earth habitable, and those that make it a good platform for scientific exploration of the universe. They say these factors are matters which are basic to the various sciences involved. You should read their book," he told Thoughtful-Woman, but the quizzical touch of her smile had segued to glazed eyes.[161]

The dog went systematically around the small group, licking everyone's hand, collecting a few strokes of petting from each human (a.k.a. "two-legged"), and Thoughtful-Woman's eyes ceased to be glazed over. "Studying the universe has gone into pretty deep matters, hasn't it?" she observed. "I heard a comment that the 'machine-like' nature of the universe had disappeared when 'quantum mechanics' replaced Newtonian physics. If things are not machine-like, the 'determinism' that people talk about ceases to be there, doesn't it?" She looked at Sci-guy, who wasn't about to mix science and metaphysics that way, although many popularizers of science never had any problem doing exactly that. (Sci-guy approached R_ later and said, "Speaking of the basic nature of the universe, let me suggest another 'convergence' to the ones you had told the folks about, before I joined you." We add it as an endnote to the Scripture Table entry "Creation.")

Thoughtful-Woman forged ahead: "The 'soul' being separable from the body used to seem scientifically absurd, but now that we see how advanced computers can become, it seems to me that our consciousness might be 'separable' from its current physical base, just as the software of a computer is separable from the hardware that runs it — if we hooked up with a superior 'source'..."[162] Her voice trailed off as the dog licked her hand again, but she was too lost in thought to pet him further.

"People have become so perplexed trying to explain how consciousness arises from the neurons of the brain," Sci-guy interjected, "that some people have seriously argued that consciousness is an illusion. Marilynne Robinson raised hell with that idea in her book *Absence of Mind*, and I don't even touch any discussions of what consciousness could be or where it could go." He looked back at the others and apologized to B-t, "Forgive me for the 'raising hell' terminology, I know you religious people feel differently about that." B-t was grinning and a pleasant quiet settled over them.

"You mentioned relativity," R_ interjected after awhile. The dog stirred uneasily. "We used to hear 'relativity' invoked quite a bit to say that conduct and morality all varied 'relative' to various cultures. But I heard a lecturer say that Einstein's Special Theory of Relativity meant that the laws of physics were *the same* in all unaccelerated frames of reference, and that Einstein's General Theory of Relativity meant that the laws of physics were *the same* in all accelerated frames of reference. So maybe 'relativity' has been misapplied?"[163]

Sci-guy's jaw set rigidly and he gazed intently out the side window. Again, take-offs from scientific theories, to make them say something about fields outside their purview, *that* was not his thing. It was popular with some atheists to say that science enabled them to deal with all of existence, but it was methodologically wrong. When that was done, the methodology was no longer sound, and a false certitude was often asserted that did not really have science with it.

Chapter 16: "Relatively" Interesting Thoughts?

Sci-guy brooded as the moon rose, glimmering through broken clouds over a river that still had patches of ice along its shore. Those patches caught the moonlight between shadows of trees. "The books you have in back," he said to R_, "show some real commitment to science as a method of seeking truths." He received a proffered cup of coffee gratefully from Thoughtful-Woman, who gave everybody one (except, of course, the dog), and he continued, "I was intrigued by Dr. Schroeder's calculation 'from the viewpoint of the universe as a whole' that the six days of creation, in your Bible's book of Genesis, *are* the billions of years of the universe's life as we measure it here on Earth."

Thoughtful-Woman's eyes crossed, and Sci-guy hastened to expound. "Einstein's theory of relativity has a lot of consequences. One is that time is affected by speed of motion. Objects travelling at an extremely high velocity, close to the speed of light, experience time at a dramatically slowed rate. The universe has been expanding, so that affects the measurement of time *as seen from the viewpoint of the universe as a whole*, which in some ways would be more of God's viewpoint. Dr. Schroeder uses cosmic background radiation (CBR) as the 'clock' for the measurement from the 'viewpoint' of the universe as a whole, and it gives a transformation factor of a million-million-to-one ratio for that viewpoint of time compared to Earth-based time measurement. He concludes that 'the division of fifteen billion years' — the age of the universe we measure on earth from our viewpoint — 'by a million million reduces those fifteen billion years to six days!'[164] The exclamation point at the end of that sentence, that you hear in my voice, is Schroeder's own," Sci-guy said with a smile.

"Do you agree with his calculations?" Thoughtful-Woman asked. Sci-guy smiled again and directed his attention back to his coffee. "Schroeder has a Ph.D. from M.I.T. — Massachusetts

Institute of Technology — which is about as a good a credential as you can get for this kind of thing. It's outside my expertise, and what you make of it, even if you agree with his analysis and his calculations, is one of those 'everything-is-debatable' sort of affairs."

B-t didn't often get a chance to play science-expert, but he had his moment now. He pulled out a newspaper clipping and waved it like a flag. "Yesterday's paper had an article saying that new calculations have changed the estimated age of the universe, and now it's 13.8 billion years." He looked intently at each listener before he continued. "I did your 'million million' division on 13.8 billion and that would give five days, not six." He had his cell-phone set on calculator, and he showed the resulting number to Thoughtful-Woman. R_ looked at B-t glumly. All he needed was for his "Bible-thumper" to shoot down one of the most interesting resolutions between Bible and science! But then, if you were going to talk science, you had to have good science...

Sci-guy sent Thoughtful-Woman to the RV's bookshelves to grab Schroeder's book, while he read the clipping carefully. "I don't think the implication falls out the way you're seeing it," he said thoughtfully. "Schroeder's transformation factor isn't simply a numerical constant that you divide the time by. It changes during the various phases of the universe's process. Look at his equation on page 66 for converting 'days' and his chart of the transformed 'time' of the Biblical days on page 67 of his book." B-t did look, but he was out of his element. Sci-guy jabbed his finger at the salient point of the chart. "Day One per the Bible, from the 'viewpoint of the universe,' maps out under the relativistic time transformation onto the earth-viewpoint period from 15.75 billion years ago up to 7.75 billion years ago, per Schroeder's 1997 analysis. Correcting the age-of-the-universe number from 15.75, what he had then to work with, to 13.8 billion years as we compute it now, would all fall within the Biblical 'Day One' because the transformation factor shifts as the universe matures."

B-t was thinking, *A lot of things shifted for me as I matured*, but he kept a respectful silence. Science had the floor... Sci-guy needed B-t for the next step, though. "Wasn't 'Day One' the day on which your Bible says light was created, and wasn't that the only thing that happened in 'Day One'?" B-t nodded — yes, it was so, although of course the opening Biblical statement, "In the beginning, God created the heavens and the earth," laced through that in a way that the Bible didn't bother to detail. *It is the glory of God to conceal a thing; but the glory of kings is to search out a matter*, B-t remembered the Bible saying (Prov. 25:2 JPS), and evidently the scientists were "kings" in their own right in this realm of finding the details.

"So whether 'Day One,' when transformed into our perceived time by Einstein's discoveries, stretched from 15.75 billion years to 7.75 billion years before the present, or if instead it was from 13.8 billion to 7.75 billion, doesn't matter, unless your theology needs to believe that light was created at the crack of dawn on day one." Sci-guy thought that was a cute word-play and B-t thought it was blatantly disrespectful, so it was a good thing that Thoughtful-Woman came back again with more coffee and some dog biscuits, which she let everyone give to the dog.

As they all manifested their own emotions (the dog manifesting his with a satisfied smile), Sci-guy segued to his own personal world: "I enjoyed Dr. Schroeder's book because of a quote in the frontispiece: 'The only path to knowing God is through the study of science — and for that reason the Bible opens with a description of the creation.'[165] That quote was Maimonides, writing in A.D. 1190." Thoughtful-Woman noticed that Sci-guy said "A.D."[166] as he looked at R_, whereas he would have said "C.E." if he had been talking to her alone. Culture, always culture...

"These deep science things are *relatively* interesting," B-t quipped, but nobody thought it was funny. "The theory of relativity erased the line between matter and energy," R_ offered. "Matter and energy are convertible under the parameters of the equation $E = mc^2$. The 'c' in that formula is the speed of light, a very large number, which means that the destruction of a small amount of matter releases an incredibly large amount of energy — hence the fantastic power of the atomic bomb." Sci-guy nodded —

that was true science — but he wasn't smiling anymore. R_ said, "Think then of the end of the universe as we know it. The New Testament says that the Lord 'holds everything together by His* mighty word of power.'[167] If that holding-together were withdrawn, what would happen? If everything 'dissolved' — 2 Pet. 3:12 in the Bible says that at the End, 'the elements will melt in the heat.'

"Well, matter disappearing into unshaped energy would create an enormous amount of energy, which reminds me of the 'Lake of Fire' that the Bible mentions in its final book, Revelation — Rev 20:14, 15." Sci-guy wasn't engaging with this — the end of his grant funding was enough of the "end of the universe" for him. B-t didn't need a scientific viewpoint on the End. But Thoughtful-Woman was pondering; the dog was unconcerned — he trusted his master, and that was that.[168]

But Thoughtful-Woman brought the dog to attention with some undertone in her voice when she said to R_, "You had been stressing Jesus as the Incarnation, the 'Word' of God become flesh, not just a man but God and human both — that 'sustaining all things' really makes that nature of Jesus' being important, doesn't it? In that other realm you guys discuss, of His* transcendent component as 'The Word of God,' your Bible John chapter 1 presentation of His pre-Incarnation role, continuing in glory." R_ nodded, and she continued: "That's another area where Jesus' being not 'only what He appeared to be'[169] is critical, if you guys are right." R_ nodded and B-t beamed, but Thoughtful-Woman was reaching for a bucket of cold water to pour into their shoes — metaphorically, of course. She looked at R_ and said, "Your 'elephant on the ice' syndrome is a real problem when you get into that territory."

B-t frowned quizzically, so R_ recapped an earlier conversation he had had with Thoughtful-Woman: "An early European ambassador to Siam, when it was still 'Siam' instead of 'Thailand,' made friends with the King, and told his majesty of the many wonders of European technology and life. The king was, 'wow, wow' — until one day the ambassador told the King that in

Europe the rivers froze so hard in the winter than an elephant could walk across the river on the ice. Siam being a near-tropical climate, this struck the King as absurd, and he jumped up and said, 'Now I know you are lying, and I will never again believe anything you say!' Well, as a former Alaskan, I have no problem believing an elephant could walk on the frozen rivers — we used to drive trucks across them — but remember what Jesus said to Nicodemus (John 3:12): 'I have spoken to you of earthly things and you do not believe; how then will you believe if I speak of heavenly things?' We have to be careful, with God's wonders, not to try to take people so far so fast into a new realm, that they fall prey to 'Elephant on the ice' syndrome." B-t's quizzical frown was replaced with a deep sorrow for the lacks caused by wrongful unbelief, and the dog sighed and slumped to the floor.

Chapter 17: Hell and the Antidote

"Your 'Lake of Fire' disturbs me," Sci-guy said. The dog came up and nuzzled his hand — the dog sensed his distress, no doubt, and was eager to dispel it with love, even if the other "two-leggeds" couldn't dispel it with alternate thoughts. "It sounds like 'writhing forever in the flames of Hell,' which I heard somebody say once. The eternal fate of everyone who didn't go to their church, if I remember right." (R_ suppressed a chuckle and the urge to say, "Some churches have been like that.") [*Esteemed reader: the inevitability of the "Lake of Fire" at the end of the universe was discussed on* *p. 102-103**, if you jumped past the prior chapter.*]

"In the first place where the consequences of alienating oneself from God appear in the Bible," B-t responded, "it says, 'the soul that sins shall die.' That was God's statement to 'Adam and Eve,' the caution put before humanity before the start of the journey we find ourselves on now." Sci-guy was listening cautiously, waiting for "the other shoe to fall," as they say. "If God is the sustainer of life — Heb 1:3; compare Psalm 104:29-30 — then that's inevitable, and a tragedy that we would hope He* would give us the way to avoid, despite our tendencies to self-will and to folly of every sort," B-t continued. "But human wickedness is a reality that cuts deeper than we like to admit, and the Bible says that God is holy, committed to the good, and with wrath against evil. Punishment/elimination of evil-doing is a theme that is clarified later in the Bible as the understanding deepens, as when Jesus compared the wicked to the trash being burned up in Gehenna, the Valley of Hinnom[170] next to Jerusalem. Everybody wants to hear that everyone will go to heaven to live forever in bliss, but that asks God to accept all manner of evil and depravity in the human heart... God's not going to do that."

Thoughtful-Woman remembered some earlier comments R_ had made about medieval theology, and there was a twinkle in her eye as she said to R_, "You should write *A History of 'Hell,'* the history of the idea." But as he looked, there was a deeper layer in her gaze, a concern to really know and to find the good and to avoid the evil — the profound concern that seemed to R_ to be innate, inherent in the most basic nature of the human being as we know it, a deep instinctual knowledge that terrible things are possible and we need help to avoid them.

R_ began, "Well, in the late 1800s, Henry Ward Beecher, one of the most influential preachers of the time, stopped preaching the doctrine of 'Hell.' He said he wanted no child to suffer again as he had in his childhood, agonizing over the threat of such suffering. That was in 1877. Fifteen years later, the American Board of Foreign Missions quietly stopped enforcing the requirement that missionaries must believe in the doctrine."[171] R_ paused to glance at B-t, who appeared less than absorbed in the matter, and continued: "The Middle Ages seem to have witnessed the elaboration of the idea, above the Biblical statements. Dante, in his *Inferno*, wrote of a tour through the areas of Hell devoted to different sins, and Milton in his *Paradise Lost* and other books also contributed to making 'conscious eternal torment' a widely-accepted understanding.

"I looked in the Index to Jaroslav Pelikan's great survey of the early Church teachings, *The Emergence of the Catholic* [universal, Church-wide] *Tradition*, and 'Hell' wasn't there at all. But the Scriptures speak of the wicked as facing 'the worm that does not die, and the fire that is not quenched.' Jesus quoted that idea several times, and the wording tracks to Isaiah, based on the forever-smoldering trash dump 'Gehenna,' the Valley of Hinnom, outside of Jerusalem — with the worms feeding on dead bodies of animals and fires always among the garbage. That imagery fits the view that marrying oneself to evil brings destruction, as the Bible's 2 Thessalonians 1:9 speaks of 'everlasting destruction.' "

"You've gone backwards through time and you've skipped the present completely — you'll never make a historian!" Thoughtful-Woman chided. R_ smiled in agreement, and tried to defend himself: "Talking about the history of human thought obscures the divine message and distracts from basic considerations — God is just, evil is to be eliminated, people have to choose..."

R_ was upset with himself. *This doesn't highlight the core problem: choosing to "be themselves" is the evil way, <u>when</u> it involves ignoring God, ignoring the guidance for the good, ignoring the help that brings the higher potentials...* B-t was remembering a Scripture from his decade⁺ of Bible reading: Deut 32:5: "They have acted corruptly toward him (God); to their shame they are no longer his children, but a warped and crooked generation."

R_ tried to "reboot," to get the basic ideas in focus: "Timothy Kallistos Ware says that human beings were created 'to advance in love.' But instead, the human race, 'blessed with the power to reshape the world and to endue it with fresh meaning... misused that power in order to fashion instruments of ugliness and destruction... [the results, especially since the Industrial Revolution] hideously apparent in the rapid pollution of the environment.' Ware speaks of 'man,' in Ware's form of language, 'caught in the vicious circle of his own lust, which grew more hungry the more it was gratified. The world ceased to be transparent — a window through which he gazed on God... ceased to be life-giving, and became subject to corruption and mortality.'[172] The result was 'God's wrath against the godlessness and wickedness of men who suppress the truth by their wickedness' — as the Bible puts it."[173]

B-t chimed in, "You can see that there is indeed real evil that merits punishment, that has to be destroyed." R_ reached to clarify: "These matters touch on the concept of 'original sin'," and he quoted Ware further: " 'Original sin' means 'we are born into an environment where it is easy to do evil and hard to do good; easy to hurt others, and hard to heal their wounds... It means that we are each of us conditioned by the solidarity of the human race in its accumulated wrong-doing and wrong-thinking, and hence wrong-being.' "

Sci-guy was still perturbed: "For punishment after death, the nature of the human being has to be different from what we started discussing — or maybe, the nature of the reality that the human being moves among. You mentioned the neurosurgeon's comment that, 'it is clear that for the mind to survive death, it must establish a connection with a source of energy other than the brain.' That makes perfect sense to me; but that human beings survive death, to be punished or rewarded or whatever, in the absence of some special connection to your God having been created — *that* doesn't compute with me." B-t felt at home discussing the nature of being: "The Bible tells us that in God, we live and move and have our being. That's Acts 17:28. We exist because of His* thoughts and by His sustaining, and if our conduct has outraged Him and demands punishment..."

R_ was, as usual, in a different place. "I think we need to take most seriously the cautions that Jesus gave us, about the seriousness of evil.[174] When I worked in Alaska, Chief Peter John was the region-wide Traditional Chief of the Athabascan Indians. Their region covers an area nearly the size of Texas. He wrote a book, *The Gospel According to Peter John*, about his life's experience living with the Holy Spirit. He described a vision he had been shown at one point — an angel showed him the path to Hell, with many, many footprints going along it. The angel took him over the path for a while, then said to him, 'From here on is not for you to see.' (B-t shuddered as these words hit him). And, just as there have been near-death experiences where people report seeing Heaven,[175] people have had experiences of seeing Hell. I think the effort of our philosophizing should be, 'How do we live in the light God gives'..." His voice trailed off, with a deep undertone of pain, and the dog put his head on R_'s thigh in sympathy.

The dog winced when Sci-guy laughed. "You may think I'm dodging the key issue," he said firmly, "but to me, eternal punishment can't be just and fitting for an action done in a finite arena." B-t responded with his own laugh: "The Scripture has always seemed pretty basic, fundamental, core and foundational to me, that 'the soul that sins, will die' — the person who refuses to ally with God, cannot continue to live indefinitely. The Bible says 'Our God is a consuming fire,'[176] and that seems to me to describe more accurately than Milton and Dante — 'conscious eternal torment' turns God into a non-consuming fire, reversing the Scripture."

Sci-guy's eyes crossed in aggravated perplexity when B-t mentioned "Milton and Dante," and B-t was perceptive enough to catch that, so he elaborated: "Milton was the great English author of *Paradise Lost* and other epics, who gave us the distorted picture of 'Adam and Eve eating the apple.' Useful in its own culture, no doubt, but not the Bible's statement. Dante's 'Inferno' was part of his epic poem on theology and showed the same sort of unending agony that Milton later portrayed. Some denominations make 'conscious eternal torment' an article of faith. Others believe that everyone will ultimately be saved and taken to heaven, given the greatness of God's love. One theologian said that there is certainty of punishment that removes all profit from sin — not necessarily eternally unending, but assuredly fully countervailing." After a pause, he added, "The only sure point, the only agreement and the one thing Scripture incontrovertibly affirms, is that connecting with God & Jesus in love now is available to avoid all 'Hell'."

"By the way," B-t continued, "In Dante's medieval classic 'Inferno,' the punishment for every sin is, 'a contrapasso, a symbolic instance of poetic justice; for example, fortune-tellers have to walk forwards with their heads on backwards, unable to see what is ahead, because they tried, through forbidden means, to look ahead to the future in life...' So the punishment is 'not merely as a form of divine revenge, but rather as the fulfillment of a destiny freely chosen by each soul during his or her life.' I got that off Wikipedia," he finished,[177] as he saw Sci-guy's wonder at hearing "contrapasso" come out of his mouth.

"I don't think a loving God, as you proclaim God to be, could possibly torment people in Hell," Thoughtful-Woman said firmly.

"They don't realize how much they demand that God 'share His glory with another,' to borrow a Scriptural phrase,"[178] R_ replied. "Look at how it would have to be with them, when God passes judgment on them: Locked in a new reality with nothing but their own evil desires[179] — and those frustrated because everything that would satisfy them is a diversion of God's creation and the resources of God are finally *fully* cut off from them — how would they not suffer?"

"I don't see your 'loving God' as condemning anyone, if 'He' is as you say," Thoughtful-Woman said with undiminished firmness. "God doesn't condemn them, they 'condemn' themselves," B-t responded. His own firmness had a gentle undertone that moved the dog to come and lick B-t's hand. "They choose and then the result of their choice, alienated from the energy source of life itself, is the outcome." R_ interjected, "Christians say that 'the gates of Hell are locked from the inside.'[180]"

B-t took up the wrestling with the terrible problem: "Should God just say, 'Sure, there's all kinds of terrible evil going on all around the earth, but hey, what do you expect?' — would *that* be a proper attitude on God's part?" "No," replied Thoughtful-Woman, but you could hear the rest of the sentence in the tone of her voice: *From there to "fry in Hell forever" is not what we're looking for... we'd like to see it all change into good...* She began to pet the dog rapidly, because the obvious follow-on sentence came, unbidden, into her mind: *That's what these guys say God is offering, "the renewal of all things" [Bible, Matthew 19:28, Jesus speaking] — the change from this traumatized planet into a "new heaven and earth" without pain, death, crying... [Bible, Revelation 21:4].*

"But you say that there's a positive resolution available," Sci-guy said. B-t had been browsing in another of R_'s old books, and he read aloud: "We have found that, both for Himself [Jesus the Christ] and for His followers, the approach to God begins with the surrender of life for the sake of others; and that in such surrender is revealed God's desire, in Him, to 'seek and save' sinners. Through that surrender He first, and His followers after Him, pass into a new and transformed life. It is the life of obedience to God's will,[181] or of self-dedication. And it is, in effect, the entry upon a new world. He has finally enlarged the horizon of human life. The kingdoms of this world have become the Kingdom of God and of His Christ. There are new powers, and new values.

Man ["human beings," this is a 1930s book] has at last been admitted into the Presence of God: for the life is found to be at once that of children in their Father's home, of subjects in the heavenly kingdom, and of worshippers in the heavenly sanctuary. And, finally, the life, first found in self-surrender and then transformed in offering, is shared. It is the life of an organic unit, running through each member and the whole; and it is communicated by food [the author speaks here of the Communion meal, receiving Christ sacramentally]."[182]

"I always feel like I almost see what you're talking about, but it comes forth as only a small patch of clarity and stretches out into an ocean of mist," Thoughtful-Woman complained. "Remember what Jesus said to Nicodemus," B-t replied. "He said, 'I have spoken to you of earthly things [the new birth! the receiving of that new life!] and you do not believe; how can you believe if I speak to you of heavenly things?'[183] Our discussions are trying to connect you with realities that are beyond your present purview, so your language and thought-structure must of unfortunate necessity be somewhat rough and inadequate for them... I don't mean any put-down and I apologize for any offense," he added.

R_ looked over at them, petted the dog thoughtfully for a moment, and put in a non-Biblical analogy: "Sometimes I think of it as being like a helicopter sent to rescue drowning people from a stormy sea — you have to grasp the hand held out to rescue you."[184]

Chapter 18: Concluding Prayer Considerations

Thoughtful-Woman pursed her lips. "If Jesus is alive and active today, as you two assert (she looked first at R_ and then at B-t), then why don't we hear of people being healed today, like Jesus healed them?!" B-t's mouth was half-open when R_ took the floor: "We do, if we listen — that's the answer. A healing miracle occurred to my friend Virginia D. If I ever were to write that 'book,' I would try to get her permission to put her picture on the cover. When you know someone personally who has had a medically-verified miracle of healing, it changes your understanding." B-t was thinking of the Scripture, "Blessed are those who have not seen and yet believe" (Bible, John 20:29), but he kept his thoughts to himself.

"Virginia had a stroke from an aneurysm in her brain. The destruction of parts of her brain meant that, as her doctors told her, she would never be able to walk again. However, she is a Christian (and a Native American Indian), and her friends prayed for her, too. The doctor returned some days later to her hospital bed, x-rays in hand. 'You're seeing a reconstructive miracle,' the doctor told her. New brain cells don't grow — but white areas on her x-rays showed that new brain cells were growing in her brain. Today she walks just like everyone else — the Lord's good grace at work, we invite you to see and to share in it!"[185]

Thoughtful-Woman wanted to look carefully at such information. "So, you've met this woman?" she asked. "I see her regularly at a church I go to locally on occasion — she's the Assistant Pastor there," R_ replied. "And she was on my staff for six or eight months, so I had a good chance to get to know her and to be able to have confidence in her." Silence graced the next hour's drive.

R_ was making notes for another "prayer" chapter during the following break in the drive, and Thoughtful-Woman looked over his shoulder (R_ appreciated her interest). R_ wrote a verse from an old hymn: ***God of mercy and compassion****, look with pity on my pain; hear a broken mournful spirit, prostrate at Your feet complain. Hold me up in mighty waters.*[186] R_ wrote himself a note: *Be sure to include, "The fullness for You, of You, by You, according to You." Tell them that God has promised to help them to pray, per Romans 8:26. Put in Copeland's thing about people wanting the blessings God has spoken about but not letting God change them in other ways. And Rev. Bunge's "Always have three things you're grateful for"*[187] *— anyone can do that, R_ thought: if nothing else, 1) that things aren't worse (if you can stop and think, there's something to this!), 2) that you're alive and therefore have hope, 3) that God's grace is above all this and lasts forever, infinitely beyond all this.* R_ himself thought of this in three levels — the great eternal blessings (offered to all, "come, whosoever will" the Bible says!), the precious "basic providing" that undergirds every day and makes life possible and often decently OK, the "sparkling above the basics" things that come and gladden many days.

Thoughtful-Woman's intense watching drew B-t in. "Are you making notes for your maybe-book?" he asked R_. "You should put in about St. Thomas Aquinas and his visions." Thoughtful-Woman turned to stare at him, so he explained: "Aquinas wrote the *Summa Theologiae*, uniting all of theology with philosophy and making, as of his age in A.D. 1200, a 'thorough wrap' — which is why Catholics sometimes call him 'the first Doctor of the Church.' But it was unfinished — he went into visions of such splendor of heavenly things, that he ceased work on that great writing.[188] It's a testimony to what great things God still has in store for us." R_ smiled. "Good point," he said. "You remind me of Bill Johnson's saying, 'We must endure the unexplainable in order to see the unforgettable.' "[189]

B-t was feeling validated. "I heard about a book," he added, "called *Accompany Them With Singing*. It discusses the parts of a Christian funeral theologically, so people can see the worship of a community, a step up from 'celebrating a life' — it seems to me to be insulting God, when He* offers so much more, to content yourself with 'a good life' for a few earthly years."[190]

But R_ wasn't listening. He was writing swiftly: *Include about prayer, the condition of the promise: "...and [if you do that] the peace of God ... will guard your hearts and your minds."*[191] *And include: Listen.*[192] The dog wished he could speak: "Add ***hesed***, the Bible's Old Testament word for faithful committed love, love like your Mom and Dad showed you as they lived the faithful path of committed and happy marriage — if you haven't learned anything else in life, you've learned that *that way* was true and good."[193]

When they resumed travel, lightly-forested hills gave way to a stretch of grassland, which opened a wide panorama of the sky for them to partake of the fullness of sunset's shifting touch upon the clouds. As darkness closed in, the RV swayed along a stretch of road oddly devoid of other vehicles. B-t spent an hour on his knees, perched between the driver's seat and the passenger seat of the RV, watching the scenery intently, sometimes visibly whispering a prayer, sometimes absorbed in the light playing over the special beauties and variety of the Creation — twilight, moonlight, starlight. "What do you think is the most terrifying verse in the Bible?" he finally asked R_. "I think one of the saddest is, 'They turn away,'[194] referring to people ignoring, neglecting, rejecting God," R_ replied. The dog was staring at R_, as if to say, *you answered a different question than the one he asked.* B-t threaded the conversation forward: "I think one of the most penetrating is when God threatens the people with this: 'I will set you face to face with yourselves.' That's Psalm 50:21 in the Septuagint translation."[195]

Sci-guy left the passenger seat to get a soda — R_ had made plain to them all that his commitment to hospitality included no-need-to-wait-to-ask snacking — and upon reseating himself, took up another version of the problem. "Suppose you do write your book someday," he said. "What you ought to explain, along with all these things you've been expounding, is this word 'holiness.' I understand that it means you don't go to movies that advocate casual sex and violence-as-entertainment, but beyond that, it seems to be a mystery. It's just not part of the vocabulary of the people I know."

B-t took the first cut at the matter. "Holiness is a matter of relationship to God. It's used when things are 'devoted to God,' like the implements in a house of worship..." R_ smiled, "That's where the cleaning-up-your-conduct level of 'holiness' comes from — you don't want Jesus to return for His Second Coming and find you sitting on your ass dead drunk in a whorehouse. That's where people get the stereotype of what it means, 'We don't smoke, we don't chew, we don't run with those who do.' But it goes far deeper — 'holy' is the adjective for the unique and perfect nature of God. It describes something that people can't experience apart from God. Andrew Murray says, 'God's Holiness is His infinite, glorious perfection, which leads Him always to desire what is good in others as well as in Himself. He bestows, and works out what is good in others, and hates and condemns all that is opposed to what is good.'[196] Because it comes from the depth of the nature of God, the word doesn't lend itself to superficial definitions, and the 'devoted to God' reflection of it at the human level, just misleads people who don't experience God's nature."

Thoughtful-Woman was eyeing R_ cautiously. *A strange guy*, she thought, *and now he demarcates territory that he labels as unknown — and unknowable by ordinary literature*. R_ went on, "Barry Lopez did long research among Arctic peoples, and he came back with some deep matters. He recounted how the Inuit/Eskimos had a deep knowledge of the land, reflected in their language, which became mere generalities or even 'misleading or imprecise abstractions' if discussed with people who lacked the intimate touch of living on the land.[197] Holiness is like that — it takes knowing, participating, being part of a certain life. With holiness, you can't explain your way into grasping it; you have to worship your way there. So, if you guys do hornswaggle me into writing a book, explaining 'holiness' won't be part of it." Thoughtful-Woman rolled her eyes as she turned her face towards Sci-guy, but he had gone back to staring out the window at the passing landscape.

(R_'s reticence about delineating "holiness" got him in trouble with B-t. While R_ was checking the tire pressures some time later, B-t took the issue up — not to expound, but to suggest prayer. "You made note of prayer to love God fully, love neighbor, worship in SPIRIT and in truth [p. 35 above] — you should add a prayer 'to live for You' per the Bible's 2 Cor 5:15." R_ was thoughtful, but the need to check the oil and transmission fluid beckoned and he heeded the call... B-t kicked the tire and wished that spiritual things were simpler. *But then the power might not be so profound,* he thought, and "purely by coincidence" the dog trotted up just then and licked his hand.

Thoughtful-Woman came up as R_ walked off and said to B-t, "I can't believe our driver sometimes. He seems so sanctimonious, and then he makes that remark about being 'dead drunk in a whorehouse' when Jesus returns..." B-t wasn't about to defend R_'s choice of illustrations, so he said, "There are a lot of places and ways that you don't want to be when Jesus returns. 'Hi, Jesus, could You hold off for two minutes? I'm just about to win this argument crushingly with my spouse...' Or, 'At last, Jesus, everything is so boring here' and He points at the beauty and kindness that you overlook every moment..." Thoughtful-Woman remembered R_'s remark about "my standing prayer, 'Thanks indeed to You, Lord, for all the things we take for granted.' " It reminded her of another remark, about "writing a love letter to God" — was that the driver or the Bible-toter? An interesting idea, for pursuing deepening the relationship... A discussion starter if she ever went to visit with a Pastor... She dropped the train of thought and went into further planning of what to say to some of her relatives.)

Chapter 19: Quoting Quotes

"Well, we're getting near to D.C.," Sci-guy observed. "Any final observations to lay on us?" R_ had been up in the middle of the night, pawing through his books by flashlight while the others slept, and the dog had sat up alertly joining the vigil. So now R_ pulled out his notes and began by addressing B-t: "Here's an example of the mysticism in Genesis chapters one through three. Remember that the Hebrew אדם "Adahm," rendered as "Adam," is also in Hebrew the word for "humanity, mankind." So, for assessing what difference it makes when you realize that, look at Genesis 2:19 in the Bible and read it that way: 'God brought the animals to Humanity, and whatever name Humanity gave each of them, that was the animal's name.' You see that the English rendition of the Hebrew might lack in scope, yes?" B-t was stoical.[198]

Thoughtful-Woman had picked up R_'s copy of Robert Short's *The Gospel According to Peanuts.* (Yes, the "Peanuts" comic strip became the launching pad for a theologian!) She read the quote of Paul Tillich on page two: "We all know the pain we suffer when we meet people who reject the Gospel ... since the Gospel was never properly communicated to them." She looked at R_: "That's been part of your concern, hasn't it?" But then she read farther down the page: "The objection *all* men have to the Church's message is fundamentally the same: it is that universal hardness of heart lying far more deeply and steadfastly within them than any objection men can usually hold consciously." She looked unhappy with that, and put the book away.

R_ seized the moment: "You might appreciate what Snoopy, the dog, says on page 34," he said. Thoughtful-Woman read the passage R_ had highlighted: "It never fails. Just *hint* that some of their troubles might be with themselves, and they get mad at you! — Snoopy." She put the book away again, looking less unhappy — not happy, but thoughtful.

"I had one that I found in your book by that scientist Denis Alexander," B-t chimed in. "He quoted Augustine about events that seem to us 'contrary to nature.' Augustine, the great ancient theologian, said, 'With God it is not so, for him "nature" is what he does.' "[199]

"Here's another," R_ continued. "From *The Emergence of the Catholic* — that is, church-wide, universal, not 'Roman Catholic' — *Tradition*: An early Christian theologian told the Greek philosophers that the soul is not immortal,' that is in and of itself, but 'it is possible for it not to die.' "[200]

Thoughtful-woman was startled. She and B-t had been browsing together in R_'s little bookshelves during one rest stop, and R_'s quote reminded her of a discovery she had needled B-t about, so she took the floor: "Hello, driver, I found one that's just what you people think: 'We are gradually becoming the kind of people we will forever be. That should send a chill down our spine. ... We live in a culture that has, for centuries now, cultivated the idea that the *skeptical* person is always smarter than one who believes. You can be almost as stupid as a cabbage, as long as you *doubt*. The fashion of the age has identified mental sharpness with a pose, not with genuine intellectual method and character.' " Her voice became strident as she continued to quote: "Today it is the skeptics who are the social conformists, though because of powerful intellectual propaganda they continue to enjoy thinking of themselves as wildly individualistic and unbearably bright.' That's from your book *The Contemporaries Meet the Classics on Prayer*, and I noticed your own note inside the front cover: 'Ah, Father! Put Your hedge of protection around us.' "[201]

R_ pulled out a magazine clipping. "Episcopal bishop John Spong asked how any thoughtful person can expect his physicist daughter to believe in a bodily resurrection. Well, the preacher William Willimon responded: 'The answer, I suppose, depends on Spong's daughter. ... How little imagination does his daughter now have? ... The text cannot be blamed if modern people ... live by epistemologies too limited to enable them to hear the text.' We cannot expect people to hear the gospel, Willimon says, when they are 'epistemologically enslaved,' to use his term."[202]

"Epistemologically enslaved," Thoughtful-Woman murmured. "I like that phrasing. Trapped by their view of the nature and grounds of knowledge..." B-t quoted Shakespeare softly: "There are more things in heaven and earth than are dreamed of in your philosophy."[203]

Sci-guy was in an unusually good mood. "I smuggled a beer into your refrigerator last night," he confided, "and I don't know if it fueled my research, but I found something I enjoyed in one of your books: I got out your *Encyclopedia of Catholicism* and read their article on 'evolution.' This I call to all you folks' attention: 'Catholic theology is comfortable with the view that God "creates" through evolution... Scientific creationism not only fails to give science its own legitimate authority, but it also trivializes biblical teachings by implicitly placing them in the same genre as scientific discourse. Biblical revelation is debased whenever it is considered another source of information that science is capable of discovering on its own.' I also noted that the same article calls on 'scientific thinkers' to 'abandon the unnecessarily materialistic and pessimistic philosophical assumptions that have tainted many of their portraits of the evolutionary process.' They say that many Roman Catholic theologians are 'grateful... that evolutionary thinking has deepened our understanding of God's and humanity's relationship to the natural world.' "[204] *Have another beer*, B-t thought, but he remained respectfully silent.

His silence was rewarded. With a glance at Thoughtful-Woman, Sci-guy brought forth his final gem: "I broke our agreement. I opened up one of your notebooks — the one on Native American clippings. The title just overwhelmed my curiosity, I'm sorry." He glanced at R_, who seemed honored by the "curiosity," and Sci-guy continued: "I found a Native American gentleman with a graduate degree in physics who said, 'No scientist has inspired me more than Albert Einstein, who was moved emotionally when he experienced the mysterious.' He noted that Einstein himself described 'the cosmic religious feeling' as being the strongest and boldest motive for scientific research."[205] (In the endnote we share the Native American writer's physics-based perception of energy and "spirit" correlating, but that discussion didn't make it into the swirling mass of "final comments and minor highlights" in the RV.)

B-t shared the sense of "wrapping it up" as their destination neared. "You have a lot of science books; there must be more of note in that regard," he told R_, who replied: "More than quoting out of those books, I would like to assert one macro-observation: Leaving God out of one's *scientific* explanations, is simply good, basic, normal science. Saying that *that* means that there *is* no God, after you've succeeded in filling your head with your own explanations, is a severe failure of thought." [206]

Sci-guy nodded in acknowledgment that this was a clear point of logic, and R_ elaborated: "I would make the point that every field of study needs to be addressed with methodology appropriate to the subject. If you searched for planets with a microscope, you would conclude there weren't any. You need the telescope instead, no matter how much good information the microscope has given you. Similarly the need for **prayer and awe**, if you want the full truth." [The astute reader may recall our comment on p. 95: Prayer, Word of God, right Christian community.]

R_ fumbled in his shirt pocket for an index card, then read: " 'We are not afraid to follow truth wherever it may lead' — the motto of the Veritas Forum, quoting Thomas Jefferson."[207]

Chapter 20: Goliath in the White House: dog and man on a leash, which reaches the prime point

B-t left the group first. Then, when they reached the Amtrak train station in D.C., Thoughtful-Woman patted R_'s hand and said, "You've made this the most interesting ride I've gotten in a long time. Well, I'm going to have a big feast dinner when I get to my friend's place, and content myself with how wonderful it is and with knowing that a loving God must have good things in store for me, if you're right."

Sci-guy was next to speak, to the dog's surprise: "You haven't been listening very carefully to what our driver has been saying! If he's right, you can't just put up your feet and coast — this God he speaks of is, according to *him*, offering you an opportunity that you need to seize or miss!" Thoughtful-Woman smiled a farewell and was off for her train. R_ drove Sci-guy to the National Science Foundation headquarters, where a friend of Sci-guy's took over the chore of temporary transportation for the duration of the visit.

And so, with his hitchhikers delivered to their immediate (albeit temporary) destinations, R_ became a tourist in Washington D.C.

The dog's full name was Goliath, so that's what R_ printed on the paper on the clipboard of the White House guard. (R_ called him "Goli" because of his amazingly sweet, gentle disposition — "Goliath" was such a harsh name, given by his previous owner). R_ had never expected to get *into* the White House — he thought a stroll nearby would be history enough - but unknown to him, when the President's "domestic summit" with gang leaders had been set up, they had found a gang leader, also from Southern California, with the same first name as R_, who also took a German Shepherd dog with him everywhere - so they had invited *that* man to the "summit" - hence the White House guard's challenge "are you R_ from Southern California?" when man and dog approached, and now the swift ushering into a very *invitation-only* meeting.

The presence of a man with a dog at the summit meeting gave the President an interesting opening. The President had wondered who to speak to first, since "precedence" of any kind would exacerbate "prominence" issues, and ego-strife was rife among these folks. "I'll ask you with the dog, my friend" (the President of the United States wasn't about to use "sir" in *this* setting - not from unwillingness to show a modicum of respect, expecting it to be returned in greater quantity, but "sir" would be quaint to a fault among *these* individuals), "I'll ask *you*, what is *your* agenda here?"

"My agenda, everywhere I go, is to pray for the people," R_ responded. Many of the assembled gang leaders snickered. The near-laughter gave the President an opportunity for alignment with the meeting by displaying a wry smile, and the President said to R_, "Are you asking me to believe you came *here* to pray?" R_ was on the spot - he didn't *come* here on any explicit purpose; he had unwittingly stepped to the edge of a vortex and it had sucked him in.

R_ decided to fulfill his purpose. "Gentlemen, I need you to bear with me for two quick points." A "V" hand gesture took their attention as he intoned "two," and that kept it all moving along OK for the moment. "First, how many of you believe there is a God in heaven Who fills heaven and earth[208] and watches over the affairs of human beings?"

A few of the ghetto chieftains put up their hands, and R_ said, "That earlier point, '*gentlemen*,' is one I need to invoke again *now*. Be kind enough to bear with me." He needed gentlemanliness for just a moment more, to give him space for "point 2" - would it work? Exhortations to kindness were rare among these people, and few of them, if any, had heard "invoke" in years. [209]

R_ looked upward and spoke without a pause: "Father God, in the beginning You created the world and the creatures in it. You revealed Yourself to us — it is not at all obvious that the world *had* a beginning, but now science has come around to teaching what You told us in Your holy word, 'In the beginning...' You *also* told us in Your word that You created us for good and not for evil, to enjoy

Your love, not to suffer and do violence. Lead us now in what is good and right in Your sight, let Your wisdom and power spread the good and flourishing peace that *You* desire, grant us the fullness of Your angels, Your truth and Your light, 'the whole armor of God for the whole people of God' [210] — in the fullness of Your most precious Holy Spirit, the Spirit of wisdom and counsel and power and might."

Now he paused, and it was quite enough for the President, who chimed in with "Amen" and moved the meeting to "business." But the thing had been spoken, which needs to go *before* Item #1 on every "agenda." The dog put his head appreciatively on R_'s thigh.

==

A note to our readers who are dog-lovers: The dog has been a silent participant in all this dialogue, often playing an important role with his emotional support. Just for dog-lovers (only!), we have an endnote at the end of all the endnotes, about dogs... [The End]

Postscript #1

Below:
A) Comments on the status of this book
B) Testimony: who your author is and my life with God over many decades

A) Comments on the book: Dear reader, this is a "work in progress," as is indeed the universe we see, and your comments may be of value in refining the book. We provide an address for inputs at the end of the Table of Contents (and a "response form" at the end in case that stimulates your thinking positively).

Virginia's testimony is included because it's important about miracle healing happening today (Chapter 18) — not just in books, but to one of my personal friends, someone I worked with for many months and still see at Church. I met others — a woman who experienced a miracle disappearance of liver cancer that had been diagnosed that it would be swiftly terminal, and a friend whose brother's fingers were cut off by machinery — but they were restored to full function by the hospital simply sewing them back on (the doctors told him, before the operation, that *that* would *not* be adequate medical care to restore them, as much elaborate inner work would be needed and their hospital would not be able to do that for him. He said, "Just sew them on." His friends gathered to pray for him, and the doctors were astonished on later check-up to find the fingers working fine, blood flowing properly through them. One doctor said to another, "We didn't do that!" — and the other doctor took him aside and said, "We *didn't* do that — God did!") Also, a friend's still-born baby was restored to life after prayer; the newspaper account said one of the doctors remembered a similar event some decades ago in the Philippines (so, hey, these things happen, you know! Well, yes, it happened right there after my friend and his believing wife prayed...)

B) **Your author**: This book is "OurBook," mine and His*. As for me, Bob, I grew up in Arizona, completed a Masters in economics, worked for Native American Indian people in Washington, Idaho, Oregon, Alaska, Canada and California (twenty-five years total), and completed a Masters degree in Theology. (This list is not strictly chronological. The people themselves generally used the term "Indian," including in the names of organizations I worked for, while "Native American" is preferred in academic circles, so I use both here. "Indian" is not clear in circles that deal with people from the nation of India).

I was given the Word of God by faithful witnesses (see "Acknowledgments" — they lived the love!) I was devoted at birth to the Lord, with infant baptism, for which I am still grateful. I made my personal conscious decision of commitment to the Lord Jesus at about age fourteen and had myself re-baptized in commitment. Prone to folly as humans are, I wandered off into spiritual darkness. After perhaps a decade and a half of living without any conscious attention to the Lord, I came into a time of deep distress — and I did something new: I prayed! After a week of this, I was standing in the kitchen, and words came into my mind with great power — "Be still and know that I am God."

I was quite overwhelmed. There was a clarity in that touch of power that showed my prayers had been answered. I bought a Bible for fifty cents at a used-book store and read it cover-to-cover. I found that those words are Psalm 46:10, probably stored up from my teenage read-through of the Bible. Yes, now, that's one of the key purposes that the Word can serve — to let God communicate with you in time of need, by the Word stored in your heart (compare Bible, Psalm 119:11). As recounted below, continuing to walk with God enabled me later to hear more directly.** That ties to my recommendation of reading a chapter a day (old Christian folk proverb: "a chapter a day keeps the devil

---

** Jesus' ministry (John 12:27-29) and Paul's "Damascus Road" encounter with Jesus (Acts 22:8-9) both show this phenomenon -- those closer hear God, those more distant think perhaps they heard thunder. Don't miss what He* has for you!

away"). If you haven't been **reading the Bible, you might start by reading Luke, John, and Acts — the basic story of Jesus (Luke), the deep spiritual meanings of Jesus (John), the early people living with the Holy Spirit of God (Acts)**. (While I'm an NIV Bible reader, I appreciate the New Living Translation — it often makes the message come through wonderfully in current language. Endnote 264 has more +/- on the NLT).

I lived, unfortunately, for many years as a child of the 1960s. After more than a decade and a half of smoking marijuana regularly (I graduated from Univ. California Berkeley without any problems, but my grades *did* go down from that), I was sitting at home, rolling a joint, when a clear thought came into my head — with the intensity of a neon sign on a dark street, and a clear sensation demarcating that it was not *my* thought. It said, "The Holy Spirit wants you to stop smoking marijuana."[211] More than thirty years later, I can still remember very clearly what it said. I was astonished! My Bible reading had brought me the verse, "test everything; hold fast to what is good" (1Th 5:21), so after this experience, I would roll a joint, pray over it, and smoke it — and my lungs began to burn! I said to myself, "In all these years, my lungs have never burned with this smoking, and now after that message they are — this *is* the word of God for me." He* not only gave me grace to quit, but saved me from cravings — ask God to do that for anyone for whom you pray drug/alcohol deliverance! (Myself and alcohol, endnote 267).

So, the Holy Spirit does talk to people, and His* guidance *is* good. He has graciously met my needs, prepared me for where He has taken me, has been "a sun and a shield" (Psa 84:11). He says to you as He said to me, "Come!" (Rev 3:20, 22:17).

The Lord has blessed me with mercy. He granted me to be high school valedictorian, and to be Phi Beta Kappa at the University of California Berkeley. He gave me grace to "stand" in my work in the Northwest and in Alaska and in California. He gave me grace to see the glory of His* creation in Alaska's special winter light and Northern Lights, in a rainbow at midnight in Alaska's "midnight sun" during the summer, and the glory of hours of moonlight over the dark Pacific when I stood midnight watch at sea. I thank You, Lord, and I pray to love You with all my heart and mind and soul and strength, and to perfectly abide in You, Lord Jesus.

[Some wanderings of further musings, if you are ready for the distraction:] Discussing logic regarding God, as we have to some degree, raises the question: What is more fundamental than God, to be used to "prove" God? For me, over seventy years of living with God has proven His* great goodness and profound reality, and it moves me to write this book. The book might want to add my analysis of the "apocalyptic" matters[212] and a special caution: if a time of great good does come forth (Rev 11:15), dear reader please: do not be lulled into soaking into momentary enjoyment and neglect to "*seek*" God. Please note my experience, when I was financially desperate, with "building towards" keeping the tithe: I set my face, even though I was too hard-pressed to start at once (the landlord *did* want to be paid!), and the Lord honored that intention/commitment: within a year, I was keeping the full tithe, and He* has since lifted me up to where a friend said, "I'm green with envy." (The journey has not been without some very harsh points; but He has been with me in them all.) The Lord *also* did indeed keep the added aspect stated in the tithe promise, "to rebuke the devourer for your sake" (that specific wording is ESV; same in NASB, LITV, NKJV, and JPS — Jewish Publication Society; my electronic text for the JPS is the old 1917 version, free on e-Sword.net. My tithe experience is discussed in endnote 49, more planned for a follow-on book, endnote 232).

I kept the tithe and my finances have been marvelously blessed; I kept the "day of rest" and my time has been blessed;[213] I commend the Lord's love to you, dear reader!

[*An update 2018*: I noted above two crises, each answered and resolved by the Word ["Scripture," Bible]: the first by Psalm 46:10 as a direct touch; the second by Malachi 3:10-11 as teaching remembered and applied, with essential counsel. Now, I seem to find myself in a "third crisis," equally deep; reserving any details for a later possible edition, I note that this crisis seems to be answered by the Word speaking again, Psalm 32:8 "I will counsel you and watch over you" — again, the faithful promise in the living Word.

Postscript #2: Taking On "The Issues"

An Eastern Orthodox deacon, who went on to become a priest, said to me: "The issues of the day are like the waves of the sea — everything bobs up and down with them, but underneath is the deep current, and that's what really moves."[214] For him, seeing eternal realities, the Gospel is the thing — "eternal destiny," the *opportunity* that becomes clear in the light of "Humanity's Greatest Discovery."

That raises the question, then: does a person who "takes pen in hand," to use a somewhat dated phrase, talk about "the issues," or just stick with "the Greatest Discovery," in the various modes in which that wants to be processed? Fareed Zakaria brought this matter into a different place: He wrote an incisive opinion piece in *Newsweek* in Fall 2009 about the "healthcare crisis." America, he said, does not have "a healthcare crisis:" America has *two* healthcare crises, one of coverage, one of cost control. That segued to my father's legacy, and a perception of a *third* crisis in the current healthcare, one worth commenting on in *this* book: the crisis of *concept.*

God sent this word to us, across more than two thousand years: "I am the LORD your God who heals you."[215] My father was a physician (G.P., then specialist), and one day as we were driving around, he said to me, "Robert, we can give them [the patients] drugs, but it's the Lord that heals them." He knew the truth of what the Scripture said, from living the experience of the healing methodologies (he was a surgeon as well as G.P. — General Practitioner — in the old days, when roles were broader, in a small town).

Americans now are, to a dangerous degree, people who "trust in therapy more than in mystery."[216] The obese person is a challenge to the doctor's ability to motivate change, but this is not perceived as an offense against the God Whose temple the body is.[217] (Similarly the smoker who puffs excessively and damages vital organs...)

America's long-term (multi-decade) success with healthcare will depend on how well this crisis is contained or resolved in all its scope. As a final aside, there was a supposedly definitive **study on prayer and healing**, based on "double blind" methodology, which was ballyhooed as proving that prayer does not work. "Double blind" is the "gold standard" for testing medicines, in which neither the medical practitioners nor the patients know which patients are getting whichever medicines or placebos. In this study, people did not know if they were being prayed for (by the participating believers) and the praying persons did not know the people for whom they were praying.

My father's medical experience comes to mind again. He worked among some people not familiar with "Western" medicine. They would take some of the pills he prescribed and decide "say, this white man medicine *is* good," then gulp the whole bottle — so he would have to rush out and pump their stomachs. "Best when used as directed" is a standard phrase for good reasons. Consider, then, what the Word of God says about how to be healed: "Is anyone sick? Let that person call for the elders, and they will pray for him and anoint him with oil..." (Bible, James 5:14).[218] Note the intense personal community involved: the sick person personally seeks God's help by recourse to the elders. (A minister teaches that this active, personal recourse gives authority for the healing.) The deeper believers, the elders, meet personally with the health-seeker. And, of course, if the person is healed, God gets the credit, not buried as a statistic in a table, but as the rejoicing of wellness goes on. Trash that community, remove that personal involvement, and say you have proven something by "using exactly *not* as directed"? And call it the application of *reason*?

A contrasting view: "...'**reason**' is the intellect choosing to live by wisdom..."[219] Surely wisdom requires the right procedure for every matter!

Acknowledgments

I acknowledge my gracious Lord and Savior, whose truth and love have made this both possible and worthwhile; my most wonderful Mom and Dad, "faithful witnesses" who introduced me to the truth of God's love and demonstrated it lifelong; and the Church, which brought me the Word and also helped me in time of trauma.

Originally, I thought two "acknowledgments" — both historical realities — might help frame the purpose of this book:

1) A Native American Indian Elder in Bellingham Washington, who told a multi-racial community planning meeting in 1970: "If we speak plainly with words that everyone can understand, we can bring peace and harmony over the whole earth." I was fresh out of college and I was tempted to snicker — "peace and harmony over the whole earth, indeed!" — but something inside stopped me, and I thought, *"If he's right, I want to be part of it, not snicker at it."* This book is an endeavor to "speak plainly."

2) An old friend B., who said he had become an atheist: "We can explain everything by evolution; we don't need a 'First Cause' anymore — but my wife and I are both carrying pistols. If there's a sermon for you in that, you're welcome to it." This book is part of that "sermon."

Since we do not have a "title page" in this self-published book, we include in this section publisher items normally called for on "title page." **Photo acknowledgments:** *Cover photo:* "Purple Mountain Majesty." Photo © by S. Cyd Read of Natural Born Hikers, all rights reserved; by permission with our gratitude! Their website naturalbornhikers.com (more on photo below). Back cover photos © 2009 Robert Keller. Clip art hddfhm.com.

Acknowledgments of the form generally made in books and major projects are due **with deep gratitude to:** *(Please note, for those who have furnished quotes, that their participation does* *not necessarily include agreement with all the opinions and thought-options in this book)*

Eric Libeu, who provided prayer support and encouragement in the early phases, the gracious touch of the Spirit of Christ. Fr. Boulos Khoury, who did that in later phases! Pastor Ron Hernandez, who prophesied over the book in Church.[220]

Rev. Bruce Engebretson — without his help in the time of trauma, I might never have come to this point (and another pastor whose name has faded into the mists of personal antiquity, but he was there and heaven will remember him). Vital in a different crisis (again caused by my own folly), Ruth Ray Kirk also gave the patience and devotion to the Lord's work in the strayed soul, and she taught me important things.

Rev. David Salmon, a Native elder, 2nd Traditional Chief of the Athabascan region, and Christian priest to his Native village in Alaska, who gave me the counsel that has led to this book.

Pastor Elder Ivory Thornton, Rev. James White, Brother David Flenaugh[221] (see footnote for his precious input on **trouble**), Deacon Ben Williams and his Mother Juanita, Brother Robert Kinnard and the other faithful members of the First Church of God in Christ (see 2 Cor. 5:19 [NKJV, KJV, NASB, LITV] re the name of this international church), who encouraged me profoundly over the years I knew them in Fairbanks Alaska. (See endnote 67 for more on Pastor Elder Ivory Thornton.)

Rita Reynolds, who was Cherokee on both sides of her family's ancestry and who was almost three-quarters Cherokee by blood, who supplied me with the Cherokee heritage book *The Cherokee People* (cited in Chapter One and elsewhere for its important contribution).

Elder Paisios of Mount Athos, the great Greek monastery complex; his writings have blessed me so much.

Rev. David Lee Byrd, a man whose victory over alcoholism and the negativity of a destructive life situation was quite impressive indeed. David was the first person to articulate in conversation with me that his own goal in life was to hear the Lord Jesus say, "Well done" when he would pass on into the next realm

(Bible, Mt. 25:21, 23). Other people are also living it, but he actually *said* it, and that was a special touch. It helped me.

In personal conversation, David credited the Lord Jesus with all his progress, which the reader should note. He made the statement that his life was transformed from "pain, fear and anger": "a miracle occurred. God's touch changed all the misery and heartache into joy."

The **front cover picture**, by Natural Born Hikers (website naturalbornhikers.com) was tagged "Purple Mountain Majesty" by them, which enabled me to find it on the web when I realized my own photography was not going to recapture the magic described in the Preface. The setting is "Flower Lake, Kearsarge Pass, Eastern Sierra, California." Photo © by S. Cyd Read of Natural Born Hikers, all rights reserved.

Your author finds that creation shows special wonders everywhere, just as every age of life shows special good things to a person. Winter in Alaska was graced by special light and colors; the student of the world finds that Victoria Falls, in Africa, is so large that the spray rises 1,000 feet above the waterfalls, and at full moon a "moonbow" rainbow can be seen! The amazing things are inexhaustible, but the "nuannaarpoc," the special joy of just being alive, is ours to grasp everywhere.[222] Thank You, Lord!

QUOTATIONS: a) *Special thanks indeed* to the Bible publishers whose versions we have quoted. (Generally, their policies permit up to 500 verses without prior permission, as long as use is acknowledged and certain conditions apply -- we cite the versions where we quote their specific language; we explain the abbreviations in the Bibliography and discuss the versions in the "Annotated Bibliography.") People gave their lives so that we might have the Word of God, and have it in the language of the people; the ongoing labors of these many to make it available now in useful forms, are deeply appreciated by those who have seen the good fruits of the Word.

b) Our deep appreciation indeed to the various publishers, authors and organizations who have graciously given permission to use their material, and to the Copyright Clearance Center (copyright.org) for vital help in arranging permission and royalty matters.

HarperCollins asks this credit in the Acknowledgments: "Excerpts [pp. Frontispiece, 84, 92, 110, 236, 237, 296, 419: 229 wds] from SIGNATURE IN THE CELL by STEPHEN C. MEYER. Copyright © 2009 by Stephen C. Meyer. Reprinted by permission of HarperCollins Publishers." (They deserve commendation for bringing this important book to the public, and they were good to work with in my endeavor.)

Many others, who may or may not be surprised not to be listed yet by name, but then ... including those who gave me the quotes that grace the back cover, and who encouraged me.

Tina Rae Collins, whose proof-reading caught some critical problems. (I didn't take all her suggestions, and if you object to any of my idiosyncratic expressions, they are *not* her fault).

A special thank you to Darin "Ambassador of Truth" Phillips, for his graphic-art cover revision contributions, and to his roommate J.J. Hardy for his help in polish-editing some of the cover text I furnished [223] (endnote: contact info, Darin's website).

Elizabeth Keating, who encouraged me about the story. Sam Demientieff, who encouraged me about the book. (These are also appreciated as some of my Native American Indian bosses).

Alas, as I start to list names, there are just too many -- if *your* name belongs here, please forgive me and comfort yourself with the obvious parallel in the Bible's great list, Hebrews 11:32 (even *David* got "short shrift" there — !)

All the "good people" whose labors and vision have given us a commercial culture which undergirds work like this, from the computer keyboard to the publishing and dissemination.

All who care about truth and goodness, who seek to live in love in the best sense of that sometimes-abused word, and all who appreciate the beauty of their pleasures in the graciousness of the Great Provider; all who perceive their need for the Savior.

The faithful dog, who loved, and brightened hard years.

Bible Publisher acknowledgments, per their wording:

(see discussion in "Acknowledgments" narrative)

NIV: "Scripture quotations marked (NIV) are taken from the Holy Bible, New International Version®, NIV®. Copyright © 1973, 1978, 1984, 2011 by Biblica, Inc.™ Used by permission of Zondervan. All rights reserved worldwide. www.zondervan.com The 'NIV' and 'New International Version' are trademarks registered in the United States Patent and Trademark Office by Biblica, Inc.™ " [NIV Study Bible, Kenneth Barker General Editor, was by Zondervan, © 1985.]

NLT: "Holy Bible, New Living Translation copyright © 1996, 2004 by Tyndale Charitable Trust. Used by permission of Tyndale House Publishers, Inc., Wheaton, Illinois 60189. All rights reserved."

NRSV: "The Scripture quotations contained herein are from the New Revised Standard Version Bible, copyright © 1989, by the Division of Christian Education of the National Council of the Churches of Christ in the U.S.A., and are used by permission. All rights reserved."

ESV: "Scripture quotations are from The Holy Bible, English Standard Version, copyright ©2001 by Crossway Bibles, a publishing ministry of Good News Publishers. Used by permission. All rights reserved."

KJV: The "Information" tab for my electronic-text KJV says: "This is the 1769 King James Version of the Holy Bible (also known as the Authorized Version)." [The reader may be interested to know that minor updatings of the KJV were done repeatedly after the 1611 publication of it under England's King James. The King James translators themselves were devoted to putting the Scriptures in the language of the people.]

NASB: "Scripture taken from the NEW AMERICAN STANDARD BIBLE®, Copyright © 1960, 1962, 1963, 1968, 1971, 1972, 1973, 1975, 1977, 1995 by The Lockman Foundation. Used by permission."

CEV: "Scripture quotations marked (CEV) are from the Contemporary English Version Copyright © 1991, 1992, 1995 by American Bible Society. Used by Permission."

GNT: "Scripture quotations marked (GNT) are from the Good News Translation in Today's English Version- Second Edition Copyright © 1992 by American Bible Society. Used by Permission."

ISV: "Scripture taken from the Holy Bible: International Standard Version®. Copyright © 1996-2012 by The ISV Foundation. ALL RIGHTS RESERVED INTERNATIONALLY. Used by permission."

NKJV: "Scripture quotations marked 'NKJV™' are taken from the New King James Version®. Copyright © 1979, 1980, 1982 by Thomas Nelson, Inc. Used by permission. All rights reserved."

LITV: "Scripture taken from the Literal Translation of the Holy Bible. Copyright © 1976 — 2000 By Jay P. Green, Sr. Used by permission of the copyright holder."

The Message (Eugene Peterson): "Scripture taken from THE MESSAGE. Copyright © 1993, 1994, 1995, 1996, 2000, 2001, 2002. Used by permission of NavPress Publishing Group."

[*The Message* follows a fairly standard practice of allowing up to 500 verses without express written permission, under certain conditions].

TPT: Scripture quotations marked TPT are from The Passion Translation®. Copyright © 2017, 2018 by Passion & Fire Ministries, Inc. Used by permission. All rights reserved. ThePassionTranslation.com

A note by your author: In the flow of the fiction narrative, the driver "R_" often quotes Scripture from memory, combining language from various versions. In these cases no version citation is given, since it does not track. As your author is mainly an NIV reader, such quotations tend to be closer to the NIV.

(Certain required acknowledgment text by other publishers, is given with the first citation of the authors to which it applies -- it may be superfluous, since we given full citation on all our sources, but "we aim to please".)

Appendix One: Scripture Table

(Your author is pleased to note that the entry on "Rejoice!" was the first item put into this Table.)

This table is *not* an effort to show how much Scripture (Bible quotation) we have used in this book. So, many verses that are discussed at various points in the narrative are *not* posted here. The items here are certain items for reference (prayer, meditation) apart from the flow of the book's narrative. See notes after the table regarding narrative discussions of Scriptures that are indexed.

	Be still, and know that I am God. Psalm 46:10 ESV
	Bring to an end the violence of the wicked and make the righteous secure. (This prayer is Psalm 7:9 NIV)
	Come... whosoever will, let him take the water of life freely. Rev 22:17 KJV
	Do not be anxious about anything, but in every situation, by prayer and petition, with thanksgiving, present your requests to God. And the peace of God, which transcends all understanding, will guard your hearts and your minds in Christ Jesus. Philippians 4:6-7 NIV
	God has compassion on all He* has made. Psalm 145:9
	He (the LORD God Almighty) will be the sure foundation for your times. Isaiah 33:6 NIV [224]
	Take words with you, and return to the LORD God; say to God, 'Receive us graciously, and we will praise You.' Hosea 14:2
	They turn away (from God): 2 Tim 4:4, Heb 12:25; see also Deut 30:17, 2 Chron 7:19, Acts 13:8. For the reverse, see 2 Chron 30:9: "The LORD your God is gracious and compassionate, and will not turn His face away from you if you return to Him." NASB
Abraham and Sarah	Abraham believed ["put his trust in" GNT wording] God: "and because of this the LORD was pleased with him and accepted him" — this language for the last part of the verse is the GNT version (Good News

	Translation) for Genesis 15:6. (The name is Abram in this verse because God had not yet changed his name per his new role in the divine work — also true of his wife Sarah, "Sarai" earlier, name changed Gen. 17:15). See also "Friends" below in this table. (Relation of Abraham and Jesus, see Gal. 3:7,9,14,16.)
Acceptance	"Who comes to Me, I will never turn away" Jesus, John 6:37. (Cf. GNB) See also "peace."
Antichrist	1 John 2:18, 22, 1 John 4:3, and 2 John 1:7 are the only places in the New Testament where this word appears. 2 Thess 2:3 "the man of lawlessness" is often considered another reference to antichrist. (*comments on that are being drafted for our possible future book, per endnote 232.)*
Believe	Jesus, manifesting Himself to "Doubting Thomas:" "Blessed are those who have not seen and yet have believed" John 20:29 [225] (& see "Abraham..." above)
Better country	... as it is, they desire a better country, that is, a heavenly one. Therefore God is not ashamed to be called their God. Heb 11:16 ESV, NRSV
Bible study	I have laid up Your Word in my heart, that I might not sin against You. Psa 119:11 (see Index, "Bible reading," and endnote 277).
Christ:	a) present with people before Incarnation: "they drank from the spiritual rock that accompanied them, and that rock was Christ" (1 Cor 10:4 NIV; of the Israelite's desert Exodus). b) Jesus' Resurrection essential to salvation: 1 Cor 15:17 (See also here "Eternal life.")
Contradiction in Scripture	Proverbs 26:4 Do not answer a fool according to his folly, or you yourself will be just like him. Proverbs 26:5 Answer a fool according to his folly, or he will be wise in his own eyes. (NIV) So, regarding the above, which is it? Is this put there to make us think?
Creation	"How:" "God made the earth by his power; he founded the world by his wisdom and stretched out the heavens by his understanding," Jeremiah 10:12. See also Prov 3:10 "by wisdom;" and, all things by

	God's Son, John 1:3, 1 Cor 8:6, Col 1:16. "By [His] right hand" Isa 48:13; cf. Psa 95:5. See also Jer 10:12; 32:17; 51:15; Psa 33:6. Heb 11:3 and 2 Pet 3:5 use the two different Greek words for "word," *rhema* and *logos*. [226] ("Information:" a convergence? see endnote). The process of creation "God said..." begins to be described in Genesis 1:3 — "God said, 'Let there be light,' and there was light." (NIV; wording is the same in KJV, NKJV, NLT, ESV, NRSV etc.) Wisdom was the first of His* creations: Prov. 8:23
Depressed P.S. do not neglect medical help when appropriate	Psalm 34. (An issue to take to your Pastor! If you don't have one, you might try three local possibles and select your Pastor, at least for a while, per trying out their responses.) Rom 15:13, Ps 43:3-5, Ps 38:15, Ps 6:2-3. Psalm 94:19: When the cares of my heart are many, your consolations cheer my soul (ESV).
Draw near	Draw near to God, and he will draw near to you. Jas 4:8 ESV. Cf. Jer 29:11-13, Heb 7:19, Psa 73:28.
Eternal life	"whoever hears my word and believes him who sent me has eternal life" Jesus, Jn 5:24. Jn 3:16, Rom 10:9
Forgive	Jesus: Mark 11:25. Eph 4:32.
Friends	"I have called you friends" — Jesus, John 15:15. Abraham believed God... God accepted him... so Abraham was called God's friend. James 2:23 GNT
God in Christ	Be kind to one another, tenderhearted, forgiving one another, as God in Christ forgave you. Eph 4:32 ESV God was in Christ reconciling the world to Himself. 2 Cor 5:19 NASB The Word became flesh and dwelt among us, and we have seen his glory... John 1:14 ESV. (See also "Son of God" below; and, Index, "Jesus/uniqueness".)
God speaks	Job 33:14: For God does speak — now one way, now another — though man* may not perceive it.[227] ... in these last days he (God) has spoken to us by his Son, whom he appointed heir of all things, and through whom also he made the universe. Heb 1:2.[228]
Good	James 1:17 Every good and perfect gift is ... from the Father of the [heavenly] lights (cf. NIV, ESV, NKJV).

Healing	See Index for where this is discussed, & "prosperity" and "well-being" below. Endnote 215 (to Postscript 2) has Scripture lists.
Joy	See "Rejoice" below. Note re Jesus: Luke 10:21 "full of joy through the Holy Spirit" and Heb 12:2 "for the joy set before Him, He endured the cross." Jesus gave the "Upper Room discourse" (John, chapters 13 - 17) so we might "have the full measure" of His joy (Jn 17:13 NIV). Also n.b. Neh 8:10 "joy of LORD your strength".
New Covenant	(The Latin for this gave us "New Testament.") Promised by God in Jeremiah 31:31, Isaiah 55:3, 61:8; Ezek 16:60 & 37:26 (and the Dead Sea Scrolls have proven that this was in the ancient text, not an interpolation in the Christian era).[229] Communion as sign/seal of: stated by Jesus in the Gospels, discussed 1 Cor 11:23-28. (Cf. Heb 13:20)
Obey	Jesus: All who love Me will do what I say. My Father will love them, and We will come and make Our home with each of them. John 14:23 NLT; cf. John 14:15, John 15:10-12, 1 John 5:3.
Peace	Isa 57:19 "Peace, peace, to those far and near," says the LORD. "And I will heal them" (NIV). Jesus: "I have told you these things so that in me you may have peace." John 16:33 (John chapters 13 - 17 are His famous "Upper Room discourse.") See also "Rest" below, and discussion of Philippians 4:7, endnote 191. N.B. 2 Thess 3:16.
Poverty	Prov 22:22 Do not exploit the poor because they are poor. (NIV) (See also Chapter Four) Prov 14:31 Whoever oppresses the poor shows contempt for their Maker, but whoever is kind to the needy honors God (NIV; & see note 34). Prov 21:13 Whoever shuts their ears to the cry of the poor will also cry out and not be answered.(NIV)[230] [Lord lifts poor: see that endnote, n. 230]
Prayer	See Index for Lord's Prayer, "worship in spirit and truth," other topics. ("Tips," endnote 277.) The Holy Spirit helps us to pray — Rom 8:26 — intercedes. (Note also "Rest" below.) More:

	Note also 1 Cor 14:15 "I will pray with my spirit, but I will also pray with my understanding;" Eph. 6:18 & Jude 1:20 "pray in the Spirit." (Re "unanswered," a note[231].) Psalm 23 should be noted as a classic resource for times of crisis. See also "Trust" below; resource books pp. 162, 187-188; endnote 277.
Pride	"The proud He* [God] knows from afar" Psalm 138:6 NKJV & LITV *(Reader, please write us if you feel we should add any illuminative commentary.)* Cf. Psa 18:27. [Note Sci-guy on our p. 92] 2 Chron 32:25 "Hezekiah did not respond according to the benefit done to him, for his heart was proud." NRSV Pride is a central sin in the Bible, distancing people from God and making them filled with self-will contrary to God; but there is also "Godly pride:" Psa 47:4, Isa 4:2, Zec 10:3, 2Co 5:12, 7:4, 7:14NLT, 8:24; Gal 6:4; Jas 1:9. "Haughty eyes and a proud heart" are called by the Word "the lamp of the wicked." (Pr. 21:4 ESV.)
Promises	**"I will never turn away anyone who comes to me... and no one can snatch them away from me"** - Jesus, John 6:37, 10:28-29 GNB; cf. John 17:11 "My grace is sufficient for you" 2Cor 12:9 "Come to me, all you that are weary and are carrying heavy burdens, and I will give you rest. Jesus, Matthew 11:28 NRSV "Come, let us reason together; though your sins be like scarlet, they shall be white as snow." Isaiah 1:18 See also "Believe" above & "Trust" below.
Prosperity	Note the prophet's clarity on a key use of prosperity: "to share your food with the hungry and to provide the poor wanderer with shelter— when you see the naked, to clothe them, and not to turn away from your own flesh and blood... Then your light will break forth like the dawn, and your healing will quickly appear (Isaiah 58:7-8 NIV). See "well-being" below.

Rejoice	"Rejoice [not in miraculous power but] that your names are written in heaven" - Jesus, Lk 10:20. The commandment to rejoice: Philippians 4:4. (See also Index entry, for where the main narrative discusses "joy" from various viewpoints. The NIV Bible has "rejoice" in 155 verses and "joy" in 295.) "Take delight in the Lord" Psa 37:4 (We are contemplating this as a possible item for a follow-on book.[232] (See that endnote if you are interested to be notified if we succeed in bringing out such a book!)
Rest	"Only in returning to Me and resting in Me will you be saved. In quietness and confidence is your strength." God's statement in Isa 30:15, NLT. Prayer: By the might of your Spirit lift us, we pray you, to your presence, where we may be still and know that you are God.[233] (Psa 46:10) See also "Peace."
Second Coming	(Visible return of Jesus Christ) Rev 1:7 "every eye will see Him." Matthew 24:44: "the Son of Man will come at an hour when you do not expect him." (NIV)
Sin	Isa 1:18 [come to God; sins covered, "white as snow"]. 1 Jn 2:1 Jesus our Advocate with the Father. 1 Jn 1:8 [if say have no sin, truth not in us]. Continuing in sin: Heb 10:26 deliberately keep on... no sacrifice for sins is left NIV. The classic summary: "the lust of the flesh, the lust of the eyes, and the pride of life" [i.e., not giving credit to God] 1 Jn 2:16 NIV-2011. (See also Index & Chapter 12. Ten Commandments, Exodus 20; Sermon on the Mount, Matthew 5:2 - 7:27)
Son of God	Jesus as "Son of God:" — His own claim: Mark 14: 61-62 and John 10:36. - Seen by the Jewish leaders in His actions: Mark 2:7; John 6:37. - Other acknowledgments: "that you may believe" this: John 20:31 (see also 1 John 3:23, command to believe this and love one another). - Other references: Note that Jesus accepted the title, John 1:49. This is a painfully selective listing, as this

	phrase occurs in 41 verses of the New Testament! See also the entry here "Translations ..." for some comments on this topic.
Suffering	Psa 138:7; Psa 91; Ps 103; 1Co 10:13 (some of these show conditions that we imperfectly meet; pray for grace! See "Prayer" and "Promises" here; "Trouble;" see also Index).
Thanksgiving	He who sacrifices thank offerings honors Me, and he prepares the way so that I may show him the salvation of God. Psa 50:23 (cf. NIV-1984, LITV). See also Philippians 4:6-7 entry at the top of this Scripture Table.
Today	"Today, if you hear His* voice, do not harden your hearts... do not refuse Him* who speaks... now is the time of God's favor." Heb 3:7-8; 12:25; 2 Cor 6:2 NIV.
Translations & versions	See endnote 6 for the comment by "B-t," the Bible-toting hitchhiker, that "They [all these Bible versions] all say the same thing: 'Jesus Christ, Son of God, Savior,'' and the comment by the *100-Minute Bible* on the importance of that. The third section of the Bibliography has some notes about differences in translation style between versions.
Trouble	But you, God, see the trouble of the afflicted; you consider their grief and take it in hand. (Psa 10:14 NIV; see also v. 17 there. Personally, I was helped greatly by Psa 138:7 — your author). 1Peter 4:19 *The Message* version reads, "so if you find life difficult because you are doing what God said, take it in stride. Trust him. He knows what he's doing." Cf. Index "victory;" book recommendation p. 187; Mt. 16:24, Acts 14:22. Some aspects: endnotes 45, 49, 70, 140. > Meditate and *do* Bible, Hebrews 4:16.
Trust	"I will never leave you nor forsake you" — the faithfulness of God's promise (Deut 31:6,8; Jos 1:5; Heb 13:5; cf. Jesus, Mt. 28:20) is illustrated by Heath Bottomly claiming it when his airplane was falling out of the sky — see Bibliography for reference. "Pour out your heart to Him*, and trust in Him with

	all your heart." Psalm 62:8
Unsearchable	"Call to Me and I will answer you and tell you great and unsearchable things you do not know." Jer 33:3 NIV
Weary	Jesus: Mt 11:28. Phlp. 4:4-8, esp. v. 6. Isaiah 40:28-31
Well-being	"The LORD be exalted, who delights in the well-being of his servant," Psa 35:27 NIV (ESV, NRSV "welfare"; NASB, NKJV, KJV "prosperity" (q.v. above). The Hebrew word is "shalom," a word which scholars note includes the broader well-being, not just absence of strife. Note also 3 John 2; Jesus per Matt. 6:33; Eph 6:3; 1Tim 6:17.

** for the asterisk on "masculine" pronouns for God, see the first lines of the Endnotes.*

Scriptures of special note, for being discussed in the narrative: The Index shows page numbers for the following items: Lord's Prayer (see "Prayer")

Healing: Scriptures for meditation for this. (Discussion of healing needs to note that it is "for today," happening now by the Lord's grace [see Chapter 18 for a dramatic example], and also that Christ's Atonement is key. Bosworth's book provides extensive discussion and more resources can be found at kcm.org.)

New birth/ "birth from above"

Worship in SPIRIT and in truth — humanity's great opportunity

Finally, let me add this: Isa 32:6 "For fools speak folly... and spread error concerning the LORD [concerning God]; the hungry they leave empty and from the thirsty they withhold water." (NIV)

(Well, any time a preacher says "finally" or "in conclusion," you tense up — is he telling the truth? Here, adding to the above some months later makes me contradict myself, but it has to be: Isaiah 30:18 "The LORD longs to be gracious to you..." [NIV]. *Put yourself in the place where He* can do that!* God calls to you: "Turn to me and be saved... for I am God, and there is no other" Isa 45:22 NIV. Note also entry "Believe" above.)

Appendix Two: *The Case for Easter*: A recap of a professional's research

Lee Strobel's research began when "the unthinkable happened — my wife became a Christian." He put his professional experience in journalism and his legal training to work, in hope that "I could liberate her from this cult!" (page 8 of Strobel's *The Case for Easter*, a 95 page excerpt from his *The Case for Christ*. His background: Strobel, "educated at Yale Law School, was the award-winning legal editor of the Chicago Tribune" — back cover of his book).

He defined the crucial issues as three questions: "Was Jesus really dead after his ordeal on the cross? Was his tomb actually empty on that first Easter Morning? And did credible people subsequently encounter him?" He started with "the medical evidence about the supposed demise of Jesus." (His initial perspective: "As a reporter, I had seen lots of dead people — and none of them had ever come back to life," p. 8.)

Question #1: The charge that Jesus did not die on the cross has ranged from the Qur'an (written more than half a millennium later; Sura IV: 156-157) to many fictional works in recent years. Strobel's questioning of a medical expert started with the Gospel's report that Jesus sweated blood as he prayed over the impending agony of the crucifixion. The medical expert — with a medical degree, Board certified, consultant to major medical institutes, published in medical journals and *Scientific American* — explained the facts of this condition, rare but definitely known — and one that would weaken Jesus' skin before the severe pre-crucifixion beatings given to condemned men (pp. 14, 15). The medical information included the correct place where the "hand" was nailed (in what we now call the wrist, but "part of the hand in the language of the day," p. 18). Strobel's medical resource person described the effects on the heart that would cause "blood and water" to come out, as per the Bible account (John 19:34) when the Roman soldier pierced Jesus' body with a spear to be absolutely sure he was dead (p. 21).

Skepticism has been applied to every part of the Gospel accounts; one published article took up the statement that Jesus' feet were nailed to the cross, and said, "there was astonishingly little evidence that the feet of a crucified person were ever pierced by nails" (p. 23). However, archaeology found a Jewish crucifixion victim with "a seven-inch nail still driven into his feet, with small pieces of olive wood from the cross still attached."

The Romans were skilled executioners, and "if a prisoner somehow escaped, the responsible soldiers would be put to death" (p. 24), so they took care not to mistake whether the victim was really dead. The ever-self-resuscitating "swoon theory" is also incompatible with Jesus' being able to walk the distance to Emmaus with disciples after his resurrection (on nail-pierced feet!). But Strobel found the ultimate clincher in David Strauss' analysis: if Jesus had survived and come out of the tomb in that manner, "he would have looked so pitiful that the disciples would never have hailed him as a victorious conqueror of death... [instead they would have] tried to nurse him back to health" (p. 26).

Strobel closed his report on this question with a quote from another medical expert, whose analysis was published in the *Journal of the American Medical Association* in 1986 and concluded: "interpretations based on the assumption that Jesus did not die on the cross appear to be at odds with modern medical knowledge" (p. 28).

Question #2: Strobel notes its importance: "The resurrection is the supreme vindication of Jesus' divine identity and his inspired teaching. It's the proof of his triumph over sin and death... *If* it's true." (p. 32).

Questions of how to view the New Testament have excited much controversy. Strobel's informant cut a path through the diverse views by taking him to 1 Corinthians 15:3-7, which even the more skeptical views do acknowledge to be "a very early creed of the church" (p. 36). It "undoubtedly goes back to within a few years of Jesus' crucifixion, having been given to Paul, after his conversion, in Damascus or in his subsequent visit to Jerusalem..." The "burial" reported in this "creed" summarizes the Gospel accounts, which give "multiple, independent attestations of this burial story, and Joseph of Arimathea is specifically named in all four [Gospel] accounts... the burial story in Mark is so extremely early that it's simply not possible for it to have been subject to legendary corruption" (p. 37). (His informant, Dr. William Lane Craig, gives analysis of reasons for that "early" assertion; the thrust of these accounts also refutes the skeptics' application of the fact that crucified criminals "were left on the cross to be devoured by birds or were thrown into a common grave" [p. 35]. The reliability of the account of "Joseph of Arimathea" giving a tomb for Jesus, is confirmed by the fact that naming such a person would have been easily refutable in the early days of the Church, if it were an invention, and by the absence of competing burial traditions).

The "early creed" statement that Jesus was "crucified, buried, and then resurrected" (Strobel's summary, p. 39) ties to first-century Jews' "physical concept of resurrection... It would have been simply a contradiction of terms for an early Jew [i.e. in Jesus' day] to say that someone was raised from the dead but his body still was left in the tomb" (Dr. Craig, p. 39). (Craig recaps the result of long scholarly arguments over an old assertion, p. 41: "The idea that the empty tomb is the result of some hoax, conspiracy, or theft is simply dismissed today." The core reason for this "state of the art" in studying the matter, is the clear situation that "the disciples sincerely believed the truth of the resurrection, which they proclaimed to their deaths.")

The statement above concerning "multiple, independent attestations of this burial story" took Strobel into another key point: The alleged contradictions in the four Gospels' accounts. Dr. Craig reviews the matters in light of the established intellectual disciples of philosophy and history: "The historian looks at these narratives and says, 'I see some inconsistencies, but I notice something about them: they're all in the secondary details.' The core of the story is the same: Joseph of Arimathea takes the body of Jesus, puts it in a tomb, the tomb is visited by a small group of women followers of Jesus early on the Sunday morning following... the tomb is empty. They see a vision of angels saying that Jesus is risen. The careful historian... says, 'This suggests that there is a historical core to this story that is reliable...' If there are some differences concerning the names of the women, the exact time of the morning, the number of the angels... those kinds of secondary discrepancies wouldn't bother a historian" (Dr. Craig, pp. 45-46).

Strobel notes that, "Even the usually skeptical historian Michael Grant, a fellow of Trinity College, Cambridge, and professor at Edinburgh University, concedes in his book *Jesus: An Historian's Review of the Gospels*, 'True, the discovery of the empty tomb is differently described by the various gospels, but if we apply the same sort of criteria that we would apply to any other ancient literary sources, then the evidence is firm and plausible enough to necessitate the conclusion that the tomb was, indeed found empty' " (p. 46 of Strobel's book)

Strobel goes on to note that, "Sometimes while covering criminal trials, I've seen witnesses give the same exact testimony, down to the nitty gritty details, only to find themselves ripped apart by the defense attorney for having colluded before the trial." Dr. Craig agrees with this assessment that the minor divergences show the Gospels "had separate, independent sources" (p. 47). Strobel goes on to reflect on a variety of fairly easy harmonizations of the remarked-on "discrepancies."

Other notes on the reliability of the narratives include the oft-cited point that the women would not have been invented as the first witnesses to the Resurrection, since in that society "they weren't even allowed to serve as legal witnesses in a Jewish court of law" (p. 50). The reason for their presence in the Bible narratives is thus "the reality that — like it or not — they *were* the discoverers of the empty tomb! This shows that the gospel writers faithfully recorded what happened, even if it was embarrassing.

This bespeaks the historicity of this tradition rather than its legendary status" (Dr. Craig, p. 50).

The empty tomb featured in early Christian preaching, from the seminal day of Pentecost (Acts 2:24), to Paul's speech recorded in Acts 13:29-31, to such other notes as Paul's statement that "if Christ has not been raised, your faith is futile," 1 Cor 15:17. Dr. Craig pointed out to Strobel that "if it weren't empty, it would be impossible for a movement founded on belief in the resurrection to have come into existence in the same city where this man had been publicly executed and buried" (p. 53). (He discusses other skeptical objections also — if the women had gone to the wrong tomb, "the authorities would have been only too happy to point out the tomb," p. 55; as to the early and reliable status of Mark's passion narrative source, "there's evidence it was written before A.D. 37," p. 53. The literary nature of the account also testifies, as it lacks the "flowery narratives" of apocryphal accounts from the second century.)

Dr. Craig argues that, "The hypothesis that God raised Jesus from the dead is not at all improbable... What is improbable is the hypothesis that Jesus rose naturally from the dead... the hypothesis that God raised Jesus from the dead doesn't contradict science or any known facts of experience... [if] God exists..." (p. 56).

Question #3: The question of Jesus' appearances post-Resurrection took Strobel to Dr. Gary Habermas, who has authored seven books on the subject. Habermas began with the 1 Corinthians passage noted earlier. "Here were names of specific individuals and groups of people who saw him, written at a time when people could still check them out if they wanted confirmation." Dr. Habermas cited five key elements in the Corinthians passage that verify it as being a "creed" of the early Church, rather than "just the words of Paul" (p. 65). That this passage is an early creed "is an assessment that's shared by a wide range of scholars from across a broad theological spectrum" (p. 66).

Paul's Greek verb in Galatians 1:18-19 indicates that he investigated the experience of Peter and James carefully when he met with them in Jerusalem after his conversion. Dr. Habermas noted that, "One of the very few Jewish New Testament scholars, Pinchas Lapide, says the evidence in support of the creed is so strong that it 'may be considered as a statement of eyewitnesses' (p. 67)... German historian Hans von Campenhausen says, 'This account meets all the demands of historical reliability that could possibly be made of such a text' " (p. 70).

The total list of appearances that Jesus made after resurrection includes: to Mary Magdalene; to a group of other women; to Cleopas and another disciple on the road from Jerusalem to Emmaus; to eleven disciples (Luke 24); to ten disciples and others, with Thomas absent (John 20:19-24); to Thomas and the other disciples (John 20:26-29); to seven disciples (John 21); to the disciples (Mt. 28) and at the Mount of Olives before his ascension. In all, "here was a wealth of sightings of Jesus... not merely a fleeting observance of a shadowy figure by one or two people. There were multiple appearances to numerous people..." (p. 72 - 73). Scholar John Drane concluded: "The earliest evidence we have for the resurrection almost certainly goes back to the time immediately after the resurrection event is alleged to have taken place. This is the evidence contained in the early sermons in the Acts of the Apostles..." (p. 73-74). Strobel framed the extent of the testimony: "If you were to call each one of the witnesses to a court of law to be cross-examined for just fifteen minutes each, and you went around the clock without a break, it would take you from breakfast on Monday until dinner on Friday to hear them all" (p. 76).

This forced Strobel to assess other possible explanations: that the reports are merely legends that grew up over time; or that they were hallucinations. But Dr. Habermas dispelled them: "Legend can tell you how a story got bigger; it can't tell you how it originated when the participants are both eyewitnesses and reported the events early... The best reasons for rejecting the legend theory come from the early creedal accounts in 1

Corinthians 15 and Acts, both of which predate the gospel material" (p. 78). For the hallucinations issue, Dr. Habermas had consulted a psychologist whose qualifications were "a doctorate, a professor for twenty years, the author of dozens of books on psychological issues, president of a national association of psychologists" (p. 79). This expert's assessment was: "Hallucinations are individual occurrences. By their very nature only one person can see a given hallucination at a time... Neither is it possible that one person could somehow induce an hallucination in somebody else... others cannot witness it." But as Dr. Habermas noted, the early records regarding Jesus showed "repeated accounts of Jesus appearing to multiple people who reported the same thing." After assessing factors influencing hallucinations, Dr. Habermas pointed out the obvious conclusion: "Over a course of many weeks, people from all sorts of backgrounds, all kinds of temperaments, in various places, all experienced hallucinations? That strains the hypothesis..." (p. 80).

Dr. Habermas quoted prominent theologian and historian Carl Braaten: "Even the more skeptical historians agree that for primitive Christianity... the resurrection of Jesus from the dead was a real event in history, the very foundation of faith, and not a mythical idea arising out of the creative imagination of believers" (p. 81).

The assessment by philosopher J. P. Moreland "clinched the case" for Strobel: "When Jesus was crucified... his followers were discouraged and depressed... they dispersed... Then, after a short period of time, we see them abandoning their occupations, regathering, and committing themselves to spreading a very specific message — that Jesus Christ was the Messiah of God who died on a cross, returned to life, and was seen alive by them. And they were willing to spend the rest of their lives proclaiming this, without any payoff from a human point of view. They faced a life of hardship. They often went without food, slept exposed to the elements, were ridiculed, beaten, imprisoned. And finally, most of them were executed in torturous ways. For what? For good intentions? No, because they were convinced beyond a shadow of a doubt that they had seen Jesus Christ alive from the dead" (p. 87).

Strobel recounts that the conclusion brought him "something exhilarating: *the rush of reason*" (p. 89, emphasis his). After he prayed to God and committed himself, "my character, values, attitude, priorities, worldview, philosophy, and relationships began to change — for the good." The change was so pronounced that his five-year-old daughter said to his wife, "Mommy, I want God to do for me what he's done for Daddy."

===================

Our short "recap" cannot do justice to Mr. Strobel's research and presentation. The book is only 95 pages including the notes, pages smaller than these — a convenient pocketbook! (My copy cost $2.99 at the local Bible bookstore). The "evidence" of personal transformation — from Strobel's self-description as "a father who had been profane, angry, verbally harsh, drunken, and all too often absent" (p. 89) to one so pleasing to his daughter — *that* is "evidence" which brings the reality of the risen Christ into the present.

As an aside, we are contemplating a follow-on book which would delve more extensively into this evidence, drawing on varied sources, from personal experience of friends, to American books, perhaps to a recent documentary done by a Chinese filmmaker about personal transformations in China today — please notify us if you would be interested. (The Chinese documentary was shown across China for better awareness of religious movements, by the bureaucracy responsible for overseeing religious affairs in China! [to bureau officials, not the public, it seems. The DVDs are available outside of China.) [234]

This current presence, of the living Jesus as evidence, was discussed earlier in this present book in terms of my own (your author's) experience, and also my friend Virginia's (Postscript #1 and Chapter 18).

The thorough Internet-surfer will find that there are people today who actually deny the historical reality of Jesus — that he in fact walked the earth, let alone who he was and is —

Strobel's larger work *The Case for Christ*, from which *The Case for Easter* is excerpted, deals with this by showing a number of non-Christian sources that document Jesus' existence.

A note from your author: We have included this Appendix as a tribute to the merit of the original work (and the other works in Mr. Strobel's *Case for...* series). We receive no marketing revenue or other consideration for doing this; like Strobel's own search, we want you to find and be blessed by the truth.

We summarize below the scope of additional information in Strobel's Case for Christ (page 179, our Annotated Bibliography).

==

For those seeking further reading on assessing the Resurrection, note that the frontispiece for N. T. Wright's *The Resurrection of the Son of God* cites Richard Ostling of the Associated Press describing that book as the "most monumental defense of the Easter heritage in decades ... a clearly organized case that confronts every major doubt about Easter, ancient and modern."

Also, Gary Habermas, mentioned above by Strobel, presents a video "The Resurrection Argument That Changed a Generation of Scholars" at youtube.com/watch?v=ay_Db4RwZ_M. His book *The Case for the Resurrection of Jesus* (2004) may be more accessible than Wright (it's under 400 pages), and is well-reported, but I have been unable to read everything that commends itself. His website is garyhabermas.com. [Habermas's books also include *The Historical Jesus: Ancient Evidence for the Life of Christ* (College Press, 1996).]

For more of what Bishop Wright covers, we might cite his conclusion on p. 718: "*The standard alternative theories have been ruled out, explicitly or implicitly, as we have made our way through this book. The common idea that, when the early Christians said, 'Jesus was raised from the dead,' they meant something like 'He is alive in a spiritual, non-bodily sense, and we give him our allegiance as our lord' is historically impossible. Not only, as we saw in Part I, did the words simply not mean that; one might as well say that 'Jesus was crucified by the Romans' meant neither more nor less than 'As I think of Jesus, I experience a sense of the crushing power of pagan empire.' If the early Christians had meant that, a belief of that kind could not explain, either within the second-Temple Jewish world or that of first-century paganism, why they hailed Jesus as Messiah and lord, or in particular, why their belief about their own future resurrection took the very precise shape it did (Part III). The suggestion that Paul's view of the resurrection (of Christians, and of Jesus) had nothing to do with what we think of as a 'body' has been shown in Part II to be exegetically unfounded. The idea that there were two parallel streams of 'resurrection' belief in early Christianity, one going from Paul to Rheginos and the other going from Luke and John to Tertullian, is ruled out by the evidence surveyed in Parts II and particularly III. The widespread belief that the resurrection accounts in the Gospels are back-projections of Christian belief from the middle or late first century simply will not work, as I have argued in Part IV... These are the major counter-proposals, the main ways in which, over the last century or so, the inference to the best explanation has been avoided... historical argument is remarkably good at clearing away the undergrowth behind which skepticisms of various sorts have been hiding. The proposal that Jesus was bodily raised from the dead possesses unrivalled power to explain the historical data at the heart of early Christianity."*

When confronting the superficial certainty of the God-deniers, the thinker might remember Habermas' penetrating insight that "the naturalistic alternatives to Jesus' resurrection favored by some were also frequently rejected by others. For example, David Strauss belittled the swoon theory held by Friedrich Schleiermacher, Heinrich Paulus, and others. Strauss concluded that such a scenario would utterly fail to account for the disciples' passionate belief that Jesus had been raised from the dead as the Lord of life."[235] The acid of scorn that you may find poured over your faith, if you choose to believe Jesus,[236] becomes even more intense when the skeptics of differing "counter" viewpoints face each other — because those analyses, as Wright assessed in such depth, just do not truly fit reality.

Appendix Three: Bibliography
Section One: Standard Listing

(An "annotated" bibliography section follows, discussing the merits of selected books. Books marked with "*" are of special remark there. In this first bibliography, we also list by *title* some key books mentioned in our narrative, in case people remember the title of the book and look for it (as your author tends to do!)

Section Three of this Appendix lists Bible translations ("versions") we have used, with comments and an example verse.

100-Minute Bible (a condensation able to be read in 100 minutes, for basic acquaintance with the Bible story): See Hinton, Michael.

Abegg, Martin Jr., et al. *The Dead Sea Scrolls Bible: The Oldest Known Bible Translated for the First Time into English.* New York NY: HarperCollins 1999 (endnote 229 discusses what this research has shown).

Accompany Them with Singing: See Long, Thomas.

Aikman, David. *Jesus in Beijing.* Washington DC: Regnery 2003.

Alexander, Denis. *Creation or Evolution: Do We Have to Choose?** Oxford UK & Grand Rapids MI: Monarch Books 2008.

Alexander, Fr. (Alexander Men). *An Inner Step Toward* ***God***: writings and teachings on prayer. Brewster MA: Paraclete Press 2014 (bold emphasis per the book. Fr. Alexander was martyred in 1990).

Allen, Leonard , Ph.D., compiler. *The Contemporaries Meet the Classics on Prayer.* West Monroe LA: Howard Publishing 2003.

ALPHA course:* Website alphausa.org (has links for other countries). The video course series is offered by various churches, which can be located from that website. Companion books are offered for the text-inclined, including *Searching Issues* (Nicky Gumbel) and others.

Apostolic Fathers: See Lightfoot, J. B.

Aulen, Gustav. *Christus Victor: An Historical Study of the Three Main Types of the Idea of the Atonement.** New York NY: Collier Books Macmillan 1986. Original publication 1931. (Collier Books edition 1986 with foreword by Jaroslav Pelikan is ISBN 0-02-083400-4.)[237]

Baker, Mark. *Recovering the Scandal*... See Green, Joel.

Bartlett's Familiar Quotations: My copy (a family heirloom) is the Eleventh Edition, *Familiar Quotations... by John Bartlett*; Christopher Morley, ed. Garden City NY: Garden City Publishing Co. 1944.

Battle of Beginnings, The: See Ratzsch, Dell.

Behe, Dr. Michael J. *Darwin's Black Box: The Biochemical Challenge to*

*Evolution.** New York NY: Free Press/Simon & Schuster 1996. Tenth anniversary edition, 2006.*

Belcher, Jim. *Deep Church: A Third Way Beyond Emerging and Traditional.* Downers Grove IL: IVP Books 2009.

Berlinski, David. *The Devil's Delusion: Atheism and Its Scientific Pretensions.** New York NY: Crown Publishing/Random House 2008.

Bettenson, Henry. *Documents of the Christian Church.* Oxford and New York: Oxford University Press, 2nd edition 1963.

Bible versions: See the third section of this Bibliography, "Bible Versions and Resources," for full titles and some comments on the differences. (Also Publishers listing, pp. 129-130. We have noted elsewhere that, "Basically, they all say the same thing, 'Jesus Christ, Son of God, Savior.'") Free "versions" (translations) available are noted in that section of the Bibliography.

Black Buffalo: See Wilson, Ray "Black Buffalo."

Bosworth, F. F. *Christ The Healer,** published in 1924, reprinted 2004 by Chosen Books/Baker Publishing, Grand Rapids MI.

Bottomly, Colonel Heath, *Prodigal Father.** Happy Camp CA 96039: Naturegraph Publishers 1975.

Brokering, Herbert, Ed. *Luther's Prayers.* Minneapolis MN: Augsburg Publishing 1967.

Bruce, F. F. *Paul: Apostle of the Heart Set Free.** Grand Rapids MI: Wm. B. Eerdmans 1977, reprinted 1998.

Burpo, Todd. *Heaven Is for Real.** Nashville TN: Thomas Nelson 2010.

Byrd, David. *Living a Spiritual Life: On the Wings of Eagles.* Baltimore MD: PublishAmerica 2006. Out of print [this update note 2018].

Canfield, Jack , et al. *Chicken Soup for the Christian Soul: 101 Stories to Open the Heart and Rekindle the Spirit.* Deerfield Beach FL: Health Communications 1997. (Website chickensoup.com has special editions for demographic groups.)

Carroll, Vincent, and David Shiflett. *Christianity on Trial: Arguments Against Anti-Religious Bigotry.** San Francisco CA: Encounter Books 2002.

Case for Easter: See Strobel, Lee.

CEV *Contemporary English Version* Bible © 1995 by American Bible Society. See Section Three of this Bibliography Appendix.

Chambers, Oswald. *My Utmost for His Highest.* Original © 1935, renewed 1963. Various editions incl. BarbourBooks.com. "Most popular book of daily devotions ever published" per its introduction to Barbour Books edition.

Cherokee People… from Earliest Origins… See Mails, Thomas E.

Chicken Soup for the Christian Soul: See Canfield, Jack. (Note website.)

Christ the Eternal Tao: See "Hieromonk Damascene."

Christianity on Trial: See Carroll, Vincent. (A different book from Mark Lanier's *Christianity on Trial: A Lawyer Examines the Christian Faith*.*)

Christus Victor: See Aulen, Gustav.

Closer to the Light: See Morse, Melvin.

Collins, Dr. Francis S. *The Language of God: A Scientist Presents Evidence for Belief.* New York NY: Free Press/Simon & Schuster 2006.

Colson, Charles. *Loving God: An Inspiring Message and a Challenge to All Christians*. Grand Rapids MI: Zondervan. Man in the Mirror ed. 2002.

Coming to Peace With Science: See Falk, Darrel.

Copan, Paul. *Is God a Moral Monster: Making Sense of the Old Testament God*. Baker Books 2011.

Copeland, Kenneth and Gloria. *Pursuit of His Presence*, Tulsa, OK: Harrison House 1998. (A daily devotional book; also, there is a 2012 special edition of their 1992 devotional *From Faith to Faith: A Daily Guide to Victory.* [238])

Copeland, Kenneth. *The Blessing of the Lord.* He quotes Prov. 10:22 (NKJV) in its entirety for his full title[239] (kcm.org), 2011

Craig, William Lane. *On Guard: Defending Your Faith with Reason and Precision*. Colorado Springs CO: Cook Communications 2010.

Cross, The: Jesus in China (DVD): See Zhiming, Yuan.

Devotionals: see "Prayerbook"

Doubts About Darwin: See Woodward, Thomas.

Eldredge, John. *The Way of the Wild Heart: A Map for the Masculine Journey** (six stages of a man's life). Nashville TN: Thomas Nelson 2006.

Elwell, Walter. *Evangelical Dictionary of Biblical Theology.* Grand Rapids MI: Baker Books 1996.

Encyclopedia of Catholicism: See McBrien.

e-Sword: free Bible-study software from website e-sword.net. A variety of translations *free*, including a more formal translation, "freer" versions, and "literal." See third section of this Bibliography.

Exodus DVD: "Patterns of Evidence," see p. 168-169 for info/website

Falk, Darrel R. *Coming to Peace With Science: Bridging the Worlds Between Faith and Biology*. Downers Grove IL: IVP Academic (ivpress.com) 2004.

Farasiotis, Dionysios. *The Gurus, the Young Man and Elder Paisios*. English edition: Platina CA: St. Herman Press 2008 (sainthermanmonastery.com). See also Elder Paisios.

Ferguson, Sinclair, et al, Eds. *New Dictionary of Theology*. Downers Grove IL: InterVarsity Press 1988.

Gallatin, Matthew. *Thirsting for God in a Land of Shallow Wells.** Ben

Lomond CA: Conciliar Press 2002.

Genesis Question: See Ross, Hugh

Gleick, James. *The Information: A History, A Theory, A Flood.* NY: Pantheon Books/Random House 2011.

GNT: *Good News Translation*, 2nd ed. 1992, American Bible Society.

Gonzalez, Guillermo, and Jay Richards. *The Privileged Planet.* Book format Regnery Publishing 2004; DVD Illustra Media 2006.

Gospel of John (DVD). Visual Bible International/Buena Vista Home Entertainment 2003. ISBN 0-7888-5919-6.

Graham, Billy. *The Journey.* Nashville TN: Thomas Nelson 2006.

Green, Joel, and Mark Baker. *Recovering the Scandal of the Cross: Atonement in New Testament and Contemporary Contexts.* 2nd ed. Downers Grove IL: IVP Academic 2011.

Guillebaud, Jean Claude. *Re-founding the World: A Western Testament,* English edition, New York NY: Algora Publishing (algora.com) 2001.

Guinness, Os. *Long Journey Home: A Guide to Your Search for the Meaning of Life.* Colorado Springs: Waterbrook Press/Random House) 2001.

Gumbel, Nicky. *Searching Issues.* Colorado Springs CO: Cook Communications Ministries 1996. This is one of several books used with the ALPHA course (see Annotated Bibliography for that).

Habermas, Gary. *The Historical Jesus: Ancient Evidence for the Life of Christ.** Joplin MO: College Press 1996.

Harris, Alex and Brett. *Do Hard Things: A Teenage Rebellion Against Low Expectations.* Colorado Springs CO: Multnomah Books/Random House 2008.

Hart, David Bentley. *The Experience of God: Being, Consciousness, Bliss.** New Haven and London: Yale University Press 2013

Heath, Chip and Dan Heath. *Made to Stick: Why Some Ideas Survive and Others Die.* New York NY: Random House 2008.

Hicks, Bishop F. C. N. "Nugent," D.D. *The Fullness of Sacrifice: An Essay in Reconciliation.* London: Society for Promoting Christian Knowledge. First published by Macmillan & Co., 1930; 3rd ed. 1944.

Hieromonk Damascene. *Christ the Eternal Tao.* Platina CA: St. Herman Press (sainthermanmonastery.com), 2004.

Hinton, Michael (the abridger). *The 100-Minute Bible.* A condensation designed to be read in 100 minutes, for basic acquaintance with the Bible story. Canterbury Kent England: The 100-minute Press, first American edition, 2006. Website: the100-minutepress.com.

Holladay, W. L. *The Psalms Through Three Thousand Years: Prayerbook of a Cloud of Witnesses.* Fortress 1993. ["Prayer-book" entry has comment.]

Homosexuality and the Christian: See Yarhouse; see endnote 237 here.

How Christianity Changed the World: See Schmidt, A. J.

Hyatt, Eddie. *2000 Years of Charismatic Christianity* (2002), & *The Azusa Street Revival: The Holy Spirit in America — 100 Years* (2006). Lake Mary FL: Charisma House.

Jeffrey, Steven, et al. *Pierced for Our Transgressions: Rediscovering the Glory of Penal Substitution.* Nottingham England: Inter-Varsity Press 2007.

Jeremiah, Dr. David. *In the Words of Jesus.* Carol Stream IL: Tyndale House 2014. His website davidjeremiah.org.

Jesus in Beijing: See Aikman, David.

Jesus: Fact or Fiction: An Interactive Journey* (DVD). San Clemente CA: Inspirational Films 2003.

John, Peter. *The Gospel According to Peter John.* Fairbanks Alaska: University of Alaska Fairbanks/Alaska Native Knowledge Network 1996. Website ankn.uaf.edu offers free PDF download, 23 June 2019.

Johnson, Bill. *When Heaven Invades Earth: A Practical Guide to a Life of Miracles.* Shippensburg PA: Treasure House/Destiny Image 2003.

Johnson, Luke T. *The Real Jesus: The Misguided Quest for the Historical Jesus and the Truth of the Traditional Gospels.* Harper SF 1996

Johnson, Phillip E. *Reason in the Balance: The Case Against NATURALISM in Science, Law & Education.* [Emphasis his]. Downers Grove IL: InterVarsity 1995.

JPS: Bible translation (Old Testament only) by the Jewish Publication Society. The 1917 edition is free with the Bible study software e-Sword (that free software is discussed in Section Three of Bibliography). There is a recent version called *The Tanakh*, which I do not have -- your author.)

Keener, Craig. *Miracles: The Credibility of the New Testament Accounts.** Baker Academic 2011.

Keller, Rev. Timothy. *The Reason for God: Belief in an Age of Skepticism.** New York NY: Riverhead Books 2008. (He is not related to the author Bob Keller of this present book.) [see also endnote 92 for a similar 2019 work]

Kelly, J. N. D. *Early Christian Doctrines.* San Francisco CA: HarperSanFrancisco 1978.

KJV: *King James Version,* Bible translated under the authority of the King of England and published first in 1611. See Index for discussion of some readings in KJV that are still particularly beneficial.

Kostenberger, Andreas, and Michael Kruger. *The Heresy of Orthodoxy: How Contemporary Culture's Fascination with Diversity Has Reshaped Our Understanding of Early Christianity. (Mentioned in Appendix 7.)* Wheaton

IL: Crossway 2010.

Lamsa, George. *Holy Bible From the Ancient Eastern Text...From the Aramaic of the Peshitta*. 1933 by A. J. Holman Co. (Harper & Row Publishers, New York NY are listed for inquiries). ISBN 0-06-064923-2. See section three of this Bibliography.

Lattimore, Richmond. *The New Testament Translated by Richmond Lattimore.** New York, NY: North Point Press/Farrar, Strauss and Giroux 1996.

Lennox, John. *God and Stephen Hawking: Whose Design Is It Anyway?* Oxford England: Lion Hudson 2011.

Lewis, C. S. *God in the Dock*. Grand Rapids MI: Eerdmans 1970 by trustees of his estate.

Lewis, C. S. *Mere Christianity*. Fount 1952.

Lewis, C. S. *The Problem of Pain*. New York NY: Simon & Schuster 1996.

Lightfoot, J. B., & Harmer, J. R., translators. *The Apostolic Fathers*, 2nd ed., Michael W. Holmes, Editor. Grand Rapids MI: Baker Book House 1989.

Lindsell, Harold. *The Battle for the Bible*. Grand Rapids MI: Zondervan 1976.

LITV: *Literal Version*, a Bible translation by Jay P. Green 1976, free at e-Sword.net. See Section Three of this Bibliography Appendix.

Long Journey Home: See Guinness, Os.

Long, Thomas. *Accompany Them with Singing: The Christian Funeral.* Westminster John Knox Press 2009.

Lopez, Barry, *Arctic Dreams: Imagination and Desire in a Northern Landscape.* New York NY: Bantam Books 1986.

Loving God: See Colson, Charles.

Luther's Prayers: See Brokering, Herbert.

LXX: See Septuagint; also see Section Three of this Bibliography.

Mac, Toby. *Under God.* Grand Rapids MI: Bethany House/Baker Publishing 2004. An unusual cover set-up adds, "Triumph and Tragedy: Stories of America's Spiritual Battle," but the publishing data does not appear to have this as part of the title.

Mails, Thomas E. *The Cherokee People: The Story of the Cherokees from Earliest Origins to Contemporary Times*. New York NY: Marlowe & Co. 1992.

McBrien, Richard, Gen. Ed. *The HarperCollins Encyclopedia of Catholicism.* New York NY: HarperCollins 1995. (This is not a Catholic church publication, as discussed in the final part of endnote 187.)

McDowell, Josh. *The New Evidence That Demands a Verdict*. Nashville TN: Thomas Nelson 1999.

McGrath, Alistair. *Understanding the Trinity* (Kingsway Publications

1987).

McGuckin, John Anthony. *The Westminster Handbook to Patristic Theology.* Louisville KY & London England: Westminster John Knox Press 2004.

Men, Fr.: See Alexander, Fr. (Alexander Men).

Metzger, Bruce M. *A Textual Commentary on the Greek New Testament.* Stuttgart: German Bible Society. 2nd ed. 1994.

Metzger, Bruce M., Ed. *The Oxford Companion to the Bible.* New York NY and Oxford England: Oxford University 1993.

Meyer, Stephen C. *Darwin's Doubt: The Explosive Origin of Animal Life and the Case for Intelligent Design.* New York NY: HarperOne/ HarperCollins 2013. His website stephencmeyer.org. [See endnote 250 for update.]

Meyer, Stephen C. *Signature in the Cell: DNA and the Evidence for Intelligent Design.* New York NY: HarperOne/HarperCollins 2009.

Midgley, Mary. *Evolution as a Religion: Strange Hopes and Stranger Fears.* London England & New York NY: Routledge Classics/Taylor & Francis Group, revised edition 2002.

Morrow, Jonathan, *Welcome to College: A Christ-follower's Guide for the Journey.* Grand Rapids MI: Kregel Publications 2008.

Morse, Dr. Melvin, et al, *Closer to the Light.* New York NY: Villard Books/Random House 1990.

Moynahan, Brian. *The Faith: A History of Christianity.* New York NY & London England: Doubleday 2002.

Murray, Andrew, D.D. *Abiding in Christ: A Classic Devotional Updated for Today.* Grand Rapids MI: Bethany House/Baker Publishing Group 2003 (original 1895; this edition a *Billy Graham Special Edition).*

Murray, Andrew, D.D. *The Power of the Blood of Jesus.* London England: Marshall Morgan 1935.

Murray, Michael J., Ed. *Reason for the Hope Within.* Grand Rapids MI: Eerdmans Publishing 1998.

My Utmost for His Highest: See Chambers, Oswald.

NASB: *New American Standard Bible.* La Habra CA: The Lockman Foundation (C) 1960-1995. Website lockman.org. See Section Three of this Bibliography Appendix.

Nee, Watchman, *The Spiritual Man.* Translated from the Chinese. New York NY: Christian Fellowship Publishers 1968.

NIV: *New International Version* Bible. See Section Three of this Bibliography Appendix. The 2011 edition is replacing the 1984 edition. Biblica, Zondervan. [NIV Study Bible, Kenneth Barker General Editor, was Grand Rapids MI: Zondervan, © 1985]

NKJV: *New King James Version* Bible. Thomas Nelson 1982. See Section Three of this Bibliography Appendix.

NLT: *New Living Translation* Bible © 1996, 2004 by Tyndale House, Carol Stream IL 60188. See Section Three.
NRSV: *New Revised Standard Version*, Bible © 1989, Division of Christian Education, National Council of the Churches of Christ in the United States of America. See Section Three.
Orthodox Study Bible (OSB), published by St. Athanasius Academy of Orthodox Theology. Elk Grove CA 2008. Uses NKJV for New Testament. Uses their own recent translation from Alfred Rahlf's critical text of the Septuagint for the Old Testament. See Section Three of this Bibliography Appendix.
Orthodox Way, The: See Ware, Bishop.
Oxford Companion to the Bible: See Metzger, Bruce.
Paisios (Elder Paisios of Mount Athos), *Spiritual Counsels*: Vol. I *With Pain and Love for Contemporary Man* (2nd ed. 2007), Vol. II *Spiritual Awakening,* 2008; *Epistles,* 2002. sainthermanmonastery.com. All posthumous (he passed on in 1994[240]). See also Farasiotis in "Annotated Bibliography" (p. 178).
Passion Translation, The. Brian Simmons. 2nd ed. 2018 BroadStreet Publishing Group, LLC. [New Testament, Psalms, Proverbs, Song]
Payton, James R. *Light from the Christian East.* Downers Grove IL: IVP Academic 2007.
Pearcey, Nancy. *Saving Leonardo: A Call to Resist the Secular Assault on Mind, Morals and Meaning.* Nashville TN: B&H Publishing Group 2010.
Pelikan, Jaroslav. *The Emergence of the Catholic Tradition (100 - 600 A.D.).* Chicago IL & London England: University of Chicago Press 1971. This is Volume 1 of his *The Christian Tradition: A History of the Development of Doctrine.* "Catholic" here refers to "universal, church-wide" rather than Roman Catholic.
Peter, Dr. Laurence J. *Peter's Quotations: Ideas for Our Times.* New York NY: William Morrow & Co. 1977.
Philokalia: The Eastern Christian Spiritual Texts: Selections Annotated and Explained. Woodstock VT: SkyLight Paths Publishing © 2006)
Pierced for Our Transgressions: Rediscovering the Glory of Penal Substitution: see Jeffrey, Steven; Michael Ovey and Andrew Sach.
Piper, J. & Taylor, J., Gen. Eds. *The Supremacy of Christ in a Postmodern World.** Wheaton IL: Crossway Books; (C) 2007 desiringGod.org.
Plantinga, Cornelius, Jr. *Not the Way It's Supposed to Be: A Breviary of Sin.** Grand Rapids MI: Eerdmans; Leicester England: Apollos; 1995.
Polkinghorne, John, and Beale, Nicholas. *Questions of Truth: Fifty-one Responses to Questions about God, Science, and Belief.* Louisville, KY: Westminster John Knox Press 2009.

Polkinghorne, John. *Belief in God in an Age of Science*. New Haven CT & London England: Yale University Press 1998.

Prayer-book: Holladay, *The Psalms...3000 Years...* above; Orthodox prayer book (Fr. Alexander, note 277) is: *Prayer Book*, Holy Trinity Monastery, Jordanville N.Y. 2011. *Book of Common Prayer* is now in updated English; & n.b. *Luther's Prayers* by Augsburg Publishing, 1967. Devotionals aid prayer; above, n.b. Copelands' & O. Chambers' *My Utmost for His Highest.* N.B. also *Drawing Near with Daily Bible Reading and Prayer,* K. Boa & M. Anders, Nashville TN: Thomas Nelson 1987 (BGEA edition. A 31-day journey.) (*In Psalms*, the reader will find places where the human-ness of the speaker comes dramatically into focus — this was before Jesus' teaching to love enemies, pray for those who misuse us. (E.g. Psa 140:9)

Pray for how to go! "The Lord is my shepherd" Ps. 23:1.

Prodigal Father: See Bottomly, Colonel Heath (note: this is a different book from Rev. Timothy Keller's *Prodigal God,* as discussed in our Annotated Bibliography section).

Qureshi, Dr. Nabeel. *Seeking Allah, Finding Jesus: A Devout Muslim Encounters Christianity.** Grand Rapids MI: Zondervan 2014

Rana, Dr. Fazale. DVD "How to Build the Case for Biochemical Design."* Covina CA: Reasons to Believe [reasons.org] © 2017 (His book *The Cell's Design: How Chemistry Reveals the Creator's Artistry* is 2008.)

Ratzsch, Dell. *The Battle of Beginnings: Why Neither Side Is Winning the Creation-Evolution Debate.* Downers Grove IL: InterVarsity Press 1996.

Resurrection of Jesus the Christ: See Strobel, *Case for Easter;* Wright, N. T., *The Resurrection...* (& end of Appendix Two here for other references).

Rienecker, Fritz. *Linguistic Key to the Greek New Testament.* Grand Rapids MI: Zondervan 1976. (English translation of a work first published in Germany in the 1930s. Further editions were published after WWII.)

Robinson, Marilynne. *Absence of Mind: The Dispelling of Inwardness from the Modern Myth of the Self.* New Haven CT: Yale University Press 2010.

Ross, Hugh. *Beyond the Cosmos: What Recent Discoveries in Astronomy and Physics Reveal About the Nature of God.* Colorado Springs CO: NavPress 1996.

Ross, Hugh. *The Genesis Question,* 2nd ed. Colorado Springs CO: NavPress 2001.

Schmidt, A. J. *How Christianity Changed the World.** Grand Rapids MI: Zondervan 2001, 2004. (Original title was *Under the Influence.*)

Schroeder, Gerald. *The Science of God: The Convergence of Scientific and Biblical Wisdom.* New York NY: Free Press/Simon & Schuster 2009. His website geraldschroeder.com.

Searching Issues: See ALPHA and Gumbel, Nicky.

Septuagint (a.k.a. "LXX"): The Septuagint is the ancient translation of the Hebrew Old Testament, the first part of the Bible, into Greek, circa 200 B.C. It was "the Bible of the early Church." A recent translation from the critical text has been done by St. Athanasius Academy, published in *The Orthodox Study Bible;* see above, "Orthodox..." (The **"critical text"**[241] is done by comparative study of all available ancient manuscripts.)

Brenton's 1851 translation (London) has been often reprinted (my copy 1997, Hendrickson Publishers, USA). It is not critical text.

Seraphim, Fr. (Eugene Rose). *Genesis, Creation and Early Man: The Orthodox Christian Vision,** 2nd ed. Platina CA: St. Herman of Alaska Brotherhood (sainthermanmonastery.com) 2000, 2011.

Sidwell, Mark. *The Dividing Line: Understanding and Applying Biblical Separation.* Greenville SC: Journey Forth/BJU Press 1998.

Smith, James K. A. *How (Not) to Be Secular: Reading Charles Taylor.* Grand Rapids MI: Wm. Eerdmans Publishing 2014. (This book is an accessible summary or guide to Charles Taylor's monumental *A Secular Age.*)

Stark, Rodney. *For the Glory of God.** Princeton NJ: Princeton University Press 2003.

Stark, Rodney. *The Victory of Reason: How Christianity Led to Freedom, Capitalism and Western Success.** New York NY: Random House 2005.

Stowell, Joseph. *The Upside of Down: Finding Hope When It Hurts.* Grand Rapids MI: Discovery House 1991, 2006 (Billy Graham Library Edition).

Strobel, Lee. *The Case for a Creator: A Journalist Investigates Scientific Evidence That Points Toward God.* Grand Rapids MI: Zondervan 2004.

Strobel, Lee. *The Case for Easter.* Grand Rapids MI: Zondervan 2003. An excerpt from *The Case for Christ... The Evidence for Jesus* (Zondervan, 1998). (*The Case for Christ* is also available as a DVD.)

Strobel, Lee. *The Case for Faith: A Journalist Investigates the Toughest Objections to Christianity.** Grand Rapids MI: Zondervan 2000.

Strobel, Lee. *The Case for the Real Jesus: A Journalist Investigates Current Attacks on the Identity of Christ.** Grand Rapids MI: Zondervan 2007.

Tac, Pablo. Pamphlet "Indian Life at Mission San Luis Rey, By Pablo Tac, An Indian Neophyte, Written About 1835." Ed./trans. from Spanish text by Minna & Gordon Hewes. Vista CA: Hutchins Printing 1998 ed., adapted from 1958 ed., pub. by the Franciscan Fathers, Mission San Luis Rey.

Thaxton, Charles, et al, *The Mystery of Life's Origin** (1984) — was a free PDF at themysteryoflifesorigin.org/ but 23 June 2019, no longer there.

Tinerino, Dennis. *Supersize Your Faith: Tapping Into God's Miracle Power.* Destiny Image Publishers, 2007. ISBN-13: 978-0768424089.

Trimm, Cindy. *Commanding Your Morning: Unleash the power of God in your life.* Charisma House 2007.

Under God: see Mac, Toby.
Unlocking the Mystery of Life (DVD), 2002; Illustra Media 2010.
Van Huyssteen, J. Wentzel. *The Templeton Science and Religion Reader.*[242] West Conshohocken PA: Templeton Press 2012.
Wangerin, Walter, Jr. *The Book of God: The Bible as a Novel.* Grand Rapids MI: Zondervan 1996.
Ware, Bishop (Timothy) Kallistos. *The Orthodox Way.* Crestwood NY: St. Vladimir's Seminary Press 1979, 1995.
Warren, Rick. *The Purpose-Driven Life.* Grand Rapids MI: Zondervan 2002. [Group study formats available.]
Warren, Rick. *The Purpose-Driven Life: What on Earth Am I Here For?** Grand Rapids MI: Zondervan 2002 (zondervan.com)
Watch for the Light: Readings for Advent and Christmas. Paperback edition Maryknoll NY: Orbis Books 2004. No editor cited.
White, James Emery. *A Search for the Spiritual: Exploring Real Christianity.* Grand Rapids MI: Baker Books 1998 (BGEA edition).
Wilson, Ray "Black Buffalo." *Smoke Signals from God.* (Buffalo Media 2009; reprinted, new ISBN 978-0-578-04457-6. Website blackbuffalo.org.
Woodward, Thomas. *Darwin Strikes Back: Defending the Science of Intelligent Design.* Grand Rapids MI: Baker Books 2006.
Woodward, Thomas. *Doubts About Darwin: A History of Intelligent Design.** Grand Rapids MI: Baker Books 2003.
World Almanac and Book of Facts 2018, The. New York NY: World Almanac Books – an imprint of Infobase.
Wright, N. T. *The Resurrection of the Son of God.** Minneapolis MN: Fortress Press, first North American edition 2003.
Yarhouse, Dr. Mark A. *Homosexuality and the Christian: A Guide for Parents, Pastors, and Friends.*[243] Minneapolis MN: Bethany House 2010.
Yohannan, K. P. *Revolution in World Missions.* Carrollton TX: gfa books/Gospel for Asia, 1986 - 2004; gfa.org or phone 972-300-7777. GFA works by indigenous missionaries in Asian societies. Free on request. gfa.org/response for their statement regarding recent lawsuit settlement.
Young, William Paul. *The Shack: Where Tragedy Confronts Eternity.* Newbury Park CA: Windblown Media 2007.
Yount, Bill. *I Heard Heaven Proclaim: Prophetic Words of Encouragement.* Hagerstown MD: McDougall Publishing 2004.
Zhiming, Yuan. DVD "The Cross: Jesus in China."* Petaluma CA: China Soul for Christ Foundation 2003 (chinasoul.org/home for English; DVD is under the "documentary" link).
"*" means this work is discussed in "Annotated Bibliography."

Bibliography, Section Two
Annotated Bibliography:
Comments on books & DVDs

This book reflects a personal journey through life, one of many decades; it reflects also a journey among books of a variety of types. There is no shortage of books in any of these areas, and many readers will feel that different books should be brought to the seeker's attention. Oh well! Comments appreciated.

This section gives my observations on a number of these books, grouped by topics. The topics are shown in bold, e.g. "**science seen more carefully,**" **"basic understandings" (of the revelation of Jesus), "trouble"** and **"adventure reading."**

For a thoughtful presentation of the story of Jesus, in His human incarnation, the DVD "The Gospel of John" (ISBN 0-7888-5919-6) was good. It brings the radiance of Jesus to scenes where other presentations do not do this as beautifully. For a basic *intellectual* overview, building the case for reasonableness, *A Search for the Spiritual*, by James White, covers things so well that I wished I had written it [see endnote 92 for a late-arriving excellent book on current intellectual objections]. For other deep cuts, Strobel's works, discussed more below; and for a deeper take on the range of human religious thought, Os Guinness' work, which surveys the scope of human thought, and processes what is the most reasonable and fruitful place to be among the many options — quoted extensively in Chapter 10. DVD's on the intellectual-focus include "The Case for Christ" and **"Jesus: Fact or Fiction."** The first is Strobel's; the latter has a number of experts testifying on the range of issues, accessible through a *"map" of the landscape of questions.* It also includes the famous "Jesus" film which has been taken all over the world, in over 1,700 languages, to introduce the story of His life, using Luke's Gospel.[244]

Well, esteemed reader, this book has brought you a lot of information, so let's list the bold topic headings of the following sections to help you navigate any areas that appeal to your interests:

Some personal observations
Church-and-society
Books on science seen more carefully
Basic understandings
On walking more closely with God
Comparative religion and philosophy
Deeper Philosophy
The **Resurrection of Jesus** the Christ
Miracles
Of note in other regards
Trouble
A **different sort** *The Bible re-presented as a novel*
Adventure reading
Considering Reality Empirically

Some personal observations: For understanding and spiritual building-up, *The Orthodox Way* has done me more good than other single book. It does not argue "the case for…" but rather it explains the Orthodox Christian understanding of God, Christ, Christ's work and His* offer to us. For clarity on the science-versus religion issue, Berlinski and Polkinghorne have provided me the deepest penetration; many others have been of great value, as discussed in that section, below, but these have fit more deeply into the overall perspective. Fascinating aspects of "Intelligent Design" take my interest, but this seems to be a field in which controversy is still valid, as discussed in the main text. See especially Denis Alexander, below (quoted on pp. 87-88 above). Also, note discussions per "information" in the Index. (Woodward's *Doubts About Darwin* was transformative for my own outlook on the controversy of interpreting biological data. He maps the flow of the arguments over the decades.)

Lee Strobel's books have covered so many issues, and I find them such stimulating reads, that a separate section is devoted to them below (pp. 178-179, after the section on "Comparative religion and philosophy").

For removing some of the shallow Bible-versus-science arguments tracking to the Bible's Genesis creation account, Hugh Ross (*Genesis Question*) has been of great value to me (note also Schroeder, our chapter 16). For present-day intellectual controversies, Rev. Timothy Keller (no relation) has some of the most advanced material I have been blessed to see. Lee Strobel's research series (*Case for Christ, Case for a Creator, Case for Faith, Case for the Real Jesus*) are very readable, engaging, and thought-provoking. (More on these further below).

A different resource is the ALPHA course, which goes through 13 once-a-week meetings centered on videos to give a *thoughtful and reasoned introduction to the whole Christian understanding* of God, Christ, life, and worship. The course is designed for a series of dinner meetings, with group viewing and conversation. It is narrated by Nicky Gumbel, whose sense of humor is more edifying than much of what is offered as humor today. (For different formats on introductory overview, the American Bible Society has a variety of materials at website americanbible.org. I was informed that this included a 40-segment **podcast**, but I have not looked into that. There are endless opportunities for research!)

In terms of **church-and-society**, tracing what the impacts have been,[245] Guillebaud's *Re-founding the World: A Western Testament* can be eye-opening, as to how much of our basic values — equality, liberty, etc. — are owed to Christ and Christianity[246] — so also *How Christianity Changed the World*, although its viewpoints are sometimes polemical. Rodney Stark's books (such as *For the Glory of God*, and *The Victory of Reason: How Christianity Led to Freedom, Capitalism and Western Success*) provide many factual counterpoints to common criticisms of the history and impacts. Lee Strobel's *The Case for the Real Jesus* debunks many current misrepresentations about Jesus in the context of world religions. His earlier works *The Case for Christ, Case for a Creator* and *The Case for Faith* provide similarly fact-intense treatment, accessibly written, on the range of issues. Personally, I have found them so readable and cogent, that a short section 4 pages further down is devoted to listing the contents of each of these works by Strobel.

Timothy Keller's *The Reason for God* assesses current objections to Christ and the faith, by a pastor who has spent years working in Manhattan with people whose intellectual questions are well-sharpened and sincere. Due to the strength of that environment (regarding bringing the issues) and his response, we devote more space to this work later.

We give **R. Stark and T. Keller** further treatment in a section devoted to Lee Strobel and them, following the "Comparative Religion and Philosophy" section below.

Christianity on Trial is a bit heavier read than Strobel's books, although perhaps not as polemical as *How Christianity Changed the World* (but then, if you've been reading/hearing anti-Christian polemics, shouldn't you absorb the "pro"?). Carroll & Shiflett discuss Christianity and slavery, science, "slaughter of the innocents," the Third Reich, charity, environment, American democracy, and "the foundation of the West." They argue that in these areas, negative stereotypes have been created as selected matters have been unfairly amplified while major positives have been allowed to fall from attention.[247] (We give a few excerpts from their material in that footnote, one of which notes a positive comment on the Apostle Paul; F. F. Bruce's *Paul: Apostle of the Heart Set Free* provides in-depth treatment of Paul, although it is not cast as an argument with the modern negativity toward him.)[248] (A similar title searches differently: Mark Lanier's *Christianity on Trial: A Lawyer Examines the Christian Faith* shows "how a top-shelf lawyer might be better suited than a faith-filled scientist" for "proving the reasonableness of the Christian account of reality" [review p. 51 of *Christianity Today* magazine, Dec. 2014]. Endnote~92 notes a late-arriving book of similar matters.)

Tim Mahoney's DVD "Patterns of Evidence: **Exodus**" is a fascinating look at archaeological and historical evidence now supporting the much-disputed historical reality of the Biblical Exodus (PatternsOfEvidence.com).

Books on science seen more carefully:

(For the reader whose eyes may glaze over long before this section is all perused, we note in the last paragraph that Strobel summarizes in less than ten pages the evidence of cosmology, physics, astronomy, biochemistry, biological information, and consciousness. That may be a useful introduction for some people. [*Case For a Creator,* pages 279 - 286] These arguments constantly "evolve," as we have said elsewhere — see Chapter 14.)

Berlinski argues that science most emphatically has not proven that there is no room for God in the picture. His perspective is informed and a stimulating read, if occasionally too "pointed." His assessment of the science is penetrating (book *The Devil's Delusion: Atheism and Its Scientific Pretensions*).

The reader will have noticed that we agree with Berlinski's conclusion as our overall assessment. The arguments that cosmology (chapter 15; even biology, ch. 14) "point to intelligence in their origin" are fascinating, but we said we would assess the state of the science, as available to your author, and consensus is obviously not obtained. [But see "information" issue, per Index.]

The *cosmology* is assessed very accessibly by Gonzalez' & Richards' *The Privileged Planet,* which is available as a DVD as well as the book. It demonstrates that Earth is not a mere dot undistinguished from the masses of planets — rather, as a scientific matter, our position and characteristics seem special and attuned both for life and for scientific observation. They touch on the "fine-tuning" issues of the universe's structure. This was discussed in Chapter 15. Also, John Lennox has done a good job of unraveling Stephen Hawking's exposition that God is allegedly not needed for creation, as a matter of physics, in his very readable book *God and Stephen Hawking*.

Stephen Meyer's *Signature in the Cell* assesses the presence of "information" in the genetic code and the implausibility of "naturalistic" origin theories in the light of this core matter.[249]

Meyer analyzes that the basic nature of "information" comes into play in making naturalistic explanations unworkable. We have noted his insights at length elsewhere (pp. 82, 90; endnotes 133, 134, 136, 150, 151). The student may be rewarded also by his careful proof that Intelligent Design qualifies as a scientific theory (an entire chapter of his work). The student of the debate will also benefit from his cataloging of predictions made by "I.D.," including the debunking of "junk DNA" in terms of the relative ratio of "signal to noise" (esp. pp. 406-7 of *Signature*...).

The reader will note that I consider Meyer insightful and intriguing, but we must say also that the "state of the art" does not foreclose other viewpoints about his expositions.

Fazale Rana is a biochemist who tells lay believers that "popular forms" of arguments for recognizing the Creator from complexity in the cell etc. "often do more harm than good" with sophisticated unbelievers. He cautions layperson believers against simplistic approaches that only alienate more scientifically-informed persons. His DVD ""How to Build the Case for Biochemical Design" gives his approach for better impact. "Bio-inspiration" gets his supportive exposition. (He cautions us that because *we* can't imagine certain complexities arising from chance, doesn't mean people with specialized studies can't imagine it.)

Dr. Rana was, as a graduate student, an agnostic; he wasn't even concerned with the question of "God." However: "When I was confronted with the elegance and the sophistication, the beauty, the ingenuity, the cleverness of biochemical systems in terms of the way they're structured and the way they function, it convinced me that a Creator must exist." (His DVD, introductory segment.) He approaches this biochemical evidence as a positive evidence for "design," rather than asserting *inability to explain* as forcing recourse to divinity for explanation. His book *The Cell's Design: How Chemistry Reveals the Creator's Artistry* goes in-depth into this exposition. [Endnote 129 here recaps his summary pages.]

Stephen Meyer also gives an in-depth treatment of a matter that Darwin himself saw eluding his theory (Darwin felt further field research on fossils would change the situation).

Darwin's Doubt explores the factors of very sudden emergence of complex life-forms in the "Cambrian explosion," without the expected predecessors slowly and gradually changing into them, per classical Darwinism. (As extensive fossil discoveries showed that their absence was not due to limited fieldwork, one renowned Chinese scientist told an American gathering that in China, "we can criticize Darwin, but not the government. In America, you can criticize the government, but not Darwin."[250] See that endnote for the "top-down" added problem in the Cambrian issues, & more.)

As science has most definitely *not* closed the door on God, we have mentioned the perspective of several scientists who believe in God and openly tell the world. Francis Collins and Denis Alexander were mentioned, whose books show that they do not quarrel with the evolutionary paradigm. Meyer's books and Behe's (below) show examples of people who believe evolution certainly has its proven points and validity, but they believe the scientific assessment itself shows intelligence clearly at work in life's origin and development. (As to not being able to show precisely "how" that worked, note that Newton could not explain *how* gravity worked when he proposed his theory, but that did not make the discovery of gravitation any less scientific).

The scientific assessment is a continuing topic that sees a ceaseless flood of books; "classics" become obsolete. One such classic is *Darwin's Black Box*, by Michael Behe, which explores the complexity that is found within a single cell, examining the question of whether this could have arisen by naturalistic "chance." (A DVD, "Unlocking the Mystery of Life," sets forth this analysis for those who prefer non-book delivery. Now, Behe has done a *tenth-anniversary edition* including a rebuttal of ten years' of critics.) Behe examines the unexpected complexity of structures *within* the cell, which he feels renders absurd the likelihood of this coming to be "by chance," without a guiding intelligence. Of much greater importance than complexity in itself, Behe examines also the interlocking aspects of complex systems, so that various parts offer no value for "natural selection" until the others are present, strengthening the argument by a new level tied to this "irreducible complexity." There are of course vigorous disputes over his conclusions (co-option of prior structures to new purposes, mentioned on p. 73 above, has emerged as a general refutation; Dr. D. Alexander says it usually takes about ten years for a refutation of an example conundrum (noted our p. 87; on our p. 77, we noted that "bio-inspiration" has put a different viewpoint on the "co-option" viewpoint, pointing some to the Creator by the positive evidence of elegance and ingenuity). *Re the implications of science, please note our Chapter 14, on the methodology and interpretation of science, as a caution about how these matters are and will be handled.* The controversies will surge back and forth, and one should be careful of too much attachment to any particular scientific analysis. ["Information in the cell" may be the deepest illuminating issue; see Index]

(The student who examines the complexity and intricacy of subcellular structures may benefit from Dr. Fazale Rana's perspective that it is "the elegance and the sophistication, the beauty, the ingenuity, the cleverness of biochemical systems" that point to the Creator, not the unimaginable complexity.)

Denis Alexander gives a special scientist's perspective when he asks, "Does the evolutionary account display properties that are more consistent with a theistic or with an atheistic account of the world?" (p. 321 of *Creation or Evolution: Do We Have to Choose).* We cited his answer in Chapter 14 above (p. 87-88). Theologian J. I. Packer, on the front cover, commends Dr. Alexander's book as "Surely the best informed, clearest and most judicious treatment of the question in its title." (See note[251] for Dr. Alexander's credentials. See also endnote 148 re this theme!)

(With my apologies for what may seem self-promotion, the person boggled by the unending and sometimes bitter controversy may appreciate Appendix Seven here, "Deeper Assessments/ Reversed Conclusions/ Same Thing.")

The Science of God...Wisdom, by Gerald Schroeder, was discussed in Chapter 16 regarding the "days of creation" and the scientists' observed life-span of the universe, and he discusses a number of other points to make Biblical faith sensible to the science-student. The book has many interesting points on Bible interpretation (including an "Adam and Eve" assessment more similar to Lewis [our Appendix Seven] than to our main text). As with our note about Dr. Meyer and Dr. Behe above, this work shows a devout believer profoundly respectful toward and supportive of science, who finds the exploration of God's universe working with faith, with careful thought.

Ross's *The Genesis Question* is a startling book, because he begins with his personal history. He came as a scientist and examined Genesis in the Bible and found it the only account in the "sacred books" that corresponds to science's findings — and he proceeds to document how that is shown, *when Genesis is interpreted correctly.* (We gave some of his analysis on p. 13.)

Falk's *Coming to Peace with Science* examines problems with not thinking carefully about Scripture, key scientific evidence for the age of the earth, etc. — a genuinely Christian view on reading Scripture without discarding science (useful for people stuck farther outside the scientific view). See endnote 120 for an excerpt of his information and perspective.

More on Dr. Collins: His *The Language of God: A Scientist Presents Evidence for Belief,* brings the viewpoint of the man who headed the Human Genome project and brought it to its successful conclusion. That marks Collins' as a scientist's scientist, yes?

Woodward, *Doubts About Darwin,* tracks the flow of the reasoning in the evolution-creation controversy. I personally found this one of the most illuminating books I read about this perennial controversy. (As noted earlier, our Chapter 14 discusses limits of the whole concept of controversy about this "issue.")

Dell Ratzsch's *The Battle of Beginnings: Why Neither Side Is Winning the Creation-Evolution Debate* gives a different perspective, one which may help to skirt the thickets of this conflict. It has a chapter "Darwin's Theory: Popular Creationist Misunderstandings" and a chapter of the misunderstandings on the other side, also a chapter on "Popular Anticreationist Mistakes" and again, the reverse. The book is rather dated — 1996, way back in the last millennium! — but I find some of the same mistakes still being offered to the seeking public. (We welcome any referrals to valuable current offerings, of course.) Similarly, "common but weak" arguments against "Intelligent Design" are assessed in some depth at the website uncommondescent.com/faq/, but I have browsed it only lightly.

Mary Midgley dedicates her book *Evolution as a Religion* "To the Memory of Charles Darwin Who Did Not Say These Things" and says in her Introduction that "quasi-scientific speculation" is "even more rampant" now (as she issued her revised edition) than when the book was first written. She writes to make us aware of "the underlying myths" (p. ix). (She is speaking of "metaphysical passages... in scientific books about evolution... presented as science," p. viii.)

The chapter "A Scientific Argument for the Existence of God" in the book *Reason for the Hope Within*, by Murray, was mentioned in endnote 160.

Thaxton et al's *Mystery of Life's Origins* is quite "dated" (1984), so we put our comments about it in an endnote, which also comments on origin-of-life research and also "scientism." [252]

We have, at the end of this "Annotated Bibliography" appendix, a sub-section on "Considering Reality Empirically" which discusses Morse on near-death experiences. To conclude our pondering on the state of science, let's take a few more glances at the "information" controversy. In endnote 226 (to our Scripture Table entry on "Creation"), we show a viewpoint on science and Scripture **converging** on "information:" some research suggests "that information forms the very core of existence." As we state in the endnote, that seems to echo the Bible's famous "In the beginning was the Word, and the Word was with God, and the Word was God... All things were made through him..." (John 1:1-3 ESV; more explanation in that endnote, of course).

Woodward, in *Doubts About Darwin*, gives his own view that the question of the origin of the **"information"** in life's genetic code may be critical: "The forming of integrated swarms of information-packed molecules seems increasingly mysterious, given our growing knowledge of the problems involved... in light of the new 'minimum genetic package' studies, the tension between scientific reality and the [purely-naturalistic] paradigm's assumptions must be approaching the snapping point" (pp. 125-126). As noted, Meyer devotes a 600-page book (*Signature...*) to the issue, which should provide a firm grounding for anyone intrepid enough to take on the field of inquiry. My issue was to assess the "state of the art," from an outsider's point of view as to the implications beyond the strictly scientific arena. We are familiar enough with the commitment to naturalism and its consequences,[253] and with the ability of people to generate alternative possible viewpoints, that *it would seem premature for me to take the "information" issue as in any sense conclusive. Dr. F. Rana, in his DVD, says many scientific papers are already suggesting that "information" can be generated by "evolutionary" processes.* Meyer's theoretical rebuttal of that solution as a logical possibility is interesting, and we haven't seen an assessment of what level of "information" is being developed by these papers or how deeply they may tie into Woodward's searching question. As we elaborated as such length (perhaps tiresomely?) in Chapter 14, the controversies sway back and forth, and deeper questioning displaces many "no room for hand of God" assertions.

Strobel's *Case for a Creator* records how he "probed six different scientific disciplines to see whether they point toward or away from the existence of an intelligent designer" (p. 279; in the following seven pages, he summarizes the evidence of cosmology, physics, astronomy, biochemistry, biological information, and consciousness. He does a better job than we did in endnote 126.)

Basic understandings:

The Orthodox Way, by Bishop Kallistos Ware, gives an overview of Christian faith. As noted above, this is a book that aids spiritual perception — it helped me more than any other outside the Bible itself.

C. S. Lewis' classic *Mere Christianity* helps to get the intellectual perception together about Christian understanding. Rev. Timothy Keller's books (e.g. *The Reason for God*) speak a similar quest from a current perspective, with perhaps less treatment of classic Christian doctrine and more current cultural/ philosophical matters.

Plantinga's *Not the Way It's Supposed to Be* discusses the concept of "sin" so that the modern reader can renew a grasp on an issue that many had hoped could be discarded. It is a thoughtful, modern mind at work, one that values human beings, not an adverse medieval morality.

Murray's *Abiding in Christ* discusses the privilege held out by Jesus in John 15:4-9, in terms of the depth available to those who most seriously commit themselves to Him.

Jesus telling us "that he was a missionary from heaven who came to minister incarnationally in an earthly culture" is discussed by Mark Driscoll in an essay in the book *The Supremacy of Christ in a Postmodern World*, p. 140 of that book. (see Bibliography, Piper, J., Editor)

Christus Victor, by Gustav Aulen, researches the early Church's understanding of Christ's atonement. Aulen argues from early church sources that the early Christians understood that yes, Christ died for us — but not so much as a "payment of the sum of all the penalties" for sinful transgressions, but as the need to establish a reality of true loving obedience to God, so that this reality would exist for human beings to be incorporated into. The book is highly recommended to any people who have a problem with the idea of blessed Jesus' *atonement* as they have heard it explained to them (it is unnecessary for those who receive His sacrifice without that particular analysis, although it might help them in talking to some people. See Chapter 12 here for discussion; endnote 112 for further depth).

The ALPHA course, discussed above on the second page of this section, is a very different approach to getting a basic grasp, one rooted in the core concept of community in Christ (a video lecture/ discussion series, done in small groups for discussion and fellowship, website alphausa.org).

In a world where skepticism flaunts itself even to try, in some cases, to deny the historical reality of Jesus, Habermas's *The Historical Jesus* is of value in presenting extensive evidence beyond the New Testament, including Roman sources, to show the reality of Jesus' earthly life.[254] Lee Strobel's *The Case for the Real Jesus* examines modern alternative theories about Jesus and restores the Biblical Son of God/ Son of Man.

On walking more closely with God:

This is a tough section — perhaps Billy Graham's *The Journey* should be first here...

My Utmost for His Highest, by Oswald Chambers, is "the most popular book of daily devotions ever published" (per Richard Halverson, former Chaplain to the U. S. Senate, in his Introduction to Chambers' book).

Payton's *Light from the Christian East* overviews faith matters from a more intellectual perspective than *The Orthodox Way*, with the obvious emphasis on Eastern Orthodox thought.

Richmond Lattimore translated the New Testament based on his acclaimed expertise in the ancient Greek language, as discussed in the third section of this Bibliography.

Note Rick Warren's *Purpose-Driven Life* (readings and discussion questions, available as a DVD study).

Comparative religion and philosophy:

Please note Os Guinness, *The Long Journey Home: A Guide to Your Search for the Meaning of Life.* In this astonishing work, Guinness surveys the vast sweep of human thought: "western" religion (including the western Asian "Abrahamic" religions), secular humanism, and eastern religions. He assesses them carefully and demonstrates that the Christian faith holds up best to reason and observed reality.

Guinness describes this in his introduction as "My best attempt to chase with words, a path beyond description." One key thread he pursues is "how the three different families of faiths respond to the dilemma of evil" (p. 74). Chapter 6 describes W. H.

Auden's experience that showed him humanity was not inherently good, "that he was encountering evil and that it must be condemned" (p. 55).

Our Chapter 10 describes much of the scope of Guinness's book in its opening pages.

Farasiotis' *The Gurus, the Young Man, and Elder Paisios* is not a philosophical view, but rather an intense personal experience of different spiritualities, as a young man raised in the Greek Orthodox Christian went to live in Hindu ashrams in India. (The experience brought him back to Christ and the Church).

In another personal journey, Dr. Nabeel Qureshi shows the family love and intense devotion to God in his Muslim upbringing. But then, he experienced the collapse of traditional Muslim arguments against Jesus as Christ and Christianity as he researched — and also the collapse of the pro-Islam arguments he had always heard, as he researched early Muslim sources. He believed God would answer his perplexity, based both on his lifelong faith and on prior supernatural experience of calling on God for personal need (pp. 104-105). Hence his calling out desperately to God, and his book's title, *Seeking Allah, Finding Jesus.*

He recounts his struggle with the issues of the Trinity, reliability of Scripture, transmission of the Qur'an, and others.

"Simplicity" of God's being is a traditional theological finding in Christian, Islamic, Hindu, and Jewish thought, discussed in depth in Hart's *Experience of God* — "simplicity" meaning without parts; Hart expounds traditional theology of God as the Being which makes all other beings possible, without Whom nothing could be — and he examines consciousness, among other points of focus, as a special indication of transcendent reality.

Lee Strobel has done such extensive work that special mention should be made of his *Case for*... series. With a degree in Law (Yale) and an award-winning career in journalism (*Chicago Tribune*), his skills lent themselves to researching the expert researchers in the areas he took under concern.

We have mentioned his *Case for Easter*, excerpted from *The Case for Christ*, and shown in Appendix 2 what sort of information Strobel accumulated. *The Case for Christ* deals also with evidence regarding Jesus from non-Christian sources, the "Jesus of History" vs. "the Jesus of faith," reliability of the Gospels, and the prophecies regarding Messiah that foreshadowed His coming from centuries before. Strobel's *Case for Faith... the Toughest Objections* deals with questions of evil and suffering, miracles as "unscientific" and evolution as all-explaining, Jesus as the unique way to God, church history as violent, Hell, and whether doubts preclude coming to Christ. (His final section includes a quote about those who "believe only in the idea of God, and not in God himself," p. 311, and his researches into the story of a violent criminal who underwent miraculous change when he came to Jesus. Strobel approached that story with "When I dig deeper, I'll find out his scam" — but the account turned out to be true).

Strobel adds an interesting study to the voluminous literature on what science, carefully assessed, says about God, with his *Case for a Creator*.[255] Fans of Strobel's approach will find this book rewarding, although the intellectual assessor may want to ponder also Denis Alexander's much different outlook (see Index for reference in this book). Strobel examines the history of the controversies, some background perspectives, and then experts' views from cosmology, physics, astronomy, biochemistry, and finally issues of biological information and of consciousness itself.

Strobel's 2007 work, *The Case for the Real Jesus: A Journalist Investigates Current Attacks on the Identity of Christ*, examines challenges that "scholars are uncovering a radically different Jesus in ancient documents just as credible as the four Gospels," that the Church has tampered with the Bible's text, that the Resurrection has been newly explained, that Christian beliefs were copied from pagan religions, and others. He includes an appendix of websites he recommends, including the note that leestrobel.com is "video-intensive" [256] (see the endnote for his full list of sites).

Rodney Stark's *For the Glory of God* opens its second chapter with a survey of the alleged religious opposition to Columbus, flat-earth vs. round earth — showing that all educated opinion of the time was round-earth, and the refusal to support Columbus' idea was (correctly) based on belief that his estimates of the size of the earth were dramatically wrong. He goes on to argue "not only that there is no inherent conflict between religion and science, but that Christian theology was essential for the rise of science" (p. 123).[257] The book covers science and religion in considerable depth, then several critical perceptions which Stark feels need to be clarified — especially regarding slavery and witch-hunts (elsewhere, we mention that the law of Moses in the Bible forbade the forced return of an **escaped slave** (Deut 23:15; noted on p. 206 here), but the Code of Hammurabi "prescribed death for anyone who helped a slave to escape").[258]

Stark's *The Victory of Reason: How Christianity Led to Freedom, Capitalism and Western Success* is equally thought-provoking and bears examination as to the validity of some strains of contemporary anti-Christian thinking. Once one becomes acquainted with the living God — an acquaintance that human books will not achieve — the idea that the Wisdom of God (Christ, per New Testament) would result in fruitfulness for the well-being of the people of God, seems almost axiomatic. However, the levels of dispute are many in today's society.

Timothy Keller founded a large church in Manhattan (Redeemer Presbyterian); he opens *The Reason for God* with discussion of his own spiritual journey, including a desperate need for "a group of Christians who had a concern for justice in the world but who grounded it in the nature of God rather than in their own subjective feelings" (he had asked, "If morality is relative, why isn't social justice as well?") (pp. xii, xiii). He answers the issues that Manhattan's keen minds have brought him, with probing essays. He opens with chapters: There Can't Be Just One True Religion; How Could a Good God Allow Suffering; Christianity is a Straitjacket; The Church Is Responsible for So Much Injustice;

How Can a Loving God Send People to Hell; Science Has Disproved Christianity; You Can't Take the Bible Literally. Later chapters are headlined "The Reasons for Faith." [See our endnote 92 for a 2019 work covering similar issues with very penetrating insights].

Timothy Keller may not be infallible, but he is very thought-provoking. On the sacrificial death of Jesus, for example, he says: "Forgiveness means bearing the cost instead of making the wrongdoer do it, so you can reach out in love to seek your enemy's renewal and change... Everyone who forgives great evil goes through a death into resurrection, and experiences nails, blood, sweat, and tears" (p. 199). On pp. 116-117 he advocates focusing on the Bible's core teachings — Jesus' deity, salvation — rather than getting "scraped up" in the controversies (such as what Biblical texts mean about gender roles).

Deeper Philosophy:

Smith and Taylor's epochal analysis of what has changed in human thinking, over several centuries, that impedes contact with the Divine, was discussed on p. 92. They also discuss the impact of a philosophy where "human flourishing" is the highest good, so that much of the range of theology is lost by default. Indeed, our society's concepts may be inadequate; the far-extended, all-encompassing "scientific" viewpoint remains "a 'take' on the world... we have come to assume that this is just 'the way things are' " [Smith, p. 45]. The result is "an overconfident 'picture' within which we can't imagine it being otherwise, and thus smugly dismiss those who disagree." Their analysis is "most interested in considering (and contesting) the 'spin of closure which is hegemonic in the Academy'. This is the spin that is dominant amongst intellectuals and elites ... [who] see their own 'closed' take as *just the way things are*... To have this stance is to be hamstrung in a way" [Smith p. 95, with an embedded quote from Taylor's p. 549].

One result they note of the concept-space shift is "cultural shifts... from talking about sin to talking about sickness... from responsibility to victimhood... What's wrong with me is more like a disease that befalls me than a disorder for which I am responsible" [p. 109]. Astonishingly, this brings us back to congruence with the oldest branch of the Christian Church, the Eastern Orthodox, where "sin is a sickness that needs to be healed" [Fr. Boulos Khoury, teaching a class 26 Oct 2010].

(*That* brings to mind Bible, Isaiah Isa 57:19 "...Peace, peace, to those far and near," says the LORD. "And I will heal them."

David Bentley Hart brings us another deep book, massive but penetrating and perceptive: *The Experience of God: Being, Consciousness, Bliss.*

In the "being" analysis, existence itself is shown to point to a cause beyond material elements. (One relevant point is that a quantum vacuum is not "nothing," but is in itself a structured "something" possessed of properties, so the idea that our universe represents an unlikely but possible "quantum fluctuation" does not get around the philosophical conundrum "nothing comes from nothing.")

Personally, I found more stimulating his fascinating analysis that the nature of consciousness points to God. I'll let him make some of his points: "Absolutely central to the mechanistic vision of reality is the principle that material forces are inherently mindless, intrinsically devoid of purpose, and therefore only adventitiously and accidentally directed toward any end... consciousness would appear to be everything that, according to the principles of mechanism, matter is not: directed, purposive, essentially rational. The notion that material causes could yield a result so apparently contrary to material nature is paradoxical enough that it ought to give even the most committed of materialists pause" (p. 154).

In saying that the phenomenon of consciousness points to a deeper reality than physical nature, he appeals to "the simplicity and immediacy of consciousness, to its extraordinary openness to the physical world, to its reflective awareness of itself, or to the liberty of its conceptual and imaginative powers" (p. 156).

The book is a "deep read," but it brings gems like this:

"There is a troubling tendency among materialist philosophers of mind and cognitive scientists to indulge in analogies that, far from making consciousness more intelligible, are themselves intelligible only because they presume the operations of consciousness. It is not uncommon to find cameras or televisions mentioned as mechanical analogies of the mind's processes of representation; but of course, a camera does not look at pictures and a television does not watch itself, and there is nothing even remotely representational in their functions apart from the intentions of a conscious mind, which is to be found not in those devices but in a person" (p. 207).

The "consciousness" analysis comes to a profound conclusion: "God also explains the transparency of the universe to consciousness, despite its apparent difference from consciousness" (p. 237).

Hart's "bliss" section incorporates discussion of the transcendent quality of beauty, and other such depths...

(Don't misunderstand his title — his book does not discuss how people have "experienced" God or "how to" do that. Rather, he's showing how we experience God's reality in various levels of our lives, matters for which God gets little overt credit.)

The **Resurrection of Jesus** the Christ: As noted in Appendix Two, the frontispiece for N. T. Wright's *The Resurrection of the Son of God* cites Richard Ostling of the Associated Press describing that book as the "most monumental defense of the Easter heritage in decades ... a clearly organized case that confronts every major doubt about Easter, ancient and modern." Thorough treatments take time; that book runs over 800 pages. (We excerpted in Appendix Two a more concise treatment; the full book is rewarding). [On the historical reality of Jesus, now sometimes challenged, note Habermas, p. 176]

Miracles (Personal healing-miracle experiences of my friends are noted and footnoted in Chapter 18 of this present book; note also the first "Postscript.") Also, *2000 Years of Charismatic Christianity*, by Eddie Hyatt, and his *The Azusa Street*

Revival: The Holy Spirit in America — 100 Years give background on the presence of Holy Spirit manifestations throughout the life of the Church.

A best-selling book *Heaven Is for Real* (Todd Burpo, 2010) set forth the report of a visit to heaven by his four-year-old child, who reported going out of his body during an operation which the child was not expected to survive. The child's report gained credibility because he was able to tell what his mother and father were doing in other rooms of the hospital while he was in the operating room, which he had no other way to know. The child's survival itself was described as a miracle by a nurse.[259] (Endnote cites other books of such experiences by medical doctors).

Craig Keener's recent book *Miracles* draws on his own experience of the miraculous presence of God and extensive investigation that he did. He finds that "majority world" (i.e. non-"Western") peoples often do not have the faith-blocking "miracles don't happen" mindset, and they experience much that we consider "incredible." His wife is from Congo-Brazzaville, and she introduced him to in-laws and others who gave personal experiences. He stated that , "I was well into this book when, having encountered so much evidence, I stopped trying to be neutral..."[260] (The work totals 1248 pages.)

Also, the personal ministry experiences in *Smoke Signals from God* by a Native American Indian author, Ray "Black Buffalo" Wilson, whose experience of the "sky and moon turned red" was given in our main text (pp. 39-40). Mr. Wilson was an enrolled member of the Cowlitz Indian Tribe in Washington State, U.S.A. He had heritage (ancestry) also from the Yakima, Chinook and Iroquois Native Americans (this per his bio, p. 215 of his book).

Miracles are described in K. P. Yohannan's *Revolution in World Missions*, from his personal experience (pages 68 & 70) and from his affiliates (healing, pp. 204-5). His organization provides free promotional copies of the book; see Standard-form Bibliography for contact information & current-events reference).

A Chinese filmmaker's DVD "The Cross: Jesus in China," by Yuan Zhiming, tells stories of lives transformed by the living presence of Jesus Christ. Available on the web, the 2003 DVD is worth the four hours' viewing, and the viewer can pick certain topical sections to focus on to save time.

Bosworth's *Christ the Healer:* Healing in modern times, by a man who received over 200,000 written testimonies to healing. Includes discussion of Christ's Atonement including healing, "How to Receive," etc.

Miracles are a "hot-button" topic. C. S. Lewis pointed out an interesting viewpoint: He says that Jesus' miracles in the New Testament reflect what God is doing around the world every day, except at a much faster pace. For example, Jesus' first miracle (John 2:11) was turning water into wine for the celebration of a wedding. Well, says Lewis, turning water into wine is what God is doing all the time — using the created intermediaries of grapevines and winemakers... Healing the sick is something that God does countless times every day, so much so that we take it for granted that we get over colds and our search is not for how to give thanks but for how to shave a couple days off the process. Bringing the dead to life (e.g. John 11:43), reflects the fact that giving life is something God does routinely and all over the earth (Psa 104:30: When You send Your Spirit, they are created, and You renew the face of the earth). Lewis' *Mere Christianity* is about half a century old now, but it still offers many interesting insights on modern contemplations; this discussion is from Chapter Two of his book *God in the Dock* (British term for a criminal defendant, as he examines modern anti-God charges).

Of note in other regards:

Christ the Eternal Tao draws on ancient Chinese perspective to tell the Gospel message in a different way, and connects Jesus the Word with perception from another culture of the ultimate spiritual reality.

Dennis Tinerino's *Supersize Your Faith* is the story of God's dealing with him. That tracks from a message from God during his youth, through a life of crime, a career as a world-famous bodybuilder, to miracles and experience of glory.

A unique Native American Indian viewpoint on living with God, a deep account of personal experience, is Athabascan (Alaska) Traditional Chief Peter John's *The Gospel According to Peter John.* Mr. John recounts experiences of his life with the Holy Spirit (as a Christian), showing the reliability of the help (we noted also in our main text, p. 108, the vision of the road to Hell that he reported being shown).

Thirsting for God in a Land of Shallow Wells (M. Gallatin) is a Protestant Pastor's account of his life journey, coming to the Eastern Orthodox branch of Christianity. (See endnote 106).

Accompany Them with Singing, by Thomas Long, discusses the meaning of a true Christian funeral. "Celebrate a life" is a common approach now, and "well, s/he had a good life" is often heard. This outlook is brutally suboptimal in light of our discovery. If God were prone to taking offense, there would be grave danger in this profound insult to the great goodness He* has offered us.

Nancy Pearcey's *Saving Leonardo* is a very erudite book, dealing with worldviews, intellectual movements and their history in our civilization over many centuries — not my sort of thing, but quite a bit of information and perspective for those who like that sort of thing. (I am confessing myself to be simple-minded. As an Indian friend once said, "Amuse me, don't confuse me.")

Johnson's *Reason in the Balance* discusses the consequences to society of our shifting worldviews. (This paragraph was written in 2010, the year during which the United States came within a week of an unprecedented default on national debt; *fifteen years* earlier, Johnson predicted a debt crisis, based on theoretical reasoning of social morality,[261] not economic projections. Interesting as prophecy?)

Fr. Seraphim's book *Genesis, Creation and Early Man* introduces itself as "The Orthodox Christian Vision," but the reader will not be surprised to find that many Orthodox Christians do not share his viewpoint. It starts me meditating on questions of interpretation...[262]

Various commentators have noted that the special love of the Father for the Son, in the blessed Holy **Trinity**, means that there is a **community of love**, a romance, at the core of the universe (cf. last of John 17:24). John Eldredge, in his *Way of the Wild Heart,* remarks that while life is much of a struggle, the romance is greater than the battle. He mentions "the stark reality that the love affair between man [human being] and God… has an enemy, who ever seeks to ruin the Romance by shutting down the heart or trapping it in any way he can" (p. 199 of that book).

Do Hard Things (Alex & Brett Harris) is a teenagers' manifesto of the importance of what we do with our lives. They subtitle it, "A teenage rebellion against low expectations."

Morrow's *Welcome to College* gives short capsules about philosophical issues that the college environment may challenge the young believer with, and books for exploration on each issue. When "brevity is the soul of wit," that approach can offer delight.

Leonard Allen's *The Contemporaries Meet the Classics on Prayer* has essays and helpful comments from time-tested authors and recent commentators. (For example, John Bunyan tells us that prayers must be sincere, sensible, an affectionate pouring out of your soul, by the strength and assistance of the Holy Spirit; according to God's promises; not selfish. See also endnote 277 for guidance from Fr. Alexander Men's 2014 book *An Inner Step Toward* ***God***. The recommended reading section of that book notes recent "ecumenical versions" of prayer books, including *Celtic Daily Prayer* and *Common Prayer: A Liturgy for Ordinary Radicals.* (I have not used those; n.b. also Bibliography, "Prayer book" entry)

McGuckin's *Westminster Handbook to Patristic Theology* lives up to a reviewer's billing as "lively and readable." ("Patristic" refers to the first five centuries of the Church's life on earth).

Trouble is a topic of universal interest. Stowell's *The Upside of Down: Finding Hope When It Hurts* deals with the perennial problem of trouble and suffering. Its quality is such that it was selected for a Billy Graham Library Edition. He emphasizes clinging to God under stress and "sticking with what we know" of God's faithfulness. (Billy Graham himself, in his *The Journey,* says that, "The real issue, however, isn't *why* we have problems and temptations but *how we will respond* to them" (p. 157). And he suggests we pray to God, "What response do You want me to make?" (p. 199). (Note also Scripture Table, Appendix One, "Suffering" and "Trouble" entries.)

A **different sort** of book: Walter Wangerin's *The Book of God: The Bible as a Novel* is exactly that. He turns the flow of people through the Bible's events, and God's working with the people, into story form, running throughout the millennia. (He finesses the controversies of interpreting Genesis by beginning the story with Abraham — per the New Testament, "the father of all who believe" Rom 4:11. The Genesis account then comes up in the Jewish people's reading of the Torah during the return from Exile. The work runs 850 pages, so it should satisfy the true novel-reader.)

Adventure reading:

See above re Tinerino's *Supersize Your Faith* (p. 185). Also, Bottomly's *Prodigal Father* recounts a number of adventures, including one of desperate peril turning to deliverance as he claimed God's promise to "never leave or forsake" him (p. 122; his airplane had lost engine power. The promise to the believer is Bible, Hebrews 13:5.) Also see Yohannan, *Revolution...*

We should note that Bottomly's *Prodigal Father* is not a similar book to Timothy Keller's *Prodigal God. Prodigal God* talks about the Bible's parable of the "prodigal son" and the true "prodigality" of God the Father, whose love is so far-reaching. It alleges that many people have trouble with the Church because in church they find "elder brother" religion, people who are confident in their own propriety of conduct — rather than Gospel love (if these terms are unfamiliar, see Jesus' parable of the prodigal son in Luke 15). *Prodigal Father*, on the other hand, is the story of a Christ-less father brought to God's love by his son during desperation, the story of a man's proud self-sufficiency being inadequate to keep him from trouble during war. War brought his self-guidance into focus as he created a crisis for himself.

Toby Mac's *Under God* ranges over the centuries for God-touched events in American history. A most unusual prolonged fog arose and allowed an American army on Long Island, outnumbered about four to one, to escape British forces; Harriet Tubman was guided by God to escape slave catchers (more than once! P. 112 of their book, "If she had not obeyed the **whisper of warning** in her mind, she would have been captured"). An abolitionist "mob" freed an escaped slave from police custody in Troy New York in 1860 (also with Harriet Tubman's involvement); a wide variety of other matters are recounted in stimulating prose. (Dwight Eisenhower's miracle healing at age 13, p. 257 of that book).

Considering Reality Empirically: Dr. Melvin Morse assesses "Near-Death Experiences" (NDE's) and their thought-provoking characteristics. He examines possible non-spiritual causes and concludes on carefully-stated technical grounds that they are not due to hallucinations, drugs, stress, etc. His discussion of alternative explanations is on pp. 183-193 of *Closer to the Light*. Interestingly, children often see themselves as adults in NDE's, not as they have known themselves. (On p. 108, Dr. Morse notes that tracing NDE experiences to a particular location in the brain does not explain *why* they occur; this knowledge does not "make it more a reflex than a spiritual experience," just as tracing vision to a part of the brain does not negate the reality of the exterior world perceived by our eyesight.)

[While older books, like Morse, will be less expensive on the web, we do incorporate some more recent books, in addition to those in this Annotated Bibliography, in endnotes; at the bottom of endnote 259, we note books on experiences by medical doctors that relate to Morse's work. We do of course welcome suggestions on what books may warrant later mention.]

A last minute addition as we rush to press: Rick Warren's *Purpose-Driven Life: What on Earth Am I Here For?* is available in a group study format as well as a book rich in the Word of God.

==================================

B-t's Shakespeare quote (p 119 above), "There are more things in heaven and earth than are dreamed of in your philosophy," is a point that will guide the truly scientific thinker to examine many of these items carefully.

Bibliography, Section Three: Bible Versions and Resources

We give comments on the variety of Bible "versions" — different translations from the original Greek & Hebrew — then, information on a free study tool that offers also a range of free "versions." An alphabetized list of certain versions and comments follows that. Finally, we quote an example verse in multiple versions to illustrate the style differences mentioned below.

Bible versions: Free web access to different Bible translations is offered by the YouVersion "app," which can be used with mobile devices or on your personal computer (more below). A more restricted range of free versions (but others for modest cost) are offered on e-Sword, which also offers commentaries and more capacity for on-screen comparison (4 versus 2 displayed). In this book, we have noted the Contemporary English Version (CEV), Good News Translation (GNT), New International Version (NIV), New Living Translation (NLT), New King James Version (NKJV), New Revised Standard Version (NRSV), Literal Version (LITV), *Orthodox Study Bible* (OSB) and Young's Literal Translation (YLT). (And LXX, although that is a separate matter.) These are discussed in more detail below. (Publishers are listed on page 134.)

"Inclusive" language (in which the translators try to avoid "he" unless the reference is to a masculine person) has been used in the NLT and NRSV (CEV appears to do this; I have not checked my electronic copy thoroughly, but it is a "freebie" at e-Sword.net and endnote 227 discusses an example of CEV's inclusive wording, comparing NLT and NRSV). Minor variations occur in the NKJV because it relies on the Greek text used for the old King James Version[263] (KJV, translated in 1611, more below). The *Orthodox Study Bible* footnotes all of these variations in the Greek text.

Special translations of note: Richmond Lattimore (New Testament per Greek expertise), and George Lamsa, using an ancient Aramaic text of the Bible — the language that Jesus spoke. More on these below.

The American Bible Society offers "engagement" tools in a variety of media forms for getting acquainted with the Bible at their website engage.americanbible.org.

Engaging with the meaning of the Bible may be done in another way, the ALPHA course (discussed in the "annotated" bibliography, 2nd page of that section).

"YouVersion" website bible.com: Free Bible downloads, versions offered work on computer or mobile device, displays two versions side-by-side if desired (Seniors take note: font size can be adjusted). Also **has audio** available for many versions (and extensive non-English versions, as does e-Sword, below). Offers Bible-reading plans, devotionals, and allows highlighting, bookmarking and notes. Audio includes NIV, NLT, and ESV. Text Bibles include those and many others.

e-Sword.net: free download of Bible versions and software. (But, for continuing study, please note our comment elsewhere that "you can get a lot of very, very helpful information from the 'study' Bibles by various publishers.")

The e-Sword website offers searchable free Bible texts including ESV (English Standard Version, similar to NRSV except not "inclusive" language, but also a more "formal" translation — versus GNT, CEV (these are more "freely" worded versions that are often clearer to the modern reader). (The Good News Translation, which we abbreviate "GNT" through this book, they call it "GNB" [Good News Bible] on the e-Sword website. "GNT" means Greek New Testament on their site). Also free is the ISV, noted below.

e-Sword's software has searchable storage for your own study notes. The free commentaries are centuries old, but I find John Wesley often helpful. NIV and NLT and other recent works are offered for modest fees (also Warren Wiersbe's 2007 New Testament commentary).

"Literal" versions offered free include the older "Young's" and the more recent Jay Green's "LITV" (© 1976 - 2000).

We alphabetize the following Bible versions for more extensive comments:

ISV We quote elsewhere the ISV's publicity statement that the International Standard Version is "the first English Bible conceived, designed, translated, and formatted primarily for a computer-literate generation" (website isv.org; also free download at e-Sword.net).

KJV *King James Version* - Bible translated under the authority of the King of England and published first in 1611. The KJV uses "thee" and "thou" (do you know the difference between those, dear reader?) and other archaic, out-of-date wording ("prevent" for "precede," "conversation" for what we call "conduct," etc.). As noted in the Index, we discuss the question of whether certain wordings in the KJV are still worthy of the student's attention, compared to modern readings, so that the seeker can be aware of those that we have found worth pondering (e.g. Psa 22:3, God "inhabits the praises" of His people; a prophet's statement that it's the anointing that breaks the yoke, Isa 10:27).

Lamsa's *Holy Bible from the Ancient Eastern Text...From the Aramaic of the Peshitta*. (We include the ISBN in the "standard" Bibliography, section 1 here, as this may be hard to find.) Lamsa notes in his Preface that "the Gospel message was first preached in the Aramaic of the Jews of Palestine," the language of Jesus' time. He grew up in that culture and believes that the understanding of Aramaic idioms illuminates many matters in the Bible. (His work was published in the 1930s, and Bible research has advanced enough since then that many of the matters he notes are now covered in good Study Bibles, or in the text of the "freer" translations. At the time he wrote, the King James version was still dominant, and much of his work corrected issues with that antiquated language.)

Lattimore: *The New Testament Translated by Richmond Lattimore:* Lattimore was "among the most distinguished translators of the Greek classics" (per Bible Collector's World, from the book cover). He was a long-time professor of Greek at Bryn Mawr. He translated the New Testament from the critical text, drawing from language expertise rather than any theological perspective.

LXX - the "Septuagint," the translation of the Hebrew Old Testament (the pre-Jesus Scriptures) done by the Jewish community circa 200 B.C. It was "the Bible of the early Church." A recent translation from the critical text has been done by St. Athanasius Academy, published in *The Orthodox Study Bible,* discussed below.

NIV - The *New International Version* has become quite widely used. The NIV sticks more closely to the Bible's original languages (Hebrew in the Old Testament, Greek in the New Testament) than some of the more interpretive versions like the NLT. For the introductory reader, this may be somewhat less clear in places, although the NIV is definitely modern language (and easier to grasp than the NKJV, in my never-humble opinion. The "2011" update of the NIV is even more modern than the older NIV-1984). The more "formal" translation in the NIV, as compared with the NLT, may give more scope to meditate on shades of meanings in some verses, and this can be helpful for the more experienced reader. Like every version, the NIV has its critics, but I find that versions preferred by some people, like the NRSV New Revised Standard Version and NASB New American Standard Version, are also open to criticism. (Some criticisms of the NIV are answered nicely at the website niv-cbt.org/niv-2011-overview.)

NIV publicity says, "The NIV has become the best-selling English version of the Bible since the King James Version. The best balance between word-for-word and thought-for-thought." (Comments on e-Sword website in offering "NIV bundle" for sale August 2009.)

NKJV — The NKJV, New King James Version, modernizes the antiquated language of the KJV, but it retains many of the wordings that are cherished by people raised on the KJV. I find it does not speak to the heart as directly as the NIV (as I said above, in my "never-humble" opinion).

NLT - The Bible in the New Living Translation makes the words of Jesus "come alive" in a special way that excited my heart, even after thirty years of steady Bible reading in other translations. It uses plain language in today's English, and has become one of the top-selling Bibles, which makes it a good one to use when you want to talk to other believers.

The NLT has a theological preference for seeing "substitutionary atonement" more strongly in some verses than the Greek requires. We discuss in the main text of this book (chapter 12) that this key theme may have been focused on and elaborated so strongly and particularly in some quarters, as to obscure the Gospel message for some people.[264]

The Orthodox Study Bible, by St. Athanasius Academy (Elk Grove, California USA) has marvelous theological notes throughout, and essays on key topics. Modern English is used for both New Testament (NKJV) and Old Testament (a new Septuagint translation by St. Athanasius Academy from the critical text of the LXX). Includes a number of full-page, full-color icons.

The Passion Translation [New Testament, Psalms, Proverbs, Song of Songs - get edition 2] is criticized as closer to paraphrase than translation, but "It expresses God's passion for his people and his world by translating the original, life-changing message of God's Word for modern readers" (page vii). (Earlier on that page, "...seek to transfer meaning, not merely words...").

An example of translation styles: In John 5:35, Jesus is discussing the prophetic ministry of John the Baptist, who preceded Him and announced His coming:

(ESV)** He was a burning and shining lamp, and you were willing to rejoice for a while in his light.

(GNT) John was like a lamp, burning and shining, and you were willing for a while to enjoy his light.

(ISV) That man was a lamp that burns and brightly shines, and for a while you were willing to rejoice in his light.

(KJV) He was a burning and a shining light: and ye were willing for a season to rejoice in his light.

(LITV) That one was the burning and shining lamp, and you were willing to exult in his light for an hour.

(NASB) He was the lamp that was burning and was shining and you were willing to rejoice for a while in his light.

(NIV)** John was a lamp that burned and gave light, and you chose for a time to enjoy his light.

(NKJV) He was the burning and shining lamp, and you were willing for a time to rejoice in his light.

(NLT)** John was like a burning and shining lamp, and you were excited for a while about his message.

(NRSVA) He was a burning and shining lamp, and you were willing to rejoice for a while in his light.

(TPT, *The Passion Translation*) John was a blazing, burning torch, and for a short time you basked in his light with great joy.

** **denotes** a version available in **audio** form from YouVersion (website bible.com), which supports mobile devices as well as computers. (Others may have been added in audio since my research.)

(*"Bible reading"* is indexed for our tips, e.g. Luke-John-Acts to start; also see endnote 277. Another way to study the Bible's wisdom and grace is D. Jeremiah's *In the Words of Jesus* — New Testament Scriptures topically, the "Person of Jesus"... "Promises of Jesus," teachings on a variety of key subjects, and classic parables. It uses the NLT.)

Appendix Four: "Out-takes"

#1 Thoughtful-Woman was in a good mood this morning. Her eyes were twinkling as she asked B-t, "Suppose I decide you're right, any *tips* on how to function as a Christian?" R_ could hear the lilt in her voice and turned to monitor the situation — but B-t's eyes were twinkling also, and the dog was grinning from ear to ear! R_ focused grimly on the road as B-t replied, "Yes... always take your Bible to church — and go to church at least every other week, even if it seems nothing is happening (over time, it makes all the difference in the world — going to a decent church or a good Christian fellowship every week or at the very least every other week, even when it's discouraging). Try to genuinely worship in your private time, read a chapter a day of Bible, like our driver said..."[265] (See also endnote 277 re spiritually-developmental practices.)

B-t saw the question in Thoughtful-Woman's eyes, and plunged into it: "The reason to take your Bible to church is that if things drag a bit, or if the sermon is quintessentially uninteresting, you can absorb yourself in reading your own Bible and have a good time."

#2 The Scripture Table didn't include this verse: "I have been a fool, but you have driven me to it." R_ was asking himself whether to include this, and when he looked up the reference, he realized he had combined language from the ESV/NRSV and the NIV for 2Cor 12:11. "If I confess that jumbling, people will laugh their heads off at me," he said to the dog, whose expression was inscrutable.

Appendix Five: Notes on Our Unsophisticated Literary Devices

The RV journey and the hitchhikers are an invention, to frame the dialogue and enhance its flow. The dog, however, is a lovingly-remembered companion, faithful and virtuous.

Chapter, **Atone/Shalom**: The "dawn chorus" highlights the human impact, for the birds are diminishing world-wide as our civilizations advance. The small towns "ungraced by architectural flair" remind us how the fulfilling at the micro level (their inhabitants, making their lives per their own visions and capabilities) can be so much less than what can be when the people are in unity with "the Great Power." This connects with the "Fall" portrayal of creation adversely impacted by human sin. (See Index references.)

Throughout the book, the scenes of nature's beauty — briefly noted in a few sentences here and there, never dwelt on with a poet's pen — alas, you will have to supply the vision. The poet's touch, I do not claim. (**Milton** wrote that it would be "an injury and sullenness against Nature not to go out and see her riches, and partake in her rejoicing.")[266]

The flow of the book puts many profound things into the "notes," because added depths that may be of interest to one reader may bog down others, yes?

We place some text in bold letters, to make Index entries easy to find on the page. Not all are treated this way, in an effort to hold down the distraction!

Our cogitations about "Markan priority," and other matters of possible interpretations, may not command the assent of all, but we hope that they will help to "attend" to the words that offer us the great hope, the true and sure salvation (Heb 2:3).

As we noted, the "dog" character comes from a real creature. We acknowledge that, with his thoughts about "hesed" (p. 114) and his tracking of the flow of the conversation in the following paragraph, the persona of the dog changed and went beyond real dog sensitivity to humans into a purely imaginary construct. But it seemed to fit what the narrative called for.

Sci-guy's two beer-drinking episodes, one leading to a headache, the other to a valuable input for everyone, are not intended as either an adverse comment against the (moderate) use of alcohol, nor as an endorsement.[267]

A sad final note:

The non-believer hitchhikers never decide whether to grasp what is held out to them or not — the busyness of life, the cares of this world, engage their attention. Scripture citations could be given, including Martha & Mary (Luke 10:41-42), or Gospel quotes "cares of this life, deceitfulness of riches" (Mark 4:19, Heb 3:13).

B-t said to R_, "Why don't you warn them, that negligence may be culpable, that negligence may be destructive beyond their imaginings?" The question stung, so R_ looked up a comment he had remembered: "...immersed in an existence that bears every indication of being limited and ending in frustration... human beings opt for what may be temporarily satisfying rather than what would be conducive to everlasting life with God." [268]

(Note Index "Warning" for R_'s other fumbling on this!)

Appendix Six: If you decide to take your Bible to Church, a modest suggestion: *Bible Books, Alphabetically*

One of the difficulties a person will face, if one takes up the Bible and Church per the promises of Jesus,** is that you will be sitting in church, the speaker will cite a Bible reference, and the old-timers will have it open before you can find the book in your Table of Contents. Somebody said, "It's embarrassing!" One way around that is to construct your own table of contents with the books within the Bible listed alphabetically. You can do that by writing the page numbers for your own Bible version, on the table below.

In noting that it does indeed go "from A to Z" ("Acts" to "Zephaniah"), it came to mind that someone said that "The Acts of the Apostles" could also be called "The Acts of the Holy Spirit"!

** To meditate on these matters, please read Hebrews 10:25 and John 14:23. (Later, Eph 5:25, re Christ and the Church.) Also, an Old Testament exhortation came to mind: "Taste and see that the Lord is good" Psa 38:4. (Note also Psa 119:11.)

<table>
<tr><td colspan="2">1 Chronicles</td></tr>
<tr><td colspan="2">1 Corinthians [Tell us: Should New Testament books be in bold?]</td></tr>
<tr><td colspan="2">1 John ("John," the Gospel, is distinct from "1 John," "First John," the epistle — first of three Epistles of John. Abbreviated "1 Jn.")</td></tr>
<tr><td>1 Kings</td><td>2 Peter</td></tr>
<tr><td>1 Peter</td><td>2 Samuel</td></tr>
<tr><td>1 Samuel</td><td>2 Thessalonians</td></tr>
<tr><td>1 Thessalonians</td><td>2 Timothy</td></tr>
<tr><td>1 Timothy</td><td>3 John</td></tr>
<tr><td>2 Chronicles</td><td>Acts</td></tr>
<tr><td>2 Corinthians</td><td>Amos</td></tr>
<tr><td>2 John</td><td>Colossians</td></tr>
<tr><td>2 Kings</td><td>Daniel (abbreviated "Dan.")</td></tr>
</table>

Deuteronomy (Dt., Deu, Deut)	Lamentations
Ecclesiastes	Leviticus
Ephesians	Luke (abbr. Lk., Luk)
Esther	Malachi
Exodus	Mark (Mk., Mar)
Ezekiel	Matthew (Mt., Mat)
Ezra	Micah
Galatians	Nahum
Genesis	Nehemiah
Habakkuk	Numbers
Haggai	Obadiah
Hebrews	Philemon (Phlm, Phm)
Hosea	Philippians (Phlp, Php)
Isaiah	Proverbs
James (abbr. "Jas")	Psalms (Ps., Psa)
Jeremiah	Revelation
Job	Romans
Joel	Ruth
John (the Gospel of John) (Jn., Joh)	Song of Solomon
Jonah	Titus
Joshua	Zechariah
Jude	Zephaniah
Judges (Jdg)	

"Bible reading" is Indexed, for our recommendations about how to proceed. The New Testament is what's offered to us, and should be the focus.

Appendix Seven: Some Theological Reflections

These are some entry points for certain controversies that do not fit into the flow of the main narrative (and a different viewpoint on the "Adam & Eve" conundrum, since it seems to perplex the mortal mind most profoundly).

Bible Scripture: Nancey Pearcey on the Text's Reliability

While sharing a cab in New York, she was asked about Dan Brown's *The Da Vinci Code*, with its "core claim — that the Bible is historically unreliable" (i.e. that the written text has been doctored and altered — quoted from p. 10 of her *Saving Leonardo*). "Over the blaring horns of New York City traffic, I explained that the New Testament can be tested by exactly the same methods that scholars use to test any other ancient documents... comparing manuscripts in different languages from all around the Mediterranean world... If variations are minor, then the texts were copied accurately and the version we have today is close to the original. And that is exactly what historians *do* find. Consequently, they have been able to reconstruct the original text with about 99.5 percent accuracy. There is no evidence that the New Testament texts were doctored or that legendary material was added later." [As to Dan Brown's claims that "the Gnostic Gospels give an earlier, and hence more authentic, account of Jesus' life," Pearcey recaps that "professional historians say the Gnostic Gospels were written about a century *after* the New Testament."] (see also Index for more explanation of "critical text.")

Neglected Items: Some aspects of the Bible's Old Testament never reach popular awareness — such as Deut 23:15 "If slaves should escape from their masters and take refuge with you, you must not hand them over to their masters" (NLT). Compare 1 Cor 7:21, Paul's comment to slaves, at that time a common status in the Roman Empire: "if you can gain your freedom, do so" (NIV).

Elwell's comment that "Every possible abuse of power finds its condemnation in what is holy" is drawn from analyzing Old Testament Scriptures, cited in the article on "Holy, Holiness." (See Bibliography for Elwell's theological reference work.)

Deeper Assessments/ Reversed Conclusions/ Same Thing:

Physics gave me a thought-provoking matter: if you drag a box over a floor, it requires force to make it move. How much force, and what factors shape that amount? Bear with me, dear reader, this will come back to shed a light on the divisive controversies of today.

Elementary experimentation: use different sizes of boxes, put different weights in them, and it will show that the amount of force is independent of the *area* of the box on the floor, and dependent on the amount of *weight* put in the box. Delve deeper: get the ability to assess the molecular level, where we find that larger weights deform the molecular structure and cause more molecular contact; and here, advanced physics research shows us that the force depends only on the amount of contact area and — for the same molecular contact areas — the force required is *independent* of the weight in the box.

So, while the analyses *look* very different — and they state different conclusions about the factors — the *force required* to move the box, *per the weight involved*, remains the same. R_ had fun explaining this to B-t and Thoughtful-Woman. B-t's eyes glazed over but Thoughtful-Woman made the obvious comment, "So, people who are comfortable with the intuitively obvious, recognizing God are OK, yes? If they really do it, of course."

Early Christianity and "Christianities"

It has become fashionable in some circles to assert that in its early phases, Christianity existed in a wide variety of alternative forms, and political power suppressed many of these to get "orthodoxy." Andreas Kostenberger and Michael Kruger do the in-depth technical analysis of the ancient data to show that as Christianity spread, the *basic* orthodox doctrines and practices were the first form in every major location, with heterodox "Christianities" coming as later evolutions. (They provide their perceptions on a CD of a radio interview as well as the book, for those who prefer alternate media. See Bibliography, Kostenberger, *The Heresy of Orthodoxy.*)

It is easy to read too much into that, for "orthodox" understanding deepened as the believers reflected on the awesome and unprecedented events of Christ's appearance. But it is also too easy to believe that the early discussions mean that "alternate Christianities" were suppressed by power plays, that the Scriptures were tampered with to build church power, etc. (We document elsewhere how the "critical text" scholarly work refutes the charge of alteration of the Scriptures when the church was able to become an institution of some power [see Index].)

Adam & Eve: A Master Thinker's View

C. S. Lewis was one of the master thinkers in relating Christian teaching to modern times. (Lewis died in 1963; his *Mere Christianity* is a non-denominational classic on understanding core matters.) His comments about Adam and Eve:

For long centuries, God perfected the animal form which was to become the vehicle of humanity and the image of Himself. He gave it hands whose thumb could be applied to each of the fingers, and jaws and teeth and throat capable of articulation, and a brain sufficiently complex to execute all of the material motions whereby rational thought is incarnated. The creature may have existed in this state for ages before it became man: it may even have been clever enough to make things which a modern archaeologist would accept as proof of its humanity. But it was only an animal because all its physical and psychical processes were directed to purely material and natural ends. Then, in the fullness of time, God caused to descend upon this organism, both in its psychology and physiology, a new kind of consciousness which could say 'I' and 'me,' which could look upon itself as an object, which knew God, which could make judgments of truth, beauty and goodness, and which was so far above time that it could perceive time flowing past...[269] *We do not know how many of these creatures God made, nor how long they continued in the Paradisal state. But sooner or later they fell. Someone or something whispered that they could become as gods... They wanted some corner in the universe of which they could say to God, 'This is our business, not yours.' But there is no such corner. They wanted to be nouns, but they were, and eternally must be, mere adjectives. We have no idea in what particular act, or series of acts, the self-contradictory, impossible wish found expression. For all I can see, it might have concerned the literal eating of a fruit, but the question is of no consequence."*[270]

Lewis' quotation was brought to me by Dr. Francis Collins on pp. 208 - 209 of his *Language of God.* Dr. Collins goes on to discuss the issue of handling Genesis as truth so as not to "eviscerate the real truths of faith" (p. 209) and that God does not "expect us to deny the obvious truths of the natural world that science has revealed to us, in order to prove our love for Him" (p. 210). (Collins discusses the relation of the Adam and Eve narrative to genetic analyses that "suggest that approximately ten thousand ancestors gave rise" to the present human race, p. 207.)

[On p. 112 we noted that "Adam, Hebrew אדם Adahm," which appears in our English Bible just as a personal name "Adam," is also in Hebrew the collective name for "humanity."]

Your author notes that Lewis' comment on humans as necessarily "adjectives" positions our existence as ultimately being only in relation to God, dependent on God. While I personally prefer the more mystical viewpoint cited in the main narrative, Lewis' thoughts may help those for whom that mysticism does not compute, yes?

"Old Testament Eyes"

These are drafting notes for a meditation on how hard it is for a modern reader to read the Bible's "Old Testament" with understanding (that section is the account from centuries before Jesus).

When living in a society where animals were core food, sacrificing animals meant sacrificing what was important to you —

just as sacrificing time would be to you now, the core of your life as you perceive and understand it.

The violence of human beings in some Old Testament sections led a British Bishop to say, "This is the social context into which God sends his own son to show a new way of living."[271] I read that the discovery of the Ebla archives debunked the critics' claim that writing was not available at the time of the Biblical Exodus (an issue as to whether Moses could have written the early books of the Bible). When I looked up "Ebla" in my *Oxford Companion to the Bible*, I found a single sentence note that "Naram-Sin, a conquering king of Mesopotamia in the twenty-third century BCE, records that he captured and burned Ebla." Just that single sentence — but if you had been there to see the horror of it... That's a non-Biblical note on how things were, back then.

This may, if writing effort permits, become a dialogue where a hitchhiker notes that there is a lot of contrary comment about the Bible's OT. B-t could note Paul Copan's book, *Is God a Moral Monster: Making Sense of the Old Testament God.* Much of the devastation reported in the OT, per Copan's research, correlates with typical ANE (Ancient Near East) language for warfare, and the Israelites, he finds, were actually less devastating than the general practices. Note that amidst widespread and unceasing war by humans, God used one of the conflicts for a positive outcome of establishing awareness of God's revelation — a revelation of concern for human welfare, and divine accessibility; *and* to lay the foundation for Messiah, the Incarnation, an ontological transformation of "God+human," transforming our possibilities.

(The argument from some archaeology, that perhaps monotheism sprang up in Egypt before Moses — and then Egypt lapsed back into polytheism — might show, *not* that revelation was not involved with Moses, but rather that it "failed to take" with those Egyptians, so that the Exodus was necessary, to use a separated people for the revelation to have impactful traction.) (Historical reality of the Exodus, see DVD noted on p. 168-169)

And this: Warfare was routine, a human commonplace then (2 Sam 11:1, 1 Chron 20:1: "In the spring, at the time when kings go off to war..." An American Indian said the same thing about ancient tribal relations [in a TV program which I cannot document for time and channel]: "Either our warriors were messing with them, or their warriors were messing with us.") The Mesha stele (c. 830 B.C.) boasts of the massacre of entire Israelite towns. Einstein said eventually war would be regarded as something barbaric and incomprehensible — well, that will be an improvement, but the people who lived in a time when it was unavoidable, need to be understood accordingly. (One might quote also Luiseño Indian Pablo Tac, the oldest account of that culture *by* a Luiseño Indian. Tac notes how common violence was in the old culture, before the Spanish came, and asks God why He waited so long to send the Gospel to them to change things).[272]

There is also what may be, when understood properly, a definitive refutation of the idea that the God of the Old Testament is prone to violence (beyond His* own clear statement in Ezekiel 18:32, "I take no pleasure in the death of anyone," repeated in 33:11. The reader may note that both verses are calls for people to forsake evil, to "repent"). The great King David was in many ways a "type," a model, a foreshadowing, of Messiah, of Jesus Christ and His Kingdom, but when it came time to build a magnificent Temple to worship God and proclaim His* glory, God prohibited David from being the one building it. He* told David, "You are not to build a house for my Name, because you have shed much blood (Bible, 1Chron 22:8, again in 28:3).[273]

Comments on reading the OT (Old Testament) need to include that the Bible sometimes does not use language as we do — e.g. Deut 15:4: "There should be no poor among you, for the LORD your God will greatly bless you in the land He is giving you as a special possession" (NLT) — and towards the end of the same chapter, "There will always be some in the land who are poor. That is why I am commanding you to share freely with the poor." Reading it for what it is actually saying, rather than what might be leveraged for objection, takes careful thought — our experience is that such thought is much rewarded. Yes, we see how both aspects can be true, and how they fit together...

Epilogue

"Of making many books there is no end," the Bible tells us (Ecclesiastes 12:12 ESV). The 100 or so books that I have used in order to do this book are a small sample in a vast universe of books and media. There will be further flood-tides of books, and some will claim they have refuted some of critical points put forth in the books we have referenced here. But those rebuttals will call forth further detailing and re-viewpointing[274] on the part of those who agree with our discovery. The fundamental matters will remain.

One of those "fundamentals," although I am unable to explore it satisfactorily, is that the God of the Bible says that He* is involved in "natural" processes.[275] So, no amount of "naturalistic" explanations will ever "prove" that God is not with us — but only that people can choose to believe that viewpoint.

The discussion of these issues continues to "evolve" throughout our society (driven at every step, we would note, by various intelligences). Terms like "constrained optimization," "bio-inspiration," and "Inference to the Best Explanation" have come on stage. My personal contribution may be the almost self-evident observation that a progression of forms (of living beings) would seem to be a logical way for a Spiritual Being to work with a material creation. Also, "under-determination" of theory by data has come up. That may confirm one of the great evolutionist's comments: "Science simply cannot adjudicate the issue of God's possible superintendence of nature" (Harvard's Stephen Gould).[276]

The uniqueness of Jesus is another over-arching issue. Our chapter "Atone/Shalom," the Index entries "Incarnation," endnote 6, and our meditation on the Bible's John 5:24 (pages 7, 17-18) show that we have tried to bring that all-undergirding matter into focus. "Prayer considerations" continue in endnote 277.

Your comments are welcomed, as noted earlier, but do not wait for the world to come to consensus before you take up the truth for yourself, for your own major and unending benefit![277]

ENDNOTES

General notes for all the book:

"B-t" is R_'s acronym for the Bible-toting hitchhiker.

" * " The *asterisk* is used in various chapters for this matter: Throughout this book, we capitalize "He*/Him*/His*" when referring to God. It is true, as some ably argue, that no special pronouns were used for God in the ancient Bible manuscripts. BUT the "pronoun wars" in our culture have fixated so much thought on "he" and "she" being distinctly and dividedly "masculine" and "feminine," that it seems necessary somehow to make the distinction that God is above this. ("God who is neither male nor female" — Aristides, a second-century Christian writer, per p. 33 of A. J. Schmidt's *How Christianity Changed the World*. See also note #227 below for an example in one Scripture text, and more perhaps-unnecessary commentary on this).

Some items in the endnotes are given in **bold type** because they are indexed items, so the reference can be more easily located.

R_'s Bible quotes are often from memory, after having read enough to fill up his modest brain, and the language of some Bible quotations has been left in his verbiage, although we have checked to be sure the meaning of the source has been faithfully set forth. (*Bible version abbreviations* are listed on p. 134 and in the Bibliography, Section Three, Bible Versions.)

Chapter One: "If someone dies, can that person live again?"

[1] The quotation is from Job 14:14 in the Bible, with the language not exact to any English version your author has in his personal library. Job is often thought to be the oldest book in the Bible, because it shows devoted religious observance (1:5) without any reference to the sacrifice system established through Moses. (The reason for not using direct quote language is that the "inclusive" language versions I have say "If mortals die..." [NLT; NRSV similar] and *that* sounds terribly stilted to me.)

The reader who absorbs the question ("if die... live?") may appreciate Guillebaud's remark that cyberculture "changes absolutely nothing in the substance of the fundamental questions..." (p. 308 of *Re-Founding...*)

[2] The neurosurgeon is Dr. Wilder Penfield, quoted from *Closer to the Light*, a book by Dr. Melvin L. Morse, p. 111. Dr. Penfield's stature is described as "the father of neurosurgery" (p. 99). Penfield, in his early work, believed that "brain studies could ultimately explain everything about the mind and body" (p. 100). He painted a graphic on a rock on his farm to symbolize that "truth"! But fifty years later, he took more paint and redid the graphic. In his last

book, *The Mystery of the Mind,* he reported that his further studies had led him to conclude that "the consciousness of man, the mind, is NOT something to be reduced to brain mechanism" (p. 100, emphasis in the original). Penfield wrote that the hypothesis that "the mind is separate from the brain seems the more reasonable of explanations... What a thrill it is, then, to discover that the scientist, too, can legitimately believe in the existence of the spirit!" (p. 101). However, Penfield felt the scientist, through science, can "really conclude... Only this: the brain has not explained the mind fully" (p. 102 of his book; see also endnote 162). ["Through science" there, cf. Methodology, indexed].

[3] The words of Jesus, as given by the New Living Translation, may be the best explanation of the "new birth," John 3:3 (or *"birth from above,"*** another way the Greek ἄνωθεν can be translated): **Bible, John 3:6: Humans can reproduce only human life, but the Holy Spirit gives new life from heaven.**

** Billy Graham says this is the better translation. Comparison with John 3:31 and 19:11, where the same Greek word appears, would appear to validate that.

[4] 57% of humanity follow the "monotheistic" (one-God believers) religions of Christianity (2,447,988,000 persons), Islam (1,752,045,000), Judaism (14,778,000), or Baha'i (8,010,000) per page 698 of *The World Almanac and Book of Facts 2018* (out of a world population of 7,405,107,650 per the same Almanac, p. 729).

(The thoughtful reader will note that that's an "Almanac statistic." The genre has its limits. We do note that when a country is reported as being 99.8% of a certain [non-Christian] religion, as a country example on page 843, it is highly unlikely that all 99.8% of those are really "true-blue" believers. We don't mention the country name, by the way, since we're critiquing, not praising – and what if I'm wrong?)

[5] For the critic, we concede that this sentence embodies an anthropological perspective rather than a Biblical one. Our approach follows the direction given to your author by a Native American Elder in Alaska, who said "you should be a preacher, and preach to your people." (He was both Athabascan Indian, holding the office of Second-Chief region-wide, and an Episcopal priest). Putting together the two perspectives, anthropological/scientific and Biblical, takes this whole present book, and we have to start by speaking with what people today understand.

[6] Jesus, Luke 23:34 KJV (King James Version, a Bible translation done in A.D. 1611 but still used by many people. There are so many translations, it may be worth noting what B-t said to Thoughtful-Woman, the key point: "They [all these Bible versions] all say the same thing: 'Jesus Christ, Son of God, Savior."

The 100-Minute Bible highlights the importance of this: "...the key to unlocking the Bible is Jesus Christ. It's as if he is the great explosion that happened in the center of history and the Bible is a record of its impact" (page 1, foreword by Bishop John Pritchard).

[7] Billy Graham, perhaps the most famous American evangelist of the 1900's, said that God is "calling out people from the world for His name, whether they come from the Muslim world, or the Buddhist world, or the Christian world or the nonbelieving world, they are members of the Body of Christ because they've been called by God. They may not even know the name of Jesus but they know in their hearts that they need something they don't have, and they turn to the only light that they have, and I think that they are saved, and that they're going to be with us in heaven."

Source: Dr. Mark Sidwell, *The Dividing Line* p. 122-123. (Dr. Sidwell is not approving of Graham's comment).

Jesus said, "Very truly, I tell you, anyone who hears my word and believes him who sent me has eternal life" Bible, John 5:24 NRSV.

[8] 1 John 4:7 NIV (New International Version, a Bible translation widely regarded positively for its balance between literalism and meaning). Consider also 1 John 2:29 "everyone who does what is right has been born of him [God]." The word **"loves" in 1 John 4:7** is the Greek αγάπη **"agape"** (pronounced "ah-GAH-pay") – **not the Greek phileo, friendship, or eros, romantic/sexual love**. This *agape* love is what Gordon Hempton, in *One Square Inch of Silence*, called "the love that connects all things" (p. 12). (Note to our readers — Hempton's book is not on spiritual issues, so it is not in our Bibliography. It is a discussion of noise as too-pervasive in our society — that sounds dull, but it's a really fun read! Also a cross-country journey.)

Agape love: the early theologian Augustine called it "self-less love".

We might ask if the woman who anointed Jesus at a public dinner, unbidden and despite hostility, was an example of this – ? She brought "very expensive perfume" and poured it on His head, drawing very negative comments. Jesus' response was to tell the detractors to leave her alone, to commend what she had done (Mat 26:10, and He noted it prepared for His burial, verse 13). Jesus said that, "**wherever this gospel is preached** throughout the world, **what she has done will also be told**, in memory of her."

The discussion of *sincerity* should include the old quote:

"You can be sincere and still be stupid." – Charles F. Kettering, quoted on page 465 of Laurence Peter, *Peter's Quotations: Ideas for Our Times.* As an example of this, I might offer a friend who told me in profound sincerity, "The Bible tells us to smoke marijuana." I said, "I must have missed that verse." My friend replied, "No, no, marijuana is a herb, right? And God says in Genesis, 'I have given you every herb to use' " (Gen 1:29 KJV).

As a further footnote on God's working with people of earnest sincerity, I might note that this friend is now a decade and a half "clean and sober," and has counseled many dozens of others to help them escape the deceitfulness of drug euphorias.

As a nod to genuine sincerity, I will explicitly note that I am refraining from documenting the times that I have been sincerely and harmfully wrong. My friend's comments did not do me any harm at all, and I wish I could say the same for the impacts of my own errors on others. (I do ask you all to forgive me.)

[9] The full quote about this is: "... aged Cherokees whose primary sources took them well back into the 1600's said that as far back as their history could be traced, the nation had been divided into at least two sects regarding their beliefs about divine beings ... [The minority] said there existed above three beings who were always together and of the same mind. The names of these beings were: first, U ha lo te qa, 'Head of all power,' or literally 'Great beyond expression'; second, A ta nv ti, 'United,' or rather 'The place of uniting' where persons agreed to meet and form a perpetual friendship; third, U sqa hu la, the meaning of which could not, in 1835, any longer be learned, but it had something to do with 'mind' or 'affection.' These three, it was said, were always one in sentiment and action** and would always continue to be the same. They created all things, were acquainted with all, were present everywhere, and governed all things. ... all prayers were directed to them. They had messengers, or angels, who came into this world and attended to the affairs of men..." — page 143 of *The Cherokee People: The Story of the Cherokees from Earliest Origins to Contemporary Times*, by Thomas E. Mails.

** compare "single will or energy" end of endnote 118

We will discuss in Part Four that in the sixth century B.C., an ancient Chinese philosopher, Lao Zi (old spelling Lao Tzu), perceived a Being which he saw as the "Source of all things" and which was "Born before heaven and earth." At least one commentator has seen this as a perception of what Christians know as the Word of God, "eternally begotten of the Father" and "through Whom all things were made" — the second Person of the Trinity which became incarnate as the God-man Jesus of Nazareth, the Christ. Lao Zi (Lao Tzu) is quoted from chapters 25 and 4 of his *Tao Teh Ching*, Lao Zi's epic work written in the sixth century B.C. (the modern spelling of this book's name is *Dao De Jing*.) These statements by Lao Zi are cited on page 6 of Hieromonk Damascene's book *Christ The Eternal Tao*. The quotation uses the translation of *Dao De Jing* by Gi-ming Shien and Eugene Rose. The quotes of Christian words for this are from the Nicene Creed and from John 1:3.

Lao Zi (old form "Lao Tzu") also left us — from the 6th century B.C., indeed! — an astonishing statement for a pre-Christian source: "the startling phrase in chapter 42 of the Tao Teh Ching, in which Lao Tzu writes, 'The Three produced all things.' " (This quote of Lao Zi is on page 255 of *Christ the Eternal Tao*.)

[Please note that the astonishment at the "startling phrase" is that of the monk who studied Taoism intensively, not *mine* — lest you think my shallow mind has mistaken the matter — your author.]

Chapter Two: The Convergence of Science and Religion

[10] The hitchhiker has condensed the message of 2 Peter 3: 9 - 13: "The Lord isn't really being slow about his promise to return, as some people think. No, he is being patient for your sake. He does not want anyone to perish, so he is giving more time for everyone to **repent**. But the day of the Lord will come as unexpectedly as a thief... the heavens will disappear in fire ... Since everything around us is going to melt away, what holy, godly lives you should be living! ... God will set the heavens on fire and the elements will melt away in the flames. But we are looking forward to the new heavens and new earth he has promised, a world where everyone is right with God." Quoted from the New Living Translation (NLT) 1996, bold emphasis added.

The scientific prospect of the earth we love ending in fire is, of course, tempered by the scientists' projection that it will be five billion years in the future when the sun sears the planet due to changes in the sun's nuclear fusion — with the discovery of a "black hole" in our galaxy, might we have a scientific basis for the apprehension that at any time the Bible's warning could come true, "This night is your soul required of you" Lk 12:20 ?

"The whole temple of Man's achievement must inevitably be buried beneath the debris of a universe in ruins." — Bertrand Russell, quoted on p. 90 of Os Guinness, *Long Journey Home*. Russell went on to say that all philosophy must now rest "on the firm foundation of unyielding despair..." (ibid). Well, not according to our discovery, dear reader!

Some feel that Russell's problem is solved by keeping a shorter-term perspective. This present life is adequate, they say. But if our "discovery" is *true*, that is a shirking. (Please note that Chapter 10 has some further discussion of this issue, including Russell's despair in later life due to his philosophy.

Os Guiness's book covers the scope of human ultimate understandings, assessing Western religion, secular humanist philosophy, and eastern religion, discussing each in a very easily-read form and carefully developing the case that the truth of Jesus Christ answers best to reality and experience. (Yes, we noted that this paragraph restates what our *Annotated Bibliography* says about his work).

[11] Leviticus 19:32 NIV. The perspective arrived at by evolutionary biologists is from a newspaper article which your author, in the absence of secretarial support, has failed to archive.

[12] Faraday "discovered electromagnetic induction and many other electrical and magnetic phenomena." The New Lexicon Webster's Dictionary of the

English Language, Encyclopedic Edition, page 341. (New York: Lexicon Publications, 1989). *See note 257 for more re "testimony of scientists."*

Checking my memory of the quote, I found that the website thinkexist.com/quotes/michael faraday (Feb. 1 2010 visit) gave Faraday's exact quote as: "Nothing is too wonderful to be true if it be consistent with the laws of nature." Here the skeptic and the believer will diverge. Consistency with the "laws of nature," per the believer, comes first and foremost from the sovereignty of God, which gives the laws of nature their normal order and also provides His* freedom to intervene (the mercy of a loving God, someone said, Who is willing to adjust the laws He* has given).

Chapter Three: The Gathering Storm

* The "*" footnote on pronouns for God is explained at the beginning of the endnotes.

[13] The description of colors glinting on the snow — on snow with water droplets and some crusting of ice in the spring sun — is drawn from your author's experience of seeing this a number of times in Alaska.

[14] Hebrews 13:2.

[15] The Bible quote ("Scripture") is R_'s memory of Bible, Hosea 4:6. Theodore Roosevelt, one of four Presidents of the United States considered worth memorializing in the massive Black Hills sculptures of Presidents' faces, said, "A thorough knowledge of the Bible is worth as much as a college education."

[16] The commentator is Hugh Ross, *The Genesis Question*, pp. 41-44. Ross perceives that *"He made the sun"* is a *recap* in Gen. 1:16.

Also, Dr. Ross argues that the great flood of Noah's Ark fame was a regional, "Local Flood" — he argues this *theologically* — and he goes into the original Hebrew language of Genesis to support this (p. 145ff). [I don't believe he responds to the question that comes to a naïve observer of the controversy: for a regional flood, why rescue animals, which could migrate back from elsewhere? We enter the realm of conjecture; it could be to teach the survivors stewardship, per Genesis 2:15 "take care of it." Or to keep them busy during a year of great stress...]

[17] Commentator is Hugh Ross, p. 65.

By the way, a major American denomination is insisting that "one day" in Genesis must mean one of our calendar days ("rotational days," some call it), as word studies in all the rest of the Old Testament show it always means that elsewhere. The flaw in this is that creation was a unique and very special time, and the use of language to describe it must therefore be expected to be unique and special.

[18] Having done two Masters degrees, one of the things your author has loved about the Bible was that 3,000 years ago, the Bible said that "of making many

books there is no end..." — Solomon's wisdom recorded in the Bible, Eccl. 12:12. (One of R_'s Seminary professors quoted that, but left off the next line: "much study is a weariness of the flesh.")

The impact of the present flow of books has moved people to say:

"The multitude of books is making us ignorant." - Voltaire (Francois Marie Arouet) (1694 - 1778), page 52 of *Peter's Quotations: Ideas for Our Times*, Dr. Laurence J. Peter

"We live in an age that reads too much to be wise." — Oscar Wilde (1854 - 1900) (ibid.)

"The Arctic expresses the sum of all wisdom: silence." - Walter Bauer (p. 66 of same book)

[19] Scripture: "Remove the obstacles out of the way of My people." Isaiah 57:14 NIV (King James Version of the Bible has "stumblingblock")

[20] Bible, John 2:19.

[21] Acts 2:22 NIV. The disciples of Jesus did their early preaching in Jerusalem, where people had indeed seen miracles performed by Jesus.

[22] R_ was especially troubled because this point reminded him of St. Augustine (about A.D. 400), one of the great early theologians — but Augustine read the Scriptures (Bible) first in a Latin translation whose literary quality was far below the works of philosophy that he was accustomed to studying, and he dismissed them as unimpressive. Later, however, when he was troubled, a child's voice floated over the garden wall, "Tolle, lege, tolle, lege" — "Take up and read, take up and read" — and the Scripture he opened to in his New Testament touched him to the core of his being and transformed his life. (Romans 13:13-14 were the verses that transformed him).

[23] The "prayer of agreement" principle takes up Jesus' promise stated in Mt. 18:19: "If two of you agree on earth about anything they ask for, it will be done for them by my Father in heaven"** (NIV). This prayer principle needs to be read in context of other prayer principles/promises in the New Testament — "if you **ask in My name**" John 14:13,14; John 15:16; John 16: 23,24,26 — that is, in accordance with the character of Jesus, with the selfless love and good work He illustrated and mapped out for His followers to do. And having another believer agree with you is a check against wrongful selfishness or other misguided requests. Another "prayer principle" is obedience: 1 John 3:22 "have whatever ask" because obey — and "His commandments are not burdensome" 1 John 5:3.

("Mt." the abbreviation for "Matthew" in the Bible, as shown in Appendix Six. We apologize for the intrusion of "technical jargon," but new terms of language come up whenever you study something new — including driving a car — so please don't hit the "brake pedal," but fasten your "seat belt" and bear with us as we hit the "accelerator.")

** This promise was made to committed, seasoned disciples, who had also the promise of the Holy Spirit to guide them; used carefully along with the other prayer principles cited, it will probably do you a world of good! (Remember God's desire for the "well-being" of His* people, see Scripture Table appendix).

[24] John 1:3. R_ is quoting from memory, not a specific Bible version. The authority lies in the underlying statement of the original Scriptures, not in a particular English wording.

[25] 1 John 4:7. The NIV text is "Everyone who loves has been born of God and knows God." See note 8 regarding the Greek of the New Testament, that this is a particular type of "love."

[26] Note 7 above cited Rev. Billy Graham on "God is calling out a people from among ..." all peoples

[27] The mystic presence of Christ is shown in the Bible in 1 Cor. 10:4, which says that during the desert journeys of the Exodus, the people "drank from the spiritual rock that accompanied them, and that rock was Christ" (NIV).

[28] The problem of "three who are one" (the Trinity of God) deepens when you find that theology insists that it is *not* a matter of three manifestations, such as water existing in three states of liquid, ice, and steam. For the answer in terms of how the nature of Being changes at higher levels of being, please see Part Four, Chapter 13.

[29] That fact (his Grandmother teaching Sunday School) gave R_ one of the treasured family artifacts, an RSV New Testament (Revised Standard Version) whose cover proclaimed, "The Most Important Publication of 1946." It had been presented to R_'s grandmother in appreciation of her Sunday School teaching. The RSV was the translation that finally dented the dominance of the venerable King James Version (KJV) of the Bible, which had been produced in 1611 and held sway for more than three centuries as *the* Bible of the English-speaking world. The p.r. for the RSV said it all: "Archaic forms of expression have been replaced by the language of today." R_'s **question to King James readers**, of whom there are still many, is: "Wottest thou what thou readest?" There, he makes the point by using the KJV's own antiquated language — the verb "to wot," which means "to know," appears in Genesis 21:26 and 39:8 and other places, and for those steeped in that language, it's fine — but speakest thou understandably when thou triest to communicate the truths of Jesus the Christ? R_ would later tell B-t that he felt the New Living Translation was one way for new believers to get a clear

presentation of what the Bible says. (But those of a scholarly persuasion may want to see endnote 264 for our caution about the NLT perhaps imposing "substitutionary" understandings on the New Testament text. The chapter "Atone/Shalom" discusses this theological comprehension issue, for those interested. Don't get hung up on it!)

B-t replied that the free Bible software at the website e-sword.net offers several free Bible versions that use this "freely-worded"** approach to make things clear, including GNB, GW, CEV, as well as a "formal" version ESV for comparison and meditation, and a "literal" version LITV, so people could work through alternate wordings for clarity, without having to spend a nickel on a Bible (and also they could save searchable notes on their studies). R_ responded that that's a fine way to start your Bible study, but for steady reading, print is nice, and you can get a lot of very, very helpful information from the "study" Bibles by various publishers. He clutched his battered NIV Study Bible close to his heart as he spoke, and the dog growled softly at B-t...

[** the technical term is "dynamic equivalence," choosing words that will convey the same meaning to the English reader as the words in the original text do in their own language.]

R_ closed the conversation by reminding B-t of an old Christian proverb, **"A chapter a day keeps the devil away"** (a chapter a day of Bible reading; the proverb is a folk proverb, not from the Bible's Book of Proverbs). R_ told B-t he thought people could *start by going through the Bible's books of Luke, John and Acts* to get a basic grasp. "If they have a pretty good feel for Jesus' human life journey (Luke), then they should read John to get the deep meaning." B-t nodded and petted the dog and peace prevailed. They agreed that a seeker should start with the "New Covenant" ("New Testament" is from the Latin version) as that is the covenant that Jesus offers to the seeker, and reading the Old Testament effectively requires "Old Testament eyes" — a mind for the context. (A British Bishop said that the Old Testament world was the world into which God sent His* Son Jesus to teach us a better way to live — this statement was in the introduction to *The 100-Minute Bible*).

B-t left the trip before they reached D.C., and R_ helped him at the ticket counter of the bus station before they parted. B-t said to R_, **"You think King James Bible readers are out of date** and ought to change, and R_ replied, "That isn't quite what I said, although it sounds like it. The King James reader comes across 'dragons' where modern texts have 'serpents,' and the KJV (King James Version) has 'unicorns' and 'steel' (the metal, in millennia B.C.!) — those are easy enough to ignore, but for someone coming to the Bible to begin to see what it says, they would be exit cues. Someone like you probably doesn't even notice those things. Also, the KJV uses 'prevent' where we would say 'precede,' and 'conversation' where we would use 'conduct' — Norman Vincent Peale's organization put out a list of *500 words* that have changed in meaning since 1611. Someone like you reads them extensively in context, so you may pick up on the correct meanings all right." B-t looked slightly cheered, but still grim, and the dog nudged R_'s hand, so he continued: "In fact, there can be a real **positive for the dedicated KJV reader**: as soon as you begin, it's clear from *the alternate language* that you've entered a special 'head space,' and that can be *a mental space of reverence* and awe and love, so it can really help, if it works that way for you."

Now B-t was smiling, and the dog was too, as R_ petted him slowly. R_ was too busy thinking to move swiftly. "There are a couple renderings in the King James that cut deep, where modern wordings seem less. In Psalm 22:3, God 'inhabits the praises' of His* people, according to the KJV (well, 'inhabitest,' to quote the antiquated verb form). That has been preached as a profound call to praise Him — and He certainly deserves it! Modern versions don't have that wording of that clear call and promise. And the King James says (Isaiah 10:27) that the anointing destroys the yoke — important for Pentecostals who have a theology of 'the anointing,' the special active presence of the Holy Spirit." B-t was thrilled at this and gave R_ a hug before he ran to catch his bus. It was one of the few times on the journey where the dog barked at one of the hitchhikers — a friendly but powerful sound.

[30] Mt. 1:6, repeating key details from the Old Testament, 2 Samuel chapters 11 and 12. Since we feel it would be rude to presume on our reader's level of Bible literacy, we will note that the Old Testament is the first part of the Bible, dealing with centuries preceding Jesus; the New Testament is the section dealing with the revelation of Jesus.

Please note also that when the prophet Nathan accosted David about this affair, David did *not* do what ancient kings were free to do: he did *not* have Nathan executed (or even put in prison, as with John the Baptist); he did *not* waive the matter aside — instead, in front of his entire court, he immediately acknowledged his sin (2 Samuel 12:13). It seems that this is important in David being called "a man after God's own heart" (Acts 13:22, restating Old Testament verses).

[31] The quotation recaps Sagan and combines commentary on his statements; obtained from the website asa3.org/ASA/PSCF/1996/PSCF3-96Isaac.html, website visited 3/15/03. *For a modern layman's recap of "what Adam and Eve did," and the remedy, see endnote 55.* (Sagan's self-description was "agnostic") [1996 quote per Wikipedia visited 26 May 2015].

[32] The Rev. Dr. King is quoted from page 16 of the Christian Science Monitor, January 16, 2009. It is noted there also that "In 1994, legislation challenging Americans to transform Martin Luther King Day ... into a day of citizen action volunteer service was signed into law."

Websites of note might include universalgiving.org, and to find opportunities for volunteer service, and CreateTheGood.org (the latter re U.S.A.; my resources are limited — your author).

Compare this: "I became angry and said to God, 'Why did you permit this? Why don't you do something about it? ... [silence; that night God replied:] 'I certainly did... I made you.' "

- Poem on seeing a hungry person, entitled "Why?" p. 40 of *Chicken Soup for the Christian Soul.*

Later, B-t argued vigorously with R_ about this at a rest-stop, saying that helping people to find salvation was the best thing you could possibly do for them...

Chapter Four: Poverty

[33] Rick Warren is quoted from an article on him, p. 162 of 3/09 *Reader's Digest.* Historian W. E. H. Lecky described **the teaching of Jesus as 'the most powerful moral lever** that has ever been applied to the affairs of man.' (Again, "man" in the old language, i.e. "humanity;" that's how he said it, so it has to be quoted that way. Os Guinness quotes him on p. 157 of *Long Journey Home* but does not give a reference for the citation. Bold added).

[34] The *Poverty and Justice Bible* has now been issued by the American Bible Society and World Vision "featuring 2,000 Poverty and Justice verse highlights" [ad October 2009]. It uses the Contemporary English Version (CEV). R_'s discussion with B-t and Thoughtful-Woman noted that this version is much like the New Living Translation (NLT) in general character of the English, although the NLT has been more predominant.

Love INC (In the Name of Christ) works to network churches to serve better together against poverty in an area. Their website is loveinc.org. Upon revisiting the website, I was unable to find the PDF again offered.

Strong's Concordance, one of the most widely available reference works, lists roughly 198 Scripture references for the word "poor" itself, with others for "destitute" and "needy." Not all relevant references contain explicit wording. For example, another key verse is "If anyone is not willing to work, let him not eat" 2 Thess 3:10 (ESV). While the Bible pleads the cause of the needy and those without market-power, it does not condone indolence or unnecessary dependency.

However, for those who suffer unjustly the accusation, "All these people want is a handout," the Bible states that the Lord will save the weak and needy "from those who malign them" Psa 12:5 NIV. See note 37 below also.

Please see Scripture Table (Appendix One) for other Bible references. Leaving aside dozens (hundreds!) of other verses, I will add: Prov. 28:27 "Whoever gives to the poor will lack nothing" (NRSV).

[35] We Americans, R_ said later, lack brutally in expressions of gratitude for how much better our children survive now. His grandfather had six children, of whom only three reached adulthood.

[36] Moses Ben Maimon ("Maimonides," A.D. 1135-1204) is quoted from his work *Charity's Eight Degrees*, cited on p. 1020 of *Bartlett's Familiar Quotations*. Two "helping" websites were cited in endnote 32, among many.

[37] The hitchhiker B-t was reminded of Job 12:5, which he had read once in the "Bible in Basic English" version: "In the thought of him who is in comfort there is **no respect for one who is in trouble**; such is the fate of those whose feet are slipping" (emphasis added).

[38] "LORD" — Old Testament covenant name for God given to the people of Israel when God brought them out of slavery in Egypt, "YHWH" when the Hebrew letters יהוה are transliterated into English letters, hence "Yahweh" (I believe George Lamsa says "Yehowah" was the ancient form. Lamsa's grounding is in the ancient Aramaic, which is the language Jesus spoke). Usually rendered "LORD" (using small capitals to give it a distinctive form) in English Bibles because the ancient pronunciation is uncertain (when God exiled the Jewish people from the "Promised Land" for persistent sin, they ceased speaking the Name to avoid possible irreverence).

"Jehovah" is derived from this but is regarded by modern scholars as not linguistically correct. The "J" for the "Y" sound appears to come from the interaction of German and English scholarship (Germans led the field for some time; compare the German word "ja" "yes", pronounced "yah.") The vowels of "Jehovah" come from the Jewish vowel pointing to show reading of "Adonai" "My Lord" instead of the YHWH name.

For discussion correcting the modern misunderstanding of "the fear of the LORD," see Index entry "Fear of God."

[39] This Scripture, when R_ went over the conversation later in his mind, reminded him of one in Revelation: "The time has come... for destroying those who destroy the earth" (Rev 11:18). [Pro. 22:23 is cited from NLT]

R_'s desire to pray ***for*** the "BTD's" (better-to-do people) is undergirded by Jesus' account of the rich man who ignored the poor beggar outside his domicile and "lived in luxury every day" (Luke 16:19). It befell him what was pronounced on another rich man: "This night is your soul required of you" (Luke 12:20). The rich man who had ignored the beggar was in hell "where he was in torment" (Luke 16:23) and saw the beggar comforted in the afterlife; the rich man was told "in your lifetime you received your good things" (v. 25).

Chapter Five: Is It Absurd?

A GENERAL NOTE FOR THIS CHAPTER: There are a number of books and websites that answer alleged **contradictions**/ discrepancies in the Bible.

Some require deep factual study, like the issue of the chronology of the kings in the Old Testament — which Edwin Thiele** finally "put to bed" with an excruciatingly detailed and analytic study. Some reflect faithfully the varying testimony of eyewitnesses (as in the count reported of how many angels at the empty tomb of Jesus Christ — Lee Strobel notes that eyewitnesses always vary; it's a human thing, and when the eyewitness accounts are perfectly in synch, they get accused of collusion (Appendix 2, see also endnote 41: Some "contradictions" seem designed to make you think — yes, Jesus said to "love the Lord God with all your *mind*" in the "Great Commandment" (Mt. 22:37, Mark 12:30, Luke 10:27) — my favorite "contradiction" is in Proverbs, where one verse says, "Answer not a fool according to his folly, lest you be like him yourself," and the very next verse says, "Answer a fool according to his folly, lest he be wise in his own eyes" (Bible, Proverbs, 26:4-5).

(** Thiele's work is summarized on paged 502 - 503 of the NIV Study Bible ©1985, from his *A Chronology of the Hebrew Kings* [Zondervan 1977]. It involves assessing periods of co-regency and other characteristics of ancient eastern kingships.)

[40] Jefferson's words are quoted from memory from R_'s reading. While they reflect accurately the analysis he made of this issue, the wording is not precisely his. The phrase "read the Bible like any other book" is his message, but Jefferson's exact words are "Read the Bible, then, as you would read Livy or Tacitus..." (assessing things as to mythological genre or historical fact, whether "evidence is so strong, as that its falsehood would be more improbable than a change in the laws of nature"). Jefferson's wording about the effect if the earth stopped revolving is that it would "have prostrated animals, trees, buildings..." Letter written to his nephew Peter Carr in 1787, p. 66 of *The Epic of Unitarianism: Original Writings from the History of Liberal Religion*, David B. Parke; Boston: Skinner House Books. My copy is in a course compendium in which publication date for that is not given.

[41] The Scriptures (Bible) differ among the several Gospels in noting one or two angels at the tomb, when the disciples discovered that Jesus Christ had been raised from the dead. The mathematician in R_ says that if there were two angels, then it is true to say that there "was an angel," although there were also more than the one noted in the other Gospel.

The sensitive soul in R_ sees in this the question of how well we humans notice the angels — were there not thousands of angels in that most special place, far above *all* our ability to perceive what we so easily neglect?

[42] The ratio is called "pi," denoted by the Greek letter "π," written in English as "pi," pronounced "pie" — it is 3.1415926535897932... to that many digits, and it cannot be expressed exactly as a decimal no matter how many digits you take it out to.

[43] With the geometry, as shown in R_'s diagram, used in the calculation, the inner circumference calculated by multiplying the inner diameter times π "pi"

is 540.35 inches (after converting from cubits into inches, at 18 inches per cubit). The Bible's reported 30-cubit measurement is 540 inches. The difference of 0.35 inches in 540 inches is less than 1 part in 1,000.

References:

The washing bowl or "bronze laver," older translations "molten sea," is in the Bible, e.g. 2 Chron 4:2-5.

The commentator's book is *The Battle for the Bible*, Harold Lindsell, p. 165. [Note that this is *not* Hal Lindsey of *Late Great Planet Earth* fame!]

Calculation: one handbreadth = 4 inches. A cubit = 18" Then the outer diameter is the 10 cubits given = 180 inches, inner diameter = 180 - 2 x 4" = 172 inches, x π = 540.35 inches for the computed inner circumference.

[44] *The Orthodox Study Bible* translates Psa 12:8 as "The ungodly walk in a circle..." and their study note says, "[walk in a circle] that is, who live only within the confined vision of their seven days each week." (They are translating from the Septuagint; this is one of those cases where determined study/analysis will find "differences" between versions, but the thoughtful student will see confirmed the basic point that core understandings and doctrines and "do/don't" commands remain the same...)

Citation note: Scripture taken from the St. Athanasius Academy Septuagint™. Copyright © 2008 by St. Athanasius Academy of Orthodox Theology. Used by permission. All rights reserved.

[45] Thoughtful-Woman teased B-t about this later: "Such language, and you a Bible man!" She said it with a grin, and B-t replied with a fact: "Father Brown at Seminary — who was also Dr. Brown, given how the Seminary was — was expostulating one day about some theologians he vehemently disagreed with: 'This is simply *wrong*... this is a bunch of baloney... this is a bunch of *crap*' — and as everyone sat up a little straighter in an unspoken rebuke, he segued smoothly to, 'I am speaking Biblically, look up *skoubalou* in your BAGD.' So I went home, got out my BAGD — the authoritative Greek lexicon, by Bauer, Arndt, Gingrich & Danker — and sure enough, when Paul wrote that he 'considered all things rubbish for the sake of knowing Christ,' he didn't really say 'rubbish,' he said 'crap.' Philippians 3:8 in the New Testament." Thoughtful-Woman looked like she was processing this at several levels, so B-t added the obvious counterpoint: "Paul was talking about dismissing cheerfully what he had been required to give up, comforts forsaken of necessity in order to do his missionary work — not advocating poverty as the lifestyle all preachers should adopt... Don't get us wrong here. Kenneth Copeland talks about THE BLESSING and 'being **blessed to be a blessing'** ** — the ***tithe*** *promise* in Malachi 3 speaks of overflowing the storehouse, which means most assuredly so that others can be assisted, I do believe."

** 3 January devotion of 2012 edition, *From Faith to Faith.*

[46] Quoted on p. 102 of *Long Journey Home* by Os Guinness. **"Suffering"** is also an item in our "Scripture Table" (Appendix One), and those statements should be pondered.

[47] P. 127 of that book. We are not endorsing *The Shack* as an overall guide to theology, although its presentation of the unity and joyfulness of the Holy Trinity are definitely worthwhile.

The reader may want to comment (form at end of book) on whether we should put more here on what the "Fall" means?? (Note discussion in chapter "Atone/Shalom" and Index entries "Fall, the, theological concept.")

Chapter Seven: Prayers: We begin...

[48] Bible, 1 Corinthians 10:13.

[49] "Obey" came into a new focus for me when a professor, during Orientation at Seminary, said, "The most violated commandment at Seminary is the 'Day of Rest.' Keep it!" I followed her advice; I kept the **tithe** (p. 127);** and, my financial situation and my time have both been amazingly blessed. Pondering, then, I ask if, in general, the most violated commandment from the Bible may be "**Rejoice**!" (Bible, Philippians 4:4; also the literal Greek for Jesus' greeting to the women upon His resurrection, Mt. 28:9 (NKJV gives the literal translation of the Greek, updated from the old KJV "All hail;" NIV has "Greetings"). It appears in the salutation of the letter to the churches from the Church council reported in Acts 15:23. The word "rejoice" in various forms occurs 42 times in the NT [New Testament, the part of the Bible reporting the life and communications of Jesus] and "joy" 82 times (NIV). (See Appendix One, "Rejoice").

** I turned to **tithing** when I was seriously financially desperate; the Lord's promise (Malachi 3:10-11 in the Bible) was faithfully kept on His* part, including the special aspect of "rebuke the devourer for your sake" (verse 11 ESV, same NASB, LITV, NKJV). I built towards the full 10% **tithe**, since I couldn't do the full amount right off; an Elder gave me her wise counsel that "a person is accepted according to what he has, not according to what he has not" 2Co 8:12, and I was given grace for that build-into. Within a year, I was keeping the full tithe. With that experience behind me, I do *not* advocate what I sometimes call the "magical" theory of the tithe — which says that if you can't make ends meet, tithe anyway and God will make money show up. A preacher on TBN Christian television said, "God doesn't need your rent money." (But Christians have been telling me that when they tithed, God *did* "make ends meet." So, I pray that all who seek Him* may receive the guidance and wisdom!)

I may put more of my story of the desperate time (that led to me coming to my senses about tithing, *putting God first in my finances* and receiving His* great promises), into my possible follow-on book; see note 232.

[50] "God does not abolish our created personhood but enhances it. Divine grace co-operates with human freedom..." (*Orthodox Study Bible* p. 1758, essay by Bishop Kallistos. He is the author of *The Orthodox Way*, discussed on our p. 166.)

[51] Wasn't it a world-class runner in a movie called "Chariots of Fire" who said that when he ran, he could feel God's pleasure in his running?

[52] For "do not lead us into hard testing," compare GNT, NRSV (also the *Bible in Basic English*, Cambridge press 1965). NLT has "don't let us yield to temptation" (cf. Mt. 26:41). George Lamsa, in translating directly from the ancient Aramaic, renders this "do not let us enter into temptation." (Lamsa grew up in an area where Aramaic, the language of Jesus' time, was still spoken. The ancient Aramaic-text Bible is called the Peshitta).

R_ mentioned that Jesus introduced this prayer with "In this way, then, you are to pray" — the "then" in that sentence, comes from His preceding statement, "Your Heavenly Father knows your needs before you ask" (Bible, Matthew 6:8). The Holy Spirit of God also helps us to pray (Bible, Romans 8:26).

The Bible's New Testament was originally sent out to the world in Greek (and the Old Testament in Hebrew). The Greek for Jesus' introductory statement is Ούτως ουν προσεύχεσθε υμείς. Young's Literal Translation renders this "thus therefore pray ye."

The 100-Minute Bible translates "The Lord's Prayer" in this way:

Our Father in heaven, hallowed be your name.
Your kingdom come and your will be done,
on earth as it is in heaven.
Give us this day our daily bread,
and forgive us the wrong we have done,
just as we have forgiven those who have wronged us.
And do not bring us to the time of testing,
but rescue us from the evil one.
(page 32 of that book)

[53] "Deliver us from the Evil One" is preferred by many modern Bible translations, but my Greek teacher was clear that the Greek "ρύσαι ημάς από του πονηρού" can be properly translated in the old way as "deliver us from evil," as the old King James and the modern NASB both do. (Jay Green's "Literal Version" says "from the evil," which is a correct word-for-word rending. There is no word in the Greek matching the English "one.")

The student may enjoy the fact that many of the scholars who insist on expanding the definite article in Matthew 6:13 (above, "*the* evil one") join together in omitting it when they translate Acts 2:42, where "devoted themselves to prayer" is more literally "to *the* prayers;" that could be understood as "the liturgy," which my Greek teacher, as a Eastern Orthodox priest, liked. Greek does not use the definite article (that is, the word "the") in the same patterns that English does — "Jesus said to him" in John 14:6 is literally "The Jesus said to him," for another example.

The conversation has highlighted the problem of the antiquated language of the King James Version (KJV). But there is another aspect to that, and R_ got into it when Thoughtful-Woman asked him about it later, as he filled the gas tank. B-t was standing beside R_, and he glowered when she brought up the issue. B-t was startled when R_ said, "For those who read it enough to understand the antiquated wording in context, the **KJV** can be a help in a special way: it can signal to their minds right away that they are entering a different thought-world, a special spiritually-minded space; if it enables them to shift gears that way, mentally, it can be good." R_ saw B-t visibly relax at this, and he added: "The **KJV wording** for Psa 22:3, that God inhabits the praises of His* people, is good and brings a special awareness of the fruitfulness of praise that the modern versions lack. And the KJV for Isa 10:27, that it is the 'anointing' that 'destroys the yoke,' has an inspired depth of meaning."

Thoughtful-Woman remembered some of R_'s previous comments, that the KJV has "dragons," "steel" (the metal!) and "unicorns" where modern translations do *not*, and the KJV uses "prevent" for "precede" and "conversation" for "conduct." She didn't look like she was about to buy a KJV to get those two verses which R_ commended. *Every translation has some nice wordings, I guess,* she thought, *and our expositor driver [that's R_, dear reader] said Richmond Lattimore translated the New Testament based on his expertise in the Greek language — that might be interesting.*

[54] Jesus was asked "What is the greatest commandment?" He answered, "You shall love the Lord your God with all your heart and mind and soul and strength." He followed the statement of it with "the second is like unto it," which is "Love your neighbor as yourself." (Matthew 22:37-39, also Mark 12:29-31 and Luke 10:27, which is followed by the story of the Good Samaritan. "Do unto others as you would have them do unto you" is Bible, Matthew 7:12.)

Jesus also, at the Last Supper, told the disciples, "A new commandment I give you, that you love one another as I have loved you" John 13:34, 15:12.

[55] 2 Chron 30:18-20. "Seeking God" brings us to the following issue:

A variant of the "prayer to accept Jesus" was the one "Bo" Bottomly used. His son "Roc" told him the background issue: "You see, man, filled with pride and misled by visions of his own power and importance, deliberately turned away from God to make his own rules, his own plans and go his own way. This grieved God deeply just as a parent is grieved when a child runs away from home.

"Yet God loved His children so completely that He chose to send His only Son to live as a human being, and to reestablish contact with men's hearts and minds and to pay the ransom for man's desertion."

Bottomly says that then: "We just prayed together: 'Lord Jesus, I need You. I open the door of my life and welcome You in as my Savior and Lord. Thank You for forgiving my sins. I have some idea of what that cost You. Please take control of my life and make me the sort of man You want me to be.' " (pp. 110, 112 of his book *Prodigal Father*).

Again, we came upon the "sinner's prayer" as Johnny Johnson led a doctor through it in a hospital: 'I love You, Lord Jesus. I have sinned and ask forgiveness for my sins. I accept Jesus as my Lord.' [from his book *Beyond Defeat*; another book I loaned out, never to see again, so the page reference is lost. His struggles as a Black man during legal segregation, and his miraculous healing by the prayer of faith, make the book quite worthwhile.]

The prayers by Josh McDowell and by his father — the town drunk until miraculously delivered by conversion to Christ — are given on pp. xxv and xxvii of *The New Evidence...* They show the same issue of the sincere opening of the heart to the Lord.

[56] Data I have seen were that the NIV, New International Version, has been for a number of years the #1 Bible in sales in the United States, followed by the King James and New King James, and New Living Translation. R_ will later commend the readability of the New Living Translation as a real help for interested people without a lot of experience in Bible study — the NLT adds some information that makes certain items understandable, and the directness of its modern language brings vividness to the chapters in John's Gospel that discuss the spiritual meaning of Jesus' work.

[57] R_ reads too much, some people think. He has combined wording from Bible translations, especially NIV and NLT; where the NIV has "Take words with you," the NLT has "Bring your confessions." People cannot expect to continue to do wrong — to abuse their neighbors and to neglect God — and find favor with God.

[58] The quote is rough; "endless asking" is probably not Rev. White's exact wording, although it makes the point for this context and carries the general sense of his remark. Clamoring at God ignores Jesus' statement that God "knows our needs before we ask" (see Matthew 6:8), and it does not show confidence in His* care and power. Rev. White was part of the Church of God in Christ (COGIC) — the name tracks to Scripture, "God was in Christ reconciling the world to Himself" (2 Cor 5:19 NKJV; see also 1 Thess. 2:14. COGIC's website is cogic.org).

[59] Since R_ never did "expand that remark" for deeper understanding, we invite the reader to write (address at end of Table of Contents) and tell us if it seems self-explanatory.

Gloria Copeland says that she experienced a great refreshing in a time of severe need, by turning to **praise** of the Lord God Almighty.

A California Elder suggested approaching God by beginning with praise of Who He* is: "You are good, and what You do is good; Your mercy endures forever, Your truth to all generations." (Bible references include "good" Psa 119:68; "mercy" 1 Chron 16:34; Psa 23:6, 52:8, 107:1; "truth" Psa 100:5. (The Hebrew word "hesed" can be translated "love" as well as "mercy" (also "lovingkindness," NASB). The word translated "truth" can also be translated "faithfulness.") "Great praise is a major key to entering into the realm of God's greatness - not necessarily loud, but what's coming out of the heart" -- Pastor George Pearsons, 27 Dec 2015, emic.tv

Chapter Eight: Destinations, Temporary; Apocalyptic Matters

[60] Page 19 of the September 13, 2009 *Christian Science Monitor* reported that the State Capitol Building was one of the properties that the State of Arizona had included in a list of properties that might be sold and leased back, for temporary revenue enhancement in the face of a massive budget deficit.

R_ was reluctant to include a factoid like that in his book — it would date the material so! But, as he pondered, he thought: *?! This pattern isn't going to stop soon. Maybe it should be in the prayers, in a special chapter, "Save!"*

[61] Washington D.C. was burned during the War of 1812. Dolly Madison performed essential service for the young U.S. government (formed by the Constitution in 1789, just over 20 years earlier) by hiding essential documents from the invader's torch.

[62] A note on "goals" — you noted that we have the word italicized as the "goals" progress through the *humans* of our story, then the *philosophers and theologians*, then our *beloved dog* — dear Reader, please do not mistake the apparent peaceful complacency of the dog's situation. He trusts in his beloved "master" to take care of the longer term — there is a dynamic moving underneath him, whose long-range sweep is beyond his comprehension and out of his control. This particular dog is well-situated, because he has the right "master" — one who will be able to feed him during the coming days, one who has the love to make sure he has plenty of healthful water, one who will go beyond that and take care of any veterinarian's bills and even provide a lot of fun experiences. (And, above all that, one who loves him and values his companionship!)

The question of "the right master" goes deeper than the dog, to all the depth of the living conscious ("sentient") beings of the universe — do they, can they, line up with such a "master" for their well-being, not only for the immediate present but for the "long haul," in fact for an unending future?

Only God could provide and guarantee such a positive answer, but since God ***has*** done exactly that, as this whole book expounds, it becomes a question of *your* participation. One of the prayers that R_ has not yet put into the "Prayers" chapters, is "to do whatever I must about ***warning*** people." Your linkage with this blessed master is not only a matter of your own blessedness — forever — it is also, like R_'s relationship with his dog, an issue of blessing others by fulfilling your part in what is possible. "For the creation waits in eager expectation for the children of God to be revealed... the creation itself will be liberated from its bondage to decay and brought into the freedom and glory of the children of God... the whole creation has been groaning as in the pains of childbirth right up to the present time" (Bible, Romans 8:19, 21,22 NIV)

[63] "moon turned blood red" is Bible, Rev 6:12 (NIV); Acts 2:20 says "the sun will be turned to darkness and the moon to blood before the coming of the great and glorious day of the Lord" (NIV). Joel 2:31 in the Old Testament says exactly the same except "great and *dreadful* day of the LORD" (NIV). ("Awesome" or "dreadful" turns on one's relation to God!)

[64] The account of this event is on pages 87 and 88 of *Smoke Signals from God*, by Ray "Black Buffalo" Wilson.

The interested reader should note that Black Buffalo wrote a song to celebrate this event. On page 89 of the same book, he recounts: "It was maybe a year later when we were in the Netherlands (Holland) ministering that I told this story and sang the song. After the meeting, a lady came up and said she was a missionary to Columbia and showed me her diary. On the same night that the sky turned red in Texas she had made an entry in her diary: 'The sky turned red in Columbia.' Is God sending us a signal of the last days?"

Ray "Black Buffalo" Wilson was an enrolled member of the Cowlitz Indian Tribe in Washington State, U.S.A. (See Bibliography for his website).

Part of the purpose of this book: (*Humanity's Greatest Discovery*) is: Proverbs 24:11 Rescue those being led away to death; hold back those staggering toward slaughter. (NIV) [and prayer point: not get in front of those given over by God to "powerful delusion" 2 Thess 2:11 NIV — that, because they deliberately "refused to love the truth" verse 10]

FROM BLACK BUFFALO'S PAMPHLET:

Why not find out what the other person thinks or understands and then use that to explain to them the way, the truth and the life? The basic law of teaching is, we teach the unknown through the known. [sixth page of undated pamphlet "Worship the Lord with Instruments, Dance and Voice,"

Ray "Black Buffalo" Wilson. Pamphlet purchased May 2009 at Kút Pokí' "House of Light" Native American church. See Bibliography for his website.]

[65] The "Incarnation" was the taking-on of human flesh by God the Logos, the Word (Bible, John chapter 1), so that Jesus was not simply a person anointed to teach in a special way, but was indeed both fully human and fully God. (Thus, able to forgive sins against God, Mt. 9:2 in the Bible; the Jewish community immediately understood this as taking on God's prerogative, and the next verse reports that Jesus was accused of blasphemy for doing this. John 10:33 reports a later incident in which they threatened to stone Jesus because "you, a mere man, claim to be God" [He didn't say, "You've misunderstood"]).

Chapter Nine: Prayers: further considerations

[66] Regarding the importance of church, a quote more than two centuries old: "To be of no church is dangerous. Religion... will glide by degrees out of the mind... [without] stated calls to worship, and the salutary influence of example." Samuel Johnson, quoted p. 233 of Bartlett's. Cf. endnote 213 (and endnote 225 discusses baptism).

[67] Pastor Elder Ivory Thornton — I always called him "Reverend Thornton," as a title of respect, but it was not his official title in his denomination, the Church of God in Christ (COGIC, see note 58). (Rev. James White, mentioned in that endnote, was his Assistant Pastor when I knew them). COGIC is the largest Black Pentecostal denomination, and these gentlemen were African-American.

Pastor Elder Thornton gave me this gem of heartfelt prayer: "We thank You, Lord, for what you have done for us on planet Earth." I keep his precious words taped to a satellite composite of Earth as seen from space, on my kitchen wall, marked with the date he spoke this: March 25, 1998.

[68] The preacher cited was Rev. Peter Edwards of the New Life Open Bible Church, San Jacinto, CA. [He calls prayer "our greatest opportunity."]

"We serve time" brings to mind Kenneth Copeland's statement that we serve our thoughts, become problem-centered and worry; the solution is to change our thoughts, line them up with the Word of God, His Word of love, of concern for our well-being, of His* ways for us to live. Compare Bible, Philippians 4:4-9; 2 Cor 12:9; a personal favorite, Psa 138:7.*

Edwards again: "The *word of faith* is 'Thank You' " [Nov. 2017]

[69] People in the Bible sometimes show both forms of "fear" toward God. They come together in God's accusation, "I thought you would fear Me and accept correction" Zeph 3:7 — either form of "fear" would have lifted the people to a higher way of living, and as God's ideas are better than ours-without-Him*, the people would have been blessed if they had done this.

Barry Lopez commented on an Arctic landscape "so beautiful it made you afraid" (*Arctic Dreams*, p. 251). We comment elsewhere on that remark as the perception of a larger, wonderful, powerful reality beyond our grasp (endnote 157). Rienecker describes "Godly fear" as "careful and watchful reverence" (his book on the Greek of the New Testament, at Heb 5:7). Note Psalm 147:11: "fear" God = hope in His* unfailing love.

As to our narrative, R_ has quoted Ps. 130:4 from memory, which he learned in the 1984 NIV version. The 2011 NIV says, "But with you there is forgiveness, so that we can, with reverence, serve you." That obscures the Biblical concept of "fear" but reads more smoothly, eh?

[70] The reference to the "armor of God" is Ephesians 6:11ff. The new Christian should note that the "weapons of our warfare are spiritual" (NIV "not the weapons of the world") 2 Cor 10:4 — the "armor" of "right standing with God and right conduct"** (the "breastplate") and "truth" and so on, are not invitations to worldly strife. (Note Romans 12:18.)

The student should compare "His* faithful promises are your armor and protection" Psalm 91:4 NLT. Someone who takes up God's offer of life, should study the promises — one expositor recommends Psalms 23, 91, 103, and 112 as key items (Kenneth Copeland, website kcm.org). One Chinese person said that during 21 years of imprisonment for being a Christian, he was sustained by only two things — Psalm 27 and the hymn "The Old Rugged Cross" (Yuan Xiangchen, a.k.a. "Allen Yuan," p. 58 of Aikman, *Jesus in Beijing*). (That's not a typo, it was Psa 27, *not* Psa 23).

** I don't seem smart enough to have supplied that modern language for the "righteousness" breastplate, but I can't find it in my Bible versions — your author.

[71] The "Jesus Prayer" is discussed on pages 341 - 350 of the book *Christ the Eternal Tao*. (The usual form of the prayer is, "Lord Jesus Christ, Son of God, have mercy on me a sinner." Matching one's speaking of it — whether overtly spoken or purely mental — with the breath, ties with the Lord as the source of life.) On pages 344-345, some cautions are firm there about not being of selfish motives, of needing counsel from older, stronger believers.

It is for these reasons of deeper layers of wording and deeper matters of caution that R_ says he's not going to expound on the "Jesus Prayer." That may seem ungracious of him, after he acknowledges that it has "done him a world of good" — but the reader will note that he *has* stated the very basic practice, for those who need to "taste and see that God is good" (see Bible, Psalm 34:8 — "Oh, the joys..." NLT).

Father Alexander Men's book, on the Jesus prayer, cautions the need for guidance (pp. 29, 70-74, 118; more on his prayer "points," last endnote).

[72] The prayer is based on Oswald Chambers' discussion of God's help in the January 9th devotion in his famous *My Utmost for His Highest*, a book of daily

devotions which has been "the most popular book of daily devotions ever published." (That's a quote from the introduction to Chamber's book by Richard Halverson, former Chaplain, U. S. Senate.)

Chambers quotes 1 Thess. 5:23 and says, "The great mystical work of the Holy Spirit is in the dim regions of our personality which we cannot get at. ... Cleansing from sin is to the very heights and depths of our spirit if we will keep in the light as God is in the light [see 1 John 1:7] ... We do not allow our minds to dwell as they should on these great massive truths of God."

Regarding this, R_ noted in later study Kenneth Copeland's exhortation, "**Expect the all-powerful goodness of God to permeate your whole being**." (in the devotional for Sept. 9th in *Pursuit of His Presence.* The seeker/explorer should note that this is definitely tied to the expectation that the person has committed to Jesus as Lord and Savior and the person is using the fellowship of the **Church** to support spiritual growth. Copeland supplies growth resources and teaching, kcm.org).

R_'s added prayer about being "where You, God, *can* bless me" refers to a proper heart toward God and turning from evil ways of conduct. One of Los Angeles' most famous criminals once expressed interest, at a special Billy Graham preaching to a private meeting of L.A. elite. This man was later led in the "Sinner's Prayer" by a Christian counselor. But when he was reproached later about not turning away from his former associates, the man replied, "There are Christian movie stars, Christian athletes, Christian businessmen. So what's the matter with being a Christian gangster?"** God is not going to bless! (See note 196 for more on this need for change.)

This brings up the question, what about a prayer, "That I may be where I can bless You"? After all, we read, "Blessed be God..." and "Bless the Lord..." (Psa 66:20, 2Co 1:3, Psa 103:1). How do we "bless" Him* — with our praise, our appreciation, by conducting ourselves so that He* can be glad to have us living the way we do? The question reminds us of the Bible phrase "rich toward God" Luke 12:21.

At the risk of prolonging unduly, I add: the reader may be as blessed as I was by Murray's *Abiding in Christ*, which discusses the privilege held out by Jesus in John 15:4-9. Murray shows the breadth and depth available to those who most seriously commit themselves to Him. (The background material of *The Orthodox Way*, applicable to other Christian communities as well as Orthodox, may help also.)

** the quote is p. 105 of *Loving God* by Charles Colson; the story of "Mickey" C. is told starting on p. 90 there. (See Index for various forms of the "Sinner's Prayer.") Colson himself demonstrated the "repentance" — he was a high official (White House!), then he was imprisoned for crimes, and when released, he dedicated himself to ministry helping the incarcerated.

Chapter Ten: Notes on Watching Human Beings Think

[73] Anne Lamott, quoted on p. 13 of Os Guinness' *Long Journey Home: A Guide to Your Search for the Meaning of Life* (© 2001; used by permission of

WaterBrook Multnomah, an imprint of the Crown Publishing Group, a division of Random House, Inc.

[74] Os Guinness kept his list of believers who were great scientists deliberately short, for flow of his narrative, so quoting the list here would actually be unrepresentative of the scope of such persons. Perhaps more noteworthy here, it was studied out whether the great scientists were merely conventional in religion per their time, or genuinely devout — finding that the deeply productive ones were largely devout (more detail, note 257 below). See the Annotated Bibliography on Rodney Stark's *For the Glory of God* (page 180 above).

While I was doing final editing on this book, I was intrigued to come upon the statement that the "Big Bang" was first proposed by a Catholic priest, the Belgian physics professor Georges Lemaitre. (He worked, of course, on the foundation of Hubble's data). Googling, I found that Encyclopedia Britannica, Wikipedia and PBS all confirmed that this is so, Lemaitre was first.

CREDIT LINE FOR OS GUINNESS quotes: From LONG JOURNEY HOME: A GUIDE TO YOUR SEARCH FOR THE MEANING OF LIFE by Os Guinness, copyright © 2001 by Os Guinness. Used by permission of WaterBrook Multnomah, an imprint of the Crown Publishing Group, a division of Random House, Inc.

[75] Re "many scientists" — one recent survey reported that 51% of scientists are believers in "God" or a "higher power." Note that this is a different framing of the question from the Wall Street Journal survey mentioned later (percentage there 40%, a more specific concept of God, see endnote 161). When B-t approached R_ at a rest stop for details and he told B-t this, B-t grimaced again — "higher power" indeed! (The 51% figure is a survey by the Pew Research Center, done May/June 2009, reported p. A25 of L.A. Times 24 Nov 2009.)

Note the mention of Newton — who revolutionized physics with his Three Laws of Motion, still valid today — and Newtonian physics still suffices to take you to the moon, for all the merits of the quantum revolution in the 20th century. Newton left us one of those tantalizing items: the great physicist was indeed a Bible student, and he meditated in the Book of Daniel in the Bible, announcing his conclusion that human beings would eventually travel faster than 50 miles an hour. The exegetical student of the Bible is stunned — Daniel never mentions 50 miles an hour — how did Newton get there? And Newton died in 1727, long before the automobile was even a glimmer on the horizon — and before James Watt's improvements in the steam engine (1765) that put humanity on its way to a well-powered existence, including in the early 1800s the railroad.

The famed French atheist Voltaire mocked Newton savagely, saying that 'the fastest horse does not touch fifty miles an hour' — yet the passing centuries have vindicated the Bible-meditating scientist. No human methodology accounts for it.

The L.A. Times article mentioned, reported also that "scientists today are no less likely to believe in God than they were almost 100 years ago, when the scientific community was first polled on this issue." In 1914, psychologist James Leuba polled 1,000 U.S. scientists, "with 42% saying that they believed in a personal God and the same number saying they did not" (L.A. Time article cited above, which went on to say that scientists today "are, if anything, more likely to believe in God today").

[76] Rodney Stark remarks on p. 291 of *For the Glory*... that "the excesses of political correctness have all but erased awareness that slavery was once nearly universal in all societies able to afford it, and that only in the West did significant moral opposition ever arise and lead to abolition... no notice is taken of ... the substantial amount of slavery** that *continues* in many parts of the non-Christian world." On the same page he states that "**antislavery** doctrines began to appear in Christian theology soon after the decline of Rome and were accompanied by the eventual disappearance of slavery in all but the fringes of Christian Europe. When Europeans subsequently instituted slavery in the New World, they did so over strenuous papal opposition... the abolition of New World slavery was initiated and achieved by Christian activists."

** Estimate 25 million slaves worldwide p. 290 of Morrow per ijm.org. [25 May 2016 website visit, 35.9 million ijm.org/casework/forced-labor-slavery; 23 June 2019 visit, estimate shown is 40.3 million on fact sheet offered for download.] U.N. estimate "21 million" Monitor 2/19/2016.

[77] This quote and the preceding one are Guinness' same book, still p. 13. He moves fast, with a light touch — it reminds me of Robert Frost's famous line, "miles to go before I sleep." (Re Guinness, see credit line at end of this endnote).

The "killing fields" were the systematic killing of a major part of the population in Cambodia (a.k.a. Kampuchea) by Pol Pot's communist regime. Your author knew a Cambodian refugee who lost 4 of his 6 children to that communist slaughter, and his wife was the only survivor of 13 brothers and sisters in her family.

Another note by your author: I was in Edmonton Canada working on a grant for a Native organization, and took a 3 a.m. break to read and refresh myself for the rest of the effort (it was pouring snow out, so no walk). I pulled down the Guinness Book of World Records, and browsing brought me to their section on great massacres. They listed Mao Ze Dong et al as the largest "massacre" in world history — so many dead, they reported, that the Russian Communists described the Chinese Communists as "bloody." (The Soviet regime was noted for its own many victims.) The Russians said the Chinese Communists' toll was 26 million dead; the Taiwanese (who had separated themselves from the mainland population during the Communist take-over) said it was 39 million; the U.S. Senate committee that investigated, said the number lay somewhere between 30 and 70 million. (The thoughtful reader will note that the Chinese regime has been through a great deal of ideological reconsideration since the Maoist period which produced those deaths).

An apology to China: We don't say the above, to point an accusing finger or to "shine a spotlight." That the world's largest country has the largest body-count, is no surprise. Woven into ALL the violence is the sinful human mind, and that is our concern. Also please note that on p. 151, we discussed the DVD "The Cross: Jesus in China" (by Yuan Zhiming) being shown throughout the country within the bureau controlling religious affairs; perhaps that DVD's account of positive human transformations by Christ will help create some more accurate perception (n.b. Annotated Bibliography pp. 184-185 & endnote 90). An ***apology*** *is due to China for the misdeeds of Western powers when China was at their mercy; the phrase "Opium War"** echoes grimly down the centuries.*

Documentation that the Nazis (Holocaust) were not Christian (beyond their obvious violation of Jesus' command "Do unto others as you would have them do unto you," see Matthew 7:12) is an important point. It has been discussed by a number of commentators — Guillebaud writes of "the radical hatred shown by the Nazis for *both* Judaism and Christianity;" he quotes Hitler saying that, "In the long run... National-Socialism [the Nazi ideology] and religion will no longer be able to coexist" and Hitler's speaking of "rooting out Christianity from Germany." (pp. 281 - 282 of Guillebaud's *Re-Founding the World*). The reader will note my concern in this book for bringing in my own observations; in studying New Testament Greek (its original language), I came upon Rienecker's statement that during his work in the 1930's in *Nazi Germany, "the ever-increasing pressure of anti-Christian tendencies* which were opposed to everything biblical made another new edition impossible" (of his book on New Testament Greek; quoted from his "Foreword to the 7th Edition"). (Further about the Nazi/non-Christian, much detailed in 2019 work noted in my endnote 92, unfortunately not received until 2020; we view the Nazi regime as having hijacked the legitimate aspirations of the German people during a time of terrible suffering).

All the massacres — from Pol Pot to the above-noted — highlight one on-going fact: People have been doing evil to each other for countless eons. There are two "large-scale" traditions of knowledge in the West; in one, the Bible says Cain bashed Abel, and that was the first murder; in the other, the scientists say they were digging in a cave in Sterkfontein, South Africa, and found the skull of an early hominid/hominin (an Australopithecus africanus) which had been bashed in, in the back, in a way they said could not have been from any accidental fall (their conclusion, not mine!) — hence a murder more than a million years ago, ? Could these two accounts be the same? Many things we do not know and will not until "the renewal of all things" (Jesus, Matthew 19:28).

Mentioning the Nazis brings up another aside: People say that the philosophy of evolution was a major factor in the evils worked by the Nazi regime. Perhaps, but take a moment for time travel: remember those old 1940's photos of columns of Nazi tanks streaming into Russia, the spear-point of an invasion that brought death to millions. Metallurgy was deeply involved there — but it wasn't that metallurgy was evil, it was the use to which it was put — the same goes for "evolutionary" understandings.

CREDIT LINE FOR OS GUINNESS quotes: From LONG JOURNEY HOME: A GUIDE TO YOUR SEARCH FOR THE MEANING OF LIFE by Os Guinness, copyright © 2001 by Os Guinness. Used by permission of WaterBrook Multnomah, an imprint of the Crown Publishing Group, a division of Random House, Inc.

** My Encyclopedic Dictionary says that one aspect of the Opium War was Britain's desire to force China to import opium from British-controlled India. That brings to mind one human transformation by Christ: A Chinese man told the missionary Hudson Taylor that he had sought relief from opium addiction in traditional Chinese practices, without any success; he was delivered from opium addiction by the power of the risen Jesus Christ, upon believing Christian prayer. *At this time I still smoked opium. I tried to break it off by means of native medicine, but could not; by use of foreign medicine, but failed. At last I saw, in reading the New Testament, that there was a Holy Spirit who could help men. I prayed to God to give me His Holy Spirit. He did what man and medicine could not do; He enabled me to break off opium smoking.* [transcribed oral testimony of Xi Sheng Mo 席勝魔 (c. 1836-1896), per the book *Days of Blessing in Inland China*, quote accessed 3 April 2013 from en.wikipedia.org/wiki/Xi_Shengmo.

[78] Guinness, p. 31. (See credit line at end of preceding endnote for this and other Guinness quotes).

[79] Guinness, p. 90. The next quote is p. 91 of *Long Journey...*

[80] Russell is quoted on pp. 93-94 of Guinness' book cited, Blackham on pp. 95-96. The phrase "creep into the first hovel" is Russell commenting on his own feelings, cited from his communications with his mistress upon being congratulated by Joseph Conrad for an essay. Russell's phrase "the terror and splendour of the night" will remind the Bible reader of Psa 19:1 "The heavens declare the glory of God."

Another famous atheist philosopher, the great French literary figure Jean-Paul Sartre, declared at life's end, "I have found my philosophy unlivable."**

"Bertrand Russell admitted that he could not live as though ethical values were simply a matter of personal taste. That's why he found his own views incredible. 'I do not know the solution,' he concluded." Bertrand Russell, "A Letter to *The Observer*," October 6, 1957, quoted in rzim.org/just-thinking/threads-of-a-redeemed-heart/ 15 Apr 2014 website visit.

We noted that the word "Gospel" comes from the Greek meaning "Good News." The open door to eternal life, created and offered by Jesus Christ, inspired the term "Gospel," i.e. "Good News," for the new message. The first century world into which Jesus came, was one particularly grim in its lack of hope beyond death's door, scholars tell us.

The Greek word is ευαγγέλιον, for those who are interested.

** Sartre is quoted by Ravi Zacharias on p. 20 of *Decision* magazine, March 2014. Zacharias' website rzim.org describes itself as "intended to touch both the heart and the intellect."

[81] Guinness, p. 211 of the book cited.

[82] For the person exposed to the swirling currents of Western thought, one of Guinness' most valuable contributions may be systematically and profoundly debunking the idea that believers construct "God the Father" out of an image of the all-providing parent from their childhood. On pages 134-135 of *Long Journey Home*, he cites Paul Vitz's *Faith of the Fatherless,* whose studies of famous atheists showed "a weak, dead, or abusive father in every case." Guinness also notes Freud's lack of clinical evidence for his psychoanalytic explanation of belief.

[83] Guinness is quoted from pages 105, 101, and 137, in that order.

Re body counts: Rodney Stark's *For the Glory of God* gives data on actual death tolls, per his research, of the Inquisition, witch-hunts... He finds them much lower than often alleged. On p. 257, he shows Spanish Inquisition statistics, for the years 1540 - 1700, totaling 44,701 persons charged, with 826 total executed. Numbers are argued, of course, and not to downplay anyone's death! But the Second World War killed about 20,000 *a day.*

Browsing about midnight one evening brought me to the death toll that got the British queen the moniker of "Bloody Mary." That perception of her has stayed active in popular history for 400 years and across two continents to reach me in America; one source credits her with martyring "some 200" and another "almost 300" Protestant dissenters. It evoked to my mind the contrast with David Aikman's note (*Jesus in Beijing*, page 26) that the Mongol invaders' massacres were not equaled until the 20th century (he cites that, "After conquering Herat in Persia, they killed 1.6 million people, after Khoresm 1.2 million..." — and a couple more, but why go on?) It raises the question of whether the harsh deeds of religious people are magnified in history while others are allowed to slide by more readily. Christopher Hitchens became famous asserting the foul deeds of religious people — but the question is inescapable, how much is due to their human warpedness...

(Please see our "Apology to China" [per Index] if you feel we are picking on the Mongols unfairly. Our perception is that human beings have been all-too-much of this nature around the world.)

[84] The quotations are from a book review of Stephen Mansfield's *The Search for God and Guinness: A Biography of the Beer that Changed the World*, p. 74 of *Christianity Today*, November 2009.

[85] p. 6 of *Christ the Eternal Tao*, quoting from *Tao Teh Ching*, chapters 25 and 4 (Translated by Gi-ming Shien and Eugene Rose). In the following paragraph, "The Three produced all things" is quoted on p. 255 of this work, there quoting from Lao Zi's writings, and "worship one's own spirit as God ... the ultimate delusion" is p. 327.

[86] Bible, Gospel of John, chapter one; compare Colossians 1:16,17; also Hebrews 1:3 "sustaining all things by His powerful word."

[87] The Christianity which arrived in China in the year A.D. 635 was Nestorian, "Church of the East." There was a later isolating of the Chinese Christian community when the rise of Islam cut them off from Christians in western Asia and Europe.

[88] The reference for the quotation is not given because recent events in China are reported as bringing enforcement of Party ideology and thinking, a call for eradication of "subversive currents", and events such as the dismissal from his job of a professor who posted remarks critical of Chairman Mao.

[89] Barry Lopez, p. 405. My 25 years working for Native American Indians (and some Inuit/Eskimo) led me to remark on Mr. Lopez as a unique author, a non-Native who could perceive that "The land, an animal that contains all other animals, is vigorous and alive" (p. 411). The student who masters the New Testament enough to begin to grasp the Old Testament will encounter the use of high mountain places to seek/meet God; Mr. Lopez mentions (p. 404) "what I had known of mountains as a child; that from them came a knowledge that was received, for which there were no words..."

All Barry Lopez *Arctic Dreams* quotes are: Reprinted by permission of SLL/Sterling Lord Literistic, Inc. Copyright by Barry Holstun Lopez.

[90] Pages 22-23 of *Christ the Eternal Tao;* these insights were discussed by Chinese persons, not Westerners. [Cf. Wikipedia on Mozi/Mo Di/Mohism: "for Mozi (c. 470-391 B.C.) the will of Heaven was that people should love one another... [this] would bring benefit to all." [accessed 22 June 2014.]

[91] With our apologies again for not having adequate secretarial staff to document everything, this may have been a *Far Side* cartoon (Gary Larson).

[92] Timothy Keller wrote *The Reason for God*, with careful analysis of key objections he hears pastoring in Manhattan. Quote is p. 176 there. (See our

pp. 180-181 for the top problems he deals with). A stunningly incisive recent work, received after "completion" of my book, *Confronting Christianity: 12 Hard Questions* by Rebecca McLaughlin [Crossway, © 2019] is noteworthy in the same arena, especially on "suffering," although received too late to do it justice [early 2020; thus, it is not in my Bibliographies].

Chapter 11: Notes on Watching Human Beings Argue

[93] *Jesus in Beijing*. My marked-up copy of the book has disappeared, so I apologize for the lack of page reference.

[94] The reader may remember our quote on p. 49 of the monk's statement that perceiving the light of one's own human spirit and taking it as God is "the ultimate delusion."

[95] R_ has somewhat misquoted Polkinghorne, as elaborated below, but the key point of the simplicity of the equations is still the same.

Greg Koukl analyzes extensively on philosophical issues and Christian truth. His dissection of **Dawkins**' argument was in the May/June 2009 issue of his "Solid Ground" newsletter, p. 2 ff. (His website str.org has some fascinating commentaries, some topics which I feel are badly off-target, but a lot of him on "how to reason the issues" is interesting. Read the New Testament, hear its own voice in total, think for yourself... The Bible said to love God with all your *mind*... Jesus, Mt 32:27, Mk 12:30, Lk 10:27).

The discussion (main text) does not do justice to Polkinghorne's analysis; he says Einstein's equation and the Dirac equation combine to "give enormously accurate accounts of a wide range of physical phenomena" according to Polkinghorne. Einstein's equation (for general relativity) is this simple: $R_{ab} - (1/2)Rg_{ab} = -8\pi T_{ab} + \Lambda g_{ab}$.** The Dirac equation is even shorter, although it has a symbol that my keyboard does not allow me. Dr. Polkinghorne says these two equations "come as close as any equations could to 'explaining' the behavior of matter." But he adds that "by Dawkins's 'argument' we should reject both equations... because 'anything that offers such an explanation must be supremely complex and improbable.' " (Pages 112-113 of *Questions of Truth*; he is quoting Dawkins in that final clause. This brief citation, like my other summaries, does not do justice to Polkinghorne's refutation of Dawkins, and I commend the original to the interested reader!)

(Wikipedia: "when fully written out," the Einstein field equations "are a system of 10 coupled, nonlinear, hyperbolic-elliptic partial differential equations" [Article "Einstein field equations," accessed 22 Apr 2013] — a different count of the number of equations, but still only a page or two, sustaining the simplicity issue.) [*For "divine simplicity" in theology,* see David Bentley Hart, *The Experience of God,* discussed in Annotated Bibliography].

** The symbols in Einstein's equation include the Ricci tensor, scalar curvature, metric tensor, stress-energy tensor, and the cosmological constant. Despite a math B.A. at U. C. Berkeley, years ago, your author would be incapable of the most elementary processing of this equation. But those who know, do... Let the reader remember the parallel in another universe, "Those who know their God..." Dan 11:32.

[96] R_ later revisited these thoughts, during a rainy, gloomy drive: The people who say "The Human One" (instead of "Son of Man") end up using "The Child" at times for other translating of the New Testament Greek regarding Jesus — and *that* is not right, he thought. "Child" carries with it by definition a connotation of immaturity, and it just doesn't fit regarding Jesus. So maybe we need not to focus so much on our self-referential concepts and just listen to what the Word really says — the precious Word, the New Testament revelation and offer from God.

(For those who prefer "the Human One," the Common English Bible © 2010 offers a more recent translation using that terminology, CommonEnglishBible.com for info.)

[97] Midgley's scathing comments about this are in endnote 132.

[98] Scripture says that King Herod *had to ask* the Wise Men when the "star" had first appeared. If, as one folk tale asserted, the Star of Bethlehem — announcing Jesus' coming — had indeed shone brighter than the sun, people in Jerusalem — only a few miles away — would not have been in the dark about it. (By the way, an astronomer worked through what conjunction in the heavens would have been interpreted in Ancient Near East symbolism as showing a King born in Judea; the astronomical events, he computes, would have led the Wise Men to Bethlehem *on December 25th* — an interesting point about Christmas. ("The Star of Bethlehem," article by Craig Chester, President, Monterey Institute for Research in Astronomy [Monterey California], Imprimis newsletter, December 1993, by Hillsdale College, Hillsdale MI.)

[99] Having mentioned Islam, let us note: One Islamic gentleman was commenting on the terrorists, some years ago, and he said, "These people who are killing people — that is not the **Islam** of my father, and that is not the Islam of my grandfather." (I apologize for not being able to provide the reference — Bob).

[100] Moynahan, Strobel and others offer much further material in support of this key matter. A recent example: Wycliffe workers in the Philippines have worked with the education system to bring mother-tongue education among minority-language communities, with the result that "children in the mother-tongue classes showed a 25 to 40 percent improvement in test scores across the board." (P. 19 of *Christianity Today*, April 2013. Wycliffe is one of the long-established Bible translation ministries.)

The scope of the works of compassion is such that "the Catholic Church is the largest health-care provider in the world, managing 26 percent of all health-care facilities." (Essay by Timothy Morgan, Senior Editor for Global Journalism, p. 57 of same). That sounds incredible, until we read the New York Times that Catholic hospitals alone account for about 1 in six of the U.S.A.'s hospital beds (3 Dec 2013 article on website, viewed 23 Sept 2014).

Chapter 12: Atone/Shalom

101 Gordon Hempton's *Dawn Chorus* CD. Mr. Hempton documents the diminishing of the Dawn Chorus world-wide as humanity impinges, and also the loss of quiet places in the United States (book, *One Square Inch of Silence*).

Human beings can also make a positive impact: A recent article on declining bird populations in the U.S.A. and Canada goes on to note that "Bluebird populations have increased thanks to nest boxes in homeowners' yards and gardens." [Christian Science Monitor 7 Oct 2019, p. 11]

102 The phrase "the sinful nature," the "fallen" state of humanity before the divine power of Christ is received to dwell in and transform the true believer, occurs 23 times in the NIV-1984 translation of the New Testament (e.g. Rom 7:5,18,25; 8:3,4,5,8,9,12,13; Gal 5:17; 2 Pet 2:10,18). The NIV-1984 for Rom 8:6&7 is "the mind of sinful man" and "the sinful mind." The Greek in those verses is literally "the mind of the flesh." The NLT also uses "sinful nature;" other translations use different phrasing. Commentators are careful to note that "flesh" here does not refer to the physical body in itself, created by God to be good. [*The Passion Translation* wording is "the self-life."]

The 2011 revision of the NIV, the new NIV-2011, comments on the matter this way: "Especially in Paul, sarx [the Greek word at issue here] can mean either part or all of the human body or the human being under the power of sin. In an effort to capture this latter sense of the word, the original NIV® often rendered sarx as 'sinful nature.' But this expression can mislead readers into thinking the human person is made up of various compartments, one of which is sarx, whereas the biblical writers' point is that humans can choose to yield themselves to a variety of influences or powers, one of which is the sin-producing sarx." [biblica.com/niv/accuracy, 28 Jan 2013. Page no longer available, use biblica.com/niv-bible/.]

103 The quote is from an unnamed student of Red Cloud Indian School, on the fourth page of poetry in their undated pamphlet "Whispers of the Lakota" (received Feb. 2011 in a fund-raising mailer from them. This school serves on the Pine Ridge Reservation — since 1888, when the famed chief Red Cloud petitioned that the "Black Robes" — Jesuits — come and educate their youth. Website RedCloudSchool.org for info on their work, needs, donations).

104 That "plan" is, in fact, what God will eventually work and sustain for eternity. Jesus' invitation to us is to be part of it!

[105] Plantinga, *Not the Way It's Supposed to Be.* First quote p. 16, others in this paragraph pp. 3 & 4.

[106] Catholic theologian Karl Rahner is quoted from his "The Divine Dawning," reprinted on page 73 of *Watch for the Light: Readings for Advent and Christmas.*

Ware makes the same point in *The Orthodox Way*: "There was a cross in the heart of God before there was one planted outside of Jerusalem" (p. 64).

The comment in the earlier paragraph, about no forgiveness without the price being paid — Thoughtful-Woman expresses that in a more negative framework, which is how it sounds to a number of people outside the Christian community, and some inside — reflects Matthew Gallatin's nagging question, "If we come to Him [God] asking pardon, why can't He Himself do what He commands us to do, and simply say, 'I forgive'?" (p. 51 of *Thirsting...*) Gallatin ministered successfully for decades as an evangelical (Protestant) pastor, but he says that question always bothered him. The alternate theological viewpoint made available in our "Atone/Shalom" chapter, for those so concerned, answered that for him, as his book recounts... (Endnotes 108 and 112 also touch on this topic area. In another view, Abelard said that Christ's sufferings show us the terrible depth of our sin.)

Thoughtful-Woman's friend's comment put the "Western" view of Jesus Christ's atonement in, arguably, a distortingly harsh light. Countless millions have received the great blessing, through a preaching mode that may want to be lifted to a higher understanding now (returning to ancient roots! The Church's older view, as expounded in the whole of this chapter). To see that sin, unremediated, brings punishment in varying forms, is an existential reality; that Christ has lifted that punishment from the suffering human "sinner," is a precious gift, and our difficulties in understanding are a reflection of our limitedness...

[107] The Sabbath laws, strictly no work on Saturday as a holy devoted day, were considered one of the central defining marks of Jewish religion** (e.g. Exo 20:8-10, Neh 13:17, Isa 56:6). Jesus healed on the Sabbath and the religious leaders were appalled (John 9:16; Mt. 12:10-12; Luke 13:14). He accused them of greed and hypocrisy in their administration of the religious community (Mt. 6:2-5, 23:25; Mk. 7:8-13). The "undercurrent of rebellion" against Rome's imperial rule, mentioned next by Sci-guy, was embodied in the "Zealots," Jewish revolutionaries. The level of strife that sometimes rose is shown by the Roman officer's question to Paul about leading "four thousand terrorists into the wilderness," Acts 21:38 NIV. The perception of Jesus as threat — that the Romans would devastate the system of local religious rule in response to challenge — was articulated by the Jewish

religious leaders of His time (John 11:48) as, " *The Romans will take our temple and our nation.*"

** When great men were to be remembered, people were set to work toiling to build impressive monuments; when God wanted to be remembered, He* gave people *rest.*

[108] In that verse, Jesus referred to Himself as "the Son of Man," His most frequent title for Himself; the language is quoted per NIV. The statement is repeated in the Gospel of Mark in the Bible (Mark 10:45). Lamsa, working from the ancient Aramaic text, renders this "to give his life as a salvation for the sake of many."** See also Mt. 26:28 (the basis of Communion in the Church) and Rom 5:18 "one righteous act resulted in justification and life for all people" (NIV).

** Aramaic was the language Jesus spoke, and Lamsa grew up in an area where it was still spoken. Scholars feel that the Aramaic New Testament was probably translated into that language *from* the Greek in which the general circulation of the New Testament was made.

Anselm's name has been attached to "satisfaction" theory or "penal substitution" in the popular mind (the popular mind that goes that far into the theological realm! There is a "popular mind" that goes not there at all!) But "penal substitution," paying the accumulated penalty, bearing the total deserved wrath, may not be a fully accurate portrayal of the medieval Anselm himself. Joel Green, in *Recovering the Scandal of the Cross*, says "Anselm does not present a wrathful God punishing Christ in our place; rather, Christ satisfies, or pays a debt we owe" (p. 169). He quotes Anselm: "What is the debt we owe to God? The whole will of a rational creature ought to be subject to the will of God... Whoever renders not unto God this due honor, takes away from God that which is his..." Living outside the will of God, Green explains, we are "depriving God of whatever he proposed to make of human nature." (P. 155.) Anselm himself said that it was needful that "either the honour taken away should be repaid, or punishment should be inflicted." His word is "or" in that sentence (Anselm, xiii of Book I of *Cur Deus Homo*, which means "Why God became man," quoted on p. 138 of Bettenson, *Documents of the Christian Church*).

Thus the hymn that says, "I owed a debt I could not pay; He [Jesus] paid a debt He did not owe." **None of the good things we do can repay the evil things**, for all those good things are in themselves simply what is due from us to God in the first place.

This analysis of Anselm may seem closer to the view articulated by the Eastern Orthodox, the ontological necessity of a perfectly righteous life, which we cite in the main text for its ancient roots.

Green also says, "Understanding **sin** narrowly as an infraction of the laws of God falls short of the biblical account of sin" (p. 242). He adds that "for Paul, salvation from sin cannot be understood primarily in terms of forgiveness... Sin is like a power that must be overcome" (p. 243).

[109] "Incarnation" summarizes the fact that Jesus, walking the earth as an ordinary-looking human being, was in fact God and human both. Jesus' divine nature is understood to be the "second Person of the Trinity," the "Word" of John 1, God the Son coming from God the Father in an eternal origination. How could two such different natures combine in one "human"? A classic analogy has been that of iron and fire: a piece of iron put into a fire receives the "fire" — more precisely, the heat of the fire — into itself, and the "fire" pervades the iron completely — combining fully throughout, while both the "iron" and the "fire" retain their own very different natures.

[110] Crucifixion, the death that Jesus died by being nailed to a cross and left to die of bleeding and exposure, was reserved by the Romans for the worst of criminals. Roman citizens could not be crucified, because this death was too degrading. We get the term "excruciating pain" from the Latin root for "crucifixion" — the nail through the wrist was placed where a certain nerve would be crushed, which would cause an explosion of incredible pain in the brain. (Reference: pp. 18 - 19 in Strobel, *Case for Easter.*)

[111] Bishop Kallistos Ware, *The Orthodox Way*, pp. 78-83.

[112] In addition to R_'s mention of the book *Christus Victor*, a web article "A Resurrection That Matters" and others have touched on this viewpoint.** See the end of this note for discussion of the Hebrew wording re the English Bible's "punishment that brought us peace." (We note there also some of the continuing theological controversy about *Christus Victor*).

** "A Resurrection that Matters" J. R. Daniel Kirk, *Christianity Today* magazine April 2010; christianitytoday.com/ct/2010/april/ allows access from table of contents. *See last paragraph of this endnote for other, more recent articles* continuing to show this meditation in Western thinking.

A BRIEF SUMMARY OF *CHRISTUS VICTOR:* Aulen argues from early church sources that the early Christians understood that yes, Christ died for us — but not so much as a "payment of all the cumulative penalties" for sinful transgressions, but as the need to establish a reality of true loving obedience to God, so that this reality would exist for human beings to be incorporated into. (Thus the Scripture's calling Him "the second Adam.") This is the "life received by His* Spirit" mentioned in the main text.

These matters lend themselves to deep argumentation, as the issues are much vaster than our ordinary disputations. Dr. Seyoon Kim discusses three main ways of understanding Jesus' sacrifice — penal substitution, Christus Victor, and "revelation" (the New Testament includes "that Christ has wrought salvation by bringing the 'revelation' of God"). Dr. Kim (an Associate Dean of a theology program, Fuller Seminary) says the three theories "coexist" in the NT and "are often coordinated with one another;"

e.g. Col 1:13-20; Col 2:13-15; Rom 8:31-39 {n.b. esp. vv 32-34, cf. Isa 53:10-12}; 1Co 15:54-57; Act 10:38; Act 10:43; Act 26:18 {this last might be considered per the "revelation" theory, ?). These per p. 18 of Fuller's magazine *Theology, News & Notes*, Winter 2008; he says on p. 19, "Just as rationalists cannot accept the incarnation of the transcendent Logos as it defies human reason, moralists cannot accept God's giving his sinless Son to a substitutionary death for sinners as it defies human moralism." Dr. Kim is strongly of the "penal substitution" view and arguing (p. 20) that "when the doctrine of Christ's penal substitutionary atonement on the cross — and the doctrine of justification that issues from it — is properly expounded, it can integrate the *Christus victor* motif in itself and provide the adequate basis for sanctification or *imitatio Christi*."

(A coordination of various viewpoints is discussed at length in *Mosaic of Atonement*, J. McNall, 2019 Zondervan Academic. It is not clear to me yet how his treatment relates to the "Eastern" viewpoint.)

Bishop Hicks' book, *The Fullness of Sacrifice*, was introduced to me by the comment that "the **ancient and scriptural idea of sacrifice** was displaced by the mediaeval [that is, "medieval"] idea that sacrifice meant primarily immolation." [from page xxiv, Translator's Preface, *Christus Victor*. See pp. 62-63 above for an all-too-brief summary of Hicks' key point].

For those whose thoughts in understanding Jesus' essential work differ from what is set forth here, we ask your understanding, your prayer that all the words and work of this present book may do indeed exactly the fullness of the good that the Lord desires. (Please consider Francis Shaeffer's exhortation to "the final apologetic," the one Jesus gave us in John 13:35 — and I ask Him* to guard me that I may so live indeed, myself!)

DOCUMENTATION OF THE IDEA IN THE EARLY CHURCH:

J. N. D. Kelly's classic *Early Christian Doctrines* documents that the early Christian writer Irenaeus was "the first to work out comprehensive theories both of original sin and of redemption." Compare the following to *Christus Victor*: Irenaeus' conclusion that "Christ by His obedience has reintroduced the principle of life and immortality"... yet at the same time, Kelly notes, "Irenaeus is quite clear that Christ redeemed us with His blood", p. 173.

As you would probably expect, R_ and B-t got into a wrangle about this. B-t took salvation seriously, and he had memorized **Isaiah 53:5 "the punishment that brought us peace was upon him** [on Christ — this was an Old Testament prophecy of the Messiah and His saving work, given hundreds of years before Jesus came]." "You can't get around *that*," he told R_. "I don't want to 'get around' it, I want to thank Him* for it — and to understand properly what He did, to help others grasp it," R_ replied. "The word 'punishment' there in the NIV, is מוסר **'musar' in the Hebrew. It means also 'discipline,' 'instruction.'** When Proverbs says, 'Get wisdom, get discipline...' (Prov. 23:23 NLT) that is 'musar.' So Isa 53 is compatible with the idea that He had to undergo the utmost discipline of fidelity to God to reverse the works of sin..." B-t was unconvinced; his understandings worked fine for him, and R_ didn't object to that — but he wanted Thoughtful-Woman and Sci-guy to be able to receive the truth. [We ask any reader who came on this little "Documentation..." section, without reading the *preceding* paragraph, to read *that* paragraph.]

CHRISTUS VICTOR AS A CLASSIC IN A CONTINUING CONTROVERSY: As with so many things that are of great importance, opinions vary and are intensely held. Some people feel that *their* theologians have refuted Christus Victor and established "penal substitution" as what the Scriptures really teach; on the other hand, an Eastern Orthodox Christian priest told me *that* theory "was a purely Protestant invention." With such a swirl of disputation, the seeker has two options: read the Scriptures of the New Testament and let them rest in your mind; or, plunge into the current flow of books. As to the latter option, Joel Green's *Recovering the Scandal of the Cross* has a discussion on p. 58-59 that the Greek for "ransom" may better be translated as "means of release... deliverance," and on pp. 242-243 he discusses the New Testament book of Romans to show that, in its presentation, "Sin is like a power that must be overcome." From the other theological camp (if we may simplify the landscape into two viewpoints only!), *Pierced for Our Transgressions* (S. Jeffrey et al) has moved many commentators to high praise for its exposition of "penal substitution." (The success of that exposition seems to me to rest on the reader's already having the Bible firmly accepted as foundational, so its utility to the questioner may be more limited).

WEB ARTICLES as mentioned above include christianitytoday.com/ct/2016/august-web-only/union-with-christ-missing-heart-of-our-gospel.html, and christianitytoday.com/women/2019/january/bibles-best-description-salvation-is-phrase-we-rarely-use.html (the phrase is "being in Christ;" she notes that we [Americans?] find it easier to apply ourselves to "being for Christ" — doing things — than being "in" Christ.

113 Mitochondria are the "power plants" of the cell, and the mitochondria of the fertilized ovum are all from the mother's egg cell, so that female-only descent can be traced by studying their genetics. (Similarly, the "Y-chromosome" is the uniquely male item.) The presence in awareness of this "Eve" issue came from "the famous '**mitochondrial Eve**' article of 1987 by the late Allan Wilson, showing that when people around the world were placed on a family tree constructed from their mitochondrial DNA, the tree was rooted in African populations, in an individual who lived about 200,000 years ago.

"Though the methodology of the paper was imperfect, its result was unchanged after the method had been corrected, and geneticists have developed a growing confidence in mitochondrial DNA dates..." (article on New York Times Learning Network, website nytimes.com/learning/

teachers/featured_articles/20001115wednesday.html. The date of 11/15/2000 was displayed at the top of the article; the article went on to the discuss compatibility of the finding with the theory of a population of human ancestors numbering perhaps 10,000 individuals at that time.) [Note our comments p. 117 above, that the Hebrew translated "Adam" is also the Hebrew for "humanity."] The web has some websites arguing that the whole "mitochondrial Eve" idea has been refuted, others maintaining that it has been vindicated. As we say over and over, when the issue is not a particular scientific matter but the larger scope, the thing is to avoid destructive blocks... More at the end of this note on the status of the debate on the web).

My meager acquaintance with the "Y-chromosome Adam" also came from popular media: "... a man who lived in Africa about 200,000 years ago..." Source was Thomas Traumann, "Veja" (centrist news magazine), Sao Paulo, Jan 31, 1996, quoted in World Press Review April 1996, p 37.

Touching on Adam and Eve brings up a theologian's comment on the threads of reality: A theologian remarked that when the Bible is being translated, "**the concepts which most stubbornly resist translation**" into a new language **are precisely those which are most important to understand."** (I apologize for remembering his/her comment without recording the source.) The "Adam and Eve" dissertation in the Bible resists translation into our present intellectual outlook (the fact that in this present book we have touched on a different viewpoint from an Indian insight, only begins to move the issue).

A variety of other reconciliations of "scientific" and "Biblical" Adam-Eve matters are expounded at the website asa3.org, differing from the outlook taken in this book. Be sure to put in the "3" or you get a very different place. Type "Adam and Eve" into the search box and you can read for hours. We're not convinced soaking your head in all that is the place to be. *C.S. Lewis on Adam & Eve, per Collins, has been appended (p. 203 here), for those who may find it helpful. Your author finds it less adequate concerning the "fruit of the tree of the knowledge of good and evil" than the "mystical" view in the main narrative here (pp. 18-20). But some may find it helpful.*

The Index entries "Adam/Adahm" have the important background note that the Hebrew word translated "Adam" is also the Hebrew word for "humanity" and ALSO some other viewpoints on understanding this.

One theologian describes systematic theologies as "cathedrals in thought." Like physical cathedrals, we feel, such theological systems are beautiful from inside, magnificent in their total aspect — but they occupy a certain "territory," and they may cease to be suitable habitations under other circumstances, yes?

In case it matters: I googled "mitochondrial Eve" to see what the current state of the argument might be. One of the top results promised me the "most robust statistical examination to date of our species' genetic links to 'mitochondrial Eve' " while another promised to inform me of "The Demise of Mitochondrial Eve." Both were replete with asserted science -- and the

"Demise" website felt their "evidence" was penetrating enough that they concluded that "a funeral" was "in order for mitochondrial Eve." As I pondered the disjunction, however, I noticed that the "Demise" website was resting on their own interpretation of 1998 and 2002 studies, while the "most robust" support *for* "mtEve" was a 2010 article -- and it showed that "10 human genetic models... using a very different set of assumptions" gave compatible results placing mtEve "about 200,000 years ago." (Website sciencedaily.com/releases/2010/ 08/100817122405.htm, accessed 12 April 2013. I do not cite the "Demise" URL since I am giving them such a bad assessment. Another source says "when all of the variables are taken into account, the current range is more like 50,000 to 500,000" years before present for mtEve.)

Chapter 13: Trinity

[114] Nicky Gumbel expounds Eddison's idea from his *Talking to Children*, writing in Gumbel's *Searching Issues*. The C. S. Lewis quote is also taken from that volume. These are pp. 112-116 there.

R_ wasn't very happy with B-t's "book" analogy, as it seemed at one level to be "Modalism" (see note 118), and at another level, if the book were different in the minds of the author and the reader, there was an issue of mis-communication, eh? But perhaps we have to start with vague analogies and gradually mature in our relationship with a Being we cannot grasp.

[115] Like the Lewis quote, the McGrath quote continues to draw from *Searching Issues*, pp. 112 ff. Original publisher's acknowledgement: MERE CHRISTIANITY by C. S. Lewis copyright © C.S. Lewis Pte. Ltd. 1942, 1943, 1944, 1952. Extract reprinted by permission.

[116] Gregory (Bishop of Nyssa) is cited on page 222 and Basil the Great on p. 223 of Jaroslav Pelikan's *The Emergence of the Catholic Tradition.* (Pelikan uses "Catholic" here in the original sense of "universal, church-wide in all places" rather than "Roman Catholic".)

[117] The late Dr. Nabeel Qureshi had his fateful revelation about Trinity when he was sitting in organic chemistry class. They were studying a nitrate molecule that has three different structures in "resonance," and his professor clarified: "Technically, a molecule with resonance is every one of its structures at every point in time, yet no single one of its structures at any point in time." She repeated that central point and Qureshi gazed upon "the three separate structures of nitrate on the wall... my mind assembling the pieces. One molecule of nitrate is all three resonance structures all the time and never just one of them. The three are separate but all the same, and they are one. They are three in one. That's when it clicked: if there are things in this world that can be three in one, even incomprehensibly so, then why

cannot God? ... I realized a triune entity was possible." (Pages 195-196 of his book *Seeking Allah, Finding Jesus.*)

His exposition is much better than my humble excerpt of it shows; he goes on to say James White's *The Forgotten Trinity* helped him to grasp the concept "that God is one being with three persons: Father, Son and Spirit." (I have not read that book, so it is not in the Bibliography.)

[118] Thoughtful-Woman's first quote is from page 1270, "Trinity," *Encyclopedia of Catholicism*, Richard McBrien, General Editor. The second is page 254 of *Christ the Eternal Tao*. The speaker is Archimandrite Sophony, who goes on to say, "Our rationally functioning mind is gripped in a vice, unable to incline to one side or the other, like a figure crucified on a cross." [*Compare the concluding comment in this endnote, below*].

Trinitarian thought has been of much discussion. Some early writers thought that "God the Father brought forth his two hands, the Son and the Holy Spirit, to serve as mediators in creating the world... This view was unsatisfactory because it tied the Trinity to the time and space framework, and because it lent itself to *modalism*, the belief that the one God appeared to man in three different modes." Augustine "used a number of analogies, of which the most significant are mind and love. A mind knows itself because it conceives of its own existence; what is more, it must also love its own self-conception. A lover cannot love without a beloved, and there is of necessity a love which flows between them but which is not strictly identical with either. From this, Augustine deduced that God, in order to be himself, had to be a Trinity of persons, since otherwise neither his mind nor his love could function." These quotes are from the article "Trinity," pp. 692-3 of *New Dictionary of Theology*, Sinclair Ferguson et al Ed.s, © 1988. We note also "the developed concept of three coequal partners in the Godhead found in later creedal formulations cannot be clearly detected within the confines of the canon [that is, the Scriptures in the Bible]" — article "Trinity," p. 782 of *The Oxford Companion to the Bible*, Bruce Metzger & Michael Coogan Ed.s, 1993.

Bishop Timothy Kallistos Ware, in *The Orthodox Way*, notes that "the two most helpful ways of entry into the divine mystery are to affirm that God is *personal* and that God is *love*. Now both these notions imply sharing and reciprocity... Egocentricity is the death of true personhood... Love cannot exist in isolation... from all eternity God knows himself as 'I and Thou' in a threefold way, and he rejoices continually in this knowledge... A favorite analogy for the Trinity has always been that of three torches burning with a single flame" (pp. 28-29). As to the three Persons of the Trinity, "None of the three ever acts separately ... They are not three Gods, but one God" (p. 30). This echoes the Cherokee statement (which was the final endnote to Chapter One). Ware notes that Synesius of Cyrene wrote, "All-pure Spirit, bond between the Father and the Son..." (p. 33; Synesius wrote c. A.D. 400. This resembles the modern commentator who said, "The Holy Spirit is the community of love between the Father and the Son" — a commentator whose name I unfortunately forget. That comment in turn resembles the Cherokee "Trinity" term "A ta nv ti... 'place of uniting' where persons agreed to meet and form a perpetual friendship"; just as the Cherokee "Trinity" term "U ha lo te qa... Head of all power... Great beyond expression" may be felt to remind us of "The Father," the third Cherokee term, "U sqa hu la, the meaning of which could not, in 1835, any longer be learned, but it had something to do with 'mind' " may remind us of the Logos, the second person or "Son" in the Christian Trinity.) [These quotes are repeating from endnote 9 above.]

Ware also notes that "As a Trinity of love, God desired to share his life with created persons made in his image, who would be capable of responding to him freely and willingly in a relationship of love. *Where there is no freedom, there can be no love*" (p. 58). One consequence is that "human beings, made in the image of the Trinitarian God, are interdependent and coinherent... We are 'members one of another' (Eph. 4:25)" (p. 62). As to the three Persons in one nature or essence, Ware says that, "by virtue of this specific unity of essence the three persons have only a single will or energy" (p. 72; he notes the two natures in Christ with two wills, and in Christ, "the human will is at all times freely obedient to the divine").

The *Philokalia* [compendium of ancient Christian spiritual writings from the East] brings this comment: *We must live the dogma expressed in a revealed truth, which appears to us as an unfathomable mystery, in such a fashion that instead of assimilating the mystery to our mode of understanding, we should, on the contrary, look for a profound change, an inner transformation of spirit, enabling us to experience it mystically*. (quoting Vladimir Lossky [died 1958] on page x of the Introduction, *Philokalia: The Eastern Christian Spiritual Texts: Selections Annotated and Explained.* Woodstock VT: SkyLight Paths Publishing © 2006)

Chapter 14: Evolution: An evolving non-consensus

119 It may be an important fact to note here that one of the early anti-religion extrapolators** of Darwin said that he wanted not to be answerable to any higher authority, to be "free" to do whatever he wanted — that issue ties to the fact that God desires good for us and He* is terribly misconstrued by such an outlook. **We achieve our best selves by uniting with God, not losing our own selves but being transformed and taking up the vast addition that God's wisdom and capabilities offer**. (Was that mistaken person one of the Huxleys? An issue for your author's further research, a fact hidden somewhere in the dozens of books that have gone into this writing...)

** "extrapolators:" they extended Darwin's theory, a scientific theory, into metaphysical matters, and one acerbic comment labeled this arena *Things Darwin Didn't Say*... (That is Midgley's comment in the frontispiece of her book. See also endnote 132 for more of her view).

120 Lest the reader suspect that I (your author), a layman, have misperceived the science, here is one of the major authority figures in paleontology, Dr.

Stephen Jay Gould: "The history of most fossil species includes... 1. Stasis... They appear in the fossil record looking pretty much the same as when they disappear... 2. Sudden appearance. In any local area, a species ... appears all at once and 'fully formed.' "

Gould is quoted by Woodward on p. 124 of *Doubts About Darwin*. The original source is Gould, "The Episodic Nature of Evolutionary Change," in his *The Panda's Thumb.* (1985, NY: W. W. Norton; no page ref. cited by W.)

This disparity of the observed pattern, versus the original Darwinian expectations, was what Gould responded to with "punctuated equilibrium" theory.

Perhaps a "higher-focus" view is shown by Darryl Falk, commenting on the fossil sequences for elephants and turtles: "Just before they make their debut, other animals with similar but more primitive features make an entry, only to leave when the 'real thing' comes along. Perhaps the whisper at the mouth of our cave is trying to tell us something — something about God's subtlety and something about how God's creation command was really carried out" (p. 105 of *Coming to Peace With Science*; on p. 107, he notes that key links have been found for the whale's development, long elusive; on pp. 116-120 he discusses transitional forms reptiles-to-mammals [cynodonts]).

[121] "Many of the discontinuities [in the fossil record] tend to be more and more emphasized with increased collecting."** But the genetic data seems to establish "common ancestry / descent with modification" on a reasonable basis. *Back to our observation* that a sequence of forms, seems a logical way for a spiritual Creator to work with a material creation! "God formed humans from the dust of the earth" (Genesis 2:7) is in that case a logical, simple summary encapsulation of that process.

** Stark, *For the Glory*... p. 180, quoting the former curator of historical geology at the American Museum of Natural History, whose name is not given in Stark's footnote reference of another book.

[122] Discussed in Johnson, *Reason in the Balance*, pp. 83, 86.

[123] Behe built his case in *Darwin's Black Box* not simply on this complexity but on interlocking aspects of the complexities of matters he cited, making a bar to the evolution of any part of the system in the absence of other required parts (since the selective advantage doesn't function till all the parts are available). As noted in discussing Dr. Denis Alexander, others feel that examples cited by Behe are yielding to further analysis. Stephen Meyer in *Signature in the Cell* joins Behe, with a great deal of data exposition, in the feeling that those who feel they are explaining these matters "naturalistically," without any guiding intelligence required, are not really engaging the depth of the details of the microbiological data now available to us. (See pp. 174-175 for what may be the deepest theoretical problem! But again, under dispute... to no one's surprise.)

[124] Some of the early enthusiasm for asserting that life could easily emerge from the chemicals of the earth, involved the initial perception that a couple billion years had elapsed during which molecules could combine and recombine randomly, to allow the first simple cells to form. But microfossils of bacteria and deposits representative of organic carbon were found which dated to the same period as the first emergence of liquid water on earth, erasing the billions of years presumed to be available for chance chemical operations. (Gerald Schroeder discusses this on p. 86 of his *Science of God*, adding the note that Francis Crick, who shared the Nobel Prize for discovering the shape and functioning of DNA, said that given the sudden emergence of life here, an extraterrestrial origin of life on earth should be considered seriously).

On his website, Dr. Schroeder discusses that in the Bible's Genesis account, water was created in verse 10 and the first life appeared in verse 11, which "had, for decades, evolutionary biologists rolling in the aisles with laughter," since everyone knew that *billions of years* had to elapse for life to emerge by chemical processes. The validation of Genesis's perspective on that issue led Sci-guy to suggest to R_ that he could add it to his list of "convergences." (Conjectures about processes that might bring naturalistic development of life during the revised time period are of course available now.) Schroeder's quote was accessed 21 April 2013 at geraldschroeder.com/wordpress/?page_id=60.

[125] As Sci-guy was noting this matter, R_ recalled a conversation he had had with a Southern California charismatic pastor: R_ told the pastor that *at certain levels*, "evolution is a proven fact; that's why you have to get a new flu shot every Fall — the germs are constantly evolving."

Evolution has become a commonplace of our language. An encyclopedic dictionary, for example, says that Egyptian hieroglyphics "evolved c. [circa] 3,000 B.C." For a while in working on the book, R_ collected examples of this kind of use of the term — *examples in which active intelligence is clearly involved in the flow of the changes.* (Reference work is New Lexicon Websters, 1989, p. 456.)

[126] We are indebted to Henry Broadbent for this "two concepts" analysis, personal conversation 2010. Henry is an M.Div. graduate of Fuller Theological Seminary, Pasadena, CA, which was founded to work for a better intellectual engagement of Christianity with the Gospel-needing world.

Something about a more supportive interpersonal atmosphere brought B-t's deeper thoughts to the surface when he talked later to R_, alone: "Look, it's like **a painting**: if it's **clearly signed** in the corner, you don't expect the signature to cover the whole canvas. And the universe *is* 'signed' in multiple places. Look at the structure of science: biology rests on chemistry, chemistry rests on physics, physics rests on mathematics. The biology testifies to the Creator: the basic, overall pattern of the emergence of forms of life turned out not to be as Darwin expected; *and,* 'information' in the cell, in the genetic 'code,' points to intelligence as its origin. Remember our travelling professor's analysis: the biology is 'signed' in the 'micro/macro/math' realms. Chemistry: Look at the non-compute of the **Miller-Urey** methodology [experiments that were at first alleged to support a naturalistic origination of life were found to have presumed an atmosphere dramatically different from the early Earth's, and it was found that the early Earth's actual atmosphere would have destroyed their reaction products**], chemistry also in the realms Kenyon proclaimed and had to repudiate [page 72 above; see endnote 136]. The universe is 'signed by its artist' again in the physics — get your DVD "The Privileged Planet" out of its cover; I see you haven't opened it — fine-tuning of the universe's key structures, and also the special habitability of our planet, mysteriously focused where the location is best for discovery [an aside - that's chapter 15 in this book]. 'Signed' again, finally, in the math — the elegance, beauty, simplicity of the fundamental laws." [This is presented better on p. 279-283 Strobel's ... *Creator*]

[** Thaxton said this in 1984 in *Mystery of Life's Origin*. Meyer gives more current documentation (2009), pp. 224-225 of *Signature*... There is no consensus with Miller, nor against his view. Woodward, *Doubts*... expounds another debunking of Miller-Urey, p. 125.]

R knew all these "signatures" drew vigorous counter- argument, and he felt that the "information in the DNA code" was probably the signature "in the corner" as B-t had said [see Index, "information"], but he wasn't prepared to redirect B-t's passion. [An aside: If B-t's analysis seems somewhat dated, Dr. F. Rana has done a *more recent* extensive survey of *"positive evidence"* from biochemical discoveries, see endnotes 129 and 130].

As he was going brain-numb from the pounding of B-t's analysis, R_ forced a break by pulling out a book and showing B-t Einstein's equation of General Relativity — one line!

$R_{ab} - (1/2)Rg_{ab} = -8\pi T_{ab} + \Lambda g_{ab}$

[see note 95 above for Polkinghorne's discussion of this equation and the Dirac equation, even shorter, also needed for "explaining the behavior of matter;" also discussion that ten equations form the theory.

B-t was respectfully silent for a moment.

R_ said, "If the science is so clear, about the 'artist's signature' on Creation, why can't scientists see it?" B-t was sullen and silent, so R_ gave his own answer: "Every analysis like that, is just a challenge to try harder and dig deeper to 'explain' naturalistically." (Anyone who reads this whole book carefully, will note that R_ may have missed the proper timing on a golden opportunity: to expound Dr. Denis Alexander's conclusion that the overall pattern of evolution, now that we have studied things in great depth, shows theism rather than atheism — see Index, "Alexander...")

B-t took this up with Sci-guy, who expounded for him the "game" danger: "People get their minds locked in the 'game.' Here's one person's description of it, my friend: 'Science, fundamentally, is a game. It is a game with one overriding and defining rule: *Rule No. 1*: Let us see how far and to what extent we can explain the behavior of the physical and material universe in terms of purely physical and material causes, without invoking the supernatural.' " [The quote is from Richard Dickerson, biochemist and elected member of the National Academy of Sciences, quoted from a published essay of his on p. 238 of *Darwin's Black Box*. Dickerson is himself a believer in God, per p. 239.] Sci-guy watched B-t wince and said, "When you stuff your mind firmly enough in that perspective, only the proverbial 'irresistible force' can move it!"

B-t took up the issue again at a later rest-stop when R_ was looking defensive. B-t grabbed Dr. Morse's *Closer to the Light* off the little bookshelf and read R_ an entry that R_ himself had flagged. "Birds do not need to learn what the sky looks like; they come equipped with an inner map of the heavens. Using planetariums that can project a changing night sky, scientists have demonstrated that birds raised in labs and never exposed to the night sky are born with a 'memory' of the stars that enables them to navigate" (p. 108-109; Dr. Morse does not cite sources for this).

B-t belabored R_ further, lest the point be evaded somehow: "That map of the sky in their genetics, is a little much to think of as something that came into being by chance mutations, and then became established by its natural-selection advantage, isn't it?" R_ had that incredible somehow-I'm-not-convinced look, and B-t was angry. "Sure, the 'selection advantage' is clear, but the arising of the map in the bird's genetic base, by chance? Come, now!" [Woodward's comment on "information," p. 174-175 here, may be more apropos in the overall picture.]

... Time went by, and later R_ read B-t a quote from Werner von Braun, "the father of space science:" "I find it as difficult to understand a scientist who does not acknowledge the presence of a superior rationality behind the existence of the universe as it is to comprehend a theologian who would deny the advances of science."** R_ told B-t: "That's the farthest you'll ever get with these people with your 'science points to...' kind of analysis — 'a superior rationality.' Beyond that, to know a personal God and receive the love, *that* takes a step beyond analysis."

** von Braun is quoted on p. 271 of Strobel, *Case for a Creator*.

(Strobel's book records how he "probed six different scientific disciplines to see whether they point toward or away from the existence of an intelligent designer," p. 279; in the following seven pages, he summarizes the evidence of cosmology, physics, astronomy, biochemistry, biological information, and consciousness. That may be a compact introduction for the seeker confronting the masses of writings on these matters).

[127] *Christianity Today* magazine, in their December 2010 issue, included an essay which stated that "C. S. Lewis's *Chronicles of Narnia* includes one of the classic depictions of a multiverse in Western literature... [the characters

observe a new universe created and] meet the one Lord over all of them." christianitytoday.com/ct/2010/december/31.46.html, page two, 3 April 2013 visit.

The same logic about a prolific Creator would obviously apply to life on other planets, yes?

The speculative issues of "**multiverse**" meet questions as to its explanatory power: A resource expert with graduate-level study in both physics and philosophy told Lee Strobel, "It's highly unlikely that such a universe-generating system would have all the right components and ingredients in place by random chance... So if a many-universe-generating system exists, it would be best explained by design." (Dr. Robin Collins, quoted on p. 144 of Strobel's *Case for a Creator*)

128 The quote is from website ncbi.nlm.nih.gov/pmc/articles/PMC4572716/, visited 8 Feb 2018.

129 First quote is Michael Denton (*Evolution: A Theory in Crisis* 1985, p. 342) cited on p. 59 of Woodward, *Doubts About Darwin*; the second is Woodward, his p. 60. Dr. Rana's quote is from the introductory segment of his DVD. Dr. Rana's quote in the following paragraph is p. 175 of his *The Cell's Design.*

On pp. 280-282 of his book, Dr. Rana recaps some of the prime points of his "positive evidence for a Creator" analysis of biochemical discoveries: "Fine-tuning, optimization, biochemical information systems, structure of biochemical information, biochemical codes*, genetic code fine-tuning, quality control, molecular convergence**, strategic redundancy, trade-off and intentional suboptimization, life's minimum complexity, molecular-level organization of simplest life, exquisite molecular logic, preplanning, molecular motors, cell membranes, designs of biochemical systems inspire human designs, man can't do it better." [Each of these items gets a paragraph on these pages of Dr. Rana's book, summarizing the detailed information given in prior chapters to support each finding. See our following endnote for a stunning example of "trade-off".]

* Dr. Rana cites "language structure and regulation of genes"

** same structural configurations arising through different evolutionary sequences, where few such "convergences" would be expected from naturalistic evolutionary theory, but a large number are found in fact

130 Dr. F. Rana notes in his DVD that "bad design" arguments have tended to fall apart in two ways: one is that further understanding shows the structure to be "good design" (his example is "junk DNA," whose uselessness was asserted to show not-intelligent-design, but now, he states, these DNA sequences have been shown to be functional). The other is that the quality of design can be misjudged because the constraints on the system, the interaction of multiple objectives, render what would seem "bad" to be part of a larger good.

A deep example of misinterpreting "design in nature as bad" is found in Dr. Rana's *The Cell's Design,* pages 264-265. The case is not trivial:

"Because of its central role in photosynthesis and its primary importance in ecosystems, rubisco is *the most abundant protein* in nature." In the early assessment, it had "acquired the reputation among biochemists as a wasteful enzyme." [Italics added]

HOWEVER, they found that the grave defects alleged in its operation come because molecular oxygen and carbon dioxide share "the small linear and symmetric nonpolar nature". So, rubisco uses a "chemical intermediate" in order "to indirectly discriminate between carbon dioxide and oxygen."

"The bottom line: Rubisco faces a trade-off between rate of reaction and discrimination between the gases. ...researchers from Australia concluded that rubiscos found throughout nature are perfectly optimized for their environments and the slow carbon fixation reaction is a necessary trade-off for this enzyme to make the difficult discrimination between carbon dioxide and molecular oxygen. These workers conclude that 'despite appearing sluggish and confused, most rubiscos may be near-optimally adapted to their different gaseous and thermal environments.' ...its deliberate design adds the necessary depth to an amazing work of art."

(As our chapter title reflects, the arguments are endlessly "evolving.")

131 The sort of maturing-transition described is shown in Dr. Wilder Penfield's own personal life journey (he is the neurosurgeon mentioned in endnote 2 and on the back cover of this book). In early life, Dr. Penfield marked a diagram on a large rock expressing his confidence that science was explaining all; 50 years later, he went out to that same rock and altered the diagram to reflect the fact that further study and reflection had taken away *that* confidence. (Morse, *Closer to the Light,* pp. 99-100; detailed more in endnote 2. Dr. Penfield was glad to find the range of his thought freed up.)

If anyone cares, more learned sources say the Twain story is a popular legend, not consistent with Twain's actual family life history.

132 Midgley, *Evolution as a Religion,* p. 126-127. She lists "arrogance, perversity and self-dramatization" as the standard vices of the "genuinely undiscriminating disbelief," a culture in which "It is always more blessed to disbelieve than to believe" (p. 126). (Earlier in the book, she attacks "fundamentalist literalism" as an unjustified concept of the Bible, and as she assesses some evolution purveyors as making it into a substitute religion, she says their products "conflict with the genuinely scientific theories which are supposed to provide their roots," p. 14, with the result that, "Bad religion is being answered by bad science," p. 15.)

133 The "God-of-the-gaps" charge is that believers say something is impossible to explain, but the negative evidence just waits for the "gap" to be filled and

then the "pointing-to-God" disappears. For a contrary viewpoint, note this from Thaxton et al: "Often it is contended that criticism focuses on present ignorance... It will be claimed that many of these problems are mere state-of-the-art gaps. And, surely, some of them are. Notice, however, that the sharp edge of this critique [their refutation of "chemical evolution"] is not what we do not know, but what we do know. Many facts have come to light in the past three decades of experimental inquiry into life's beginning. With each passing year the criticism has gotten stronger. The advance of science itself is what is challenging the notion that life arose on earth by spontaneous... chemical reactions." (p. 185 of their 1984 book *Mystery of Life's Origins*, under "Thaxton" in Standard Bibliography). [*see endnote 250 re Cambrian*]

Meyer (*Signature*..., 2009) places the larger question in a deeper philosophical context as he examines the "historical sciences" (which include origin of life research) and their special methods, and he details the process of "inference to the best explanation." (See our Index for that).

See Woodward on the status of the "information" issue (p. 174-175 here) for an illustration of Thaxton's methodological view.

[134] The "top-down" pattern is assessed, with other "Cambrian explosion" issues, in Meyer's *Darwin's Doubt*. It involves the rapid emergence of a wide variety of fundamental body plans for animal types, with elaboration within those types afterwards. We quote Meyer on that in endnote 250. The issue is that gradual accumulation of small changes would be expected to give a radically different pattern of how new forms emerge, as contrasted with the actual Cambrian record.

Meyer's title reflects Darwin's own highlighting of the Cambrian explosion as one item *not* explained by his theory. As a scientist, Darwin did not try to hide or minimize the issue, but he looked for it to be resolved by further fossil explorations. Those have, however, only sharpened the problem, as Meyer discusses (with, of course, other viewpoints being taken by other people).

[135] Collins is quoted from pp. 1-2 of his *Language of God*. The student should note that Collins says, "No serious biologist today doubts the theory of evolution to explain the marvelous complexity and diversity of life" (p. 99), yet Collins is an enthusiastic believer in a personal God, and recounts his own "journey to faith" in that book, as well as many informed ponderings on the relation of science and faith.

Bill Gates is quoted on p. 12 of Meyer's *Signature in the Cell*, drawing from Gates' *The Road Ahead*, p. 188 (NY: Viking/Penguin 1996).

[136] Meyer notes that, "At the close of the nineteenth century, most biologists thought life consisted solely of matter and energy. ...[after Watson and Crick they] came to recognize the importance of a third fundamental entity in living things: **information**. And this discovery would redefine, from that

point forward, what theories about the origin of life would need to explain." [Page 84 of *Signature...*; he notes on p. 85 that "information" is now a routine concept in biology.]

Meyer expands on p. 92 the insights we have mentioned about the sequencing of the "code letters:" "The chemistry of the molecule [DNA] allowed any one of the bases to attach to any one of the sugar molecules in the backbone, allowing the kind of variable sequencing that any carrier of genetic information must have." *That means that chemical properties do not give rise to the "code" being in place*, and the enormous number of code "letters" makes probabilistic emergence inconceivably unlikely.

Meyer clarifies thoroughly the difference between order as seen in crystals, vortices etc., and the specified complexity in the genetic information. He notes (p. 110) that, "Sequences and structures exhibiting either redundant order or *mere* complexity are common in the chemical substrate of nature. But structures exhibiting specified complexity are completely unknown there apart from DNA, RNA, and proteins."

Also described is how the famous *Biochemical Predestination* author Dean **Kenyon**** had worked from amino acid affinities in the "chemical evolution" theory but new research showed that "these differential affinities do not correlate with actual sequencing patterns in large classes of known proteins" (p. 236).

Meyer also deals at length with the inability of "self-organizational" theories to explain the matter, and why no such theory, in his informed judgment, will be able to succeed. (Since physical and chemical properties do not shape the ordering of the bases, i.e. the sequencing of the "letters" of the DNA code, therefore such theories will never work, see Meyer's pages 240, 245).

** Meyer recounts (his p. 237) that Kenyon had announced that further research had led him to "doubt all theories of 'chemical evolution' " (life forming itself from chemicals by unguided natural processes), "not just his own" famous theory.

137 The previous quote was NIV. This one, R_ is quoting from memory of the meaning, not from a particular version. That's what happens when you read a number of versions — but it helps you to grasp things!

138 Bible: everyone considers their own interests, not those of the Lord Jesus (Phlp 2:21).

We mentioned "the tsunami" in the main text. Why didn't God stop the tsunami? Or, are there other questions that should be asked? What about last month, when there wasn't any tsunami; what about the month before that, when there wasn't any tsunami. Did you hear anyone thanking God that there wasn't? Isn't it true that God does a lot better by human beings, than they do for God? If you haven't been relating to God, try thanking Him* daily in a thorough manner for three weeks (and let us know what results).

Psalm 50:23: "giving thanks is a sacrifice that truly honors Me. If you keep to My path, I will reveal to you the salvation of God" (NLT). Sci-guy's comments on Taylor/Smith, p. 92, may illuminate here, also. (Please see also the next three notes, including comments on Preacher Copeland.)

[139] *The reader may remember our earlier recap of* ***God's*** *view of the suboptimality of the present "world/nature" — "because they desire better ... God is not ashamed to be called their God," per Bible, Hebrews 11:16, discussed in this present book on p. 31.*

[140] One reason for this, R_ told Thoughtful-Woman later, is that God is a God Who "delights in the well-being of His* servant" (Psalm 35:27 NIV). (Athabascan Indian Chief Peter John again: "If you do things God's way, things are going to go for you."**)

The "**prosperity gospel**" can be terribly twisted to sound like indulgent wealth while others suffer — but preacher Kenneth Copeland says that the power and goodness of God mean that those who will dwell in His* presence, can count on Him to meet their needs. Copeland asserts that the "Blessing" (Gal 3:14, Jesus bringing blessing of Abraham to Gentiles) is BOTH the power of God to salvation eternally, AND the well-being in this life noted above — for those who put the promises to work, which many Christians do not do (per Kenneth and Gloria Copeland). "Believe in your heart and confess with your mouth" (compare Rom 10:9) — if he is right about "the Blessing," that extends not only to salvation but to much attainment of well-being on this mortal passage, with due regard for the assaults and impacts of the ungodly world, the fallen nature, and the devil. *Not for selfish self-interest, but to serve others and bless God by showing His* goodness*... (see endnote 238 for Copeland's "live to give;" also endnote 45). Kenneth W. Hagin says God told him that "if you learn how to follow Me, troubles and afflictions ... will only mean greater victories." We might to explore these themes more in a follow-on book with a more devotional focus, also recounting my own experience with the tithe [see Index] and restoration of "prosperity" — not superfluous wealth, but well-being — your author.

For the Christian's expectation of trouble and suffering, see Acts 14:22, that we "*must go through many hardships to enter the kingdom of God*" (cf. Jesus, Mt. 16:24). Note God's underlying promise in Psa 31:19-24, so that we can overcome these tribulations. (Compare Jesus' words in John 16:33.)

** With my apologies to the reader, I had a copy of *The Gospel According to Peter John* which I had carefully read and marked up, so I would have been able to cite the page reference -- but I loaned it out and it is gone.

[141] Cindy Trimm, *Commanding Your Morning*, p. 46. Her exact quote is "Since the spirit realm is the causal realm, Goliath [the hostile menacing giant] was dead long before he was struck down by the stone [from David's slingshot] and beheaded by the sword." (A Native American's comment, note 205.)

[142] Johnson, *Darwin on Trial,* pp. 153-54, quoted in Woodward, *Doubts About Darwin*, p. 109.

[143] In later conversation, B-t said to Sci-guy, "Name one," and Sci-guy responded, "Denis Alexander" and told R_ to be sure to put that author in his Bibliography. (B-t made the obvious move and said, "Name two," and Sci-guy said, "Francis Collins — and Michael Behe believes that evolution is real, even while countless people label him an IDiot." ID in that word stands for "Intelligent Design;" the term is a labeling by its detractors — just in case you hadn't been treated to that derogatory technique).

[144] Richard Dawkins has lived up to the nickname "Darwin's Rottweiler"** by coming up with what he himself regards as an incredibly penetrating and irrefutable argument against the existence of God. We noted the gist of it on p. 53 above and noted the refutations given by some of our betters in endnote 95. That is as much exposition as we will engage in on that argument; Thoughtful-Woman's desire for more talk about it and Dawkins' other inputs (he writes massively), we have to leave to our betters, and many of them are engaged in their own writing more massive than ours here. (The book *The Dawkins Delusion* and D. B. Hart's *Atheist Delusions* sound like classics in that field, but they are among many I have not had time to read). We need to cover our own set of inputs...

Dawkins brings to light a fundamental problem that transcends scientific analysis — he reports that he gets letters from people who feel "liberated" by his perspective, and *that* is a commentary on the mistaken image of God that some have taken in. We have noted elsewhere our belief and experience that it is a great benefit to have God in our lives.

Dawkins comes in for some more of our direct commentary in note 154 below.

** The term "Darwin's Rottweiler" is easier to understand if you know that one of the earlier aggressive "Darwinists" was known as "Darwin's Bulldog."

[145] p. 321 of Denis Alexander's *Creation or Evolution: Do We Have to Choose.* The next quote is p. 322. Endnote 251 recaps some of his scientific credentials, directing one Institute and Senior Affiliated Scientist at another.

[146] Alexander's quote is "Though each supposedly 'irreducibly complex' system is proposed by ID proponents as being, in principle, inexplicable by normal evolutionary mechanisms, all we need to do is wait for a decade or so, often less, and a coherent evolutionary account begins to emerge," p. 304 of *Creation...* My attention was drawn to his book by an Amazon.com reviewer who said this was the best refutation of "ID" ("intelligent design," if I am not

insulting your intelligence by spelling that out). [However, the "origin of information" issue may re-cast all this; see Index, "Information."]

[147] Quotes are pp. 322, 330, 331 of the same book. ("Op. cit." is a little pompous for a work like this present book, isn't it?)

[148] Same book, p. 311.

A similar touch from a different source: "[Alvin] Plantinga argues that in fact the theistic worldview is as a whole deeply consonant with the goals and successes of contemporary science. ... identifies a number of features of our world, and our cognitive relationship to that world, that are much more likely, and make much more sense, on a theistic than on an atheistic picture: the reliability and regularity of nature, and its working in accordance with law; the role of mathematics in the understanding of nature; the possibility of induction; the appropriateness of theoretical virtues such as simplicity; and even the empirical nature of science, which Plantinga argues is underwritten by the contingency of divine creation. In all these respects modern science is deeply compatible with theism, a fact that renders unsurprising the further fact that all the great founders of modern science were theists, working from a deeply Christian background." Plantinga is quoted by permission from an essay by Christopher O. Tollefsen, Professor of Philosophy at the University of South Carolina, at website thepublicdiscourse.com/2012/06/5612. Copyright 2012 The Witherspoon Institute. All rights reserved.

[See Index, "Science/pioneers more devout" for reference documenting the assessment of genuine faith status of major "founders".]

[149] Profound disputes rage over the issue of whether "micro-evolution," the movement of characteristics within the range of a gene pool, extrapolates to "macro-evolution," the change between species.

Our comment is that all of this risks a neglect of the perception of the levels of reality involved in life — note the comment we quote elsewhere that "the spiritual realm is causative" (p. 83).

One commentator says that Michael Behe's 2008 book, *The Edge of Evolution*, sets evolution in its proper place — indeed *part* of the history of life, but not *all* of that. Dr. Behe, famous as one of the derogatorily-labeled "IDiots," does indeed believe that evolution is real.

Anyone who pursues this commentator's insight and agrees with Behe's perspective, should be cautioned as we have assessed before: These are matters intensely in flux, and such a perspective will lead to massive books "refuting" the matter. But those in turn will lead to equally fact-dense and specialized books carrying the argument further, and to reach the knowledge of God, none of this will do. **Only the methodology that fits the matter will work.** [As p. 95, "Prayer, Word of God, Christian community."]

[150] "Inference to the best explanation:" Meyer explains this method of "abductive reasoning" on pages 154-59 and 343-44 of *Signature in the Cell*. It is a common method in "historical sciences," where past events are to be explained and experimental replications are not feasible.

Meyer's website is noted in endnote 274.

The assessment of what biology teaches us by Denis Alexander (pp. 87-88 of this present book) give a dramatically different resolution to the "God of the gaps" issue, which we also commend to the reader's attention.

See also note 133.

[151] Uniformitarianism, or the principle of uniformity, is the doctrine that everything is to be explained in terms of the natural forces that we see at work today — for example, erosion is by wind and rain as experienced in today's world, not by a catastrophic flood of dimensions different from today.

This scientific principle takes a new focus when philosophers of science note that the creation of ordered, specified **information** is, in the universe of our experience, always done by intelligence. The enormous "information" stored in the genomes of cells exceeds that of the Encyclopedia Britannica by a wide margin, and this has become one of the fields of contention for intelligence-acknowledging theories. (For the term "specified information" see Meyer's book *Signature in the Cell*.)

[152] Smith, p. 52, with his embedded quotation from Taylor's p. 233.

[153] Smith/Taylor quotes are p. 77 of Smith with his embedded quotation of p. 365 of Taylor. Guillebaud quote is p. 152.

[154] John Lennox has demolished Hawking's error at much greater length in his very readable book *God and Stephen Hawking*. [Our comments about Hawking were written while he was still alive; "God bless us everyone."]

Hawking asserts also another view, which Richard Dawkins agrees with: "determinism" — the movements of atoms and molecules determine everything, there is no "free will," no independent agency on the part of human beings. **Dawkins** asks the obvious: "Doesn't a truly scientific, mechanistic view of the nervous system make nonsense of the very idea of responsibility?" But when challenged on this during one of his book tours, he said, "I blame people, I give people credit ... it is an inconsistency that we sort of have to live with, otherwise life would be intolerable" [quoted on p. 153 of Nancy Pearcey's *Saving Leonardo*].

Perhaps, B-t mused, the reason why that interpretation of science makes life "intolerable" is that it isn't true, it doesn't fit reality. He asked Sci-guy, "Doesn't quantum mechanics, the latest physics, make determinism absurd, since there is openness at the bottom of everything?" "I think you're right, but I'm not a quantum mechanic," Sci-guy quipped, "so I can't turn the nut for you on that one."

Marilynne Robinson has put a famed rebuttal of determinism into her 2010 book *Absence of Mind.* One point she makes is that as the system grows in complexity, it acquires a character not solely of its components. For example, a computer may indeed be operating in a series of binary codes, 0's and 1's comprising all the information of its elements, but the resulting activity transcends that.

In terms of "not taking the universe [or some substrata] for granted, D. B. Hart notes in his epic tome that a quantum vacuum is not "nothing," but is in itself a "something," so the idea that our universe represents an unlikely but possible "quantum fluctuation" does not get around the philosophical conundrum "nothing comes from nothing."

[155] R_ is quoting from memory again; Paul quoted this in Acts 28:27, and it is quoted five other times in the New Testament. The Old Testament citation is Isa 6:9-10; compare Jer 5:21, and Deu 29:4!

[156] Meyer is quoted from his *Signature...* p. 244. [For reference, our initial discussion on the "information" nature of DNA was p. 82 of this present book.] Fong was quoted by Thaxton from his essay on p. 93 of *Biogenesis, Evolution, Homeostasis*. Ed., A. Locker. New York: Springer-Verlag 1973.

One comment we offer about Fong's essential concern for the "source" of the information that shapes all things is in our endnote 226.

Chapter 15: The Universe and You: notes on studying it

[157] *Arctic Dreams*, p. 251, stated re icebergs in Melville Bay. "Fear" is a word in the Bible that excites much discussion (see Index, "Fear of God"); Mr. Lopez notes that the Eskimo (p. 7, his word there rather than "Inuit") have two words for "fear:" *ilira* and *kappia*. He expounds these: "*Ilira* is the fear that accompanies awe; *kappia* is fear in the face of unpredictable violence." (He notes also on p. 404 an Arctic "beauty you feel in your flesh. You feel it physically, and that is why it is sometimes terrifying to approach. Other beauty takes only the heart, or the mind." It raises the question of whether "primitive" people experienced much more totally than we do, perhaps?)

[158] Dr. Francis Collins headed the Human Genome project on its successful quest to map the genetic code of human beings, one deep penetration of our science into a sector of reality unsuspected by the ancients. He tells on page 225 of his book *The Language of God: A Scientist Presents Evidence for Belief* of being gripped by the beauty of a frozen waterfall in the Cascade Mountains, the capstone to much spiritual searching (including reading C.S. Lewis on whether Jesus could be considered only a great spiritual teacher): "the majesty and beauty of God's creation overwhelmed my resistance."

[159] "above the sway of contention:" the next discussion is simple facts. These constants are measured values; they are not specified by the laws of physics

to be required to have these values; they just "happen" to be what life requires, within a very close precision. Interpreting what that *means* is of course a matter of the utmost contention — but the astonishing "coincidence" is beyond dispute.

[160] A few examples may be useful to illustrate the point: "If the initial explosion of the big bang had differed in strength by as little as one part in 10^{60}, the universe would have either quickly collapsed back on itself, or expanded too rapidly for stars to form. (As John Jefferson Davis points out, an accuracy of one part in 10^{60} can be compared to firing a bullet at a one-inch target on the other side of the observable universe [billions of light years away] ... and hitting the target.) ... Calculations by Brandon Carter show that if gravity had been stronger or weaker by one part in 10^{40} [ten to the 40th power, more than a trillion trillion trillions], then life-sustaining stars like the sun could not exist" (from the chapter "A Scientific Argument for the Existence of God," p. 49 of *Reason for the Hope Within*, Murray).

[161] The book is *The Privileged Planet*, G. Gonzalez & J. Richards. In the DVD presentation, Gonzalez and Richards highlight seven critical factors whose precise numeric values make the universe able to host life; science/philosophy writer Jay Holt says "20 or so parameters" in the fundamental laws of nature appear in such fine-tuning that "against astronomically unfavorable odds, conscious organisms could emerge." Holt's comment appears in a *Wall Street Journal* article "Science Resurrects God," in which he reports a survey in the journal *Nature* that showed "40% of American physicists, biologists and mathematicians believe in God — and not just some metaphysical abstraction, but a deity who takes an active interest in our affairs and hears our prayers" — a percentage "exactly the same as it was in 1916, when an identical poll was taken," he reports. (Holt's article was in the December 24, 1997, *WSJ*; the *Nature* journal he cited as having been "a few months" earlier.) Holt notes that the discovery in the 1900s that the universe did indeed have a beginning jolted the philosophy that the universe's "existence was just a brute fact requiring no further explanation."

Gonzalez and Richards also bring in a key concept: **constrained optimization**. "God's design" is criticized often that "this could have been better, that should have been done differently." But the issue involves what constraints the design has been shaped by, as well as "desirable" matters. An often-used example is a laptop computer: a larger screen might seem like an improvement, but it has to be balanced with the constraints of overall size for carrying convenience, weight and power consumption. *The perfection of the design cannot be assessed until the objectives of the designer and the constraints involved are considered.*

[162] This concept we owe to Jay Holt in the *WSJ* article mentioned in the preceding note.

Lee Strobel mentioned a medical study that about 10 percent of clinically dead heart attack victims who were revived, had "well-structured, lucid thought processes, with memory formation and reasoning, during the time that their brains were not functioning." The "once-skeptical" researcher said findings "would support the view that mind, 'consciousness,' or the 'soul' is a separate entity from the brain." He "speculated that the brain might serve as a mechanism to manifest the mind, much in the same way a television set manifests pictures and sounds from waves in the air." (The study was presented in 2001, per p. 250 of Strobel, *Case for A Creator*. See also endnote 2.)

[163] While I can't recall where I first heard this, Nancy Pearcey documents it in *Saving Leonardo* (p. 230): "Einstein emphatically denied that his theory implied relativism. He even wanted to label it *invariance theory*, because his calculations showed that physical laws *do not vary* from one reference frame to another." (Emphasis hers.)

The same point is documented in *Made to Stick: Why Some Ideas Survive and Others Die*: "The theory was designed to explain how the laws of physics are *identical in every frame of reference*... In 1929, Einstein protested, 'Philosophers play with the word [relativity], like a child with a doll... It does not mean that everything in life is relative.' To Einstein's chagrin, the number of people trying to tap into the resonance of 'relativity' began to exceed the number of people who were trying to understand relativity." P. 172 of 2008 book by Chip Heath and Dan Heath, Random House publishers.

Chapter 16: "Relatively" Interesting Thoughts?

[164] Dr. Schroeder expounds this in Chapter Three of *The Science of God*, and the quote is from p. 60 (p. 58 of the first edition). His chapter four discusses the changes in the transformation factor for time, as the universe's process matures. He has an appendix on CBR "as a universal clock."

The interested reader should note that the transformation factor changes during the process of the universe's expansion; Schroeder maps the "days" of Genesis 1 to "earth-based time" [my phrase, not his] accordingly and shows the correspondence between the developmental eras of life on earth, per the scientific account, and the steps of the Genesis "days" (pp. 61 - 67 of his book.) A critical point in this is that the "plants ... seed-bearing," of verse 11, he understands per 700-year-old *kabalah* interpretive tradition as being the *beginning* of the plant development process, understood to continue throughout the following "days" (p. 68; the phrase in Gen 1:11 "God said, 'Let the earth bring forth [plant life-forms]' " [NKJV] strikes me, as it does Schroeder, as having an evolutionary ring — some translations are less direct in Gen 1:11, but it returns in verse 24: "God said, "Let the earth bring forth living creatures...livestock... beasts... [ESV. Cf. NKJV, NLT, NRSV, NASB,

JPS, GNB. Some have "produce" instead of "bring forth." NIV has "land" instead of "earth"]). Newspaper re the universe's restudied age: March 2013.

165 Lest this seem quaintly antiquarian, given the modern tendency to see the Bible's "Genesis" creation narrative as brutally conflicting with "science," the reader is reminded of our revisiting Genesis with a more careful understanding of how it is to be read, discussed on p. 13 of this book per Hugh Ross, particularly the shift in Gen 1:2 to the viewpoint of the surface of the earth. (Dr. Schroeder agrees with Dr. Ross in taking the Bible/Genesis appearance of the sun in Gen. 1:14, "Day Four," as being the full manifestation of it as the atmosphere cleared on the forming planet Earth.)

166 A.D. Anno Domini "in the year of our Lord," dating from the old tradition's date of Jesus' birth — which is now generally acknowledged to be off by several years. The Gospel of John 2:20 provides one date: since the Temple had been, then, under construction "46 years" and was begun in 20 B.C., that conversation (John 2:20) took place in A.D. 26. (The Temple was not completed at that point; it was completed in A.D. 64 — per my NIV Study Bible, © 1985). But this seeming certainty flexes when we think that the starting year as pegged by scholars now, may not have been the point which the populace of those days reckoned as the start of the rebuilding process.

This is the Bible's frustration for scholars and debaters: we are told what we need to know, if we are searching and receiving in a humble spirit; we are NOT told all the intricacies, the extensive defense of points that strike some people wrong, etc.

167 R_'s unfortunate inexactitude as a Bible student has merged Col. 1:17 and Heb. 1:3 — both of which seem to say essentially the same thing (the final clause in Heb. 1:3, that is). The KJV has "consist" in Col. 1:17 where other versions have "hold together" (NIV, NASB, NRSV, ESV, NLT).

168 In case the reader takes interest in this "Lake of Fire" analysis, we should note that it is not part of Dr. Gerald Schroeder's application of the theory of relativity, but your author's input.

It is also something, as I reflect on it further, that is an interesting idea — but it seems that it dramatically under-portrays God's plans for creation [see Rev 21:1 - 22:7 for "a new heaven and a new earth, also 2Pe 3:13; in the OT, Isa 65:17 and 66:22].

169 Thoughtful-Woman is referring to an earlier conversation in which R_ quoted Theodore of Mopsuestia's account of how John's Gospel came to be written, and the apostle John's comment recounted there "that they who discourse on the coming of Christ in the flesh ought not to omit to speak of His divinity... lest in the course of time men who are used to such discourses might suppose that Christ was only what He appeared to be" — that is, a

human teacher with a gift for miracles. Theodore, a fourth-century writer, is quoted in J. I. Packer's *Bible Almanac*, p. 585.

Chapter 17: Hell and the Antidote

[170] "Hell" in the New Testament is most often the Greek word γέεννα ge-enna "Gehenna," from the Hebrew Ge Hinnom, the Valley of Hinnom (Hinnom "lamentation"). *Thayer's Greek Definitions* says, " 'Gehenna' or 'Gehenna of fire'. This was originally the valley of Hinnom, south of Jerusalem, where the filth [excrement] and the dead animals of the city were cast out and burned; a fit symbol of the wicked and their future destruction." In that valley fires smoldered continuously through the trash, and smoke arose unendingly... γέεννα occurs 12 times in the New Testament, ᾅδης "Hades" 10 times (also translated "hell," or sometimes "the grave") and Τάρταρος "Tartarus" once (the Greeks' term for the lowest level of hell). These word-counts are using the King James Version, as translations vary, as we have previously noted, and more reference works where our reader might research this are prevalent among the populace based on the KJV.

"Hell" in the Old Testament is used only in some translations, for the Hebrew "Sheol," the general "abode of the dead" for all persons.

[171] These informational tidbits are out of my notes from my Seminary journey (M.A. Thcology, 1999). We apologize for the lack of more specific source references.

The "history of hell" resurfaced in conversation between Thoughtful-Woman and B-t, when he told her that, "the 'history of hell' in the New Testament starts with John the Baptist, the great counter-establishment prophet who baptized Jesus: John said the Messiah would "burn up the chaff with unquenchable fire," Mt. 3:12, Lk. 3:17 (Bible abbreviations, please see Appendix Six. John Wesley's commentary understands this "chaff" as a reference to the Church, which has within its nominal membership both truly-transformed and not-really people, but B-t saw it as a wider paradigm of the elimination of evil).

That got them into an argument based on the modern "discoveries." Thoughtful-Woman brought up "**Markan priority**," the textual theory that the Gospel of Mark was the first to be written. The scholars conclude this by studying the text of the Bible narratives, in which Matthew and Luke both include many verses from the much-shorter Gospel of Mark. She was fishing for the idea that the later writings might have added something in, less authentic than earlier traditions... B-t believed in God and so he felt that the Holy Spirit watched over all the New Testament writings, and "earlier/later" was a bogus issue — to say nothing of the fact that "late dating" (of the Gospels' composition) is based on conjecture rather than definitive evidence. But he was possessed of a more gripping idea: the old traditions of the Church say that Matthew wrote first, "in the language of the Jewish people" (a mixture of Hebrew and Aramaic; Jesus' words in Matthew 27:46 are two

Hebrew, two Aramaic, according to Perschbacher's Lexicon). Well, trace that back through the traditional understanding that Mark accompanied Peter in Rome, and wrote as a condensed compilation of Peter's preaching — when Mark came to visit in Jerusalem, then, given the stature of Peter, this writing would naturally be used to compare and revise and strengthen any other writings already completed (Matthew's first writing in Hebrew/Aramaic, we posit) or in progress (Luke's, the great research that Luke himself noted in Lk. 1:3). [Perhaps using Mark's esteemed material, then, Matthew revised his own writing and it made the transition from Hebrew/Aramaic to Greek -- conjecture, but it harmonizes textual analysis and ancient tradition...]

Thus, B-t concluded, the tradition is *not* overthrown by the text-based analysis that produced the "Markan priority" theory — and the role of tradition is highlighted as something that we often need to study more carefully than our first impetuses. Sci-Guy had come by and listened to some of this, and B-t added gratuitously that the prominence given to "Markan priority" reflected the dynamic of scholarship today, the need for people to come up with something new to say, if they want recognition as "scholars" — "otherwise," B-t said, "you're a clerk, if you just teach again what has been said for centuries."

B-t pointed out also that the unquenchable fire appears from Jesus' own lips in Mark 9:48 (quoting Isaiah 66:24).

[172] These quotations are p. 59 of *The Orthodox Way*. The following paragraph's quote on "original sin" is page 62.

[173] Romans 1:18. At a rest stop, Sci-guy jested with R_ about this, and told him, "That must make you feel good about being religious." R_ replied, "That Scripture makes me uneasy, talking about wrath against those who suppress the truth, because I find myself 'suppressing' the truth by not letting the joy and peace shine as they should, by not being able to speak it forth in a way that people can receive... Negligence suppresses the truth, doubt can also, as well as active denial." Sci-guy shrugged and made a mental note not to try to make jokes with religious people.

Ah, the perplexities of the mortal passage! A note from your author: The Word of God tells us to confess our sins to one another and be forgiven (James 5:16, 1 John 1:9). If I confess that I do not "let" the joy and peace shine as they should, what is the remedy? Berating myself for the lack is worse than useless! But it seems that the Lord has led me to the answer: earlier this week, I came "by coincidence" on this on the web:

"Unlike exercising a muscle repeatedly where it gets stronger with extended use, exertion of your mind in ***prayer*** *will concentrate* ***too much power to your known faculties*** *and may cause less reliance on what your spirit is saying. Lead in with your spirit. Experience the wisdom of praise.*
*I** can reach your depths when you enter in to My presence in holy surrender. Your depths of your spirit know far more in time of praise than hours of*

pondering and questioning. Your most profound insight is most often the product, or byproduct, of the deepest times of prayer.

"Once your mind grasps what the spirit is telling it, now you have true direction. It never works in reverse—mind first speaking to spirit. The mind is too finite to probe the deeper things of God.

"So, again, I say, lead in with your spirit and connect with My Holy Spirit. I will show you truth."

Perhaps another Native American view will help: "You've got to make sure that you're doing it with your heart open to God." Peter John, p. 48 of his book *The Gospel...*

** "I" phrasing, and "My:" the words are a prophecy given to a believer to speak "during a worship service" per the website peterkreeft.com/faqs.htm (visited 27 July 2011). They are therefore phrased as the Lord's message. The webmaster of that site invites readers, "For more about this... visit my site: davenevins.com/loveofgod."

If applying this "works," I may report it in a possible follow-on book to this one. (Send SASE to the "Comments" address, end of Table of Contents, if you want to be notified. Thanks.)

Added information: in obtaining permission to quote this, I was told the author is Dan Goggin and the source should be cited as davenevins.com.

[174] For Jesus on the "seriousness of evil," see for example the brutal-sounding metaphors in Matthew 18:9, repeated also in Mark.

[175] Dr. Melvin Morse assesses in his book *Closer to the Light*, the alternative explanations given for these "visions" or experiences, showing that logical assessment does not support the alternatives as being more likely, or in many ways even plausible (pp. 183-193 of that book).

The discussion of *Chief Peter John* needs to mention his comment about understanding: "There are many things Athabascan Indian way that are hard to understand if your mind is fixed another way" (in *The Gospel According to Peter John*; see Standard Bibliography for free download, June 2019). This touches *one of the fundamental problems of our time*: many people's minds are "fixed in ways" that make some important things hard for them to get a hold of. See Index for "epistemologically enslaved," a commentator's penetrating discussion that one's "ways of knowing" can be limited and become a barrier to perceiving.

[176] Deut 4:24, Heb. 12:29. Compare 2 Sam 22:9; Psa 18:8; Isa 30:27, 30:30, 33:14; Mal 4:1; Mt. 3:10. Note that in Exo 24:17, the appearance of the glory of the LORD on top of Mt. Sinai "looked like a consuming fire."

Malachi 3:2 says, "But who can endure the day of his (the Lord's) coming? Who can stand when he appears? For he will be like a refiner's fire or a launderer's soap."

[177] Quote is from website en.wikipedia.org/wiki/Inferno_(Dante), visited 5 July 2011. (The observer interested in the state of our culture may appreciate the note that this entry is the third most popular "result" for "Dante's Inferno" on Google — the top two links are for a video game which now bears that name!

The same article showed us a deeper cut on Dante's "inherent justice" analysis — the Bible portrays Satan's initial sin as aspiring to rise to the height of being equal with God, and Dante's portrait of Satan's final destiny is that Satan is locked chest-high in solidly-frozen ice, which was chilled by the flapping of his wings as he tried to soar usurpingly.

The Bible student will recognize a theoretical problem with that portrayal, as the Bible says Satan's final destiny is in the Lake of Fire (Rev 20:10). That contrast may lend an added edge to our question of whether the medieval theologians brought too much of their own cogitation to bear on explaining things.

[178] Scripture references for "I will not share My glory with another:" God speaks in the Bible:

Isa 42:3 A bruised reed he will not break, and a smoldering wick he will not snuff out. [*Here "he" is referring to Messiah, to the predicted and promised Christ {Jesus}, in prophecy hundreds of years before His coming*]. In faithfulness he will bring forth justice;

Isa 42:4 he will not falter or be discouraged till he establishes justice on earth. In his teaching the islands [i.e. the farthest reaches of human habitation] will put their hope."

Isa 42:5 This is what God the LORD says — the Creator of the heavens, who stretches them out, who spreads out the earth with all that springs from it, who gives breath to its people, and life to those who walk on it:

Isa 42:6 "I, the LORD, have called you in righteousness; I will take hold of your hand. I will keep you and will make you to be a covenant for the people and a light for the Gentiles [i.e. the assorted nations],

Isa 42:7 to open eyes that are blind, to free captives from prison and to release from the dungeon those who sit in darkness.

Isa 42:8 "I am the LORD; that is my name! **I will not yield my glory to another or my praise to idols.**

Isa 42:9 See, the former things have taken place, and new things I declare; before they spring into being I announce them to you."

Isa 42:10 Sing to the LORD a new song, his praise from the ends of the earth...

And later in the Book of Isaiah in the Bible, God declares:

Isa 48:9 For my own name's sake I delay my wrath; for the sake of my praise I hold it back from you, so as not to destroy you completely.

Isa 48:10 See, I have refined you, though not as silver; I have tested you in the furnace of affliction.

Isa 48:11 ... **How can I let myself be defamed? I will not yield my glory to another**.

[179] In *Beyond the Cosmos,* Hugh Ross has related thoughts that someone could read up on, but I don't find them fruitful. Regarding "desires," n 175 below...

[180] This is not a Biblical phrase but a common assertion of many Christian thinkers. Bishop Timothy Kallistos Ware is cited in endnote 184, as one example. C. S. Lewis is also reported to have said it.

[181] Remember what that will (God's will) entails: it is often distorted in misapprehension, but God says, "I teach you what is best for you." Bible, Isaiah 48:17.

[182] Page 223 of *The Fullness of Sacrifice: An Essay in Reconciliation*, F. C. N. (Nugent) Hicks, London: Macmillan and Co., first published in 1930, quoted from Third Edition, 1944. [Page 66 above cited one key point of Hicks'.]

"Communion" is of course the central ritual of the followers of Jesus. At the Protestant churches I am familiar with, it is often done on the first Sunday of every month, with "open" Communion available to all who desire it. The Roman Catholic and Eastern Orthodox Churches restrict Communion to people who have become formally members of their particular churches. Jesus said "Do this in remembrance of Me" (Luke 22:19* and other Gospel parallels; 1 Cor 11:24-25), and He said, "If you love Me, you will obey My commandments" (John 14:23). His Presence for the Communion service is guaranteed by Matthew 18:20 and John 14:23, but there is intense theological argument (of course?) over what the "real presence" of Jesus means. It would seem that if you read the Gospels of Luke and John, your mind will have enough material, if you are prayerful about it all, that you will be set to talk to Pastors in your area and be led to where you should "find church." (Pray first, then trust! And seek.) Be careful about the people who tell you that you can sit home by yourself and **"church"** doesn't matter — the New Testament speaks of the "Body" with all its parts needing each other (1 Cor 12:8-27).

* The precision of the wording in 1 Cor 11 to the wording in Luke has been argued to support "early dating" of the Gospels; for Paul to be quoting Luke, in a work (1 Corinthians) which my Study Bible** dates "c. 55" A.D., Luke's Gospel must have been much earlier than some scholarly conjectures like to place it.

***The NIV Study Bible New International Version*, Kenneth Barker General Editor, Zondervan 1985.

[183] John 3:12.

The reader may want to cue us for more reflection on these matters: the analysis of reality comes into discussion — the idea that "we are spiritual beings having a physical experience"** is a different cut from our opening chapter's citation of NLT John 3; the varying views of annihilationism, the evident over-extrapolation of Gehenna in Western classics (Dante, Milton) etc, need to be seen in light of a theory of reality that acknowledges "in Him* we live and move and have our being" (Bible, Acts 17:28), "to Him* all are alive" (Jesus, Luke 20:38).

** *That* (spiritual beings having physical experience) is *not* a Biblical statement; it comes from some alcoholic's statement concerning spirituality and the suffering in this mortal world, as I remember. It is much repeated in the sobriety movement, in my limited experienced with it (your author has been "alcohol-free" since Dec. 7, 1992, see endnote 267).

184 Ware, in *The Orthodox Way*, says: "Christ is the judge; and yet, from another point of view, it is we who pronounce judgment upon ourselves. If anyone is in hell, it is not because God has imprisoned him there, but because that is where he himself has chosen to be. The lost in hell are self-condemned, self-enslaved; it has been rightly said that the doors of hell are locked *on the inside*" (p. 135, emphasis his).

Chapter 18: Concluding Prayer Considerations

185 The great philosopher David Hume said, "We know miracles don't happen." How did he *know*? At one level, he had a wide web of human connections, and he could assert that neither he nor his friends witnessed any miracles (see the New Testament** regarding why this would be so indeed!). But he had more than just possibly-limited experience — he had a theoretical rationale also. The laws of nature cannot be violated, he asserted (how could he prove that?). But Bertrand Russell, an atheist's atheist, showed the lie in that analysis: Facts which obey one set of laws, Russell explained, will under other circumstances obey another set of laws. (The quote is: "facts which obey one law will also obey others, hitherto indistinguishable but diverging in the future." From a 1912 paper of his. Quoted by Timothy Williamson, *Times Literary Supplement* 2/23/96, p. 27).

Hume was a famed Enlightenment philosopher, 1711-1776.

** Mark 6:5-6, which says that Jesus could work no miracles there (Nazareth) because of their unbelief.

For discussion of a number of miracles actually experienced in the present time, see Bill Johnson's *When Heaven Invades Earth,* and F. W. Bosworth, *Christ the Healer.* Also, a deliverance from paralysis is described on pages 204-5 of K. P. Yohannan's *Revolution in World Missions* (as per Bibliography, book is free on request from his organization). I have had my healings and deliverances — and in addition to Virginia's astounding restoration, another personal friend recounted a dramatic healing from the on-air ministry of one of the much-ridiculed, oft-despised televangelists (healing an injury that had been threatening to keep him from working, at a time when finances meant he really *needed* to work). Other miracle accounts are in *Smoke Signals from God* by Native American Indian author Ray "Black Buffalo" Wilson.

People attribute some healings to "coincidence" — but one person said, "When I pray, 'coincidences' happen; when I don't pray, they don't happen."

186 The hymn is called "Autumn." It was sung on the decks of the *Titanic* as that ship was sinking.

187 Rev. John Bunge was a pastor in the Evangelical Lutheran Church in America, in Southern California.

188 "On December 6, 1273, Aquinas, while attending mass, fell into a prolonged and rapturous mystical state. Thereafter, he ceased to write. When urged by officials of the Catholic Church to continue his work on the *Summa*, which he had left unfinished, he replied, 'I can do no more. Such secrets have been revealed to me that all I have written now appears to be of little value' " p. 66 of *The Devil's Delusion: Atheism and Its Scientific Pretensions* by David Berlinski, published by Crown Forum / Random House.

189 Bill Johnson is a pastor in Redding, Northern California (Bethel Church).

190 The book is by Thomas Long (Westminster John Knox Press, 2009). He has a discussion of the Christian hope versus the Platonic concept of the "soul," which he says has snuck widely into our consciousness. He also had a meditation on the realities of time, as an item under God's sovereignty, which puts in new light the question of the state of the departed. (If there is inherently no time with God, then those departed to Him don't have to "wait" for the blessed state(s) that we see as "future." That's as counter-intuitive as curved space, one of the basics of modern physics, and equally impossible for me to explain...)

191 Philippians 4:7 in the Bible (NIV translation). The **condition** is in the previous verse: "Do not be anxious about anything, but in every situation, by prayer and petition, with thanksgiving, present your requests to God."

That is the condition stated for "The peace of God... will guard your hearts and your minds in Christ Jesus."

192 B-t told R_ that he had heard somewhere of a preacher who was watching the people come into the meeting, and he said to God, 'Lord, I feel Your presence so strongly, why don't these people feel it?' And he says God informed him, 'When I let them *feel* My presence, their minds immediately go to their list of requests. What I want is to really spend some time with them.' That all ties in with the way you introduced the Lord's Prayer, that God 'knows your needs before you ask.' How about that idea of spending time with the Lord, person-to-person, instead of 'praying'?" R_ nodded at B-t and

said, "**A Cahuilla Indian pastor, Gabriel Ward, said, 'When you're praying, don't always be the one doing the talking.'** " **

That discussion moved R_ to remind B-t, "There's also the fact that God delights in meeting His* people's needs, like a father delights in seeing his kid open birthday presents -- when they acknowledge Him, so there's reciprocal love, not just selfish gratification."

** Test what you think you hear against God's revealed Word, the New Testament in particular — because, deceitful thoughts will try to come...

[193] **Hesed** חסד, faithful committed love, is a central word in the Old Testament in the Bible. It is a Hebrew word, of course, the Old Testament (pre-Jesus Scriptures) being almost all Hebrew (with minor Aramaic portions), and the New Testament Greek uses αγάπη agape (pronounced a-GAH-pay) for the same love.

Regarding the concept of faithful committed love in the marriage context as a wisdom concept blessed by God, it's interesting to note the research on happiness reported in the Reader's Digest: "When people commit to something that's expensive or hard to get out of, they report feeling happier." [The speaker reports applying this research to his girlfriend:] "...those findings seemed so clear to me that I went home and proposed. Now we're married, and I do love my wife more than I loved my girlfriend, even though she's the same person. **Commitment** isn't just a sign of love; it's a cause of love." [The speaker is Harvard psychologist Daniel Gilbert, author of the bestselling *Stumbling on Happiness*. Quotations are from pages 16-17 of the February 2010 *Reader's Digest.*]

R_ was telling B-t that this matches ancient Indian wisdom: the Luiseño Indians, when performing a marriage, admonished the couple that "Chingichngish has given you your spouse and you must be faithful." Thoughtful-Woman looked at B-t with a quizzical glance, as his brow was furrowed, and B-t added the obvious but vital point: "You have to research big decisions carefully, get sound counsel, not just follow a passion."

[Psychologist Gilbert also notes, "when people were given money to spend, those who spent it on others were happiest. Giving is literally a joy," also page 17 of *Reader's Digest*].

[194] For Scriptures (Bible verses) on this, see the first page of the Scripture Table (first Appendix).

R_ noted in his studies that "The Indifferent Generation" is the title of Chapter One of Elder Paisios' *Spiritual Counsels*, Volume II: *Spiritual Awakening.*

See also note 44 above for "walking in a circle" when focused on our human world, our seven-day week of worldly matters.

[195] As quoted in an early church letter — "First Clement," Clement of Rome:

The **Septuagint** (LXX) is the first major translation of the Old Testament Scriptures from their original Hebrew, into Greek, done about 200 B.C. The abbreviation "LXX" comes from the seventy translators who worked on it according to what history survives about the provenance of the work. (LXX is the Roman numeral for 70.) The Septuagint went out around the Mediterranean-circling world of the Roman empire, making a vast international reach of the Word of God, to people who found it *"a creation parallel to the creation of the world itself... both are the work of the same Creator."* (The quote is from p. 50 Ernst Wurthwein's *The Text of the Old Testament*, English translation 1995 Eerdmans/Grand Rapids MI. He is citing A. von Harnack.)

The Septuagint was the "Bible" of the early Church. B-t's quotation of Psalm 50:21 comes from language used by one of the early Church leaders in quoting the Septuagint for that verse — quoted by the early leader Clement in *The Letter of the Romans to the Corinthians*, which Lightfoot and Harmer say is perhaps the earliest Christian document we possess outside of the New Testament. (Source: *The Apostolic Fathers*, translated by Lightfoot & Harmer, p. 48 of 2nd ed.)

196 Page 33 of *The Power of the Blood of Jesus*, by Andrew Murray.

The discussion of "holiness" may bear this commentary on the implications of the whole complex of ideas there: "It demands that we recognize the sin in our lives and that we acknowledge and **repent** of that sin. This is the first major intersection on the spiritual pilgrimage. Many prefer to turn off at this point, or think they can live the Christian life on their own terms** — that is, without the conversion in attitude and action that must follow the conversion of heart." P. 85 of *Loving God.*

** a note by your author — see Index for "Christian gangster," one man's effort to do exactly what this paragraph describes!

Repentance (the Greek word means a turning, to turn from wrong ways to the good & right way) was the first of Jesus' preaching (Matthew 4:17, Mark 1:15; compare Jesus, Luke 24:47).

For a final aside on the implications of holiness, consider: "Every possible abuse of power finds its condemnation in what is holy" (p. 342 of Elwell's *Evangelical Dictionary of Theology).*

And some comments by the monk bear repeating: "If one's intention (conscious or unconscious) is not to face one's sin-condition, repent and thus be reconciled to God, but instead to 'be spiritual' while continuing to worship oneself ... the ultimate delusion. ...They do see a light but it is not the True Light... It is the natural light peculiar to the mind of man created in God's image... mental light... might just as well be called darkness... God is not in it."

"Doing the Jesus Prayer in order to feel spiritual and distract ourselves from our sin-condition is of course a contradiction in terms. It works against the very aim of asking Christ, 'Have mercy on me.' [Praying properly] we begin to realize all the subtle, hidden passions and resentments of which we have to repent."**

(Now, if you're a typical "modern," you may think, "Sure, I've done some things, but I'm not a bad person, those were just ..." Well, lay them before God in a genuine seeking prayer, tell God you want to be what He* desires...) [If you *do* perceive your sins as quite serious, remember that "the Blood of Jesus cleanses from all sin" for those who receive Him (1 John 1:7).

** Quotes are pp. 327, 348 of *Christ the Eternal Tao.* (Hieromonk Damascene, the author, says also that the Jesus Prayer comes out of the [Eastern] Orthodox tradition and the one praying it should be under the discipline & support of that tradition, that Church community, to be safeguarded and blessed [not his precise words]. This gave me pause about mentioning it, because access to the Orthodox is very limited [they are only 10% of "Christendom"] – but I have found that, although my contact with them has been small in some regards, it has been very fruitful and positive.

[197] *Arctic Dreams*, p. 273-4: Mr. Lopez discusses the Inuit/Eskimos' deep knowledge of the land and creatures, "an intricate, long-term view ... corroborated daily" as it is constantly refined. "Outside the region this complex but easily shared 'reality' is hard to get across without reducing it to generalities, to misleading or imprecise abstraction."

Note also the blunt statement: "The key terms are not translatable." This comes from "Brody, discussing Eskimo concepts of intimacy with the land..." (p. 276).

This issue of the adequacy of our concepts, for discussion of God and holiness, may be highlighted also by: *The profound skepticism of our age, the mistrust of all that has been handed to us by our grandfathers and grandmothers as tradition, has led to a curious failure of the imagination, manifested in language that is thoroughly comfortable, and satisfyingly unchallenging. A hymn whose name I have forgotten cheerfully asks God to "make our goals your own." A so-called prayer of confession confesses nothing but whines to God "that we have hindered your will and way for us by keeping portions of our lives away from your influence." To my ear, such language reflects* ***an idolatry of ourselves, that is, the notion that the measure of what we can understand, what is readily comprehensible and acceptable to us, is also the measure of God****. (Bold emphasis mine — your author. A nice point re "**Trinity**" conundrums, yes?) — from* Kathleen Norris, "Annunciation," one of the essays in the collection *Watch for the Light: Readings for Advent and Christmas* (no editor listed). This is from pp. 45-46.

Chapter 19: Quoting Quotes

[198] Denis Alexander gives a discussion of this issue on pp. 191-200 of his book *Creation or Evolution, Do We Have to Choose?*

The issue of how to translate the Hebrew terms, including אדם **Adahm**/"Adam," goes back at least as far as the Greek "Septuagint" translation, circa 200-250 B.C. Speaking of *that* translation, one Jewish commentator said, "that day was as ominous for Israel as the day on which the golden calf was made,** since the Torah could not be accurately translated." P. 86 of *The Psalms Through Three Thousand Years: Prayerbook of a Cloud of Witnesses*, William L. Holladay; Fortress 1993. He quotes it from Sopherim 1.7, one of the "appendices to the Babylonian Talmud."

(** The "golden calf" was a falling into idol worship, Exo 32:1-19; "Torah" is the term for the first five books of the Bible, including Genesis.)

[199] Denis Alexander, *Creation or...*, p. 305. Augustine was circa A.D. 400.

[200] The quote is from page 30 of *The Emergence of the Catholic Tradition* by Jaroslav Pelikan. "Catholic," Greek *katholikos*, "universal," became part of the liturgy of the Church in the Nicene Creed, more than half a millennium before the Roman Church and the Eastern Church split.

On the doctrine that all souls are immortal, consider this:
"Plato gave a strong focus on the inherent immortality of the soul. At first this was resisted by many Christians as incompatible with the Gospel message, and the concept of the 'conditional immortality' of the soul was preferred: namely, that God would elevate the human being into immortal life (and not merely the soul but the body too), if (and only if) the creature was obedient to the covenant. Only after the third century did the presupposition of the soul's immortality became [sic] more commonly accepted in the Christian world." — p. 317 of McGuckin's handbook on Patristic Theology. ("Patristic" — the early centuries of the church. A reviewer described this work as "carefully documented, yet lively and readable," and that has proven to me to be true — your present author.)

[201] Quote is p. 158 of that book, quoting Dallas Willard. "Hedge of protection:" Bible, Job 1:10, Zec 2:5. (Rev. Tim Keller, pp. xvii - xix of his book, has a positive perspective on searching and thoughtful "doubt.")

[202] Christianitytoday.com/ct/2000/april24/4.86.html?start=5. Willimon is a United Methodist Bishop; per Wikipedia, a "theologian, writer, former Dean of the Chapel at Duke University... one of America's best known preachers... Per a Pew Fndn Survey, one of the two most frequently read writers by pastors in mainline Protestantism (Henri Nouwen also noted)... [Another survey, 1996:] one of the 12 best preachers in the English-speaking world."

(Regarding "epistemologically challenged," see also note #175 above for *an Athabascan Indian leader's comments on having one's mind "fixed" in ways that limit understanding.*)

(Epistemology: "the branch of philosophy dealing with the nature of knowledge, its origin, foundations, limits and validity" — The New Lexicon Webster's Dictionary, 1972, 1989.)

Also regard "epistemologically enslaved," Willimon's wording, note our comment on p. 30 that "people became entangled in thickets of thought that held them from the light." (The pessimist might compare this with the New Testament's statement that "the things they understand by mere brute instinct, these are the very things that destroy them" Jude 1:10. That may connect also with our comment on p. 111 about the situation being like a helicopter being sent to rescue a drowning person, but the person has to grasp the hand held out to save...)

The question of our regard for "epistemology" was set in context nicely by Barry Lopez in his summary of "the formal divisions of Western philosophy — metaphysics, epistemology, ethics, aesthetics, and logic — which pose, in order, the following questions. What is real? What can we understand? How should we behave? What is beautiful? What are the patterns we can rely on?" (p. 202 of *Arctic Dreams*)

[203] The quotation is spoken by Hamlet.

[204] On p. 498, the *Encyclopedia of Catholicism* describes animals, plants and humans as "a single earth community." (The multi-faceted term "catholicism" *is* Roman Catholicism here — the professed allegiance of more than half of the world's Christians).

Sci-guy is quoting from the article on "evolution." (The article opens with the definition of evolution as "the descent of all forms of life, with modification, from earlier forms," discusses Darwinian natural selection and the "modern synthesis" of molecular biology, genetics, and Darwinian principles, and notes "an extended usage" which uses the term for "the unfolding of the entire cosmic story." Please note that their definition is a very different perspective on "evolution" from the perspective that if "evolutionary" explanations work, God's out of the picture.)

B-t never got Sci-guy another beer, but he did pull out that *Encyclopedia* and noted an number of quotes on other topics that he found worth reading to Thoughtful-Woman and Sci-guy while R_ refilled the gas tank later on:

"...two truths have to be kept in balance: the universality of God's call to salvation and the apparently unequal response of people to this call. The [Roman Catholic] Church ... teaches that baptism of desire ... may substitute for water baptism (that of one preparing for baptism, or that of a person of goodwill who simply is unaware that God is calling the person to the Church)... may substitute... The salvation of unbelievers remains a matter of theological discussion" (page 138).

"God's purpose the unification of all creation in loving communion. For fallen humanity this goal required the incarnation of the Word of God, so that in Christ the human will could act freely and fully in harmony with the divine." — article on Maximus the Confessor, who lived c. A.D. 600.

"The effect of original sin... distorted contour to the moral playing field... However, human beings are not predestined toward evil; any such predestination would compromise both human freedom and the goodness of God." (Article "evil," p. 496). (Compare article "evil, moral:" "the doctrine's assertion that human nature remains basically good serves rather to emphasize the mysteriousness of moral evil than to explain it.")

Thoughtful-Woman took the Encyclopedia from B-t and perused several matters before she exclaimed with delight, "Here's the wording our driver has been looking for! The 'Enlightenment,' they say, 'was characterized by a sometimes uncritical confidence in the powers of human reason, an optimistic view of human nature, and a passion for human freedom.' P. 249," she concluded with a flourish. B-t's old KJV Bible furnished him with the wording, "oppositions of science falsely so called" (1 Tim 6:20), which made him think of R_'s language about "over-extrapolating."

R_ finished refilling the thirsty vehicle, waved for the dog to jump back in, and stumbled upon the conversation. He frowned at B-t and told the group that, "The interested student of reality should be aware that the *Encyclopedia of Catholicism* is not an *official* product of the Roman Catholic Church. Its General Editor [Fr. McBrien, p. vi] *is* a theology professor at the University of Notre Dame, and President Emeritus Hesburgh of Notre Dame wrote the foreword in which he notes that 'few institutions around the world are so closely identified with Catholicism' as Notre Dame, *but* the book bears no 'imprimatur' or 'nihil obstat,' the marks of official hierarchical approval by the Roman Catholic Church." Nobody was really interested in what he had to say, and they "put it on the road."

We should note that your author is *not* (Roman) Catholic.

205 The speaker quoted is Phillip H. Duran (Tigua tribe), p. 12 of *Native Peoples* magazine, Nov-Dec 2007. At the time of that article, he had completed master's degrees in physics and computer science, and extensive further studies in theoretical physics (he also served as vice-president of the organization Hamaatsa (hamaatsa.org). In the article, Mr. Duran stated that, "The sterile attitude toward nature that prevails in academia infects all of us who are educated in science... Native people relate to a universe that is alive with spirit, recognizing that Nature has its own authoritative system with spiritual and moral principles essential to leading a life of wholeness."

Speaking editorially, we recognize, believe and assert, with the **Church** of the ages, that the unifying & governing "Principle" of all those "principles" is Christ, the Wisdom of God. (Please note that this is your author's statement, not Mr. Duran's). This is the Christ of the Word of God, not necessarily the Christ that has been mirrored to Native peoples in their dealings with non-Native peoples ...

In getting permissions for quotations, I was able to be in contact with Mr. Duran. To my joy, he wrote that it is "often said in Indian country that all things are imbued with spirit. Modern physics confirms that the visible world is sustained by an invisible world and that energy manifests as matter... The spiritual universe, then, is manifest to Man as the Creation... Thus, I have come to understand that the physical universe is the manifestation of its spiritual existence, implying that the physics term *energy* corresponds to ***spirit***. I am a follower of the Christ and believe this assertion agrees with the work of the Creator-Son described in Colossians chapter 1 and with the fact that God/Creator is spirit (John 4:24)." [letter of July 2, 2012, quoted by permission; bold emphasis added for indexing.]

Native Peoples magazine described itself as "... devoted to the arts and cultures of the Indigenous peoples of the Americas... a respected, consistent and reliable voice ... bridging the gap between the historical traditions of the past and today's Native realm", inviting readers to "journey with us and explore the rich evolving lives of American Indians: where they came from and where they're going." (from their website nativepeoples.com, May 1, 2012). 2019 update: it appears that this magazine has gone out of business; the "rich evolving lives" of native peoples continue!

[206] J. B. S. Haldane: "My practice as a scientist is atheistic. That is to say, when I set up an experiment I assume no god, angel or devil is going to interfere with its course... I should therefore be intellectually dishonest if I were not also atheistic in the affairs of the world."** But, B-t told Thoughtful-Woman, that was carrying a mentality which was appropriate in one domain, into other domains without any warrant for doing so, except inertia. It would be like a swimming instructor saying he wears his swimsuit all day to teach, and he has to wear his swimsuit to dinner to be consistent.

Thoughtful-Woman didn't enjoy the analogy, and replied with a quote from Schopenhauer: "Every man takes the limits of his own field of vision for the limits of the world."

** en.wikipedia.org/wiki/J._B._S._Haldane, accessed 5 April 2013.

Arthur Schopenhauer is quoted from p. 1063 of *Bartlett's*.

(This is the last of several citations from Wikipedia; finding them quite useful and versatile, I would like to note for the reader's possible interest that I am a donor to them. Donations go to The Wikimedia Foundation, a 501(c)(3) nonprofit, P.O. Box 98204, Washington DC 20090-8204, USA).

[207] The quotation is taken from p. 198 of Johnson's *Reason*... Johnson goes on to state that, "In all the world there is no greater dogmatist than 'everybody knows.' "

Chapter 20: "In The White House"

[208] Bible, Jeremiah 23:24. Cf. Acts 17:28.

[209] A note on certain sectors not hearing certain words: I worked for a non-profit that visited in the local prison to encourage the people to make better of their lives, and I was talking on the phone to an inmate friend that I had

met in this way. He was discussing the case of a man on trial, who had — unprovoked — stabbed a pregnant woman in the belly. That man had decided he wanted to hurt someone, and when he went looking, she seemed to him as someone he would like to hurt. My friend was saying that community organizations should support this man, not the woman's desire for a long jail term for him. I said, "G., first he has to repent." My friend "G." laughed out loud and said, "There's a word I haven't heard in years and years." Now I ask you, dear reader: a medium-security prison, a *Correctional Center*, and the word "repent" hasn't been heard in years?

[210] See Bible, Ephesians 6:11-19. [Now that the RV journey has closed, see endnote 277 for tips for your journey; "Church," endnote 66.] Re the quoted verses, some pastors advocate using these verses for daily "morning prayers" — you say "I take the shield of faith, with which to quench all the flaming darts of evil… [go on through each 'piece of armor'] … I thank You, Lord, that I am fully covered and the devil can't defeat me!" Another key element is thanking God for being our healer (see Index for His* promises re healing, & Scripture table "well-being;" endnote 70 for another approach.)

The End: The *"final end-note"* mentioned in this chapter, is placed indeed at the end of all the endnotes, below.

Postscript #1

[211] Recounting this vital help from God, reminds me of the monk's words: "…sensual distractions, from love of comfort… to drug and alcohol use. Among these, the use of marijuana is perhaps the most sinister, for it gives the illusion of being 'spiritual' while making one unable to concentrate and thus practice watchfulness and face oneself." Pages 354-355 of *Christ the Eternal Tao*, Hieromonk Damascene.

Marijuana lingers in the system longer than alcohol, with traces up to 30 days after intake; the person who smokes it every weekend is thus never completely free of its effects. That is one significant difference from alcohol (your author is now "alcohol-free" also, see endnote 267 for the account). [Note: people have called marijuana "the zero-ambition drug"…]

For another Holy Spirit deliverance from drug addiction, see the last lines of endnote 77. [My own freeing from marijuana usage, p. 126]

[212] Your author's inputs about "apocalyptic matters" — the "coming to the End" and the Biblical "AntiChrist" — are planned for a following book. (See endnote 232). The reader concerned for apocalyptic matters should pray over the information on page 39-40 by the Native American Christian preacher named Black Buffalo.

[213] A third "principle" might bear citing, that of community, attending church regularly. I was blessed to find people to help in my various crises, and to encourage me. My conclusion from over thirty years' experience now, is that

over a decade or so, it makes all the difference in the world. Go to Church, find a Bible-believing good one and go, even if it seems nothing is happening on a week-by-week basis! ("Tips," p. 196; endnote 225 discusses baptism).

Postscript #2

[214] Deacon Scott Gillis, now Fr. Michael, working now in British Columbia.

[215] Exodus 15:26. Psalm 103:3, 1 Peter 2:24, and Psalm 147:3 are other Scriptures on this. Isaiah 58:8 connects **healing** with concern for the poor. Other meditation Scriptures on healing include Prov 4:20-22; 2 Kings 20:5; 2 Chron 30:20; Jer 17:14; Matthew 4:24; Luke 5:15; Acts 5:16; James 5:16; 1Pet 2:24; Psalm 91:9-16; Psalm 103:1-5; Isaiah 40:29,31; Isa 53:4-5; Jer 30:17; John 10:10; 2 Cor 10:3-5; Phlp 1:6, 4:6-7; 2 Tim 1:7. This list combines lists from Marilyn Hickey Ministries and Kenneth Copeland Ministries (kcm.org has a topic search box that will pull up videos on "healing" for your interest; I myself had a healing from watching a series of Copeland videos).

Hosea 11:3 in the Bible records God's statement that "they did not realize it was I who healed them" (NIV).

Note our important caution in endnote 218. (Cf. Mat 9:12, Lk 5:31!)

[216] Kathleen Norris, in her essay "Annunciation," p. 45 of the essay collection *Watch for the Light: Readings for Advent and Christmas* (no editor cited for collection).

In advocating the essential attention to the spiritual dimension of health and healing, let us also repeat what we said on p. 138: do not neglect medical help when appropriate.

[217] The human being is called to be the dwelling place of the God Who said, "I will dwell in them... and they shall be My people" (2 Cor 6:16 NKJV) — see 1 Cor 6:19 "your bodies are temples of the Holy Spirit" (NIV), also 1 Cor 3:16. For the promises about "I will dwell with ..." see for example Ezek 37:27; Heb 8:10; see also Jer 24:7, 31:33, 32:38; Ezek 11:20, 14:11, 34:30, 37:23(!); Zec 8:8.

[218] The phrase "anoint with oil" in James 5:14 is interpreted by some commentators to refer to the use of all appropriate medicine(s), as olive oil was used as a medicine in the first century. Jesus (Mat 9:12, Luke 5:31) obviously commends using physicians and medical care where appropriate.

[219] The definition of "reason" by the author of 4 Maccabees, per commentator p. 481 of *The Oxford Companion to the Bible.* (4 Macc 1:15. The books of the Maccabees are some of the books found in the Catholic Bible but not the Protestant Bible — the variations occur only in the Old Testament, with Catholics, Orthodox and Protestants all using exactly the same books in the New Testament. The books of the Maccabees — the intertestamental revolts

of the Jews against sacrilege and oppression — are believed to vary in historical value, and the acceptance of them varies. The Catholic *New American Bible* has Maccabees 1 & 2, the *Orthodox Study Bible* has 1, 2 and 3. Brenton's *Septuagint* has all four Maccabees, as does the NRSV-A [A: "with Apocrypha"] that I purchased for my e-Sword Bible software, e-sword.net.)

Acknowledgments

220 Pastor Ron Hernandez is in the Foursquare denomination, founded by the trailblazing female pioneer Aimee Semple McPherson. I met Fr. Boulos when he was OCA (Orthodox Church in America), an autocephalous Eastern Orthodox Church ("autocephalous" meaning that the American church is self-governing, separated from the oversight of the original Eastern country of origin — in this case, Russia. The Russians were in Alaska before the Americans undertook to fight for their independence. The Orthodox Church in Russia, by heroic endurance, survived the evils of Soviet communism.) Fr. Boulos ministers now in Escondido California.

221 Brother David Flenaugh (a member of the Church of God in Christ) gave me a lesson I struggle to remember and apply: When I was going through something that utterly "fried" me — perplexed me and troubled me and totally wiped me out — he listened patiently and then said, **"It's going to be very interesting to see how God works this out."** The trouble was indeed resolved; the specifics have faded from memory; what was so large at the time has proven forgettable — but Brother David's gentle, solid trust in God bears my perpetual remembrance. Yes, the Scripture tells us, "Pour out your heart to Him*" (Psa 62:8) — but then, having done that, let us remember to "trust and obey." [Yes, He* leads us to do *our* part!]

The "Trouble" section in the Annotated Bibliography (p. 187) has some comments and a book that may be of interest.

222 The "moonbow," a rainbow made by the rays of the moonlight in that location, is documented in a book on natural wonders which I unfortunately have loaned out. "Nuannaarpoq" is an Inuit/Eskimo word which Barry Lopez discusses in *Arctic Dreams*, p. 202. *(Note: "Inuit/Eskimo" is used throughout my writing here, because in Alaska "Inuit" was used — in my 13 years working for the Alaska Native community** — only for Canadian and other non-Alaskan Eskimos. [If proper sensitivity was desired for Alaskan Eskimos, the distinction between Inupiat and Yupik was always observed.] The Alaska Federation of Natives, for example, defined their membership as "Eskimos, Aleuts and Indians."*

*** "working for" here means working in Native organizations, for Native supervisors and contract managers, for goals serving the Native community.)*

223 Darin did great work on the redesign overhaul of the cover I furnished - see his WEBSITE theinvinciblesoldier.wixsite.com/theambassadoroftruth

You can also look for "The Ambassador of Truth" on YouTube or EMAIL Ambassadoroftruth@disciples.com. (Proofing/editing, contact J.J. thru Darin)

Appendix One: Scripture Table

[224] For "LORD" see endnote 38.

[225] Jesus, John 6:29: The work of God is to believe in the one He* has sent. (Cf. 1 Thess 2:13; 1 John 3:23.) Then, the next step for decided-belief is baptism. Essential per Mark 16:16, Acts 22:16. (Not just "fire insurance," re possible hell-fire, but a life commitment...) Endnote 277 has information for spiritual growth. ("Church," endnote 66).

[226] The Greek word "rhema" is often used of the spoken word, "logos" of the idea or message (e.g John 17:20: NIV, GNB, ISV "message," ESV and others "word").

"Information" is one of our profound modern concepts. James Gleick did a massive tome on the history and details of humanity's interaction with information. His research showed: "... **as scientists finally come to understand information, they wonder whether it may be primary: more fundamental than matter itself. *They suggest that information forms the very core of existence.*"** (P. 10 *The Information...* — emphasis added. More:)

Doesn't that sound like **a modern echo of John 1:1-3's famous declaration, "In the beginning was the Word, and the Word was with God, and the Word was God... All things were made through him**..." (ESV Bible). [This "Word" refers to the second Person of the Trinity, Who became **incarnate as Jesus the Christ**. The Greek is λογος "logos" in these verses.]

[227] Job 33:14 re "God speaks" has been quoted in the Scripture Table from the 1984 version of the NIV, for reasons discussed below. The reader may question the asterisk on "man" in the NIV-1984 language cited. It *is* a different usage, to some degree, than our pronoun asterisking elsewhere, but it rests on a similar concept that "masculine vs. feminine" does not apply in this particular place. The old language, for all its objectionable aspects, had a coherence in regard to human/divine that sometimes merits caution in "correctness." (The CEV for this verse does "inclusiveness" on the human side by saying, "we don't always recognize his voice." It isn't entirely the same, is it?) Now that women are 51.4% of management/professional employees, constitute the majority of the American workforce, and earned 60% of new B.A. & M.A. degrees (in 2010),** maybe at times we can let the "old language" speak for its meaning rather than placing its articulation amidst the language wars — "Father-Mother" for God is awkward at best and playing with the language revealed, in order to make matters much larger than ourselves fit our human concerns, is risky, conceptually.***

Returning to the quoted language above, does the CEV wording preserve the thought-provoking aspect of the NIV-1984 language? Some other "inclusive" rewordings do not: GNT "no one pays attention to what he says;" NRSV "though people do not perceive it." (NLT is similar to NRSV; GW "God's Word" version is similar to GNT; NKJV still has "man" used in the old sense, for "humankind.")

(NIV-1984 & NIV-2011: The widely-respected NIV Bible translation has been revised to bring more compatibility with modern usage including "inclusive" structuring; the update was issued November 2010 and is being referred to as the "2011" version of the NIV. The language quoted for this verse in the Scripture table is NIV-1984. The "2011" language for the verse is: "For God does speak—now one way, now another — though no one perceives it." But like the CEV, the meaning slides in that construction — many times someone does perceive it, as foreshadowed in the 1984 NIV's use of the verb "*may*." If I am reading the Hebrew correctly, it does not differentiate between the two ways of translating that clause — Hebrew verb tenses do not match up with English ones. The new NIV edition is discussed at the website thenivbible.com/.)

None of the versions cited here change "Son of Man" (a title for Jesus) into "The Human One," as the new "Common English" New Testament does (as did the 1995 Oxford "Inclusive" New Testament). Since His* incarnate identity was combined Divine-Human, that does not read well to me. It loses the beautiful parallelism of "Son of God, Son of Man," and the tie to Bible, Daniel 7:13. Also, this terminology seems to box the translators into using "the Child" for "the Son" in the New Testament, and *that* seems inappropriate for Jesus — the word "child" has an inescapable connotation of immaturity. There is a point at which our human concepts fail us, and centering ourselves in them becomes counterproductive...

** The statistics cited are per Los Angeles *Times* OpEd p. A19, Oct 20, 2011, citing statistics from a story published in *Atlantic* magazine in 2010 entitled "The End of Men." I have not read that story and this citation is not to recommend it.

*** Do I never cease to belabor these matters? But it cannot be helped (Bible, 2 Cor 12:11). The "Father-Mother" verbalization is wrapped in human beings' working from their own gender-based-ness; it is a reaching for wholeness, but it seems to suffer from our self-based-ness. The reaching for comprehension showed a different verbalizing re "Father" when Hieromonk Damascene processed Lao Tzu's question, "Is the Way a Child of something else?" (p. 78 of *Christ the Eternal Tao*). The monk writes, "The Sage [Lao Tzu/Lao Zi] had not seen the Mind Who had given birth to the Word outside time," and the monk thus comes to write of "the Father-Mind."

So I have "Father-Mother" brought to me by some, and "Father-Mind" from another quarter, and I listen respectfully and gratefully write of "Father*."

When Jesus said, "ἐγώ εἰμι ἡ ὁδὸς καὶ ἡ ἀλήθεια καὶ ἡ ζωή I am the Way, the Truth and the Life," each of those three key terms — Way, Truth, Life — is feminine in the original Greek. It was to a woman that Jesus first revealed Himself as Savior of the world (John 4:26), a woman whom He spoke to outside the empty tomb (John 20:16,) and women special in Mt. 26:13, Luke 1:48. (The attempts to rework the language bring some Bible prefaces to say that "inclusive language is used for humans but not for God" — which forces me to the awkward thought, *Could God be any more "inclusive" than He* has been in the Gospel — what is more inclusive than "come, whosoever will" ?*)

[228] This ("God speaks," p. 138) brings us to the "cosmic Christ," the Jesus Who is more than a human being walking the earth, Who is God incarnate. See Index re "Incarnation."

[229] The Dead Sea Scrolls, discovered 1947-1956, gave scholars copies a thousand years older than previously-known Old Testament texts. This gave rise to a spate of sensation allegations, which have fallen by the wayside as the texts have been released; Martin Abegg and collaborators have published *The Dead Sea Scrolls: A New Translation* (Harper SanFrancisco 1996; this has the non-Biblical texts) and *The Dead Sea Scrolls Bible*, which notes variants in the scrolls from the generally-used Masoretic Text of the Old Testament. The latter book says (p. 213), "Arguably the single *most dramatic passage among the newly discovered biblical scrolls*" comes in 1 Samuel 11, where "the atrocities of King Nahash of the Ammonites" are documented as to mutilations among other communities before Nahash threatened this to the Israelites (1Sam 11:2) [italic emphasis mine — your author]. The non-specialist may be forgiven for feeling that the teachings of the Bible are not impacted by this. There are many variants that may be interesting to ponder — on p. xix, Dr. Abegg et al note that, "Several possibilities exist for the multitude referred to in Isaiah 29:5... 'your strangers'... 'the ungodly'... 'your enemies'..." Again, the careful work through the ancient texts is most commendable, but it does tend to show that the alleged "unreliability" of the current Scriptures is *refuted* rather than established by these researches.

See Index for discussion of "the critical text," a massive scholarly work of decades by different teams, which has demonstrated the reliability of the New Testament text. (Also discussed by Nancy Pearcey on p. 201 here).

The person interested in these matters should remember how eager some commentators are to leverage any minor difference in historical Biblical texts into a major item. One wrote that "the Catholics and Protestants even have different Ten Commandments!" So I put my Catholic Bible and my (Protestant) NIV side by side — the verses are broken up differently, so the writer could justify the assertion, but it distorts the matter terribly: what is commanded to be done, and what is commanded *not* to be done, those matters are entirely the same.

[230] This Scripture Table entry on Poverty has been dealing with the Lord's injunction to take concern for the poor. If you are **suffering poverty**, relevant Scriptures include Psalm 113:7 "He [the Lord] raises the poor from the dust," and Psalm 12:5, 40:17. ***Pray* such Scriptures** as Psalm 69:13, 70:5, 74:21, 86:1 (reading through Psalms and Proverbs will bring you many more! And the Scripture tells us that the Lord is "watching over His* word to perform it" (see Jer 1:12).

[231] "Unanswered prayer:" Bill Yount, who claims a prophetic ministry, reported a vision of a bowl in Heaven that had filled over "many long years" with "prayers that seemingly didn't get answered," and in his vision the bowl was poured out and great blessings were wrought on earth (p. 136 of *I Heard Heaven Proclaim: Prophetic Words of Encouragement*, McDougall Publishing 2004, mcdougalpublishing.com).

"Waiting on the Lord" is a common phrase in Scripture, and *perseverance* to see prayers answered is a key item of living for God. (Note also issues of motive in Bible, James 4:3).

[232] For a possible **follow-on book**, topics might include: "Delight yourself in the Lord" (Psa 37:4); "AntiChrist" (e.g. 1 John 2:18, 4:3); personal transformation (on page 150-151, we mentioned the transformation of Lee Strobel by the presence of the living Christ; Chapter 18 and Postscript 1 in this book show more of the "present evidence of His* Presence." Yuan Zhiming's DVD series has many examples; Lee Strobel has a new book *The Case for Grace*). As noted in Postscript #1, I should offer a fuller write-up of my experience with the "tithe" bringing me from desperation to profound blessing, and the fullness of that promise being kept *including "rebuke the devourer* for your sake" - Malachi 3:11 ESV, NASB, NKJV. (Our Index entries about the "prosperity gospel" have some important qualifiers that are sometimes omitted from adverse discussions).

If you would like to hear when such a book may become available, please write us with SASE "self-addressed stamped envelope" (that is, of course, with a "forever" stamp, as the world does continue to turn in its present ways! Our contact address is at the end of Table of Contents).

[233] This prayer is from the *Book of Common Prayer* (BCP), found in Bartlett's, p. 1128, citing the BCP reference as "Family Prayer, For Quiet Confidence," 1928 BCP. I have updated "thy" and "thou" to modern English. Cf. Psa 46:10, a life-changing experience for me (your author) as discussed in "Postscript."

Appendix Two: Easter, A Professional's Research

[234] The DVD was "The Cross: Jesus in China," by Yuan Zhiming, available on-line in English. See note 232 above for comments about our contemplated follow-on book and how to tie into the possibility of it, if you are interested.

[235] Web URL garyhabermas.com/articles/trinityjournal_latetwentieth/trinityjournal_latetwentieth.htm#ch0. The article is "The Late Twentieth - Century Resurgence of Naturalistic Responses to Jesus' Resurrection" by Gary R. Habermas. Originally published in the Trinity Journal/2001 (TRINJ 22NS (2001) 179-196).

[236] This book is not an academic study; so, a note here in a completely different vein from the source citations. We mentioned "scorn" against believers — you may appreciate as much as I have the prayer, "Do not make me the scorn of fools," Psa 39:8 NIV. The first part of that verse is "Save me from all my transgressions," reminding us that if we are wiser than the scorners, seeing Jesus' precious truth, it is a gift from God (1Cor 4:7).

Appendix Three, Bibliography: Standard Form

[237] This ISBN is provided in case someone wants to hunt various booksellers for *Christus Victor*; I believe it is out of print, and it took me literally years to find it.

The ISBN is also provided for some other books which might be hard to find but which I thought were worth the extra attention.

[238] The Copeland's January 3 devotional in *From Faith to Faith* has the vital concept, "*Blessed to be a blessing.*" Kenneth says, "Today, I literally 'live to give.' " This is a vital note for those who misunderstand the "**prosperity gospel**" to mean self-indulgence and focus on self-gratification instead of the praise of God by the well-being of His* servants.

At the risk of de-emphasizing *that* point, we add that Kenneth Copeland says in another place, "God pointed out to me that there was something I'd been leaving out. The force of joy. He told me I have no right to walk by faith and love and just leave joy dormant in my spirit. It's too important... joy is an important part of a life of victory" [otherwise, only "an occasional triumph now and then" and he cites Bible, Neh. 8:10 that joy is the key to strength, to "staying power," to overcoming the assaults of evil]. The quote is from the May 15 meditation in *From Faith to Faith: A Daily Guide to Victory*.

The word "victory" there is not victory "over" those around you, but **victory** *for* the "shalom," the harmony and flourishing (in reverence) that is God's design and desire (see chapter Atone/Shalom. Compare the usage in the Bible, "Death has been swallowed up in victory," 1 Cor 15:54 NRSV).

[239] Bible, Proverbs 10:22 NKJV: The blessing of the LORD makes one rich, And He adds no sorrow with it.

[240] The Eastern Orthodox say that he "reposed" rather than "passed on." That tracks to the Scripture of "entering God's rest" (Heb 4:3); to say someone "passed away" is inaccurate if that person was a believer in the saving Lord.

[241] Hand-copying of ancient manuscripts has brought in minor errors, sometimes added notes by copyists, etc. The **"critical text"** of an ancient document is based on using principles of text criticism to assess all the available manuscripts and arrive at the best understanding of exactly what the original document said.

For the New Testament, the "critical text" research has worked through about 5,000 ancient Greek manuscripts, and also the extensive citations of Bible quotes by early Church leaders (one scholar said that these are so extensive that if we had *no* New Testament manuscripts whatsoever, the New Testament could be reconstructed from the totality of these quotes in sermons and other citations). The scholars also assess the ancient translations into other languages, including Aramaic, Arabic, Coptic, etc., as these show the form of the text in ancient times. They also use lectionaries, ancient compilations of Scripture for religious services. More than 15,000 documents in total enter the analysis.

Citations of large numbers of divergences among these documents come from the scholarly requirement to count even spelling errors as "variants." The refinement of the "critical text" has proceeded by two major study groups, the Nestle-Aland and the United Bible Societies. Continued application of the critical principles has led to a convergence of these two efforts into a single "critical text" (first published as the third edition of the UBS Greek New Testament and the 26th edition of the Nestle-Aland).

The UBS Greek New Testament is published with the "critical apparatus" in the front, showing the *major* documents used and their ages; this table, while not showing all the 15,000+ resource documents, lists so many that predate the Council of Nicaea, as to refute clearly the charge that the Scriptures were altered by the Church when it became "established" under the Emperor Constantine (his Edict of Milan, A.D. 313, brought the **Church** out of its quasi-"underground" status).

[242] The Templeton Foundation specializes in study of the relations between science and religion. The reader perusing Van Huyssteen's book should note Reinhold Niebuhr's meditation on sin on p. 196 there, and the comments on the following page on human intelligence as more complex than the analytic intelligence of computer software.

On p. 114 there, authors of that particular essay mention "agape love, seen uniquely in the self-giving and self-emptying of Jesus Christ. The self-giving of Christ was unique, and it is by faith that we affirm that the ultimate act of Christ's self-giving, by its nature, sets him and it apart from all others." But the book in general does not deal with such perceptions; the question on the back cover "*Why* did we evolve the way we did?" shows more the tone of the treatment. That's why this Reader (Van Huyssteen's) is not in the Annotated Bibliography.

[243] Dr. Yarhouse has a mediating viewpoint which I appreciated.

Regarding the high-volume and unceasing controversies, we must add (not quoting Yarhouse): The misconception exists that homosexuality is spoken against only in a few "Old Testament" Scriptures. It is a New Testament concern -- 1 Cor 6:9-10, 1 Tim 1:10, especially Rom 1:1 - 2:8. We hear the deceiving concept that "if you try it and you enjoy it, you are" — no, the fact that you enjoy sexual release just means your genitals are wired normally in your brain. (Jude 1:10 bears consideration in this regard, as well as in the general sexual focus on self-gratification rather than living for God.)

Appendix Three, Bibliography: Annotated Section

[244] Re: "The Jesus Film:" I don't resonate with their visual treatment of the Holy Spirit descending on Him in baptism (I think "The Gospel of John" DVD does a much better portrayal). Other than that, it's a great introduction to Jesus!

[245] Impacts include social matters (the *Encyclopedia of Catholicism* notes that Christians established the first hospitals and schools in many areas; Moynahan, Stark and others discuss more). Impacts include personal transformations like Viggo Olsen — "a brilliant surgeon whose life was steeped in science." He and his equally skeptical wife began their study — to answer believing relatives — by labeling a sheet of blank paper "Scientific Mistakes in the Bible." Their research of *that* brought them to faith, and they left the U.S.A. after asking God "to send them to a place devoid of both Christians and medical care" — spending 33 years "in the poverty-wracked nation of Bangladesh," founding a hospital and being so appreciated by the Government of Bangladesh that Olsen "was honored with Visa #001 in gratitude" (recounted pp. 287-291 of Strobel, *Case for a Creator.* As noted in my Postscript, your author has experienced the personal transformative touch, and seen it in others. Strobel notes one of Viggo Olsen's three books, *The Agnostic Who Dared to Search*).

[246] Gerald Schroeder quotes another reference on this issue, which I have not read: "As Paul Johnson articulated so incisively, the Bible is the earliest identifiable source of the great conceptual discoveries essential for civilization: equality before the law, sanctity of life, dignity of the individual, individual and communal responsibility, peace as an ideal, love as the foundation of justice." This is from p. 18 of Schroeder's "Science...;" he is restating exposition by Paul Johnson, *History of the Jews* (NY: Harper & Row, 1987).

[247] *Christianity on Trial* deals in quantities of factual material, set in a sharp perspective on the current culture. For example, the authors observe that "when the *New York Times* reported on Professor John L. Heilbron's revelations about the medieval church's unappreciated support of astronomy — it often has a man-bites-dog tone of wonderment," page ix. In commenting on **male-female matters** in early Christianity, they note that pagan Roman women were three times more likely than Christian women to have married before age 13, and "Christian women also exercised far more choice in whom they wed, and were less likely to be forced into an abortion (a frequent cause of death for women of the time)" p. 4. On page 5, they make a comment provocative to the modern ear: "In those days, you would have been hard put to find anyone who believed in 'sexual equality' in the modern sense, and the person who comes closest to it is, strangely enough, Paul." (They are quoting A. N. Wilson, and they give the reference. See also the following endnote.) Another comment on the Epistles given through Paul: "Paul's writings help bring about the idea of individual dignity" per a "historian of Europe, Larry Siedentop," p. 34, Monitor 19 Jan 2015.

[248] The controversy over gender roles in "Paul's" writing is set in an interesting light in the *Orthodox Study Bible*, a repository of tradition: their study note regarding Eph 5:21-31 says, "Paul writes three sentences to wives, but writes at greater length to impress on husbands that they should love their wives. Just as the wife's submission is to accept the headship of the husband, the husband's submission to his wife is to sacrifice himself for her."** (We put "Paul's" in quotation marks because we believe that "all Scripture is inspired by God," 2Tim 3:16, and so the frequent practice of treating this as Paul's personal philosophy is off-the-mark. (The preceding note has a commentator's observation on Paul's outlook in the context of that time).

** The husband's sacrifice was clear in the family life in the traditional pattern, as I saw it, growing up in the old culture of the 1950s. The man worked all his life to support his wife and family, turned away from opportunities for sexual adventures outside the marriage bond — and was labeled an oppressor by some of the heralds of cultural readjustment. Yes, some were oppressors, some terrible oppressors — but I saw those who were not, who were nurturers and protectors and a blessing in great depth.

[249] Meyer's chapter on "RNA first" (as an explanation for the origins of life; his Chapter 14, "The RNA World" — "now probably the most popular theory of how life began," p. 296) is a good example of his analysis that the alternative explanations *fail to engage with the details* which are now known about the level of complexity of these matters. (He goes in detail into five key areas where the "RNA first" theory fails, according to his analysis. Meyer, like Behe in his tenth-anniversary update of his famous book, feels that the critics do not really work with the details of the biological data, when they assert

that naturalistic explanations are adequate. Dr. Dean Kenyon's repudiation of his own "chemical evolution" theory is one example of further data, extensive detail of it, disabusing an extrapolated naturalistic theory; see endnote 136.)

As one example of Meyer's thought, I quote from his p. 419: "the activity of a designing intelligence does not necessarily break or violate the laws of nature. Human agents design information-rich structures and otherwise interfere with the 'normal workings of material objects' all the time. When they do, they do not violate the laws of nature; they alter the conditions upon which the laws act."

Other gems of thought besides the microbiology include his pointing out that the "fruitfulness" of "intelligent design" thinking, included the very genesis of science in a culture which attributed the universe to a rational and law-giving God, and his comment that scientific discovery often brings discernment before details of causation (Newton described the "laws" of gravity without being able to show what caused gravity — analogous to the present situation of asserting the discerning of intelligence at work in the structures of nature *without* being able to demonstrate on empirical grounds what the nature of that "intelligence" is). His review of "origins of life" theories is worth the price of the book for those unfamiliar with the later rethinking of the celebrated Stanley Miller - Harold Urey demonstrations, and the extrapolations which took those experiments to mean that "the origin of life was not a chance event, but was inevitable" (a 1984 science writer cited on p. 57 of Meyer. Meyer reports that the Miller-Urey viewpoint has since been challenged as the early atmosphere of earth was found to be different than assumed, and for other factors that Meyer cites).

(One of Meyer's frontispiece quotes says his "refutation of **Dawkins** will have all the dogs barking and the angels singing." Your comments on that, patient reader, would be of interest.) [The dogs aren't barking in MY neighborhood, but the coyotes have been howling in the open fields across the street!]

[250] "Renowned Chinese paleontologist" J. Y. Chen, a lecture given in 2000, quoted on p. 52 of Meyer's *Darwin's Doubt*.

The massive expansion of fossil data on the Cambrian and pre-Cambrian has surfaced another issue: The fossils do "not show the gradual emergence of unique species followed slowly but surely by the emergence of representatives of ever higher and more disparate taxa, leading to novel phyla. [Rather] body plan-level disparity arising first and suddenly..." "Major innovations in body plans precede minor variations on basic designs. This 'inverted cone of diversity' also suggests intelligent design." (Meyer, *Darwin's Doubt*, pp. 74, 371. Meyer uses the terms "top-down" as opposed to the expected "bottom-up" appearance of taxonomic groups.)

As we have discussed at several points, all these perceptions evoke intense debate. The debates are chronicled in the more recent *Debating*

Darwin's Doubt: A Scientific Controversy That Can No Longer Be Denied by David Klinghoffer (2015).

For the patient reader, we excerpt some of the best of the Cambrian processing:

The Cambrian "Explosion:" Looking at what is the basic issue:

Stephen Meyer's analysis of the issues of the "Cambrian Explosion" provoked intense controversy (if you've studied the argumentation over whether science points toward or away from God, you would say "of course" to that). There was a fascinating ray of light that slashed through the strife: Some of the fiercest critics of Meyer's "intelligence-manifesting" analysis said that people who wanted to understand the Cambrian "explosion" issues should read Douglas Erwin and James Valentine's *The Cambrian Explosion: The Construction of Animal Biodiversity* (2013).

Erwin and Valentine were cited by Meyer's critics as "two of the leading mainstream scientific authorities on the Cambrian explosion." One of Meyer's fiercest critics called Erwin and Valentine's work "a good account by real paleontologists who know what they're doing."

But then, we find that Erwin and Valentine said that *there is indeed* an "explosion" and that it does indeed stretch beyond the normal Darwinian analysis of evolution's workings. They themselves stated that "the Cambrian explosion can be considered an adaptive radiation only by stretching the term beyond all recognition... the scale of morphological divergence is wholly incommensurate with that seen in other adaptive radiations."

Erwin and Valentine state that they "strongly hold to" the position that "evolutionary theory needs to be expanded to include a more diverse set of macroevolutionary processes." They put forward the conclusion about the explanatory reach of evolutionary theory "that microevolutionary processes are not sufficient to explain macroevolutionary ones, stating: 'the move from micro to macro forms a discontinuity.' "

Erwin and Valentine also state a key factor that Meyer observes in the Cambrian, that the "cone of increasing diversity" (Stephen Jay Gould's term) – expected as the gradual accumulation of small changes drives new "body plans," under traditional Darwinism – is not observed in the Cambrian.

These top-of-the-scientific-field viewpoints confirm the foundation for what Meyer does, in assessing what should be considered in the "more diverse processes" beyond traditional, received Darwinian analyses. Meyer took up the traditional "uniformitarian" outlook to assess what new causation could be best assessed to account for the Cambrian phenomena. The issue, he says, is that these new "body plans" are brought into being by DNA genetic codes that focus the *information* needed to build the organism (and also by some higher-level regulatory structures, "epigenetic"; we are not your source for a full-bore technical analysis here, sorry!) Those DNA codes and related structures involve *major amounts of new information* in the Cambrian developments. So, what do we know about the sources of information? For centuries now, the principle has been to look for *known causes* that *produce the type of results* observed ["uniformitarianism," or "uniformity"].

Meyer points out the unavoidable: we have, today, massive amounts of information - always produced by an intelligent agent. Thus, the best explanation of the swift appearance of the "new information" for new body plans in the Cambrian (swift in terms of geologic time), is the involvement of an intelligence - what sort, still to be determined, just as Newton had no explanation of the mechanism for gravity when he elucidated its basic laws (gravitational force proportional to masses involved, inverse to square of distance, etc.).

[Quotations are from *Debating Darwin's Doubt,* in order of appearance above, pages 363, 197, 368 [quoting p. 341 of Erwin and Valentine's book], 366-67 [citing pp. 9-10 of E. & V.], 368 [per 339-340 of E. & V.]

[251] Dr. Denis Alexander is the Director of the Faraday Institute for Science and Religion, St Edmund College, Cambridge (website faraday-institute.org), and is also a Senior Affiliated Scientist at the Babraham Institute, Cambridge — from first page inside front cover of his book.

[252] Thaxton et al's pattern of argument is interesting as showing the origin of "intelligent design" as a scientific analysis, not a religious concept. (This 1984 book is credited by some as starting the I.D. movement; others feel Denton's 1985 *Evolution: A Theory in Crisis*, was that.) Thaxton's demolition of the conjectured "prebiotic soup" is still hotly disputed, although various current writers defend his view with updated analyses (cf. Meyer, *Signature*... or Woodward, *Doubts*... p. 125. Dr. Rana, in his 2017 DVD, says that such a prebiotic or primordial soup of chemicals should leave chemical traces in the oldest geological formations on earth, and "The fact is we see no evidence" of this [19:14ff of his DVD].)

An interesting comment on origins-of-life research was: "In fact, a recent survey of the scientific literature shows that every step in the proposed pathway from prebiotic amphiphilic compounds [components for cell membranes] to contemporary cell membranes strictly depends on exacting compositional and environmental factors." (June 2007 publication, cited p. 242 of Rana, *The Cell's Design*. Suggestive, eh? Although, to some, simply a springboard for more work...)

Thaxton touches on the interpretation issues, including this: "The philosophy of experimental science ... began its discoveries and made use of its method in the faith, not the knowledge, that it was dealing with a rational universe controlled by a Creator who did not act upon whim..." (p. 206, quoting Eisley).

Pondering that brought your author back to the "**scientism**" issue, on which another source: "Scientism involves the use of scientific forms and categories in order to give the appearance of science to unscientific ways of thinking..."* Compare James Smith on those who say they dropped faith "because of science": "what's usually captured the person is not scientific evidence per se, but the *form* of science... the underlying epistemological stance... seen as the stance of maturity, of courage..." (p. 77 of *How (Not) to Be Secular*). [Cf. comments, our pp. 118-119, "epistemologically enslaved."]

* Roger Scruton, "Scientism in the Arts and Humanities," *The New Atlantis*, Number 40, Fall 2013, pp. 33-46. From thenewatlantis.com/publications/scientism-in-the-arts-and-humanities, Feb 2014. [June 2019, the search box on their website accesses that article.]

[253] For example, Woodward quotes an author on cell biology and life who says, "We should reject, as a matter of principle, the substitution of intelligent design for the dialogue of chance and necessity..." (*Darwin Strikes Back*... p. 176; quote is 2001). However, if that is where the data take us, such "principle" becomes a rejection of empiricism itself. (That acerbic comment does *not* exclude the viewpoint that considers other explanations adequate; it takes Meyer's 600 pages to argue the "adequacy" issue in one area alone, so *this* book cannot do more than assert the Divine's right to be heard.)

[254] The denial that Jesus actually lived, is asserted from a reported survey of local historians in His region and time. These sources (if the deniers have accurate research) do not mention Him, so He must not be real, eh? Well! The person who absorbed what the New Testament says, sees the fallacy — those local areas were governed by people and structures with an intense opposition to Jesus and His followers, so silence from them is "of course."

[255] As to what can be learned about God from nature, it matters much with what eyes we look. An eminent scientist summarized the observational data, in *his* viewpoint, as showing that "God has a special preference for beetles." This comes from the data that the number of species of beetles outnumber other insect orders, and insect species outnumber other forms of life. (It does not seem to be the most penetrating assessment of the facts of nature!)
[The wording of the quote is as reported by Stephen Gould, quoting Vol. 10 of the *Journal of the British Interplanetary Society*, reporting on a 1951 speech by J. B. S. Haldane — per en.wikiquote.org/wiki/J._B._S._Haldane, April 5, 2013.]

[256] In addition to leestrobel.com, other **websites** listed in appendix B of *The Case for the Real Jesus* include: Jesuscentral.com, "a place to learn and dialogue about what Jesus said" (these quoted comments are Strobel's from the book); tektonics.org, "a feisty site that answers critics of historic Christianity" (note "k" not "c" in the name); reasonablefaith.org, "scholar William Lane Craig defends historic Christianity"; markdroberts.com, "a wealth of material from a Harvard-educated scholar"; metamorpha.com,

"where the focus is on how to become more like Jesus." (Strobel being smarter than I am, that's his full list. I would have gone on for several pages and it wouldn't have done anything but confuse people — your author.)

We mentioned Ravi Zacharias' thoughtful website rzim.org at the end of endnote 80.

The **website** myhopewithbillygraham.org has on-line programs, including people's accounts of God meeting them in desperate need.

[257] Stark expresses his conclusion on p. 147 that "Christianity depicted God as a rational, responsive, dependable, and omnipotent being and the universe as his personal creation, thus having a rational, lawful, stable structure, awaiting human comprehension." He noted on p. 124 that "some of my central arguments have already become the conventional wisdom among historians of science [but unfortunately] unknown outside narrow scholarly circles."

On p. 160ff, he assesses the "scientific stars 1543-1680," the leaders who made the largest contributions to science. Stark studied the evidences of "especially deep religious concerns" on the part of these persons, separating such persons from those "whose piety does not stand out as other than entirely satisfactory to their religious associates" in an age when much religion was conventional (p. 162). Conclusion? "Those who made the 'Scientific Revolution' included an unusually large number of **devout** Christians — more than 60 percent," p. 163 — and only 4% "Skeptic" (table, p. 162). Again, as discussed in the main text, a finding that would be expected by those who "know their God" (Bible phrase, e.g. Dan 11:32 NIV) — but a finding incomprehensible in many "educated" sectors, is it not so?

(Stark says, "What the great figures involved in the sixteenth- and seventeenth-century blossoming of science — including Descartes, Galileo, Newton, and Kepler — did confess was their absolute faith in a Creator God, whose work incorporated rational rules awaiting discovery" p. 157 of *For the Glory*... Here's one specific, from a different source: Johannes Kepler, the great astronomer who discovered that the planets' orbits are ellipses, wrote of his studies that "through my effort God is being celebrated in astronomy." Cited on p. 29 of *Christianity Today* magazine, March 2013, article by David Wilkinson, "Bigger Than We Think: The doctrine of creation goes deeper than just explaining how the world began." Kepler's statement was in correspondence to one of his teachers, in A.D. 1595.

[258] Stark, p. 325. The prohibition in Deuteronomy is made stronger in the following verse: "He shall live with you, among you, in the place which he chooses inside one of your gates, wherever it is good to him. You shall not oppress him" (LITV, Jay Green's LITeral Version). Some commentators say this applied only to Israelite slaves, not to slaves from outside communities; the language in Deuteronomy 23 does *not* make that limitation. *The NIV Study Bible* says it does apply to "a foreign slave" [Bible is by Zondervan, ©

1985]. Stark is pointed in his prose and fun to read, but please expect protracted controversy over everything in such arenas. (Anyone who has waded in much of such controversy may appreciate Rev. Timothy Keller's comment that, "Each side demands that you not only disagree with but disdain the other as (at best) crazy or (at worst) evil" — page ix of *The Reason for God.*)

The following chapter of Deuteronomy prescribes death for anyone kidnapping a fellow Israelite for slavery (i.e. slave trader) Deu 24:7. The "not-return-slave" provisions of Deuteronomy 23:15 have been described as "unparalleled in the legislation of the ancient Near East," p. 400 of F. F. Bruce, *Paul: Apostle of the Heart Set Free.*

[259] See pp. 147-8 of Burpo's book. The nurse told Burpo that when the doctors "tell us someone isn't going to make it, they don't make it." Burpo told her of the prayer group the church had mobilized during this crisis, but she seemed uninterested. Burpo said, "I think maybe she didn't want to hear a sermon from a pastor. But the truth was, she didn't need a sermon — she'd already seen one."

The credibility of the child's account (of visiting heaven) was buttressed by his reporting that he met there a sister he had never known he had — that one had died tragically before he was born and his parents had never mentioned her to him, so this was a shock to them. Other credibility-boosting matters that his father, a Pastor, reported in the book included the child describing what his father and mother had been doing in other parts of the hospital while he was anesthetized on the operating table, and correspondence with Bible Scriptures about heaven.

Medical doctors have experienced journeys to heaven, which makes an interesting source! One commented that his experience, while his body was in a coma, was inexplicable per his lifetime work in neuroscience (*Proof of Heaven* by Eben Alexander, 2012). Orthopedic surgeon Mary Neal's *To Heaven and Back* was also 2012, describing an experience of heaven while unconscious, trapped underwater during a kayaking trip. (I have not read these, so they are not in the Bibliography.)

[260] Quoted in an interview in *Christianity Today*, December 2011, p. 36

[261] Johnson, *Reason* ..., p. 148: "In economic terms the moral deficit is the difference between what people feel morally obligated to put into society's treasury and what they feel morally entitled to take out." [He felt Americans were feeling more entitled to benefits, less inclined to pay into government expansion; more, p. 149: the issue of perceived] "redistribution to other persons toward whom the taxpayers feel no sense of moral obligation. ... A financial crisis is inevitable." [He wrote that in 1995!]

[262] Fr. Seraphim presents a vast array of scientific information, much of it stimulating. His fundamental perspective, however, is "What did the early Church leaders ['Church Fathers'] teach about the six days of Genesis 1?" That whole issue opens the question of *looking to the Bible for what it teaches*, not for what people read into it. Fr. Seraphim's critique of the assumptions of long-term radioactive dating is interesting, as are other presentations, but we feel that backing into the "young earth" corner is a mistake and not required by the Bible. (The Hebrew "begot," as in the generations lists in Genesis, can span a number of generations, not always "immediate descendant." Study of Matthew 1 shows this as a caution flag right at the beginning of the New Testament: The 14-14-14 generations that Matthew lists are "those of note," not *all* the generations, as comparison with the Old Testament shows some omissions.**

Fr. Seraphim notes that the early Church used the Septuagint for the Old Testament, and the Septuagint has 5,500 years in the genealogical entries specifically documented between creation and Christ, whereas the standard Hebrew text ("Masoretic") gives 4,000. Fr. Seraphim notes that the early church "Fathers" never bothered themselves about that difference, which to me says that the number of years is not the issue. It seems to me that the Fathers never had to think about the questions now "on the table," and drawing on their viewpoint to answer those questions is therefore most open to question.

** Regarding that "son of" or "begot" can span generations, note in Matthew 1:20 that the angel, seen in his dream, addressed Joseph as "Joseph, son of David," when telling him not to reject Mary as his wife — even though the great King David was more than 20 generations earlier. (Similarly, Mat 1:1 calls David "the son of Abraham," although verse 17 says there were 14 generations from Abraham to David).

Appendix Three, Bibliography: Bible Versions Section

[263] For example, the NKJV still has the "Book of Life" in Rev 22:19, although *The Orthodox Study Bible* footnotes that verse to say that both the "Majority Text" and the critical text ("N-U," in their terminology) have "tree of life" there. Metzger, *Textual Commentary* p. 690, notes that: "The corruption of 'tree' into 'book' had occurred earlier in the transmission of the Latin text when a scribe accidentally copied the correct word *ligno* ('tree') as *libro* ('book')." (The "Majority Text" is the one derived by counting the majority of existent ancient documents on any textual issue, rather than applying critical textual principles.) The minor (and theologically insignificant) corruption noted, became part of some later-centuries Vulgate Latin Bibles in the hand-copying days, and from there was picked up when the King James Bible was translated into English in A.D. 1611. (It came into the King James because Erasmus, in creating the first published Greek New Testament, was working from Greek manuscripts that didn't have the last verses of the last book of the Bible, Revelation, and back-translated them from a Latin manuscript).

The "theological insignificance" of changing "tree of life" into "book of life" can be supported by Philippians 4:3.

[264] That discussion was in Chapter 12. As to the NLT's interpretive handling of Scriptures giving, in some cases, what may be added emphasis on the "substitutionary punishment" element:

Examples I found: Psa 111:9 NIV "He [God] provided redemption for his people," but NLT says God "has paid a full ransom." Col 1:14 may show this issue; in Heb 10:20 NLT has added "by his [Christ's] death."

The later NLT changed the wording of its translation in one verse that reflects this realm of concern: NLT 1996 edition: [God] "sent Jesus to take the punishment for our sins and to satisfy God's anger against us." NLT 2004 edition: "For God presented Jesus as the sacrifice for sin" (Romans 3:25). The latter reading is much closer to the NIV's reading, "God presented Christ as a sacrifice of atonement..." Compare Jay Green's *Literal Version* (free at e-Sword.net) which reads, "[Jesus] whom God set forth *as* a propitiation through faith in His blood, as a demonstration of His righteousness through the passing over of the sins that had taken place before..."

The 2004 NLT wording also opens up space for the reflective reader to ponder these things in light of Bishop Hicks' re-illumination of the meaning and nature of sacrifice [p. 66 our main text], which the 1994 wording did not what do you think? (Endnote 102, another NLT "good")

For an alternative viewpoint, at Galatians 2:20 *The Orthodox Study Bible* has this note: [Justification] "constitutes substantial union with Christ, not just an abstract position of the believer with respect to God."

R_'s discussions with B-t about these matters put him in remembrance of theologian J. Gresham Machen's "False ideas are the greatest obstacle to the reception of the Gospel" (quoted by Nancy Pearcey, p. 15 of *Saving Leonardo*).

Appendix Four: "Outtakes"

[265] B-t is referring to the remark given in Postscript One that "you might start by reading Luke, John, and Acts — the basic story of Jesus (Luke), the deep spiritual meanings of Jesus (John), the early people living with the Holy Spirit of God (Acts)." (I commend the New Living Translation — it really makes the message come through wonderfully in current language. It's also popular enough, as one of the top four Bible translations in sales, that you will find other people who use it. The prior note discussed one theological issue where the NLT may constrain the reader's outlook more than the original Greek NT.)

"Church at least every other week, even if nothing seems to be happening" — we want results NOW, but when you look back after a decade or two of **church**-going, you'll find it makes all the difference in the world.

Appendix Five: Notes on Our Unsophisticated Literary Devices

[266] Bartlett's, p. 162.

[267] Your author's own alcohol status: I quit (1992) when a counselor noted some significant problems and said, "I wish I had quit when I was no farther into it than you are." What depths that remark speaks to! If it applies to you — alcohol or whatever ...

[268] p. 112 of *Light from the Christian East*, James R. Payton Jr. The quotation from Peter John at the bottom of the Preface comes to mind in this regard! [While we are "warning," we should candidly warn the seeker that life in Jesus will involve times of endurance... The New Testament will tell you much about that, perhaps more than will ever apply to *you,* but it will also remind you of the joy and speak of the peace, even in this life — ! [2 Th 3:16]

Appendix Seven: Some Theological Reflections

[269] People who like C. S. Lewis' approach to interpreting Adam/Adahm may enjoy a comment that Dr. Gerald Schroeder brings from the medieval commentator Maimonides. Maimonides "described animals co-existing with Adam that were identical to humans in shape and intelligence, but because they lacked the *neshama*, they were animals." The Hebrew word *neshama* is in Gen 2:7, usually translated "breath," but understood by Schroeder's commentators to be "the human soul... instilling free will."** Maimonides' comment was penned more than 600 years before Darwin, at a time when hominid/hominin fossils had not become part of the intellectual conundrums of the European mind.

** p. 17 of Schroeder's *Science...* Maimonides quote accessed 21 April 2013 at geraldschroeder.com/wordpress/?page_id=79.

[270] C. S. Lewis, The Problem of Pain, pp. 68 - 71. [Publisher's requested statement: THE PROBLEM OF PAIN by C. S. Lewis copyright © C.S. Lewis Pte. Ltd. 1940. Extract reprinted by permission.]

[271] Bishop John Pritchard, Preface to *The 100-Minute Bible.*

[272] Tac discusses the violence of the former days and on p. 11 of "Indian Life..." he says, "O merciful God, why didst Thou leave us for so many centuries, years, months and days in utter darkness after Thou camest into the world?** Blessed be Thou from this day through future centuries." (The antiquated language must be ascribed to the translator, translating from a Spanish-language record of Tac's writing.)

** This is referring to Jesus' Incarnation.

Pablo Tac was writing in the early 1800's, which in Southern California was early in the "contact" period.

The Mesha stele information is from the NIV Study Bible, p. 365.

[273] We hope the argument is clear. If the "God of the Old Testament" were of the character His* maligners attribute to Him*, it would have been to David's *commendation* that he had "shed much blood." It would have qualified him more highly for being the Temple-builder, but instead, it was a prohibitive block against him having that manifesting role.

Epilogue

[274] Dr. Stephen Meyer, for example, continues to engage with the evolving arguments of his critics at his website stephencmeyer.org/research.php, which as of my 12 April 2013 visit included a "must-read" article on "the history and the current state of intelligent design theory." ("Must-read" is his term, not mine, although it certainly has its place in the intellectual landscape of these issues!) Another article has his response to "a series of objections" that critics have made. (The "state of the art" of human intellect will be endlessly "evolving"! -- your author Bob Keller.) "Intelligent design" is certainly not the only thought that believers have; see Index for Denis Alexander's radically different assessment of how evolutionary science supports belief in God.

[275] Please see page 82-83 "rain in the springtime" for that discussion. My feeble attempts to enlighten that matter is on pages 83-84.

Endnote 138 comments on the vexing question, "Why didn't God stop the tsunami?"

[276] "Under-determination" means that several theories can explain the given data. Wikipedia and other technical references explain it, as it has become an issue in the whole discourse.

Dr. Gould was quoted by Gerald Schroeder on p. 18 of his *Science of God.* The original source, per Schroeder's notes, was Gould's July 1992 *Scientific American* article "Impeaching a Self-Appointed Judge." Gould is credited with the "punctuated equilibrium" theory of evolution.

[277] Forgive me, I beg you, dear reader: Here I go again, writing in an endnote some material that will be important to some, but which may want not to interrupt the thoughts of some who will be guided by the Spirit (of God) to skip this. "*Your own major and unending benefit*" understates the matter: it affects also *others*, whom you will touch upon, by the unavoidable manifestation of God's great work in *you*, if you receive it.

Pray! And seek Him* in His* Word, the "living and active" memorial of Jesus' monumental Incarnation (see Index to pursue "Incarnation;" "living and active" is Bible, Heb 4:12).

Father Alexander's book suggests "6 to 10 minutes," as the *minimum*: That, once for prayers read from the prayer book,** prayers proven over the centuries, and 6-10 again for Bible reading; and *above* that, "prayerful fellowship with God" (p. 14 of *An Inner Step Toward **God***). Also,

"The Eucharist," i.e. Communion; he says: "Four things. This is not a theory. It has been tested practically." (Regarding "minimums," n.b. 2 Cor 9:6. On p. 31, Fr. Alexander says the most exhausted of us "can always find seven minutes*** some time before bed"). Also, on p. 67 he cautions that prayer without serving others "risks degenerating into self-delusion."

More on **prayer**, below... From my betters! ("Church," endnote~66)

A note for the modern thinker on **"repentance:"** D. B. Hart notes that] "for us, it is a largely negative term that means something like 'regret and repudiation,' ...which say nothing of the real inner transformation that is a far larger part of the word's sense [in the New Testament] ... a positive and genuinely transitive power... an interior change *'toward'* (God, salvation, life...)" [p. 560, his Postscript, of his NT translation [Yale University Press, 2017].

Bible reading: we have noted elsewhere our recommendation to read the New Testament first, perhaps starting with Luke - John - Acts. The grace in the New Testament is what is offered to us ("the new covenant," in theological terms) and should be the focus. [Another approach, p. 44]

We mention below the commendation of "half an hour" of Bible reading, and a believer's success with 15 minutes Bible reading, 15 minutes prayer, daily. (Don't forget endnote 225 on baptism!)

Also noted earlier was a translator's comment that the Bible concepts which are most difficult to translate into a certain language and culture, are the most important for them to receive as new information (endnote 113). In that regard, the "modern" person may find the discussions of "spirits" most difficult in the New Testament; it may help to think of them as "energies," per one commentator ("structures of thought" was an Elder's comment to me in earlier days; she was most helpful in a terrible crisis, mentioned in the Acknowledgments. See also endnote 205).

Another interesting way to take up a broad acquaintance with the Bible has come to my attention: Dr. David Jeremiah's *In the Words of Jesus*, which arranges New Testament Scriptures topically, the "Person of Jesus"... "Promises of Jesus," teachings on a variety of key subjects, and classic parables. It uses the NLT Bible.

** The *function of the prayer book* is to lift us above the simple pleasure of expressing ourselves better and better, and to ground us in fundamental truths. (The simplest practice might be the Lord's Prayer morning and evening, using it as the foundation for personal prayer; another person's pattern, further below.) A good devotional can help; the Bibliography, under "Prayer-book," lists several, as well as various prayer-books (and an interpretive caution on Psalms for the new reader).

*** "twelve minutes of attentive and focused prayer every day for eight weeks changes the brain significantly enough to be measured in a brain scan. [Page 15 of *What Your Body Knows About God* by Rob Moll, IVP Books 2014. While any continued activity leads to changes in the brain, prayer changes areas associated with compassion and empathy; p. 16:] these scientists have discovered that the spiritual circuit that gets exercise in prayer or in church has all kinds of positive effects. It's as though God created our bodies to live to their fullest when we love him and love our neighbors as ourselves. This is what our bodies are *built to do."*

The reader should be cautioned to note, at some point, the message on "endurance" that we have added to endnote 268 above.

A blessing for the diligent endnotes reader: An ancient promise that still waits its time:
Isa 11:9 לא־ירעו ולא־ישחיתו בכל־הר קדשי כי־מלאה הארץ דעה את־יהוה כמים לים מכסים׃
They will neither harm nor destroy on all my holy mountain, for the earth will be filled with the knowledge of the LORD as the waters cover the sea. (NIV)

Finding myself with 250+ footnotes (well, properly, "endnotes"), I added another quotation: "He wrapped himself in quotations — as a beggar would enfold himself in the purple of Emperors." Rudyard Kipling, "Many Inventions...," p. 786 of Bartlett's. ["Woodrow Wilson once quipped, 'I not only use all the brains that I have, but all that I can borrow" — quoted by Dr. Francis S. Collins on p. 281 of his *The Language of God: A Scientist Presents Evidence for Belief.*]

Well, your author is sometimes self-indulgent. Putting the above material in, led me to include another "endnote" not tied to the main text: "*For ignorance of the Scriptures is ignorance of Christ*" — quoted on inside front cover of the Catholic *New American Bible,* quoting Second Vatican Council (New York: Catholic Book Publishing Company, 1970). On p. 4 of the Preface, they commend most highly Bible reading of at least half an hour. A Protestant author who, in his earlier working career, experienced **powerful blessings** on his endeavors, would **every morning read 15 minutes, pray** 15 minutes, then go off to work. (My apologies to Brother Gilbert of Sun City CA, whom I met at his book-signing, for forgetting his last name). An old Christian folk proverb says (about Bible reading), "A chapter a day, keeps the devil away."

Having indexed "ignorance: relative and absolute," I wanted to be able to "index" that "ignorance" as italicized above. (For first-steps out of any such "ignorance," we discussed above reading Luke, John and Acts in the New Testament of the Bible, as a manageable amount with a broad content.)

PRAYER, again, in closing: it is, after all, **perhaps the greatest privilege**. Most simply, starting with the Lord's Prayer (q.v. Index) and then what Father Alexander calls "prayerful fellowship with God" (above; and he says, *"Prayer is much more God's action upon us, than it is our own personal efforts."* P. 58 of *An Inner...*, italics his). **May the Lord bless you!**

======================================

The End: **A final endnote (as promised at the end of Chapter 20):** [More imagined journey: R_ did finally write the book. When he finished, the dog came up and put his paw on R_'s knee — segue to:] a bit of true personal history: My cousin asked, "You studied theology — I had a dear, dear dog years ago that I really loved. Can I hope to have my beloved dog in heaven?" And I replied what I was given at the moment to say (not a previously developed opinion): "My understanding of what God is doing, is that God is developing an eternal community of pure love. So I would think that your dog would fit right in, and it would be incomplete without the creature."

In one tradition, a disciple is talking with the Creator Almighty, and expresses difficulty believing that people can live again, after death. The Creator Almighty replies, "Creating them in the first place is what's difficult. Once you have created them the first time, making them live again is easy."

(The thinker exploring this may enjoy considering p. 137 in *The Orthodox Way*: "In the 'new earth' of the Age to come there is surely a place not only for man but also for the animals: in and through man ["humans"], they too will share in immortality, and so will rocks, trees and plants, fire and water." The four-year-old's visit to heaven was noted to include seeing dogs and other animals there (*Heaven Is for Real,* T. Burpo, see Annotated Bibliography, "Miracles" section). Endnote 204 here cited a leading Christian writer from about 600 A.D. proclaiming "God's purpose the unification of all creation in loving communion".

R_ was surprised to get a positive response on these matters from "B-t," the Bible-toting hitchhiker. B-t started quoting Scriptures — *Rom 8:19-22, 32 re creation liberated; Mark 16:15 (KJV) "preach the gospel to every creature"; Col 1:23 (KJV) "hope of the gospel... preached to every creature which is under heaven."* R_ was cheered to find one of the most recent versions, an earnestly scholarly and modern version, saying: *"proclaim the gospel to the whole creation"* for that Mark 16:15 reference (this was the ISV, "the first English Bible conceived, designed, translated, and formatted primarily for a computer-literate generation," isv.org — a free download at e-Sword.net).

Index

--- Response form ---

(You may wish to comment on: 1) What *should* R_ have said to the people? As to what he and they *did* say, what does it speak to you? 2) Did you find anything to commend? 3) What further should have been, or should be, said? *Overall, and especially,* how did this touch you? (Mailing address at end of Table of Contents)

www.ingramcontent.com/pod-product-compliance
Lightning Source LLC
Chambersburg PA
CBHW030251290526
45785CB00001B/41